100 GIRLS

Adam Gallardo
WRITER/LETTERS

Todd Demong
PENCILS/INKS

Lucas Marangon
WITH Marina Quevedo
CiL
Josh "Bee" Perez
COLORISTS

SIMON PULSE

NEW YORK LONDON TORONTO S...

This book is a work of fiction. Any references to historical events,
real people, or real locales are used fictitiously. Other names, characters,
places, and incidents are the product of the author's imagination,
and any resemblance to actual events or locales or persons,
living or dead, is entirely coincidental.

SIMON PULSE
An imprint of Simon & Schuster Children's Publishing Division
1230 Avenue of the Americas, New York, NY 10020
Copyright © 2005 by Arcana Studio, Inc.
All rights reserved, including the right of reproduction
in whole or in part in any form.
SIMON PULSE and colophon are registered trademarks
of Simon & Schuster, Inc.
Manufactured in the United States of America
First Simon Pulse edition June 2008
2 4 6 8 10 9 7 5 3 1
ISBN-13: 978-1-4169-6109-3
ISBN-10: 1-4169-6109-7

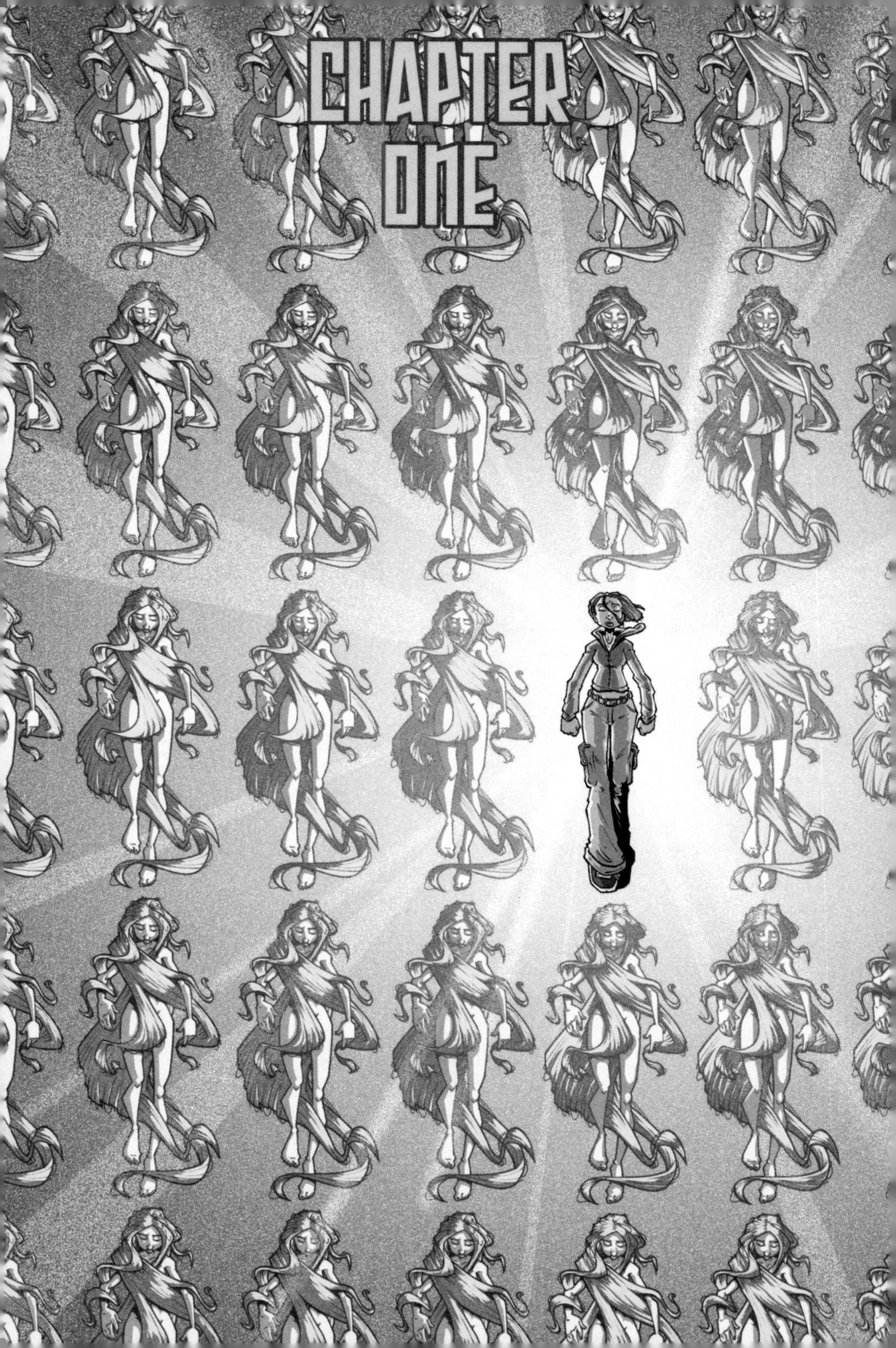
CHAPTER
ONE

"Yeah, the last thing I want
to do is cause trouble."

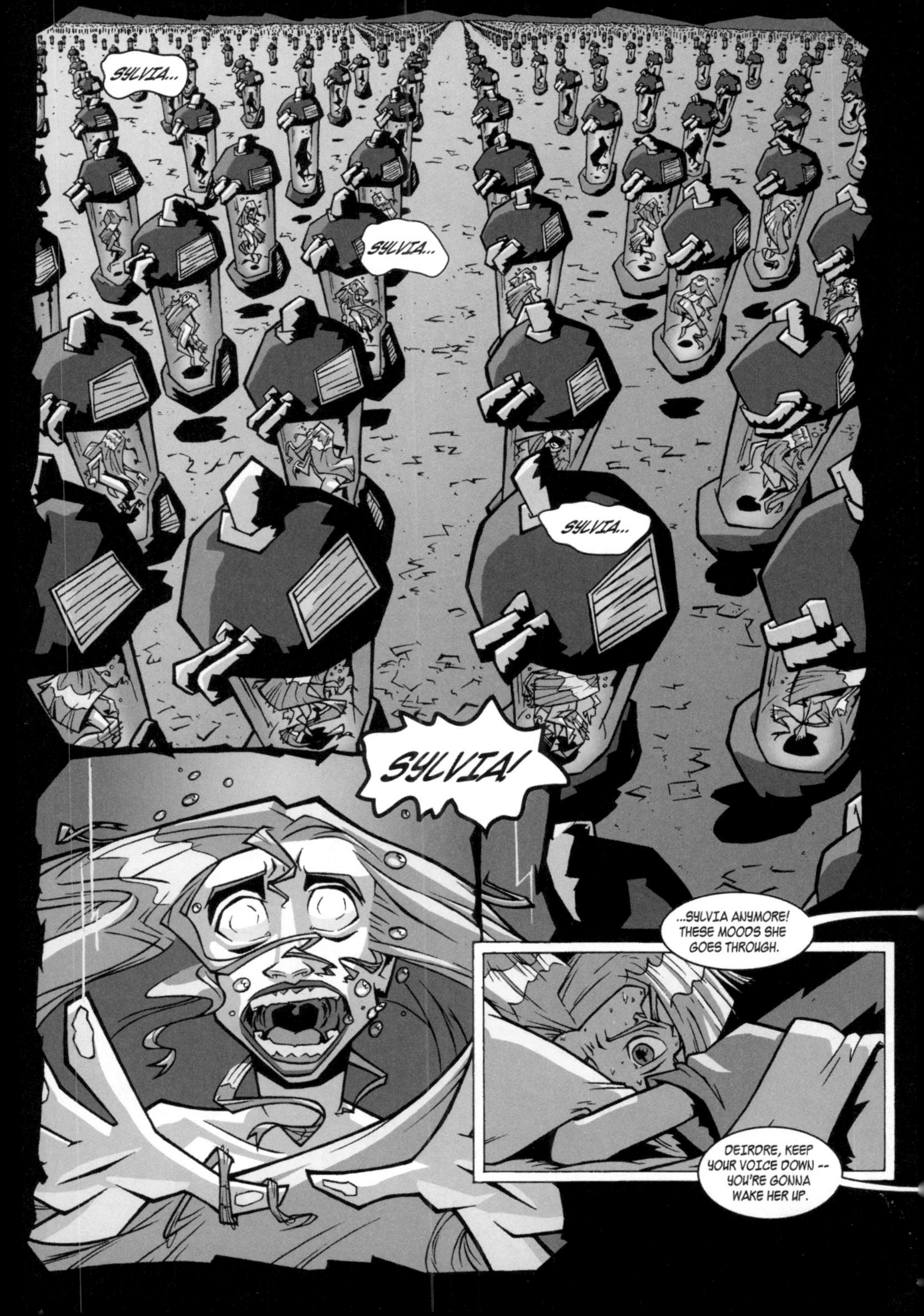
SYLVIA...
SYLVIA...
SYLVIA...
SYLVIA!
...SYLVIA ANYMORE! THESE MOODS SHE GOES THROUGH.
DEIRDRE, KEEP YOUR VOICE DOWN -- YOU'RE GONNA WAKE HER UP.

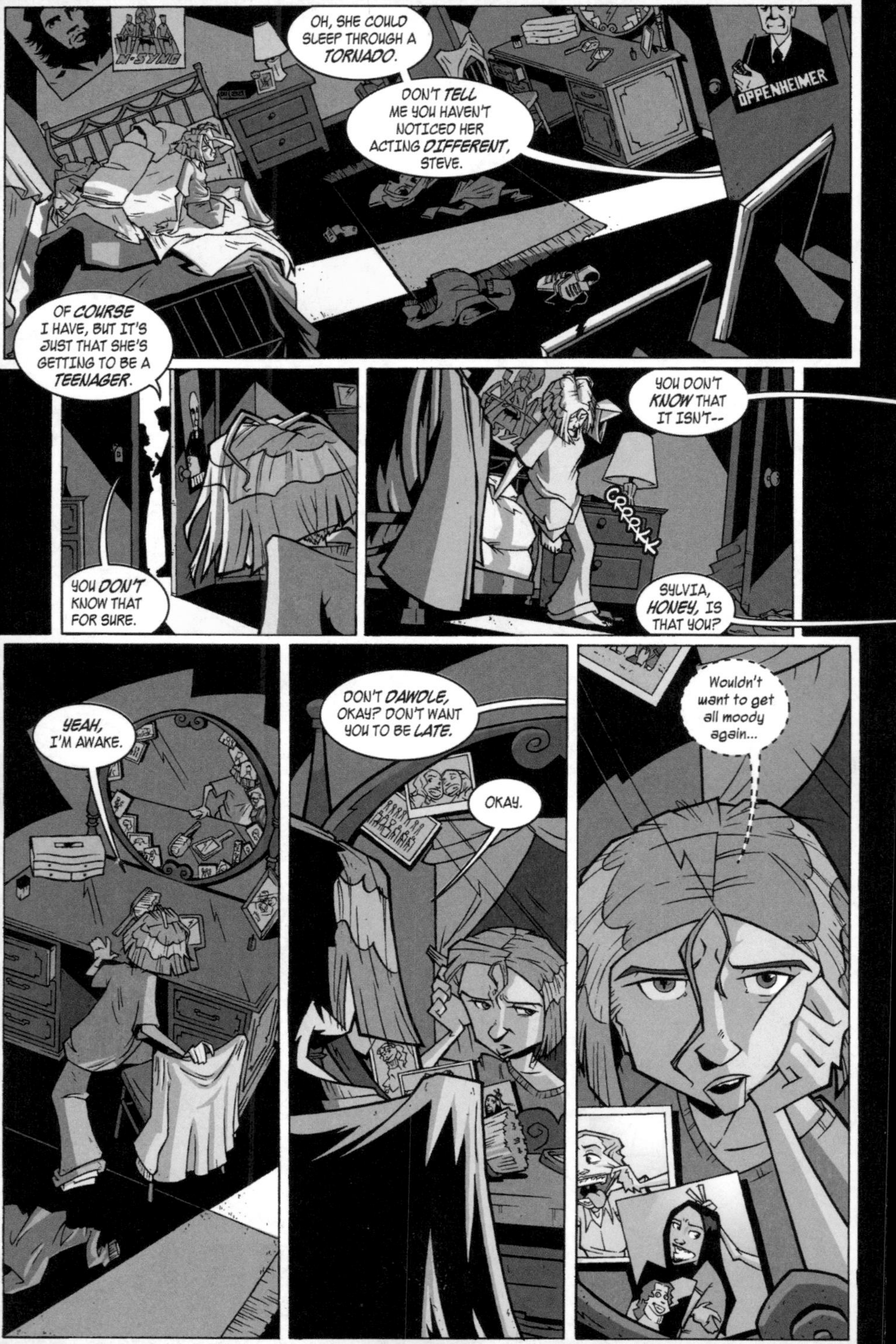
N-SYNC
OPPENHEIMER
OH, SHE COULD SLEEP THROUGH A TORNADO.
DON'T TELL ME YOU HAVEN'T NOTICED HER ACTING DIFFERENT, STEVE.
OF COURSE I HAVE, BUT IT'S JUST THAT SHE'S GETTING TO BE A TEENAGER.
YOU DON'T KNOW THAT FOR SURE.
YOU DON'T KNOW THAT IT ISN'T--
CRRRKKK
SYLVIA, HONEY, IS THAT YOU?
YEAH, I'M AWAKE.
DON'T DAWDLE, OKAY? DON'T WANT YOU TO BE LATE.
OKAY.
Wouldn't want to get all moody again...

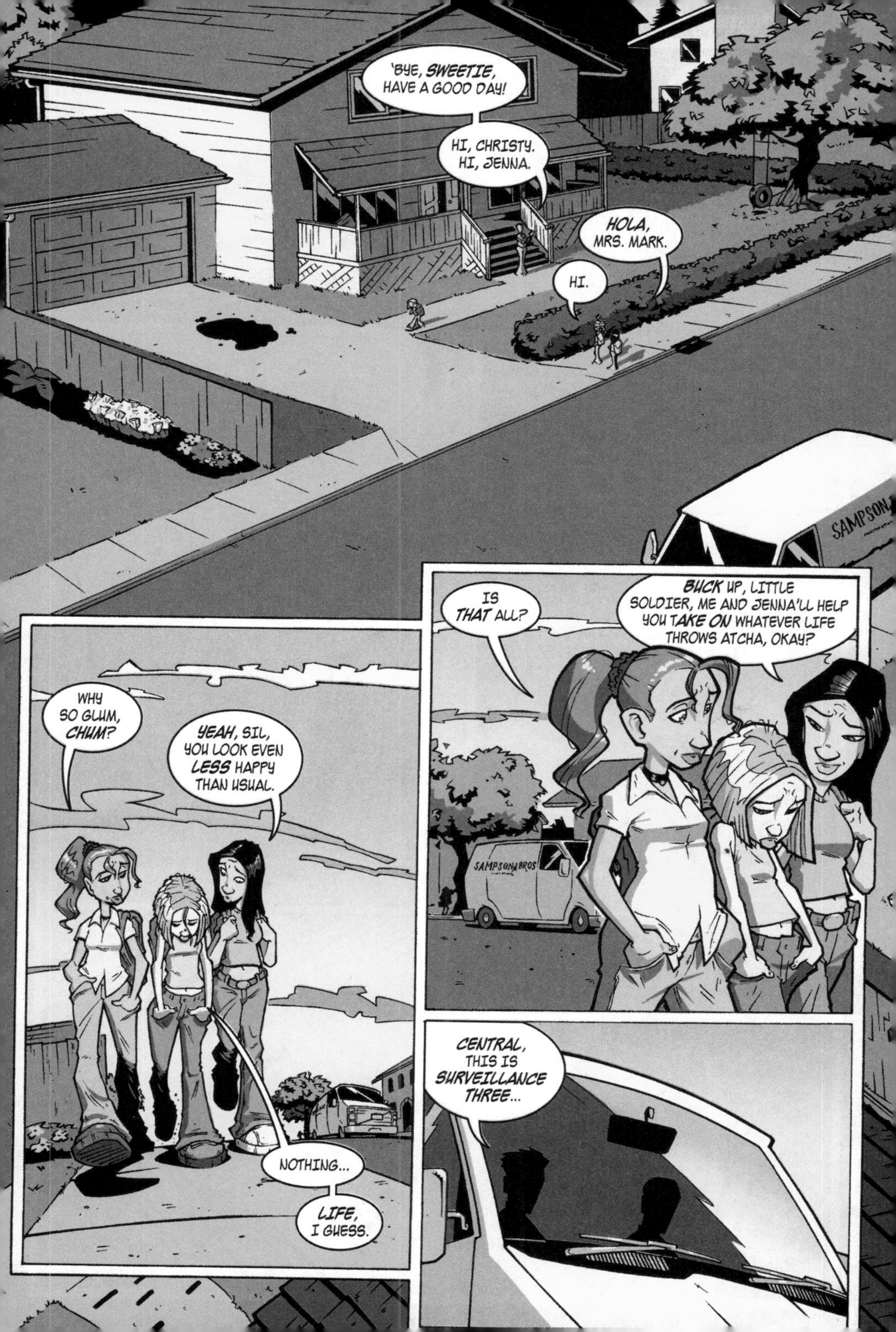

'BYE, SWEETIE, HAVE A GOOD DAY!
HI, CHRISTY. HI, JENNA.
HOLA, MRS. MARK.
HI.
SAMPSON
WHY SO GLUM, CHUM?
YEAH, SIL, YOU LOOK EVEN LESS HAPPY THAN USUAL.
NOTHING...
LIFE, I GUESS.
IS THAT ALL?
BUCK UP, LITTLE SOLDIER, ME AND JENNA'LL HELP YOU TAKE ON WHATEVER LIFE THROWS ATCHA, OKAY?
SAMPSON BROS
CENTRAL, THIS IS SURVEILLANCE THREE...

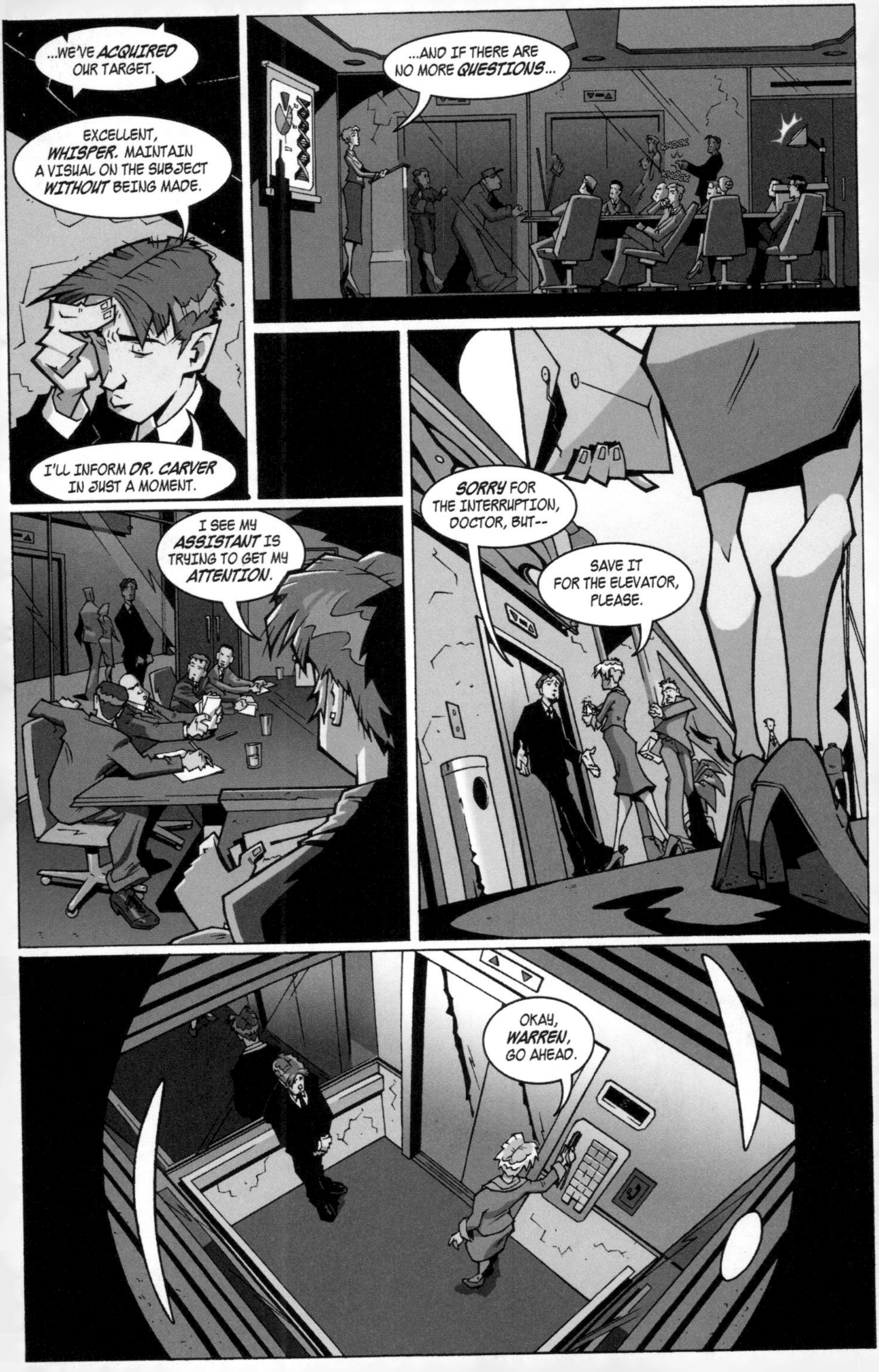
...WE'VE ACQUIRED OUR TARGET.
EXCELLENT, WHISPER. MAINTAIN A VISUAL ON THE SUBJECT WITHOUT BEING MADE.
I'LL INFORM DR. CARVER IN JUST A MOMENT.
...AND IF THERE ARE NO MORE QUESTIONS...
KNOCK
KNOCK
I SEE MY ASSISTANT IS TRYING TO GET MY ATTENTION.
SORRY FOR THE INTERRUPTION, DOCTOR, BUT--
SAVE IT FOR THE ELEVATOR, PLEASE.
OKAY, WARREN, GO AHEAD.

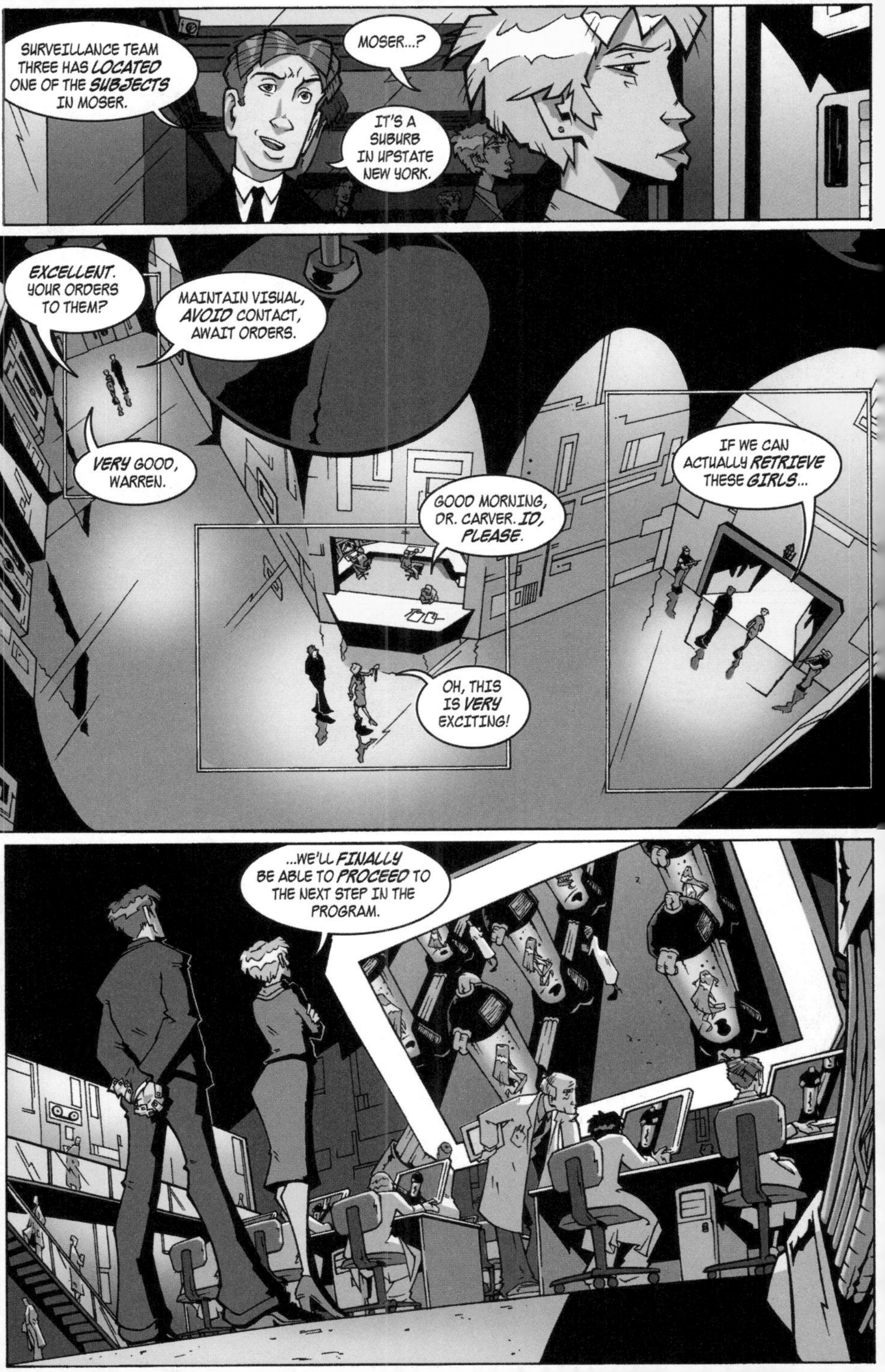

SURVEILLANCE TEAM THREE HAS LOCATED ONE OF THE SUBJECTS IN MOSER.
MOSER...?
IT'S A SUBURB IN UPSTATE NEW YORK.
EXCELLENT. YOUR ORDERS TO THEM?
MAINTAIN VISUAL, AVOID CONTACT, AWAIT ORDERS.
VERY GOOD, WARREN.
GOOD MORNING, DR. CARVER. ID, PLEASE.
OH, THIS IS VERY EXCITING!
IF WE CAN ACTUALLY RETRIEVE THESE GIRLS...
...WE'LL FINALLY BE ABLE TO PROCEED TO THE NEXT STEP IN THE PROGRAM.

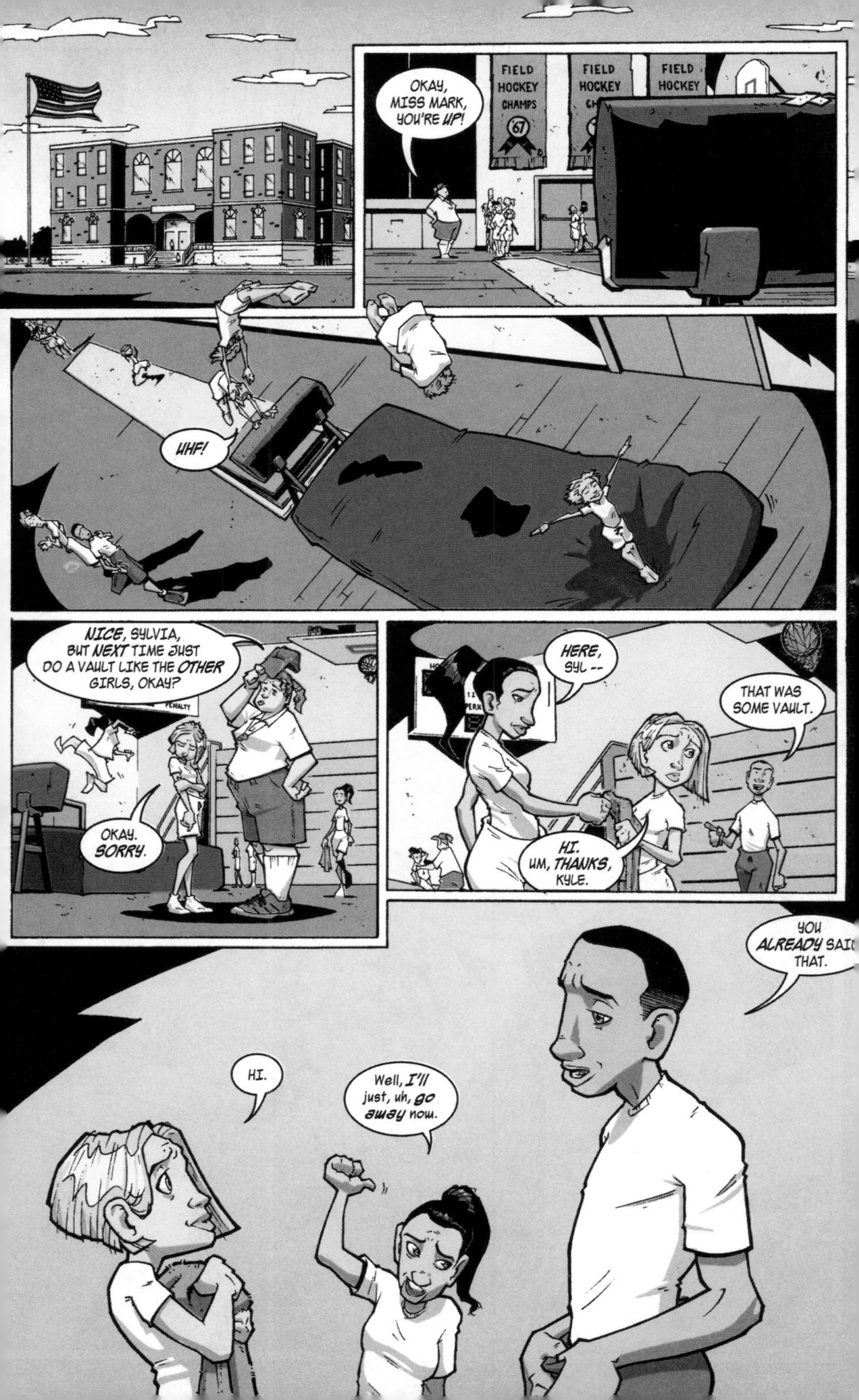
FIELD HOCKEY CHAMPS '67
FIELD HOCKEY
FIELD HOCKEY
OKAY, MISS MARK, YOU'RE *UP*!
UHF!
NICE, SYLVIA, BUT *NEXT* TIME JUST DO A VAULT LIKE THE *OTHER* GIRLS, OKAY?
PENALTY
OKAY. *SORRY*.
HERE, SYL --
HI. UM, *THANKS*, KYLE.
THAT WAS SOME VAULT.
YOU *ALREADY* SAI THAT.
HI.
Well, *I'll* just, uh, *go away* now.

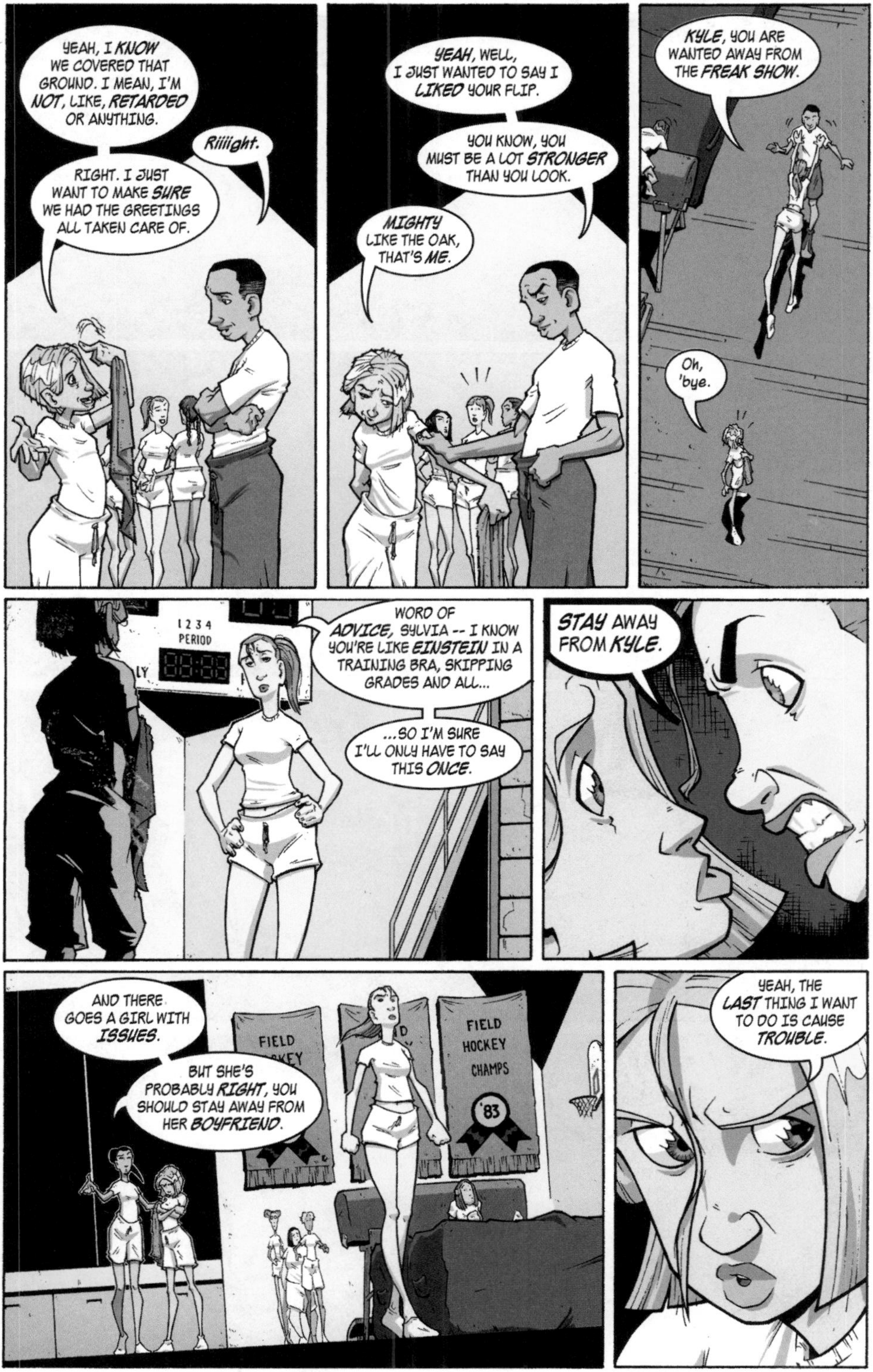
YEAH, I KNOW WE COVERED THAT GROUND. I MEAN, I'M NOT, LIKE, RETARDED OR ANYTHING.
Riiiight.
RIGHT. I JUST WANT TO MAKE SURE WE HAD THE GREETINGS ALL TAKEN CARE OF.
YEAH, WELL, I JUST WANTED TO SAY I LIKED YOUR FLIP.
YOU KNOW, YOU MUST BE A LOT STRONGER THAN YOU LOOK.
MIGHTY LIKE THE OAK, THAT'S ME.
KYLE, YOU ARE WANTED AWAY FROM THE FREAK SHOW.
Oh, 'bye.
1 2 3 4
PERIOD
WORD OF ADVICE, SYLVIA -- I KNOW YOU'RE LIKE EINSTEIN IN A TRAINING BRA, SKIPPING GRADES AND ALL...
...SO I'M SURE I'LL ONLY HAVE TO SAY THIS ONCE.
STAY AWAY FROM KYLE.
AND THERE GOES A GIRL WITH ISSUES.
BUT SHE'S PROBABLY RIGHT, YOU SHOULD STAY AWAY FROM HER BOYFRIEND.
FIELD HOCKEY CHAMPS
'83
YEAH, THE LAST THING I WANT TO DO IS CAUSE TROUBLE.

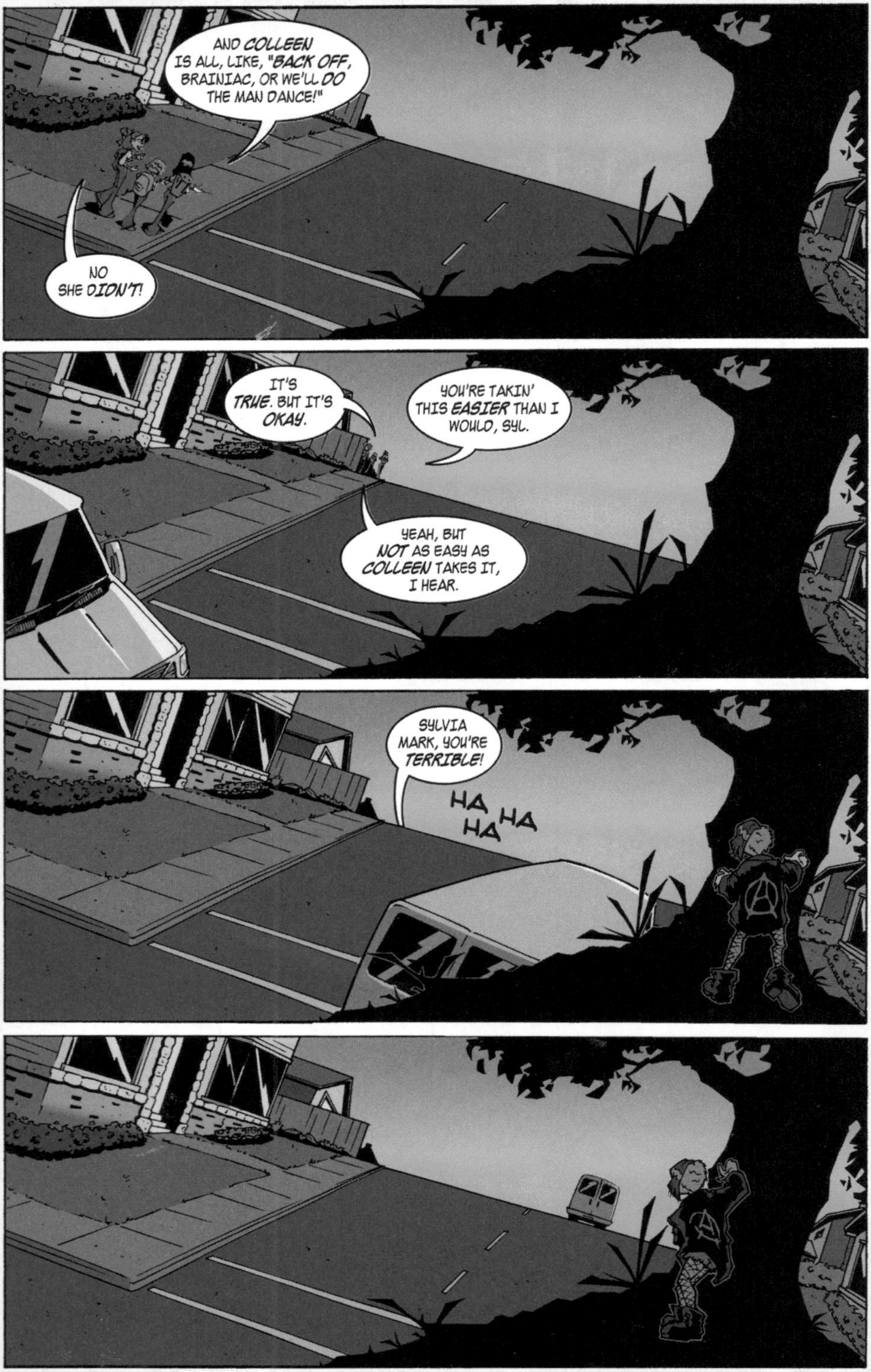
AND COLLEEN IS ALL, LIKE, "BACK OFF, BRAINIAC, OR WE'LL DO THE MAN DANCE!"
NO SHE DIDN'T!
IT'S TRUE. BUT IT'S OKAY.
YOU'RE TAKIN' THIS EASIER THAN I WOULD, SYL.
YEAH, BUT NOT AS EASY AS COLLEEN TAKES IT, I HEAR.
SYLVIA MARK, YOU'RE TERRIBLE!
HA HA HA

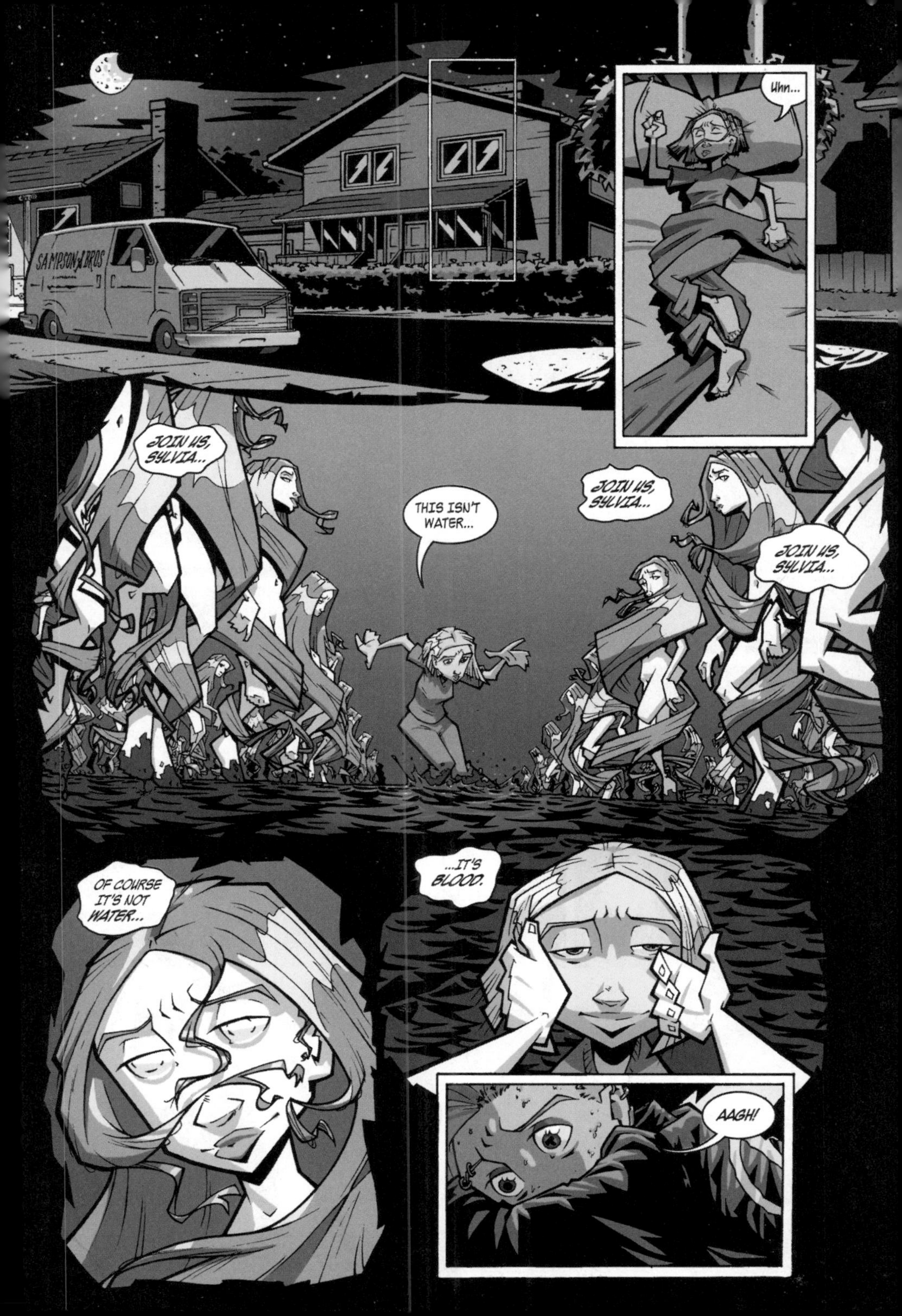
SAMPSON BROS
Uhn...
JOIN US, SYLVIA...
THIS ISN'T WATER...
JOIN US, SYLVIA...
JOIN US, SYLVIA...
OF COURSE IT'S NOT WATER...
...IT'S BLOOD.
AAGH!

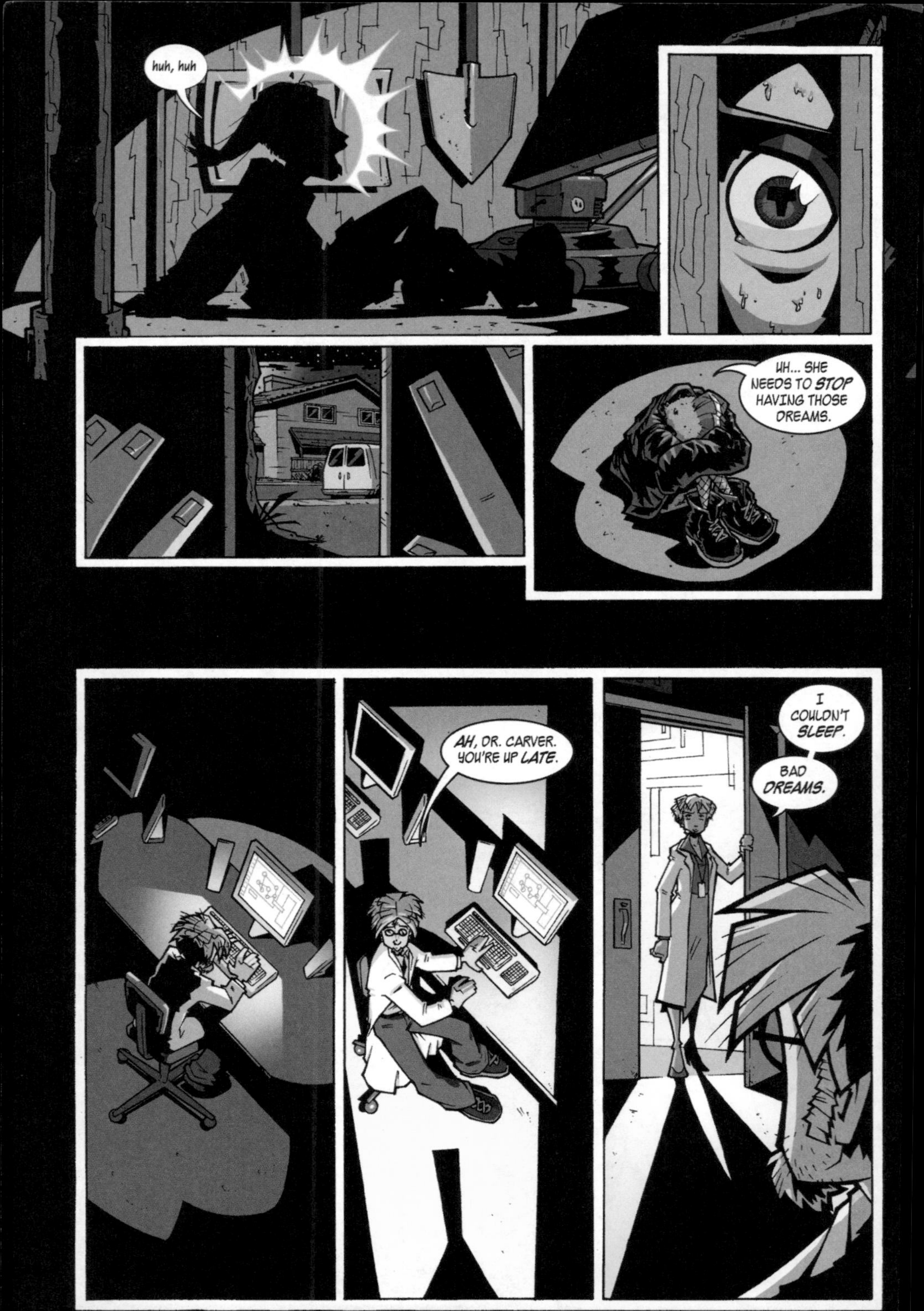
huh, huh
UH... SHE NEEDS TO STOP HAVING THOSE DREAMS.
AH, DR. CARVER. YOU'RE UP LATE.
I COULDN'T SLEEP.
BAD DREAMS.

OH, MAY I *GET* YOU--

NO...

...I *JUST* WANTED TO COME *LOOK* AT THEM.

DO YOU *KNOW* WHAT THIS ONE *DOES*, EDGAR?

NO, DOCTOR, BUT I'LL LOOK IT UP FOR YOU.

SHE *FLIES*.

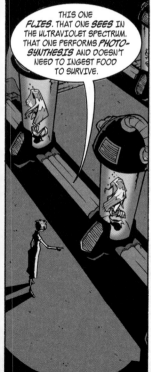

THIS ONE *FLIES*. THAT ONE *SEES* IN THE ULTRAVIOLET SPECTRUM. THAT ONE PERFORMS *PHOTO-SYNTHESIS* AND DOESN'T NEED TO INGEST FOOD TO SURVIVE.

WE *HAVE* TO *FIND* THEM AND BRING THEM BACK TO *ACTIVATE* THEM, EDGAR.

I DON'T KNOW WHAT KINDS OF *DAMAGE* THEY'LL CAUSE IF THEY START TO MANIFEST OUT IN THE WORLD...

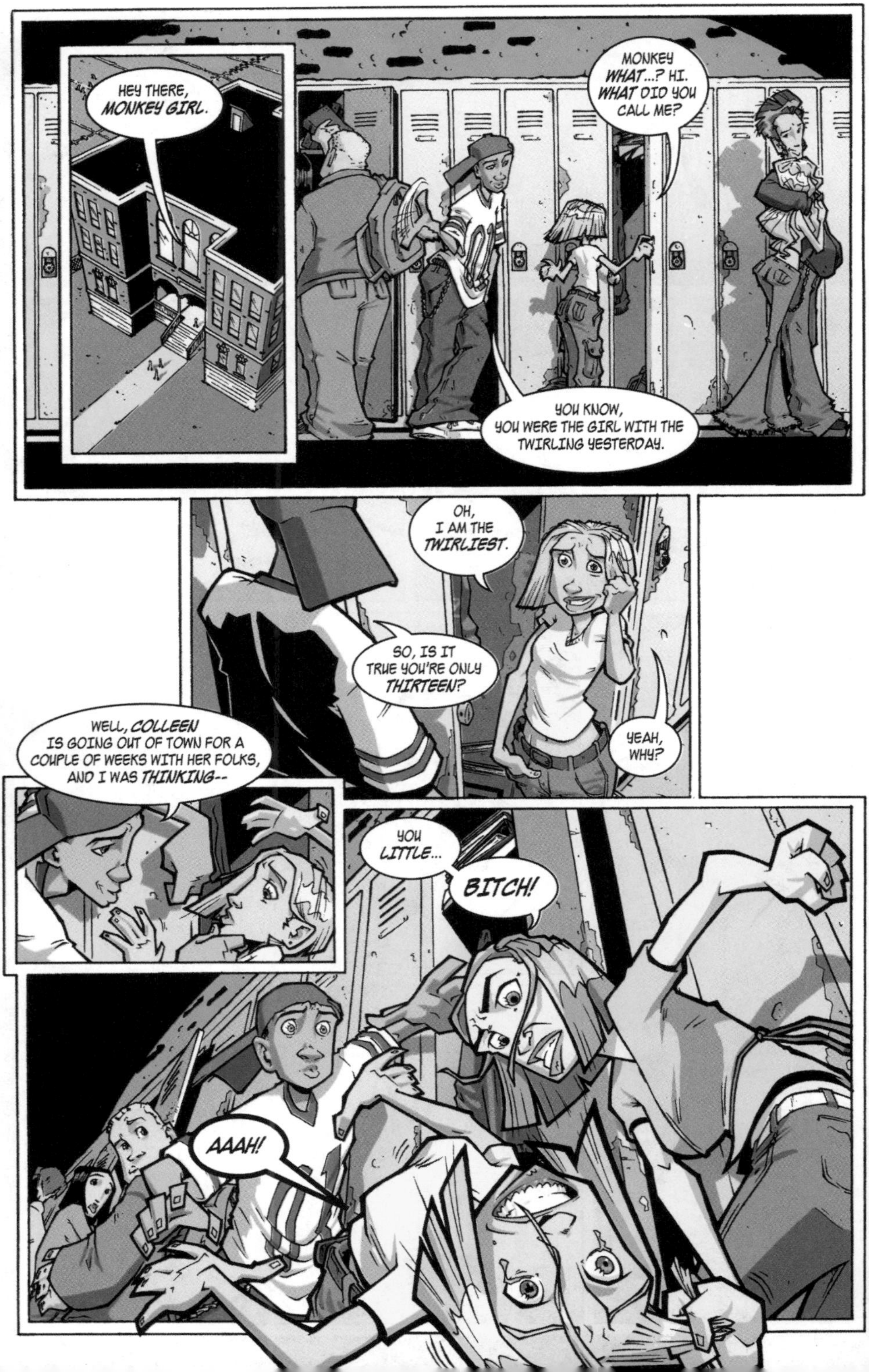
HEY THERE, *MONKEY GIRL*.
MONKEY *WHAT*...? HI. *WHAT* DID YOU CALL ME?
YOU KNOW, YOU WERE THE GIRL WITH THE TWIRLING YESTERDAY.
OH, I AM THE *TWIRLIEST*.
SO, IS IT TRUE YOU'RE ONLY *THIRTEEN*?
YEAH, WHY?
WELL, *COLLEEN* IS GOING OUT OF TOWN FOR A COUPLE OF WEEKS WITH HER FOLKS, AND I WAS *THINKING*--
YOU *LITTLE*...
BITCH!
AAAH!

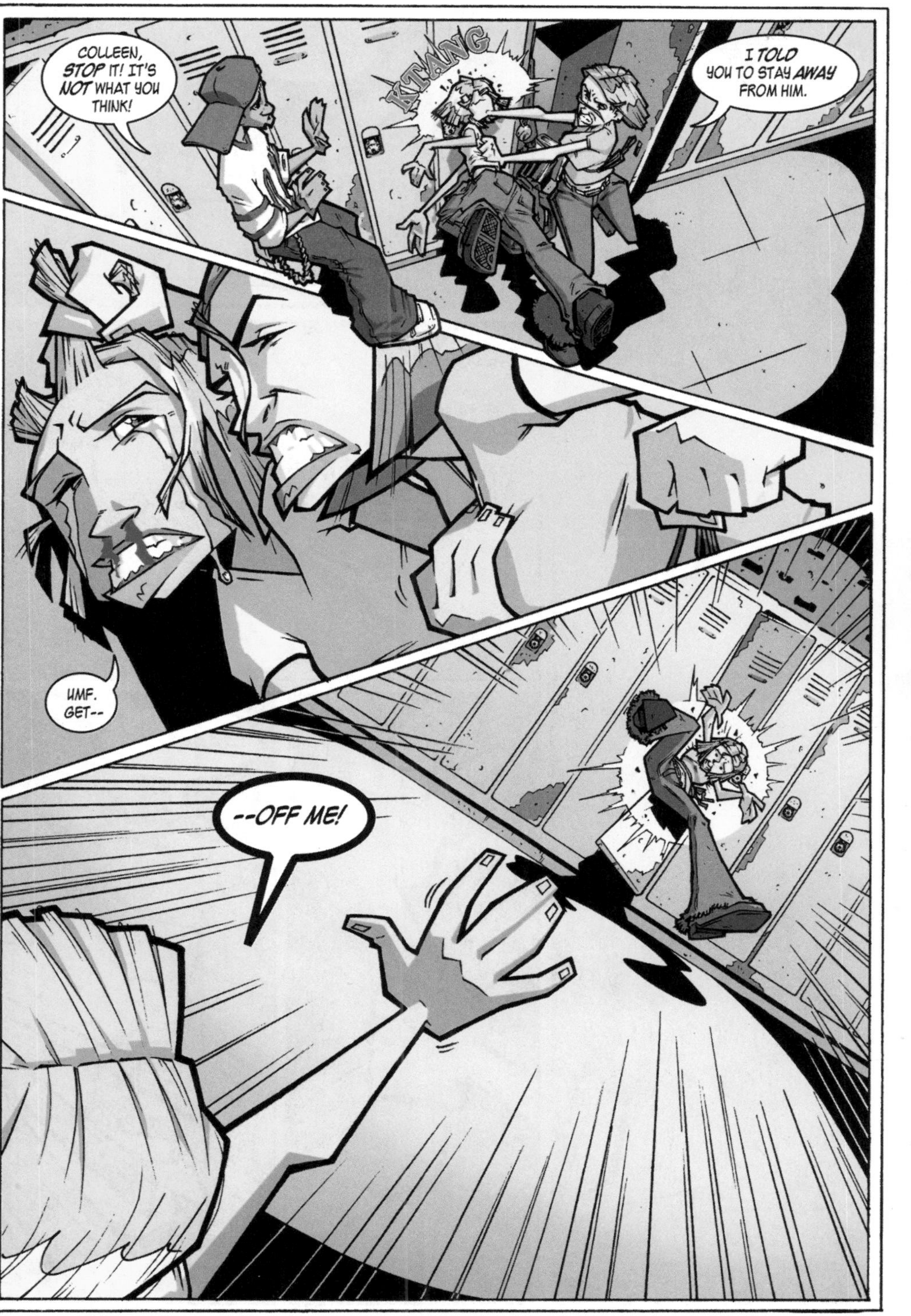
COLLEEN, STOP IT! IT'S NOT WHAT YOU THINK!
KTANG
I TOLD YOU TO STAY AWAY FROM HIM.
UMF. GET--
--OFF ME!

COME ON! GET OUT OF THE WAY!
KILL YOU!
GET OFF ME.
Please...
SNAP!
AAAARGH!

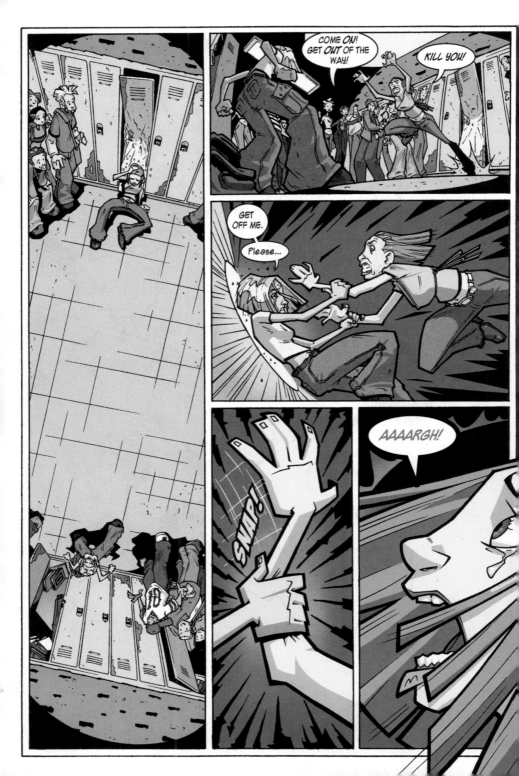

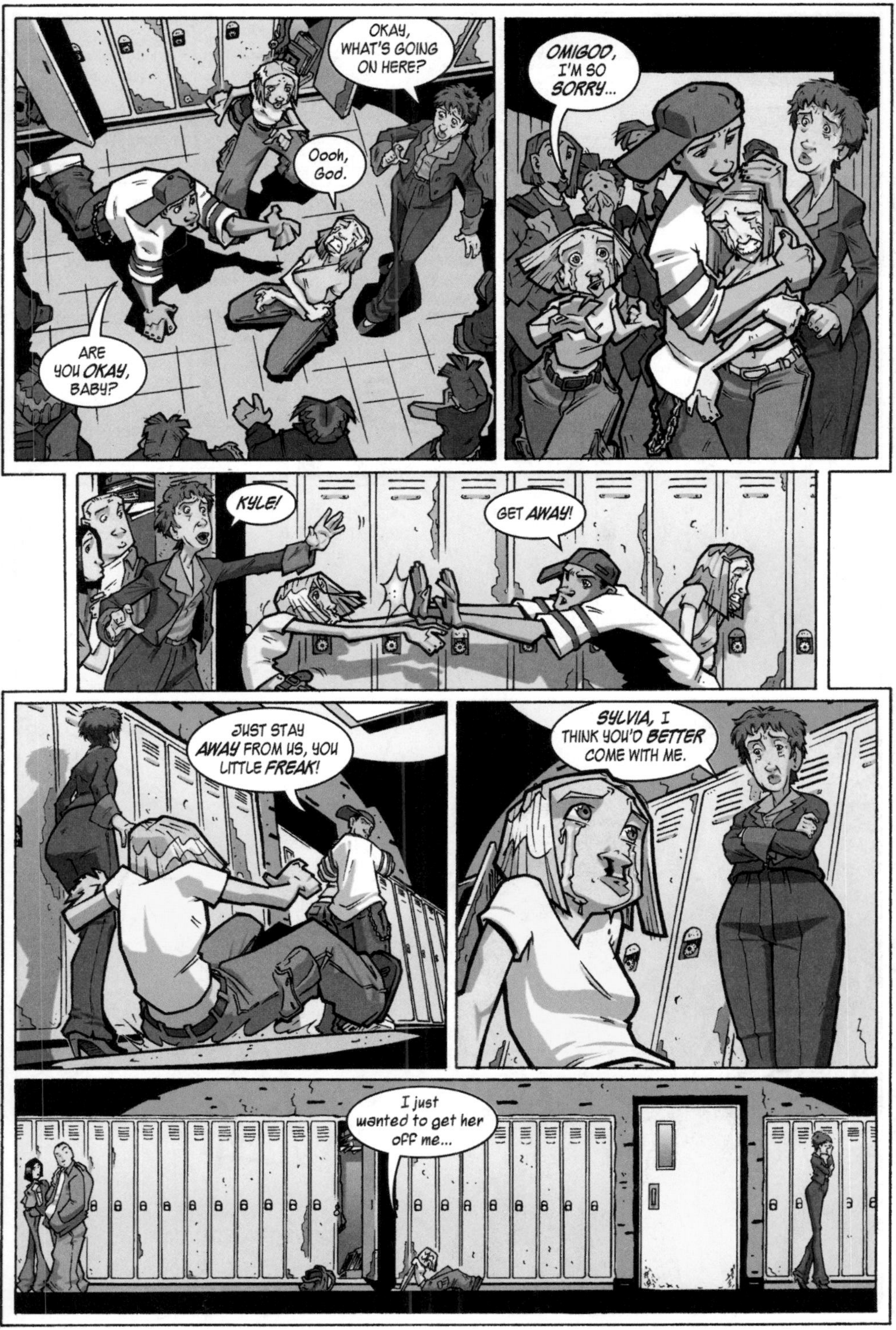
OKAY, WHAT'S GOING ON HERE?
Oooh, God.
ARE YOU OKAY, BABY?
OMIGOD, I'M SO SORRY...
KYLE!
GET AWAY!
JUST STAY AWAY FROM US, YOU LITTLE FREAK!
SYLVIA, I THINK YOU'D BETTER COME WITH ME.
I just wanted to get her off me...

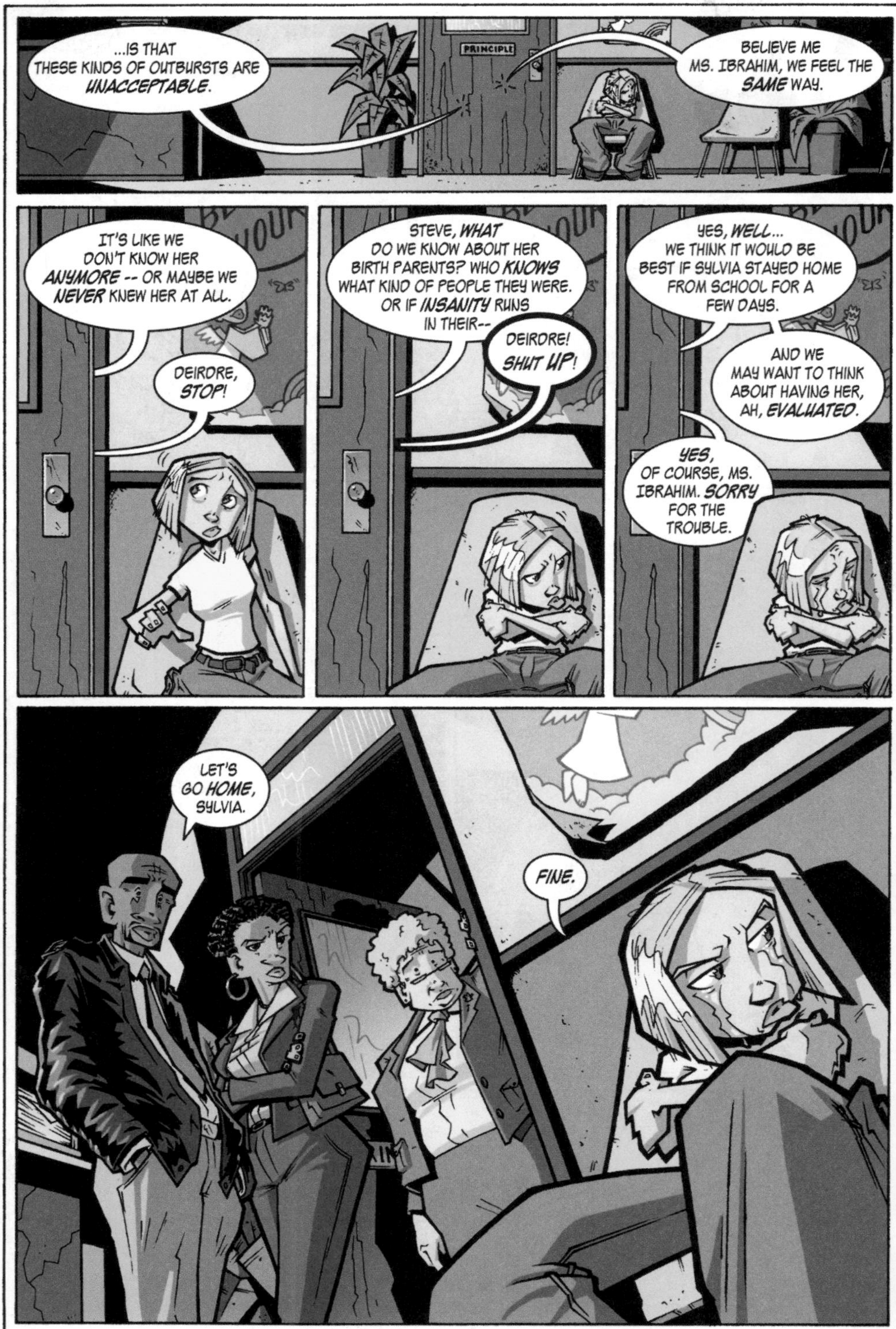
...IS THAT THESE KINDS OF OUTBURSTS ARE UNACCEPTABLE.
PRINCIPLE
BELIEVE ME MS. IBRAHIM, WE FEEL THE SAME WAY.
IT'S LIKE WE DON'T KNOW HER ANYMORE -- OR MAYBE WE NEVER KNEW HER AT ALL.
DEIRDRE, STOP!
STEVE, WHAT DO WE KNOW ABOUT HER BIRTH PARENTS? WHO KNOWS WHAT KIND OF PEOPLE THEY WERE. OR IF INSANITY RUNS IN THEIR--
DEIRDRE! SHUT UP!
YES, WELL... WE THINK IT WOULD BE BEST IF SYLVIA STAYED HOME FROM SCHOOL FOR A FEW DAYS.
AND WE MAY WANT TO THINK ABOUT HAVING HER, AH, EVALUATED.
YES, OF COURSE, MS. IBRAHIM. SORRY FOR THE TROUBLE.
LET'S GO HOME, SYLVIA.
FINE.

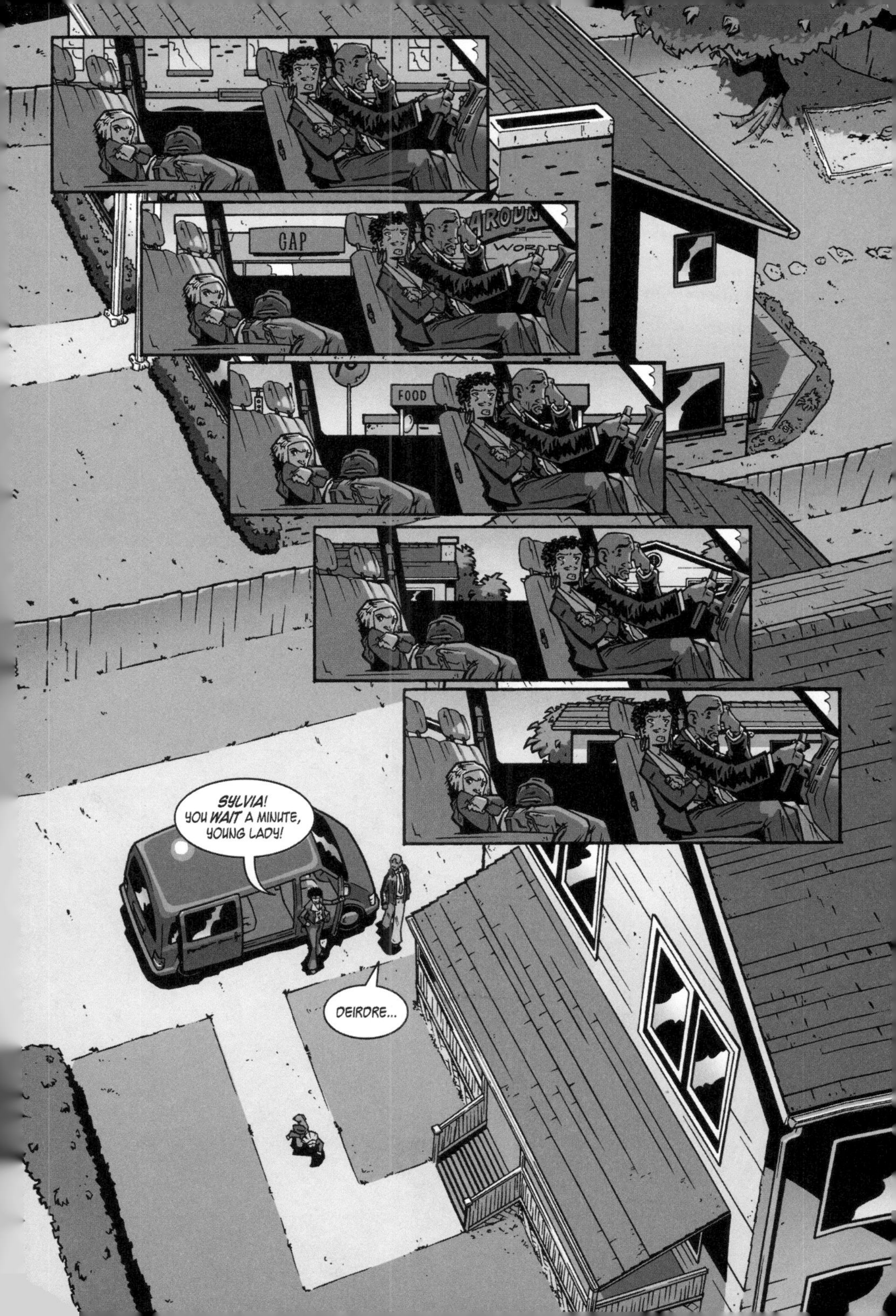
GAP
FOOD
SYLVIA! YOU WAIT A MINUTE, YOUNG LADY!
DEIRDRE...

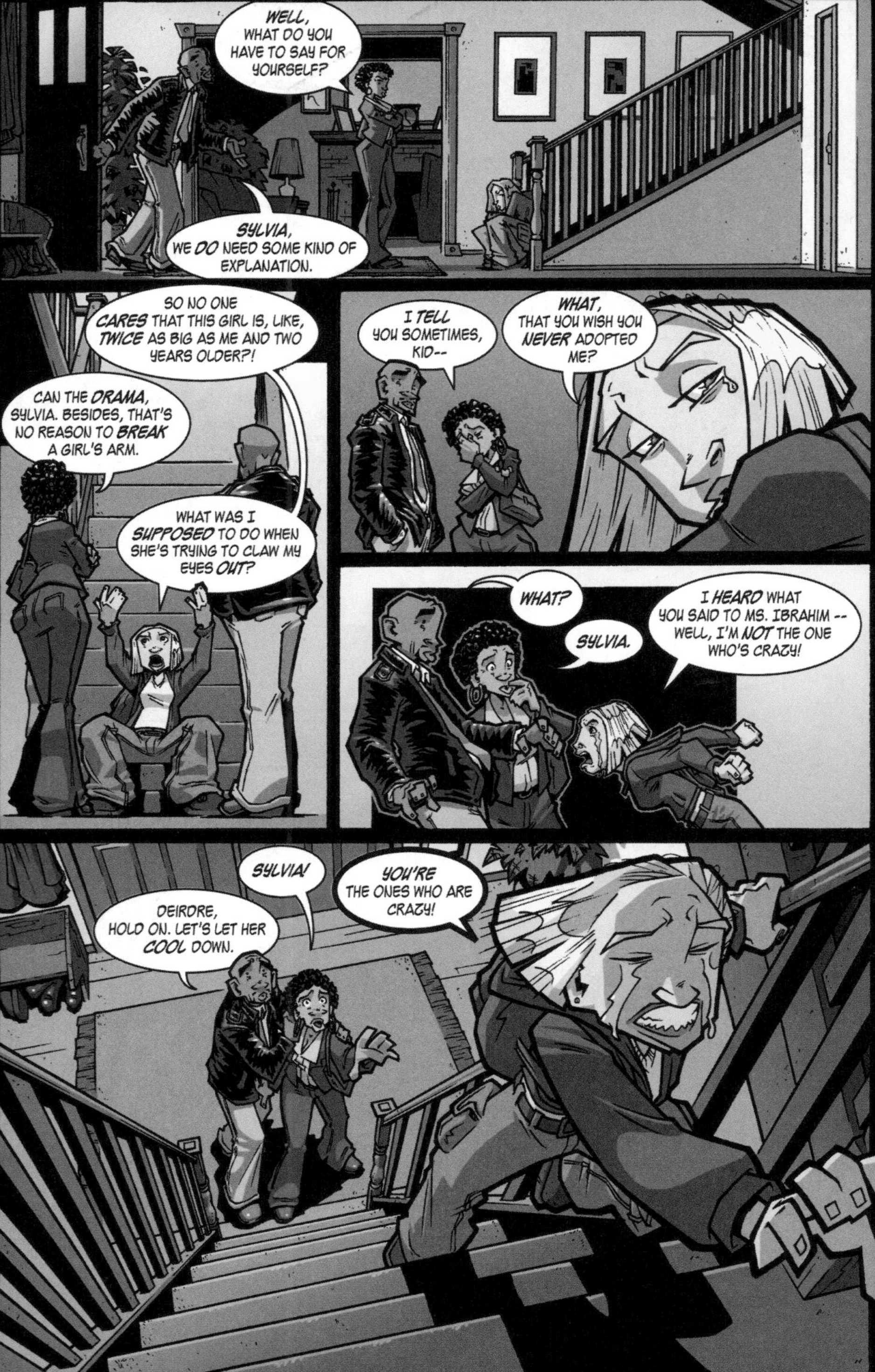
WELL, WHAT DO YOU HAVE TO SAY FOR YOURSELF?
SYLVIA, WE DO NEED SOME KIND OF EXPLANATION.
SO NO ONE CARES THAT THIS GIRL IS, LIKE, TWICE AS BIG AS ME AND TWO YEARS OLDER?!
CAN THE DRAMA, SYLVIA. BESIDES, THAT'S NO REASON TO BREAK A GIRL'S ARM.
WHAT WAS I SUPPOSED TO DO WHEN SHE'S TRYING TO CLAW MY EYES OUT?
I TELL YOU SOMETIMES, KID--
WHAT, THAT YOU WISH YOU NEVER ADOPTED ME?
WHAT?
SYLVIA.
I HEARD WHAT YOU SAID TO MS. IBRAHIM -- WELL, I'M NOT THE ONE WHO'S CRAZY!
SYLVIA!
DEIRDRE, HOLD ON. LET'S LET HER COOL DOWN.
YOU'RE THE ONES WHO ARE CRAZY!

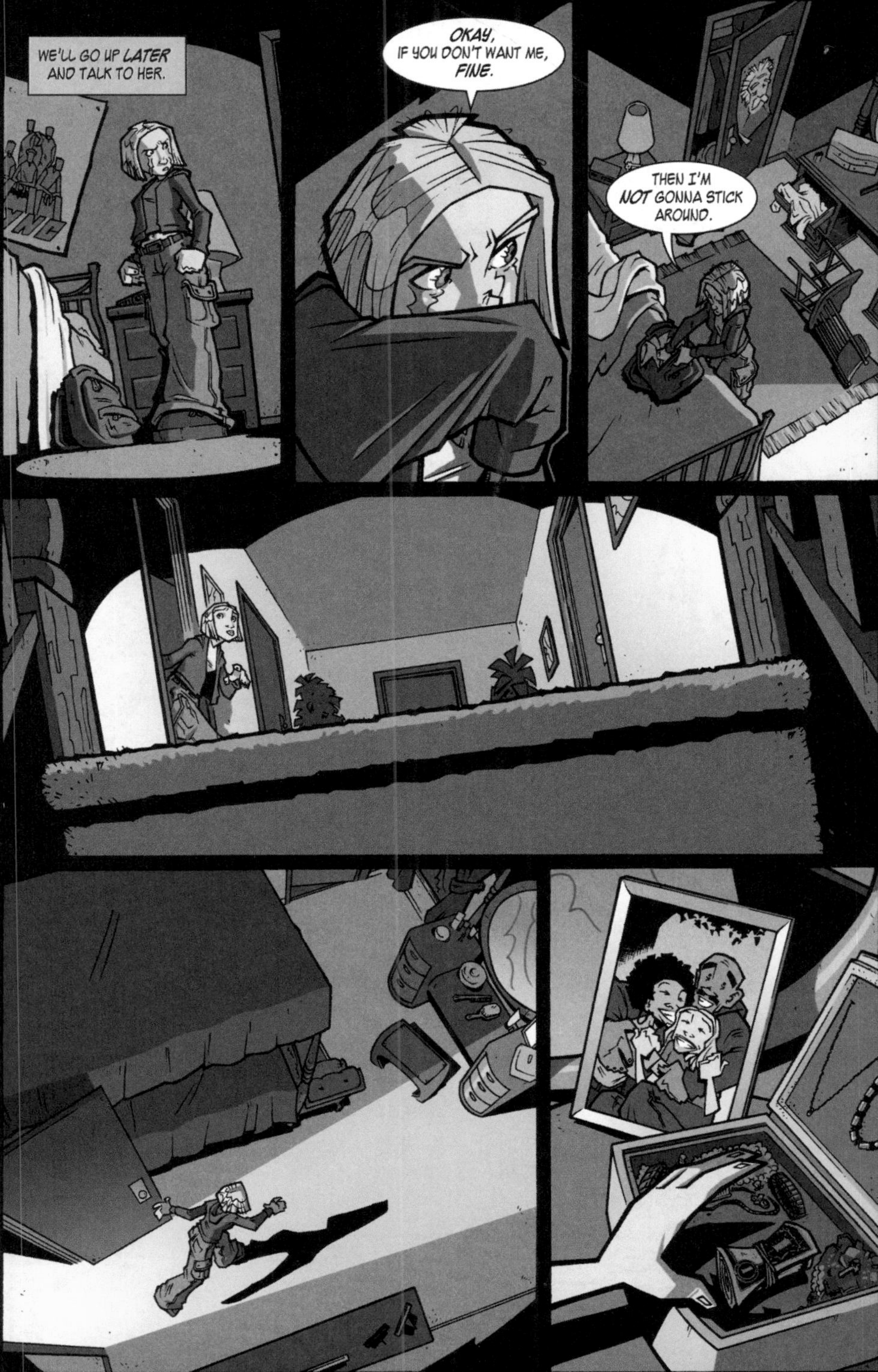
WE'LL GO UP LATER AND TALK TO HER.
OKAY, IF YOU DON'T WANT ME, FINE.
THEN I'M NOT GONNA STICK AROUND.

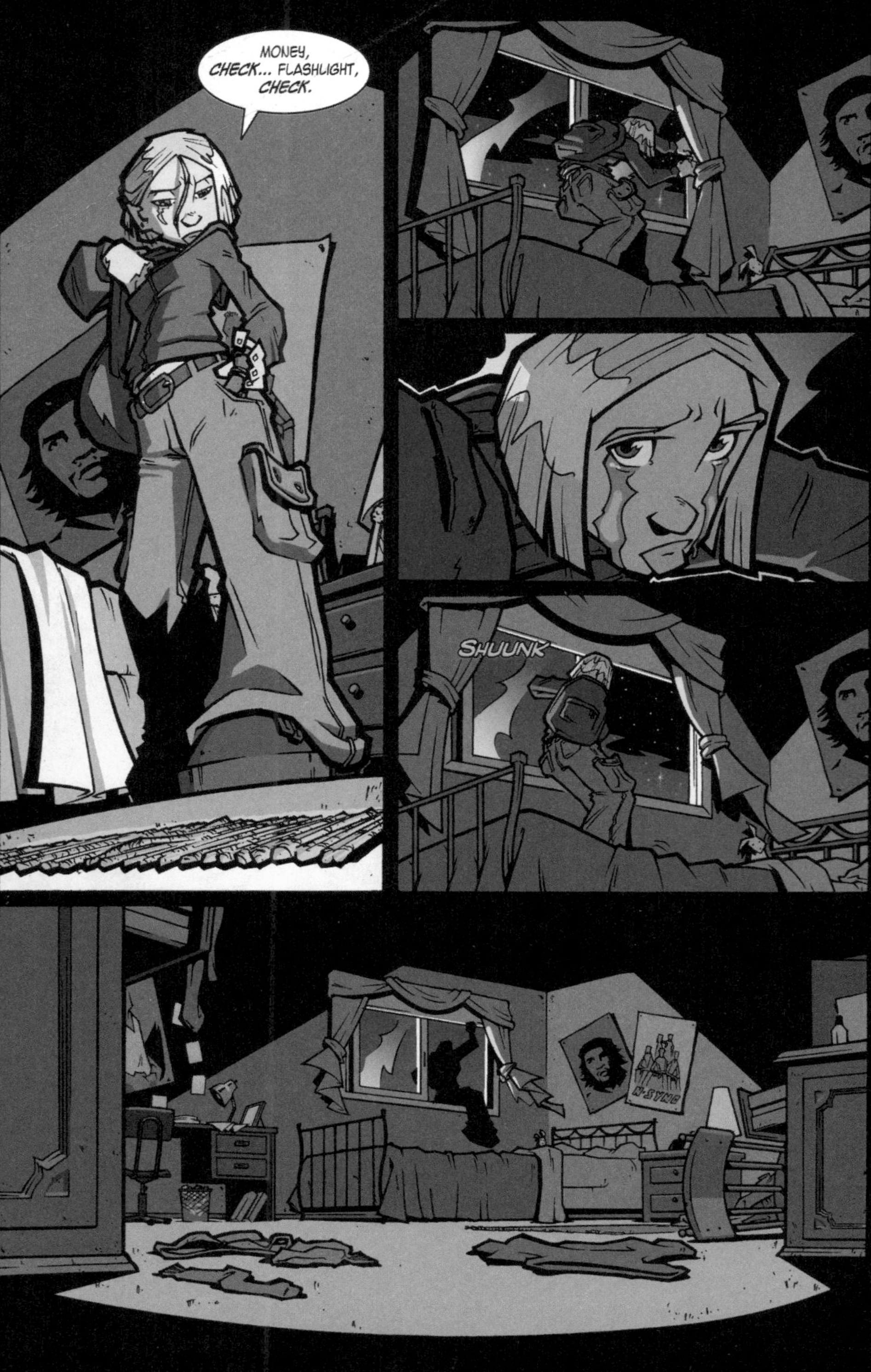
MONEY, CHECK... FLASHLIGHT, CHECK.
SHUUNK
N-SYNC

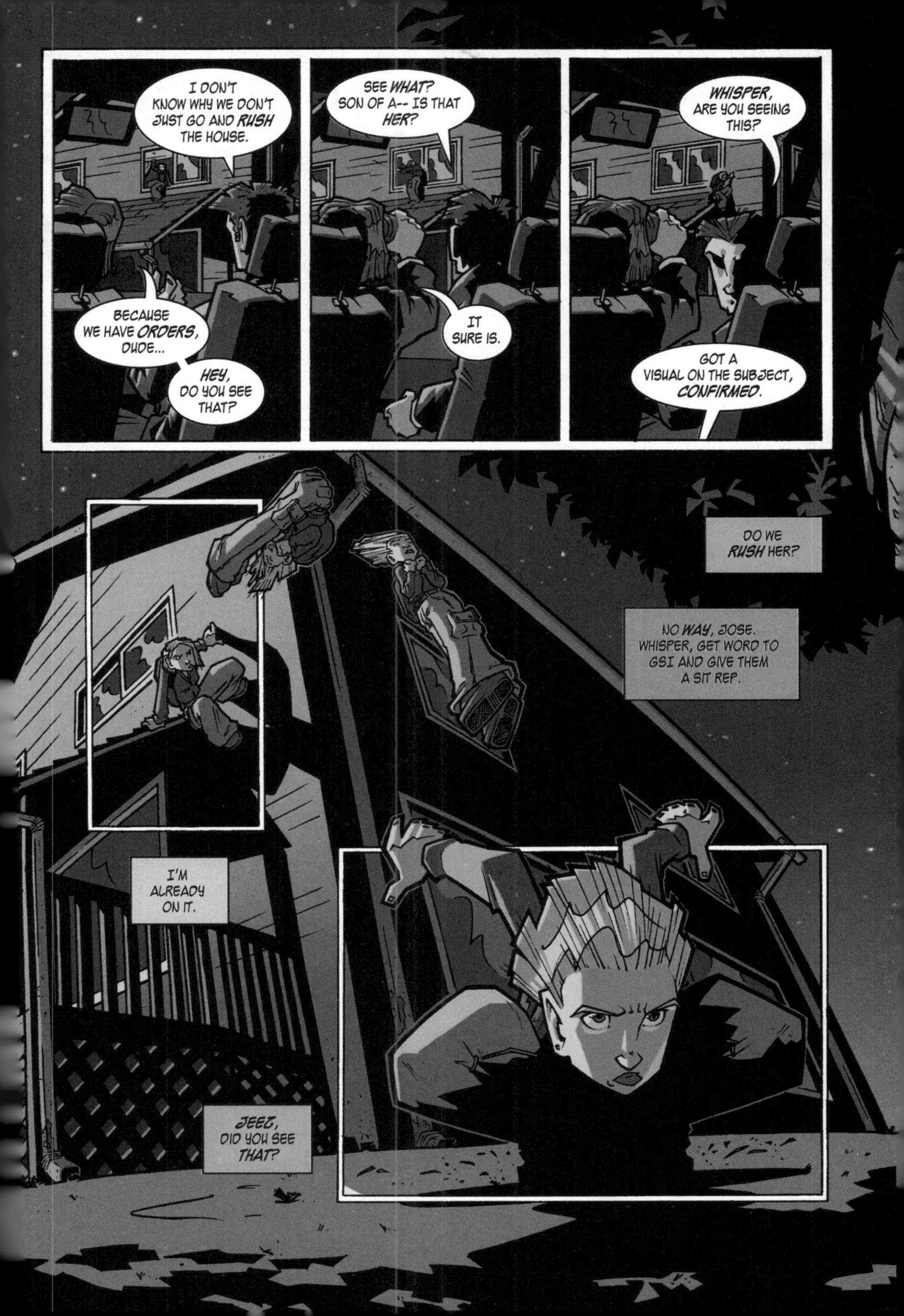
I DON'T KNOW WHY WE DON'T JUST GO AND RUSH THE HOUSE.
BECAUSE WE HAVE ORDERS, DUDE...
HEY, DO YOU SEE THAT?
SEE WHAT? SON OF A-- IS THAT HER?
IT SURE IS.
WHISPER, ARE YOU SEEING THIS?
GOT A VISUAL ON THE SUBJECT, CONFIRMED.
DO WE RUSH HER?
NO WAY, JOSE. WHISPER, GET WORD TO GSI AND GIVE THEM A SIT REP.
I'M ALREADY ON IT.
JEEZ, DID YOU SEE THAT?

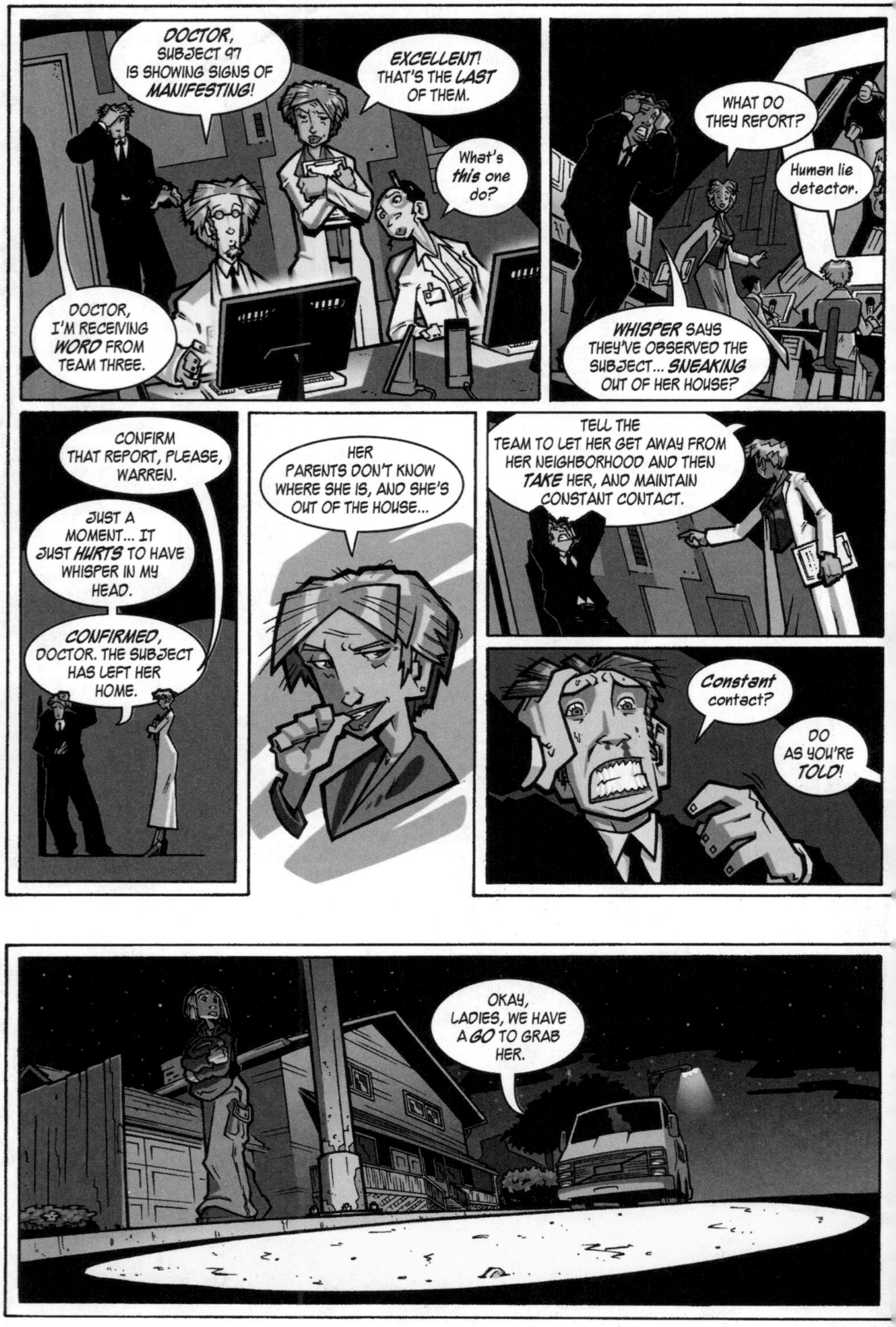
DOCTOR, SUBJECT 97 IS SHOWING SIGNS OF MANIFESTING!
EXCELLENT! THAT'S THE LAST OF THEM.
What's this one do?
DOCTOR, I'M RECEIVING WORD FROM TEAM THREE.
WHAT DO THEY REPORT?
Human lie detector.
WHISPER SAYS THEY'VE OBSERVED THE SUBJECT... SNEAKING OUT OF HER HOUSE?
CONFIRM THAT REPORT, PLEASE, WARREN.
JUST A MOMENT... IT JUST HURTS TO HAVE WHISPER IN MY HEAD.
CONFIRMED, DOCTOR. THE SUBJECT HAS LEFT HER HOME.
HER PARENTS DON'T KNOW WHERE SHE IS, AND SHE'S OUT OF THE HOUSE...
TELL THE TEAM TO LET HER GET AWAY FROM HER NEIGHBORHOOD AND THEN TAKE HER, AND MAINTAIN CONSTANT CONTACT.
Constant contact?
DO AS YOU'RE TOLD!
OKAY, LADIES, WE HAVE A GO TO GRAB HER.

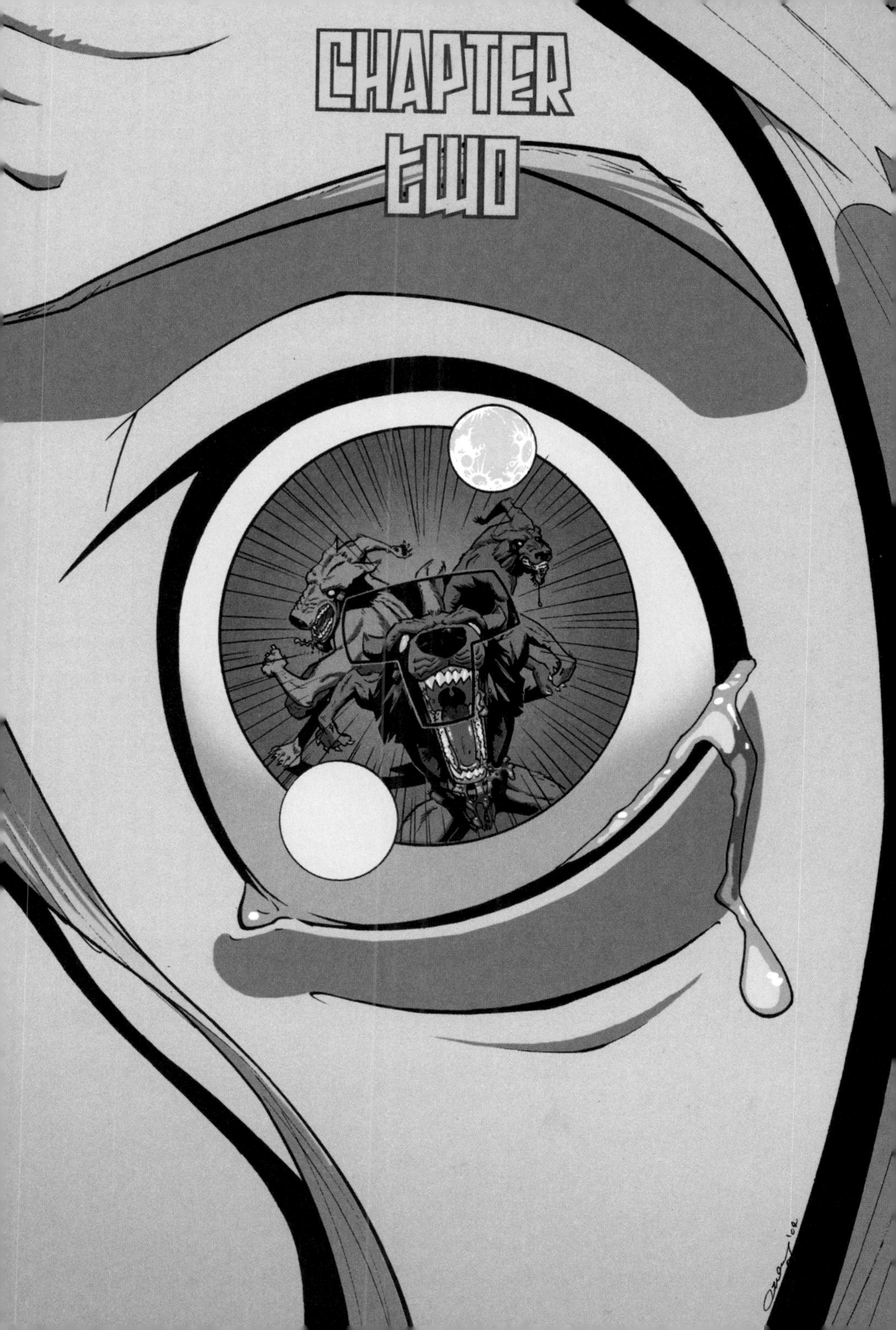
CHAPTER
TWO

"okay. I'm ready."

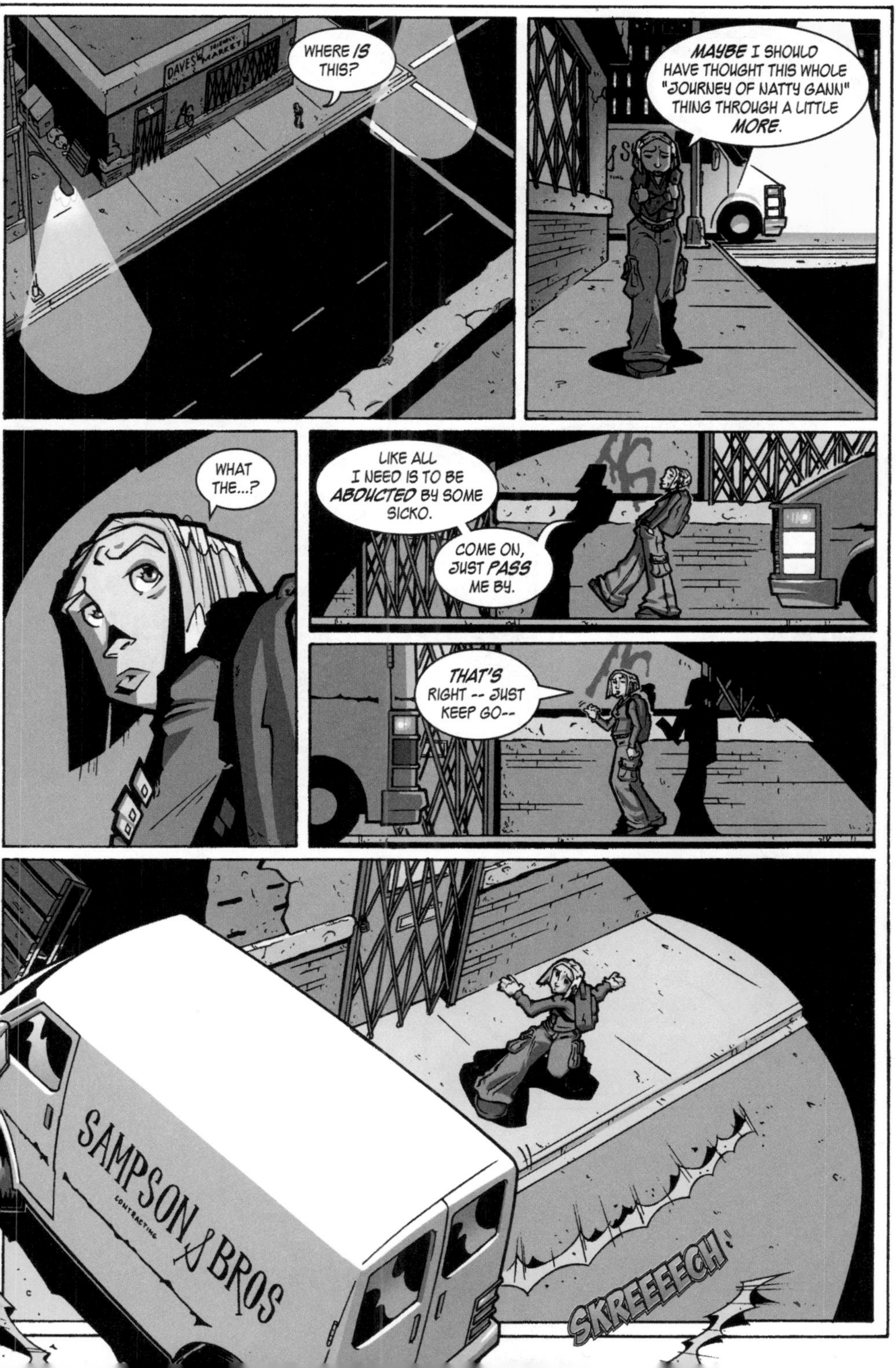
DAVES
MARKET
WHERE *IS* THIS?
MAYBE I SHOULD HAVE THOUGHT THIS WHOLE "JOURNEY OF NATTY GANN" THING THROUGH A LITTLE *MORE*.
WHAT THE...?
LIKE ALL I NEED IS TO BE *ABDUCTED* BY SOME SICKO.
COME ON, JUST *PASS* ME BY.
THAT'S RIGHT -- JUST KEEP GO--
SAMPSON BROS
CONTRACTING
SKREEEEECH

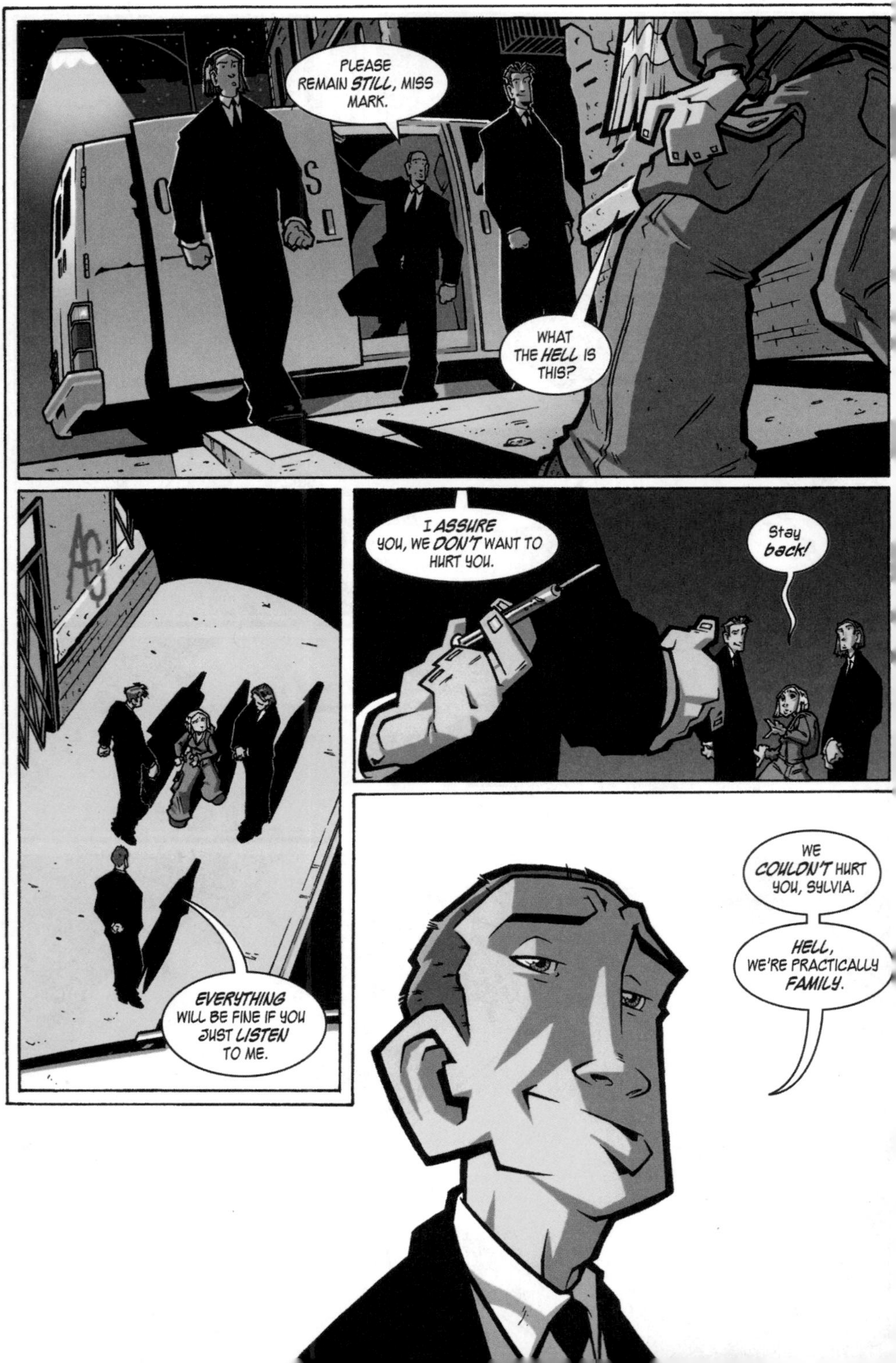
PLEASE REMAIN STILL, MISS MARK.
WHAT THE HELL IS THIS?
EVERYTHING WILL BE FINE IF YOU JUST LISTEN TO ME.
I ASSURE YOU, WE DON'T WANT TO HURT YOU.
Stay back!
WE COULDN'T HURT YOU, SYLVIA.
HELL, WE'RE PRACTICALLY FAMILY.

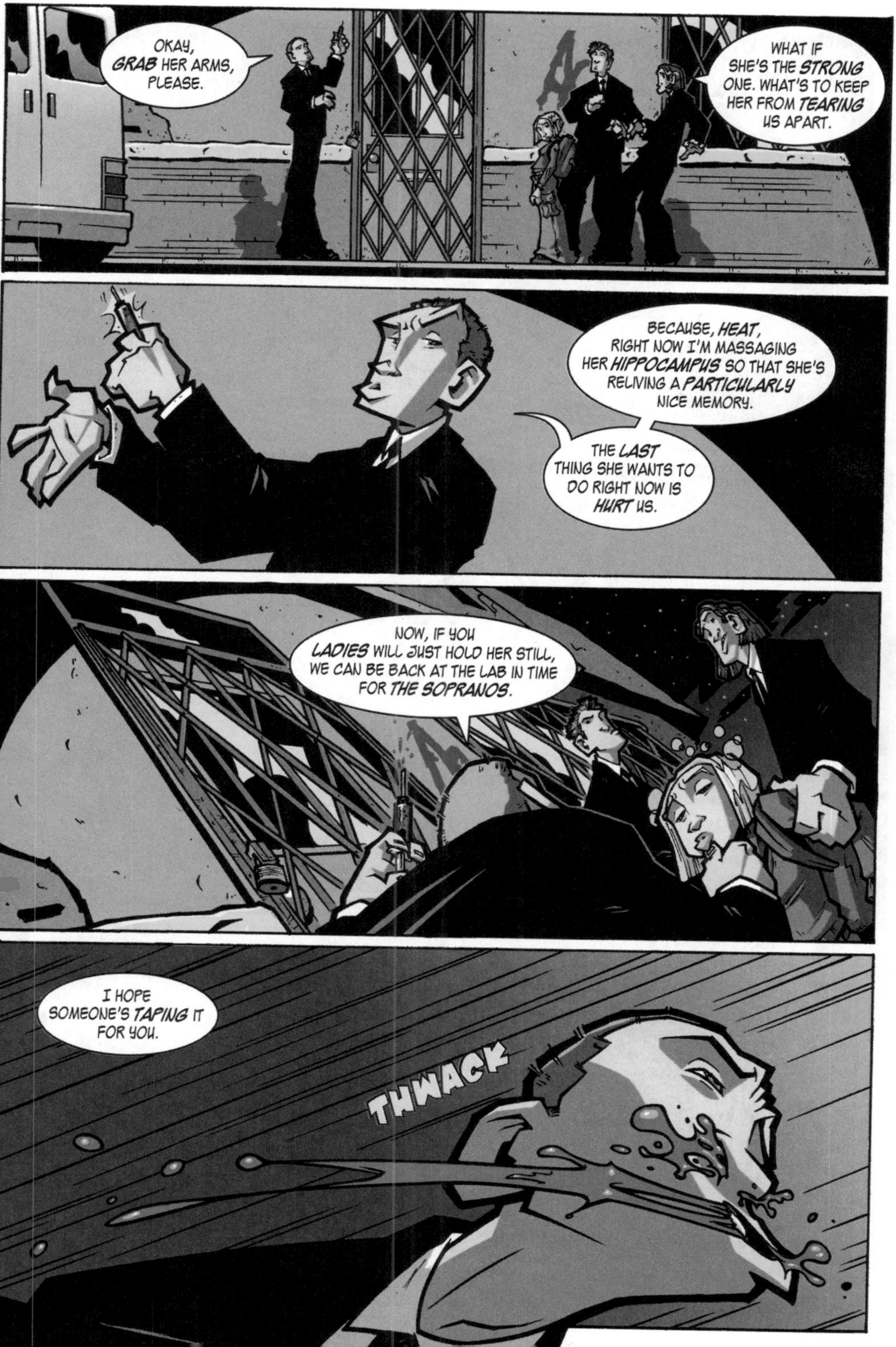

OKAY, GRAB HER ARMS, PLEASE.
WHAT IF SHE'S THE STRONG ONE. WHAT'S TO KEEP HER FROM TEARING US APART.
BECAUSE, HEAT, RIGHT NOW I'M MASSAGING HER HIPPOCAMPUS SO THAT SHE'S RELIVING A PARTICULARLY NICE MEMORY.
THE LAST THING SHE WANTS TO DO RIGHT NOW IS HURT US.
NOW, IF YOU LADIES WILL JUST HOLD HER STILL, WE CAN BE BACK AT THE LAB IN TIME FOR THE SOPRANOS.
I HOPE SOMEONE'S TAPING IT FOR YOU.
THWACK

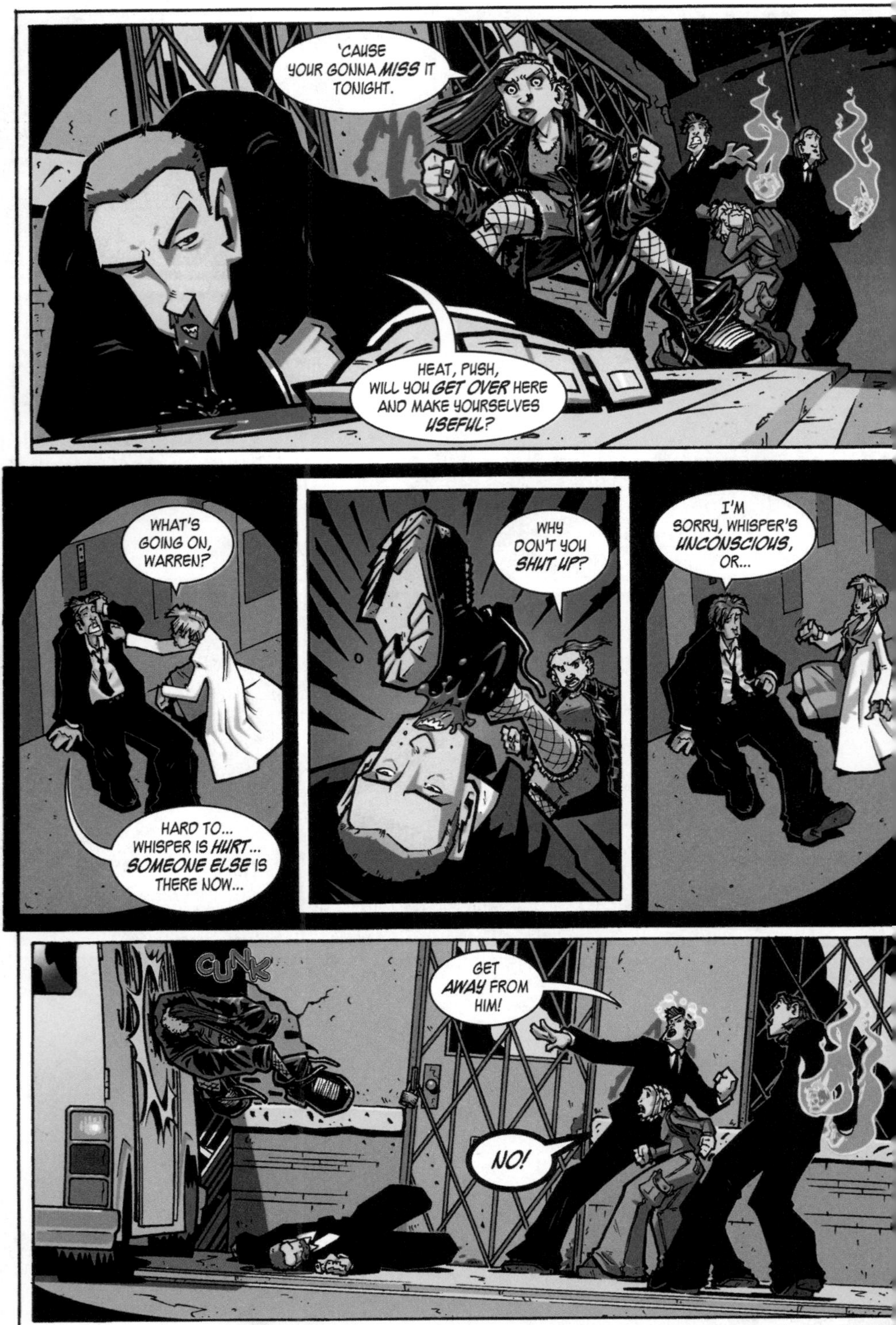
'CAUSE YOUR GONNA MISS IT TONIGHT.
HEAT, PUSH, WILL YOU GET OVER HERE AND MAKE YOURSELVES USEFUL?
WHAT'S GOING ON, WARREN?
HARD TO... WHISPER IS HURT... SOMEONE ELSE IS THERE NOW...
WHY DON'T YOU SHUT UP?
I'M SORRY, WHISPER'S UNCONSCIOUS, OR...
CLUNK
GET AWAY FROM HIM!
NO!

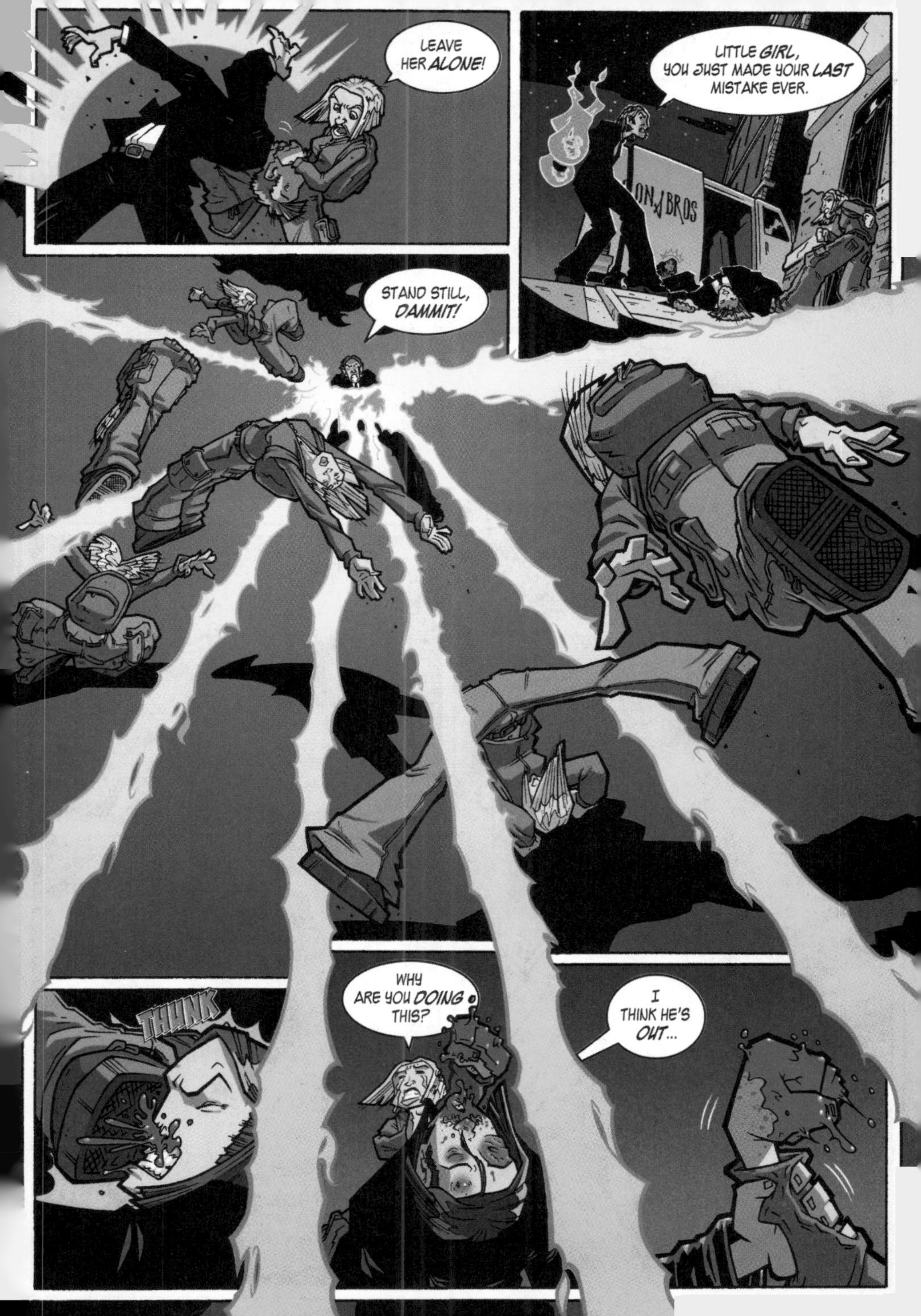
LEAVE HER ALONE!
LITTLE GIRL, YOU JUST MADE YOUR LAST MISTAKE EVER.
ON BROS
STAND STILL, DAMMIT!
THUNK
WHY ARE YOU DOING THIS?
I THINK HE'S OUT...

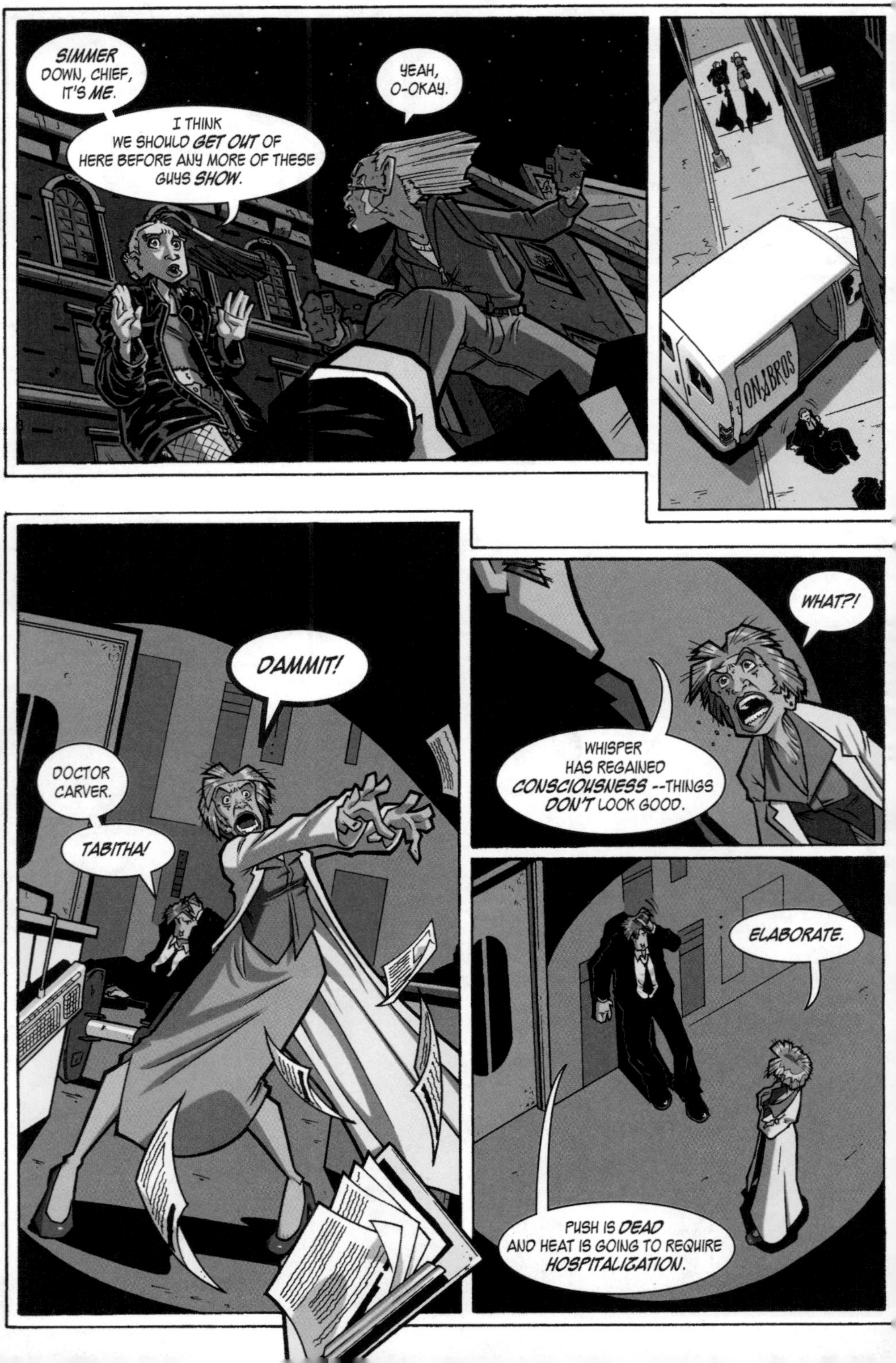
SIMMER DOWN, CHIEF, IT'S ME.
I THINK WE SHOULD GET OUT OF HERE BEFORE ANY MORE OF THESE GUYS SHOW.
YEAH, O-OKAY.
ONABROS
DOCTOR CARVER.
TABITHA!
DAMMIT!
WHAT?!
WHISPER HAS REGAINED CONSCIOUSNESS --THINGS DON'T LOOK GOOD.
ELABORATE.
PUSH IS DEAD AND HEAT IS GOING TO REQUIRE HOSPITALIZATION.

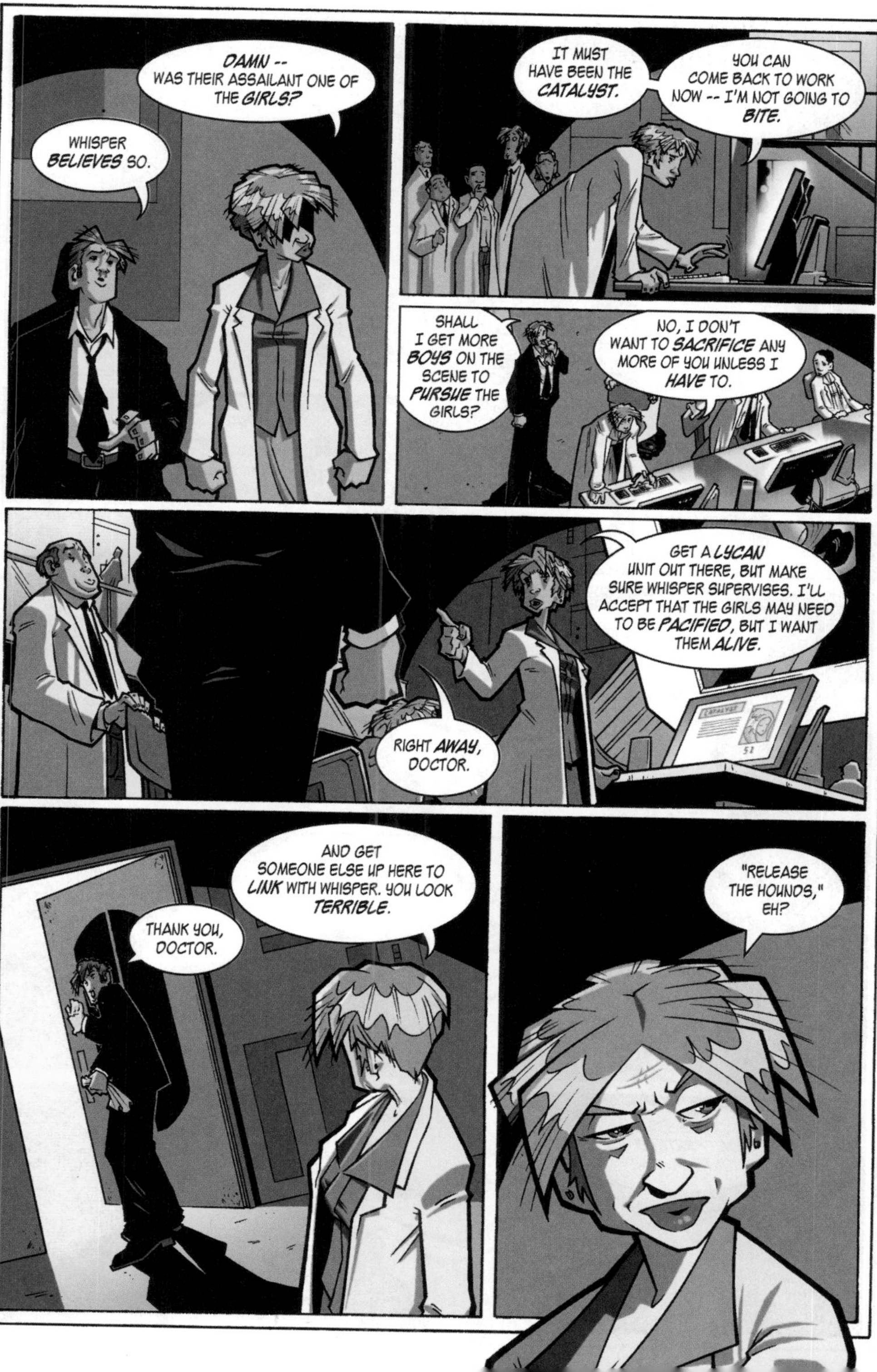
DAMN -- WAS THEIR ASSAILANT ONE OF THE GIRLS?
WHISPER BELIEVES SO.
IT MUST HAVE BEEN THE CATALYST.
YOU CAN COME BACK TO WORK NOW -- I'M NOT GOING TO BITE.
SHALL I GET MORE BOYS ON THE SCENE TO PURSUE THE GIRLS?
NO, I DON'T WANT TO SACRIFICE ANY MORE OF YOU UNLESS I HAVE TO.
GET A LYCAN UNIT OUT THERE, BUT MAKE SURE WHISPER SUPERVISES. I'LL ACCEPT THAT THE GIRLS MAY NEED TO BE PACIFIED, BUT I WANT THEM ALIVE.
RIGHT AWAY, DOCTOR.
CATALYST
51
AND GET SOMEONE ELSE UP HERE TO LINK WITH WHISPER. YOU LOOK TERRIBLE.
THANK YOU, DOCTOR.
"RELEASE THE HOUNDS," EH?

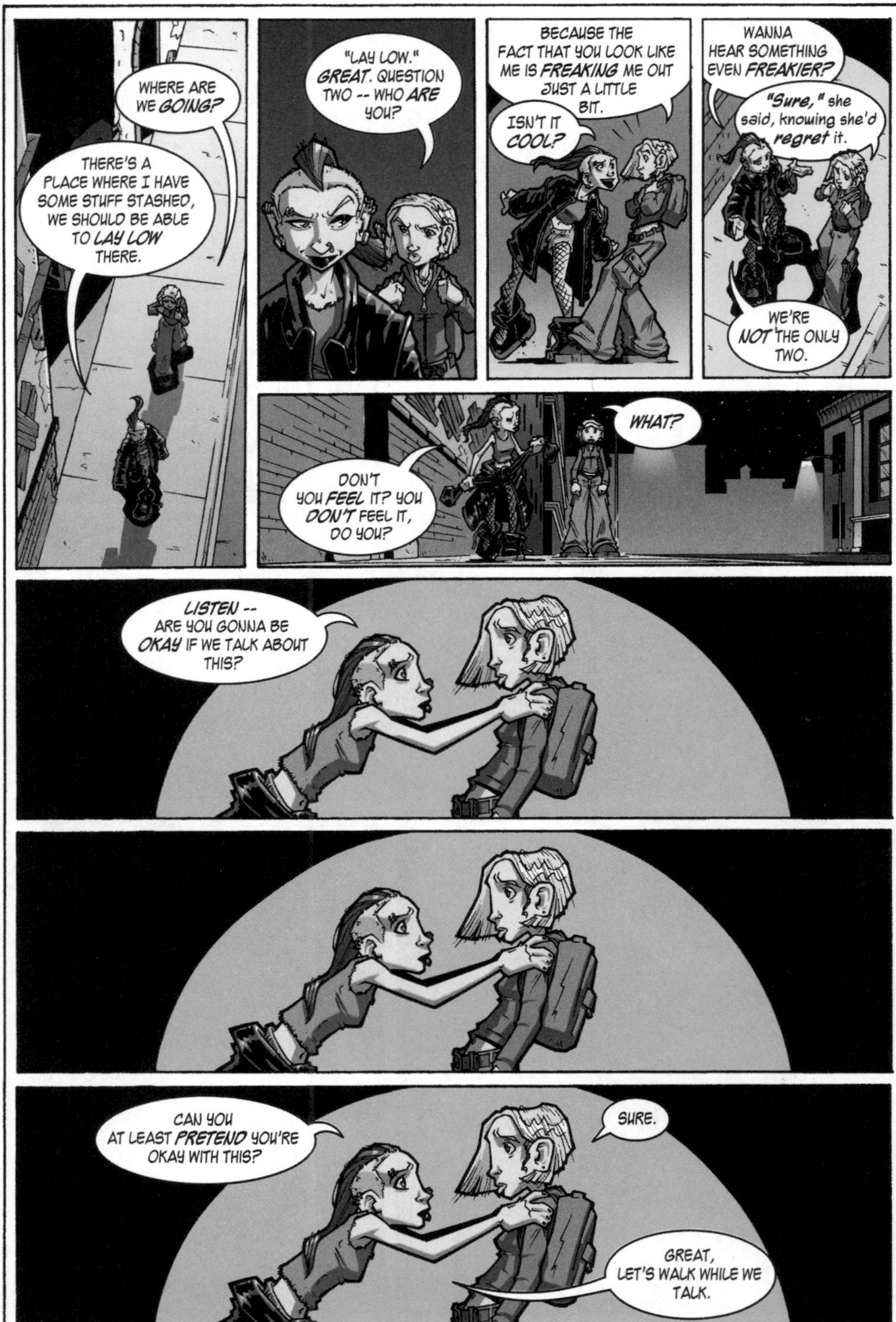
WHERE ARE WE *GOING?*
THERE'S A PLACE WHERE I HAVE SOME STUFF STASHED, WE SHOULD BE ABLE TO *LAY LOW* THERE.
"LAY LOW." *GREAT*. QUESTION TWO -- WHO *ARE* YOU?
BECAUSE THE FACT THAT YOU LOOK LIKE ME IS *FREAKING* ME OUT JUST A LITTLE BIT.
ISN'T IT *COOL?*
WANNA HEAR SOMETHING EVEN *FREAKIER?*
"Sure," she said, knowing she'd *regret* it.
WE'RE *NOT* THE ONLY TWO.
WHAT?
DON'T YOU *FEEL* IT? YOU *DON'T* FEEL IT, DO YOU?
LISTEN -- ARE YOU GONNA BE *OKAY* IF WE TALK ABOUT THIS?
CAN YOU AT LEAST *PRETEND* YOU'RE OKAY WITH THIS?
SURE.
GREAT, LET'S WALK WHILE WE TALK.

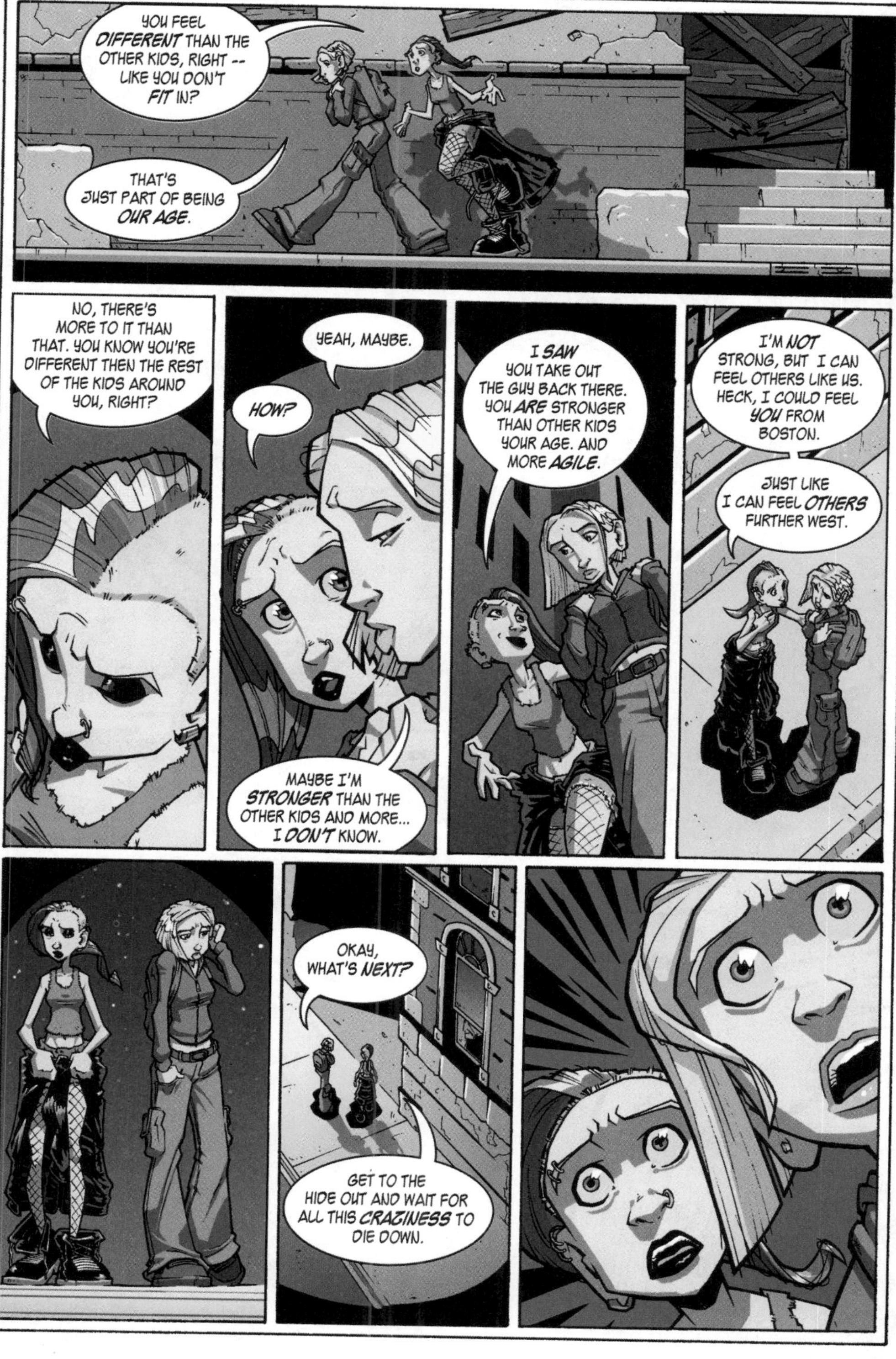
YOU FEEL DIFFERENT THAN THE OTHER KIDS, RIGHT -- LIKE YOU DON'T FIT IN?
THAT'S JUST PART OF BEING OUR AGE.
NO, THERE'S MORE TO IT THAN THAT. YOU KNOW YOU'RE DIFFERENT THEN THE REST OF THE KIDS AROUND YOU, RIGHT?
YEAH, MAYBE.
HOW?
MAYBE I'M STRONGER THAN THE OTHER KIDS AND MORE... I DON'T KNOW.
I SAW YOU TAKE OUT THE GUY BACK THERE. YOU ARE STRONGER THAN OTHER KIDS YOUR AGE. AND MORE AGILE.
I'M NOT STRONG, BUT I CAN FEEL OTHERS LIKE US. HECK, I COULD FEEL YOU FROM BOSTON.
JUST LIKE I CAN FEEL OTHERS FURTHER WEST.
OKAY, WHAT'S NEXT?
GET TO THE HIDE OUT AND WAIT FOR ALL THIS CRAZINESS TO DIE DOWN.

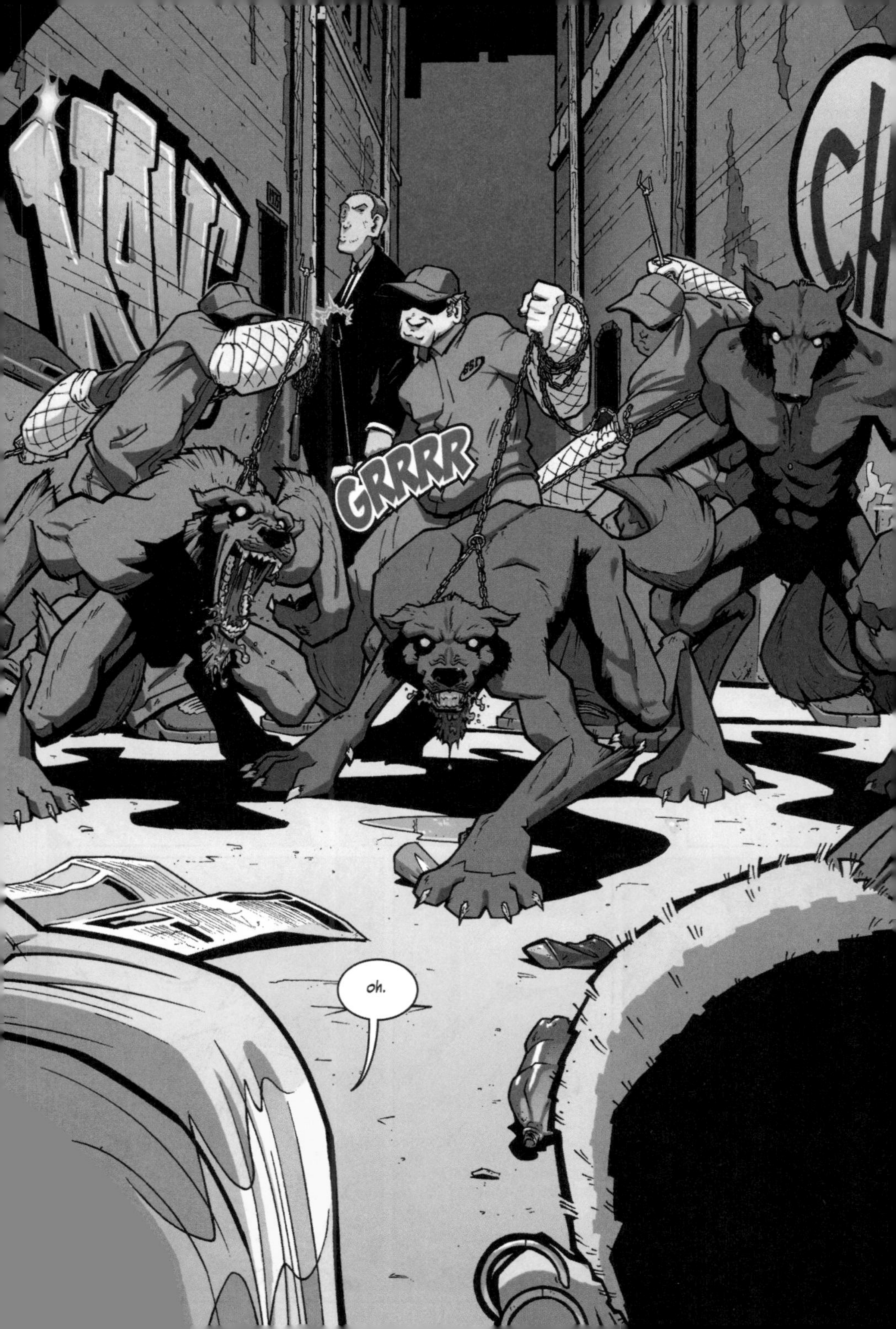
GRRRR
oh.

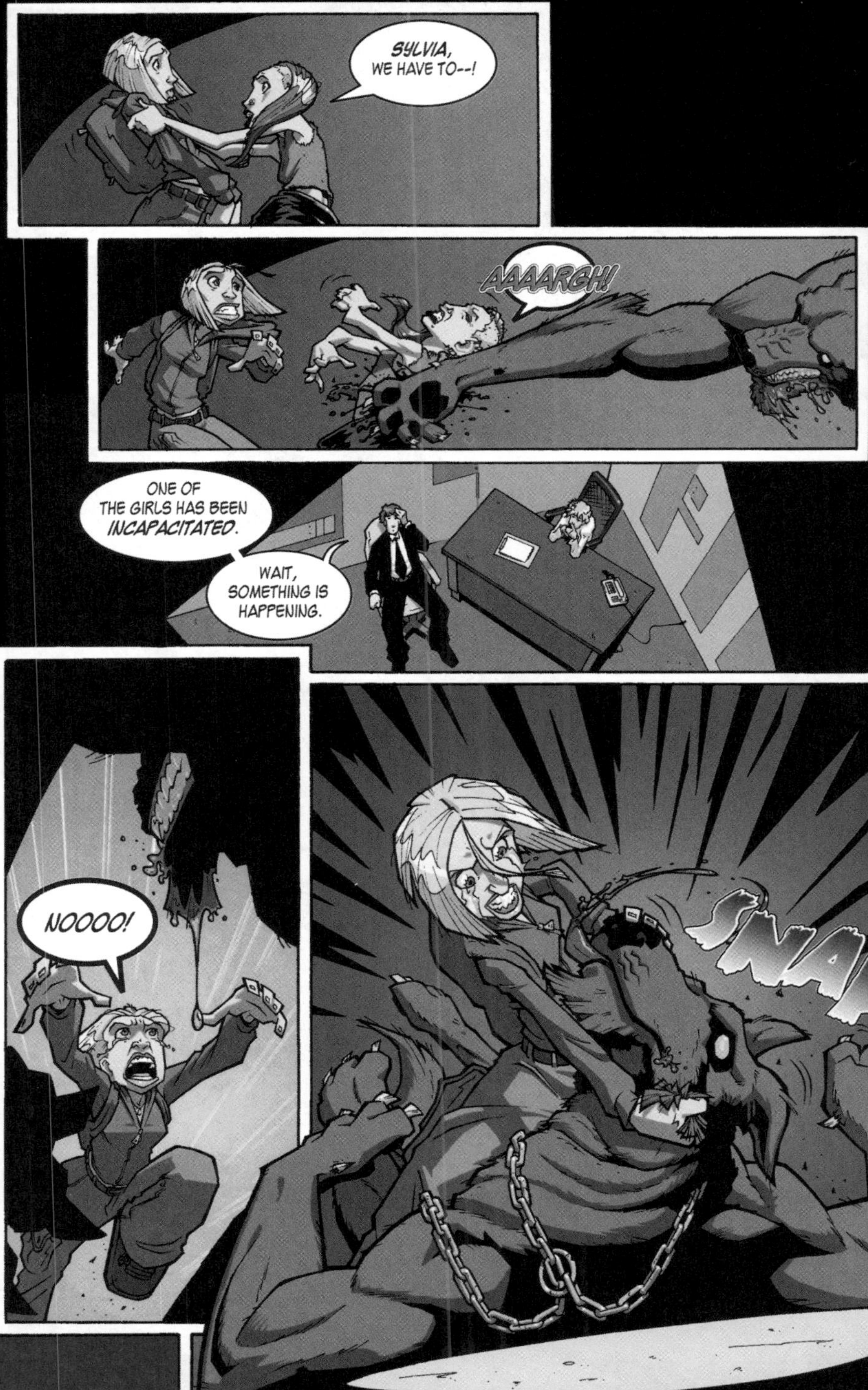
SYLVIA, WE HAVE TO--!
AAAARGH!
ONE OF THE GIRLS HAS BEEN INCAPACITATED.
WAIT, SOMETHING IS HAPPENING.
NOOOO!
SNAP

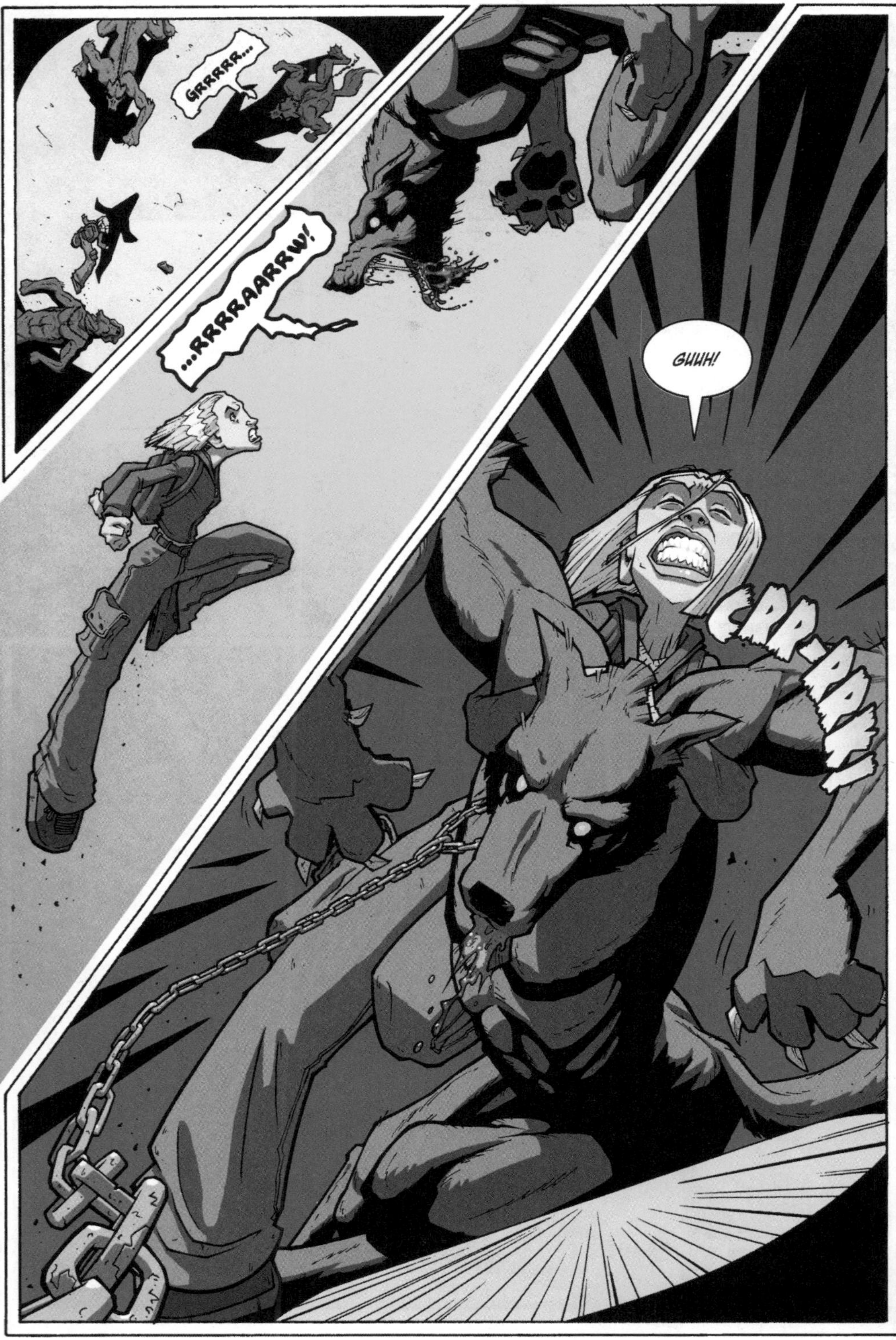
GRRRRR...
...RRRRAARRRW!
GUUH!
CRR-RAK!

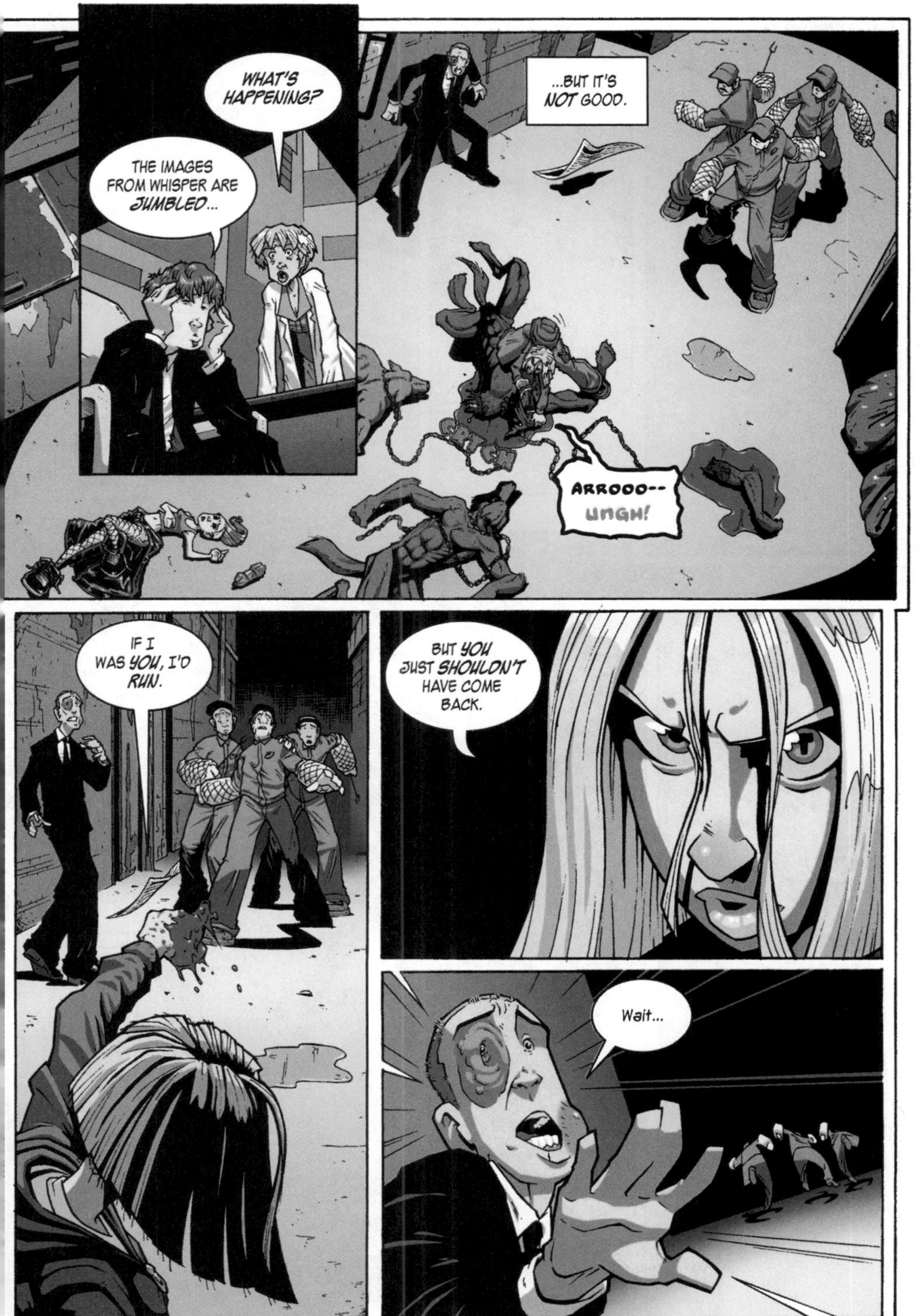
WHAT'S HAPPENING?
THE IMAGES FROM WHISPER ARE JUMBLED...
...BUT IT'S NOT GOOD.
GRTCH
ARROOO-- UNGH!
IF I WAS YOU, I'D RUN.
BUT YOU JUST SHOULDN'T HAVE COME BACK.
Wait...

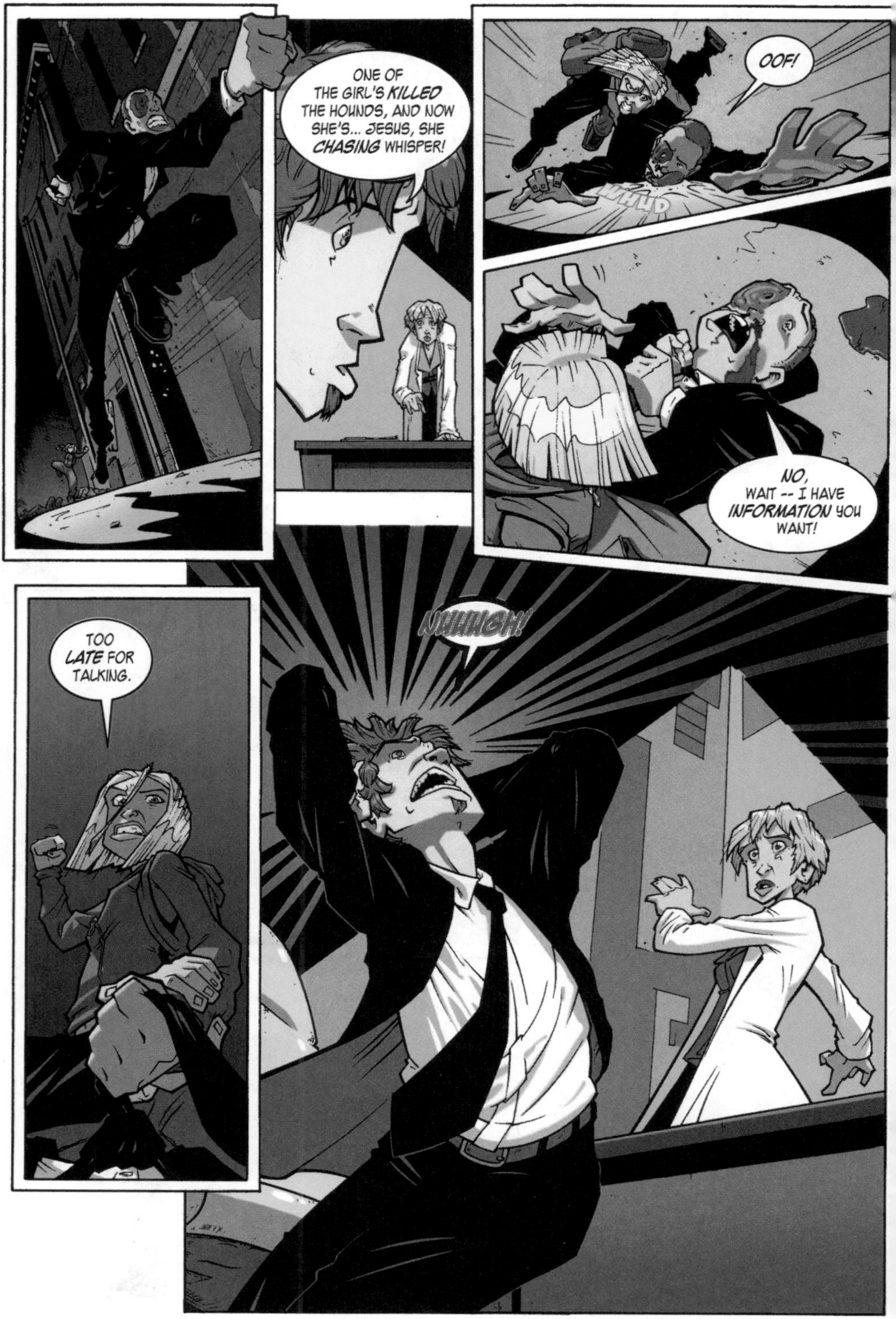
ONE OF THE GIRL'S KILLED THE HOUNDS, AND NOW SHE'S... JESUS, SHE CHASING WHISPER!
OOF!
WHUD
NO, WAIT -- I HAVE INFORMATION YOU WANT!
TOO LATE FOR TALKING.
NUUUGH!

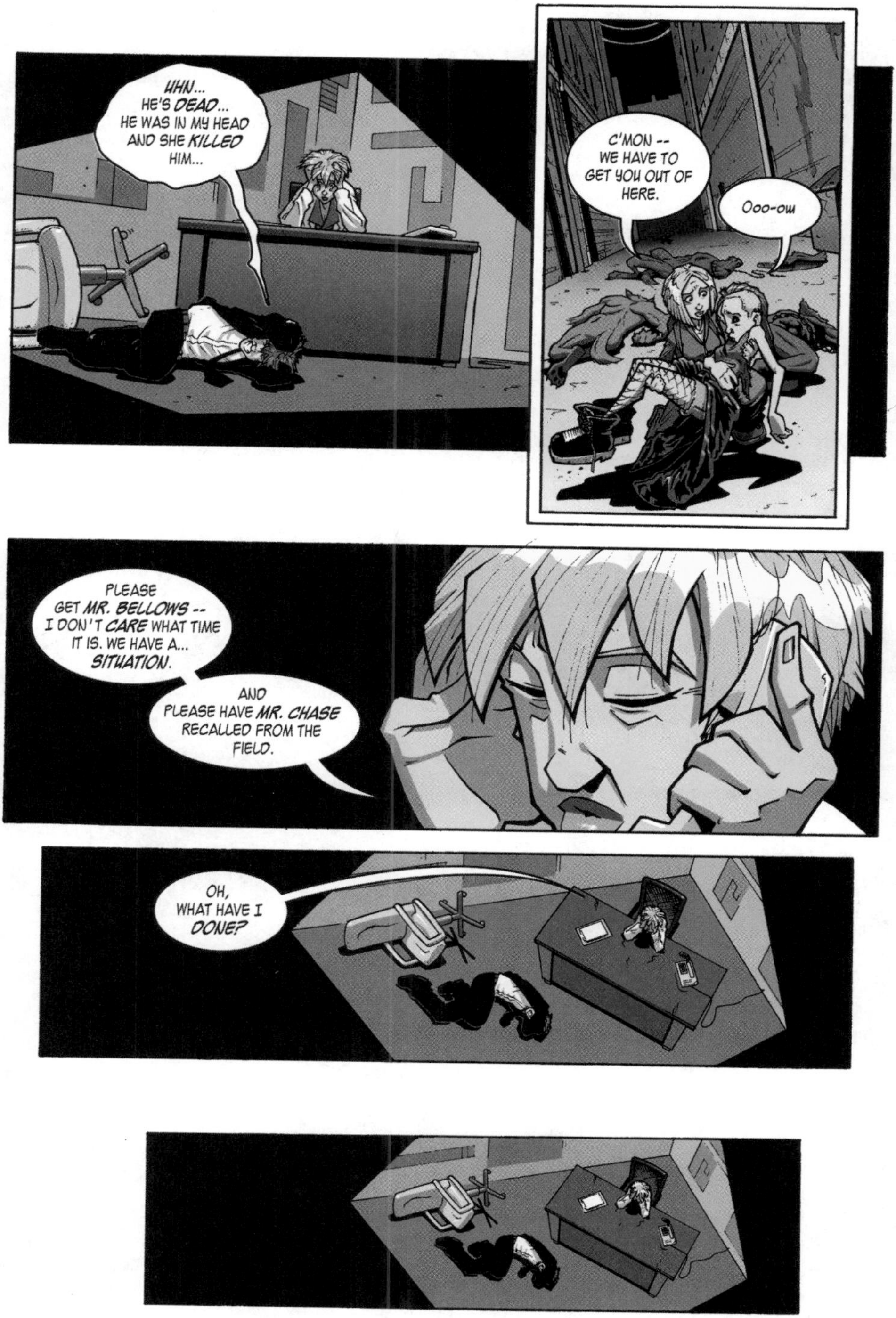
UHN... HE'S DEAD... HE WAS IN MY HEAD AND SHE KILLED HIM...
C'MON -- WE HAVE TO GET YOU OUT OF HERE.
Ooo-ow
PLEASE GET MR. BELLOWS -- I DON'T CARE WHAT TIME IT IS. WE HAVE A... SITUATION.
AND PLEASE HAVE MR. CHASE RECALLED FROM THE FIELD.
OH, WHAT HAVE I DONE?

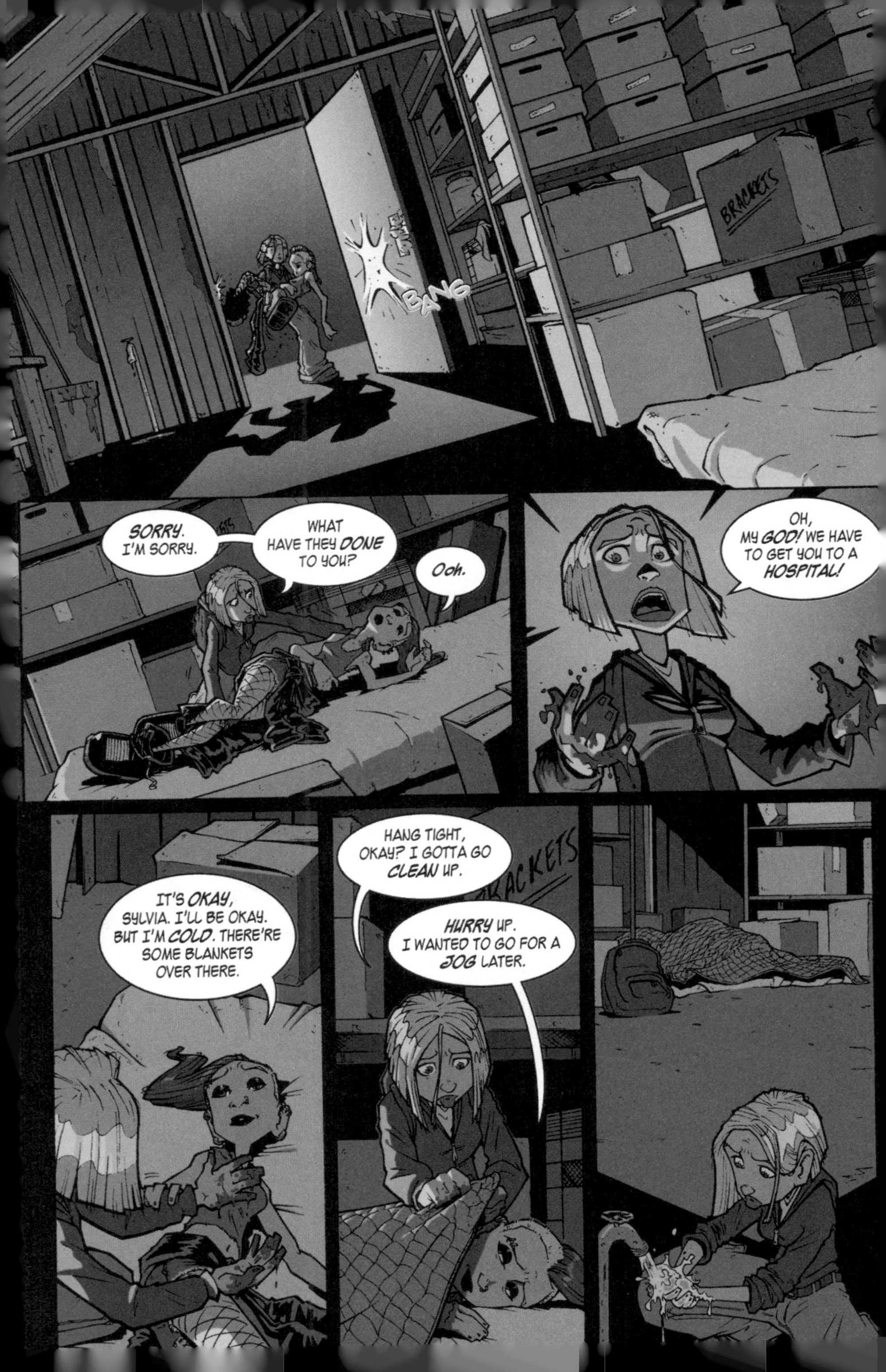
BANG
SORRY. I'M SORRY.
WHAT HAVE THEY DONE TO YOU?
Ooh.
OH, MY GOD! WE HAVE TO GET YOU TO A HOSPITAL!
IT'S OKAY, SYLVIA. I'LL BE OKAY. BUT I'M COLD. THERE'RE SOME BLANKETS OVER THERE.
HANG TIGHT, OKAY? I GOTTA GO CLEAN UP.
HURRY UP. I WANTED TO GO FOR A JOG LATER.

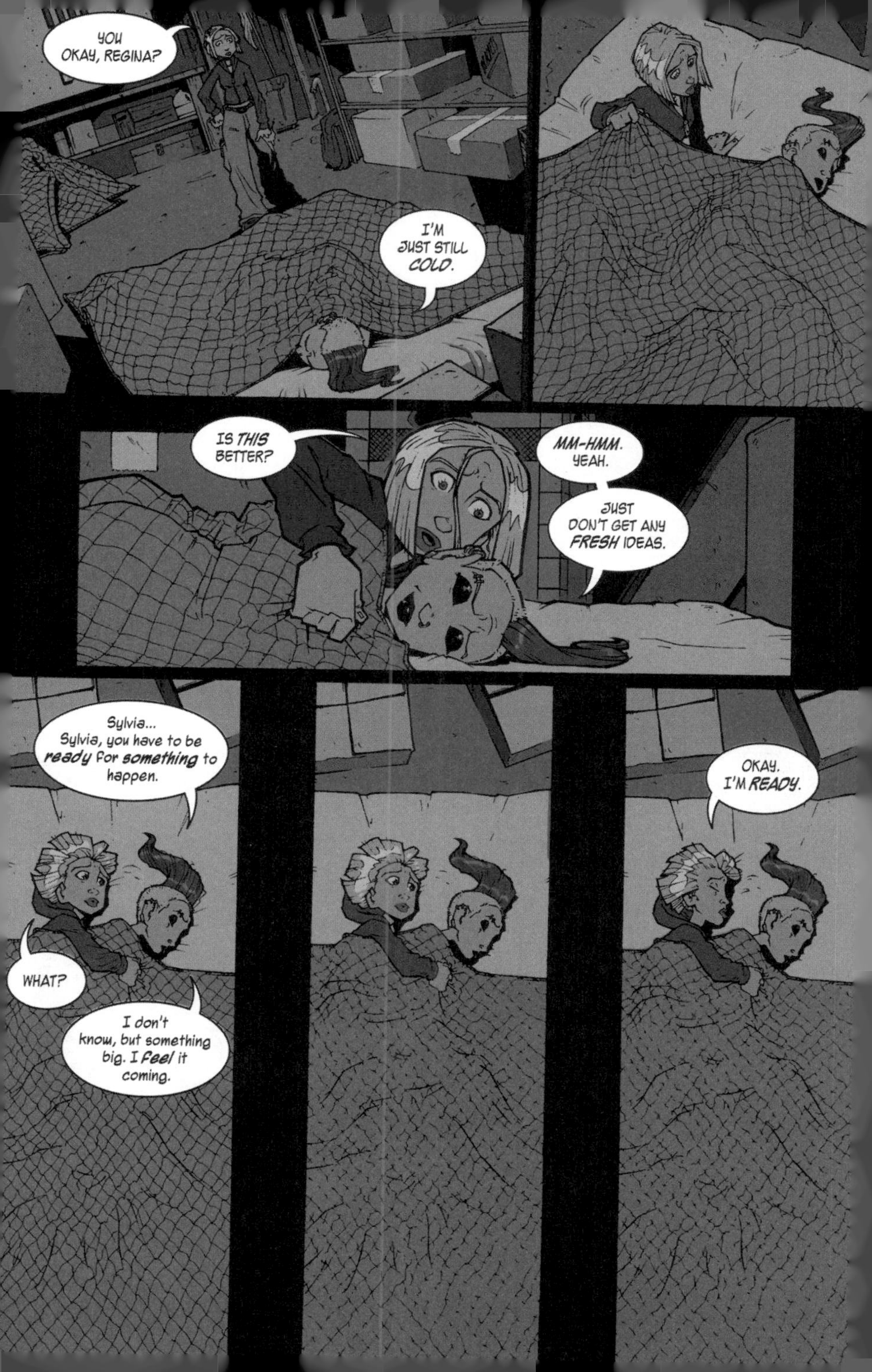
YOU OKAY, REGINA?
I'M JUST STILL COLD.
IS THIS BETTER?
MM-HMM. YEAH.
JUST DON'T GET ANY FRESH IDEAS.
Sylvia... Sylvia, you have to be ready for something to happen.
WHAT?
I don't know, but something big. I feel it coming.
OKAY. I'M READY.

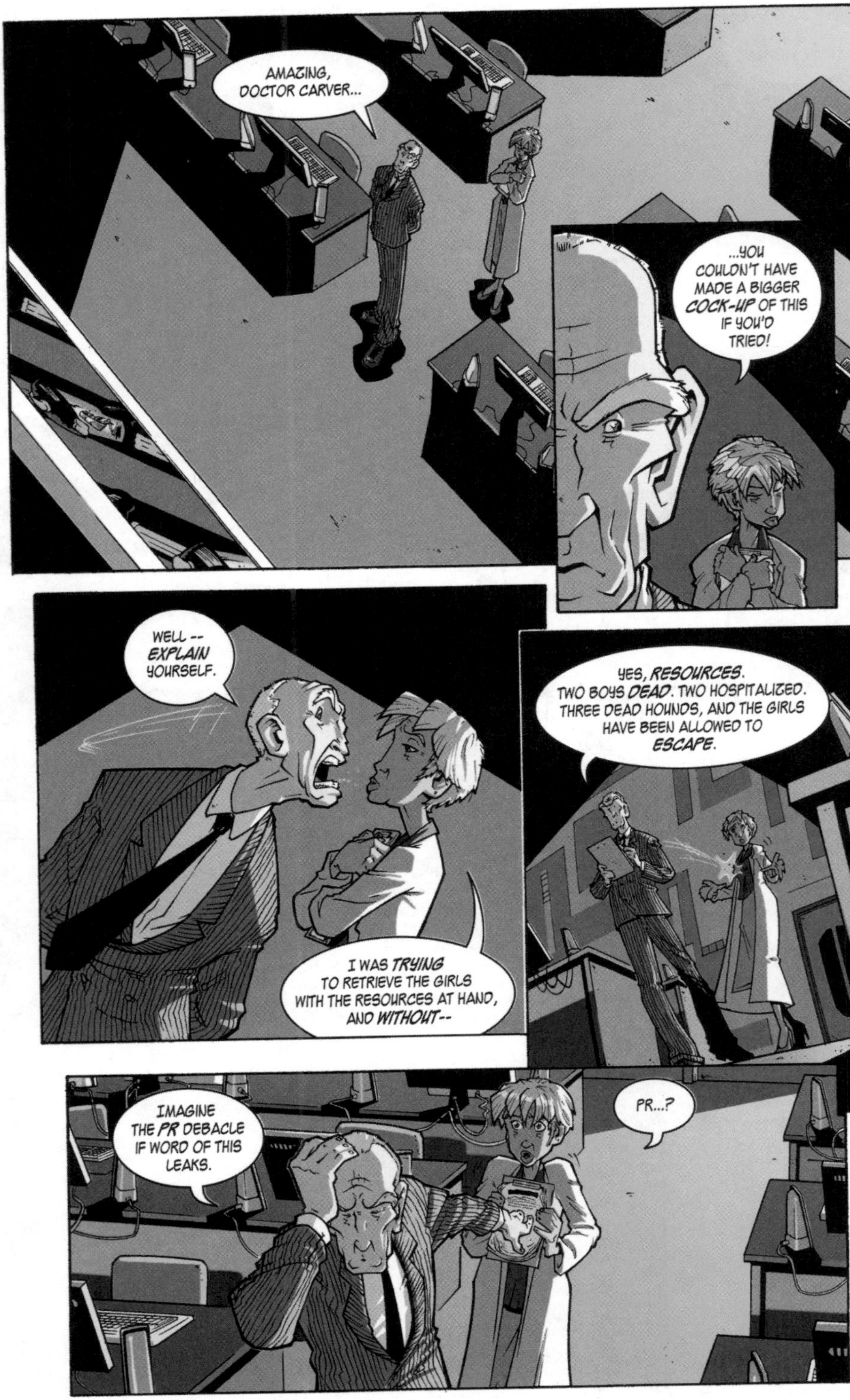
AMAZING, DOCTOR CARVER...
...YOU COULDN'T HAVE MADE A BIGGER COCK-UP OF THIS IF YOU'D TRIED!
WELL -- EXPLAIN YOURSELF.
I WAS TRYING TO RETRIEVE THE GIRLS WITH THE RESOURCES AT HAND, AND WITHOUT--
YES, RESOURCES. TWO BOYS DEAD. TWO HOSPITALIZED. THREE DEAD HOUNDS, AND THE GIRLS HAVE BEEN ALLOWED TO ESCAPE.
IMAGINE THE PR DEBACLE IF WORD OF THIS LEAKS.
PR...?

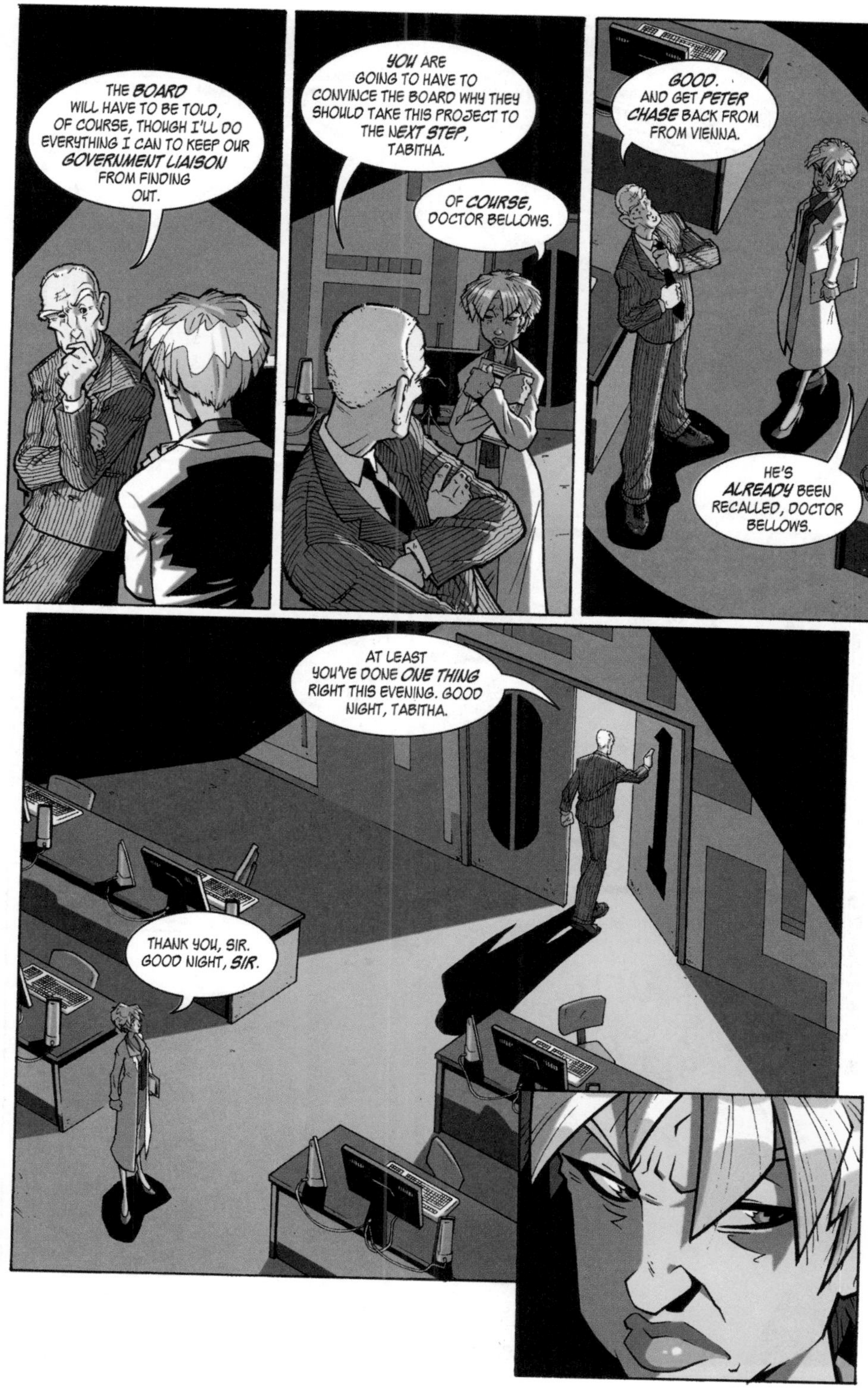
THE BOARD WILL HAVE TO BE TOLD, OF COURSE, THOUGH I'LL DO EVERYTHING I CAN TO KEEP OUR GOVERNMENT LIAISON FROM FINDING OUT.
YOU ARE GOING TO HAVE TO CONVINCE THE BOARD WHY THEY SHOULD TAKE THIS PROJECT TO THE NEXT STEP, TABITHA.
OF COURSE, DOCTOR BELLOWS.
GOOD. AND GET PETER CHASE BACK FROM FROM VIENNA.
HE'S ALREADY BEEN RECALLED, DOCTOR BELLOWS.
AT LEAST YOU'VE DONE ONE THING RIGHT THIS EVENING. GOOD NIGHT, TABITHA.
THANK YOU, SIR. GOOD NIGHT, SIR.

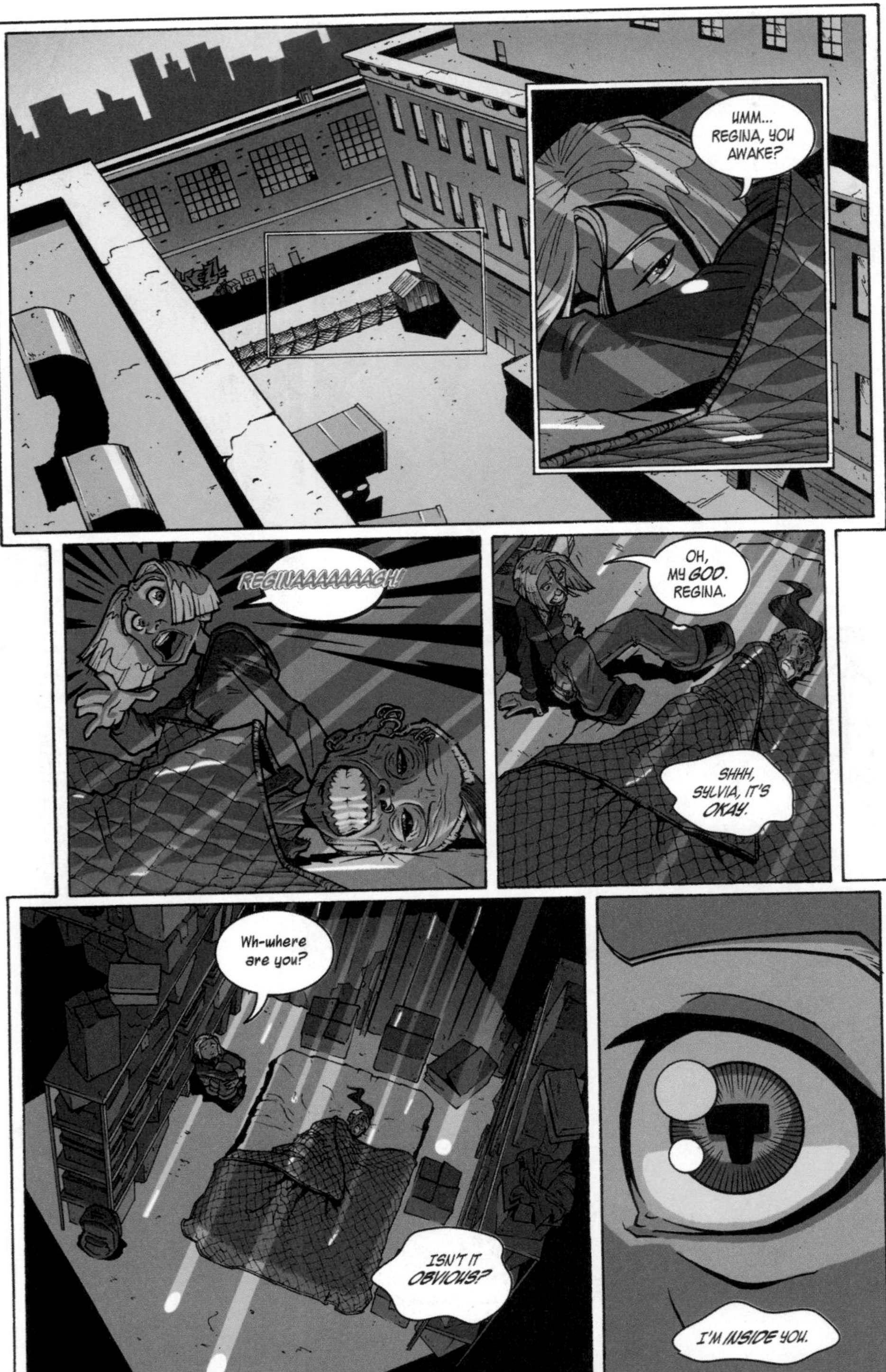
UMM... REGINA, YOU AWAKE?
REGINAAAAAAAACH!
OH, MY GOD. REGINA.
SHHH, SYLVIA, IT'S OKAY.
Wh-where are you?
ISN'T IT OBVIOUS?
I'M INSIDE YOU.

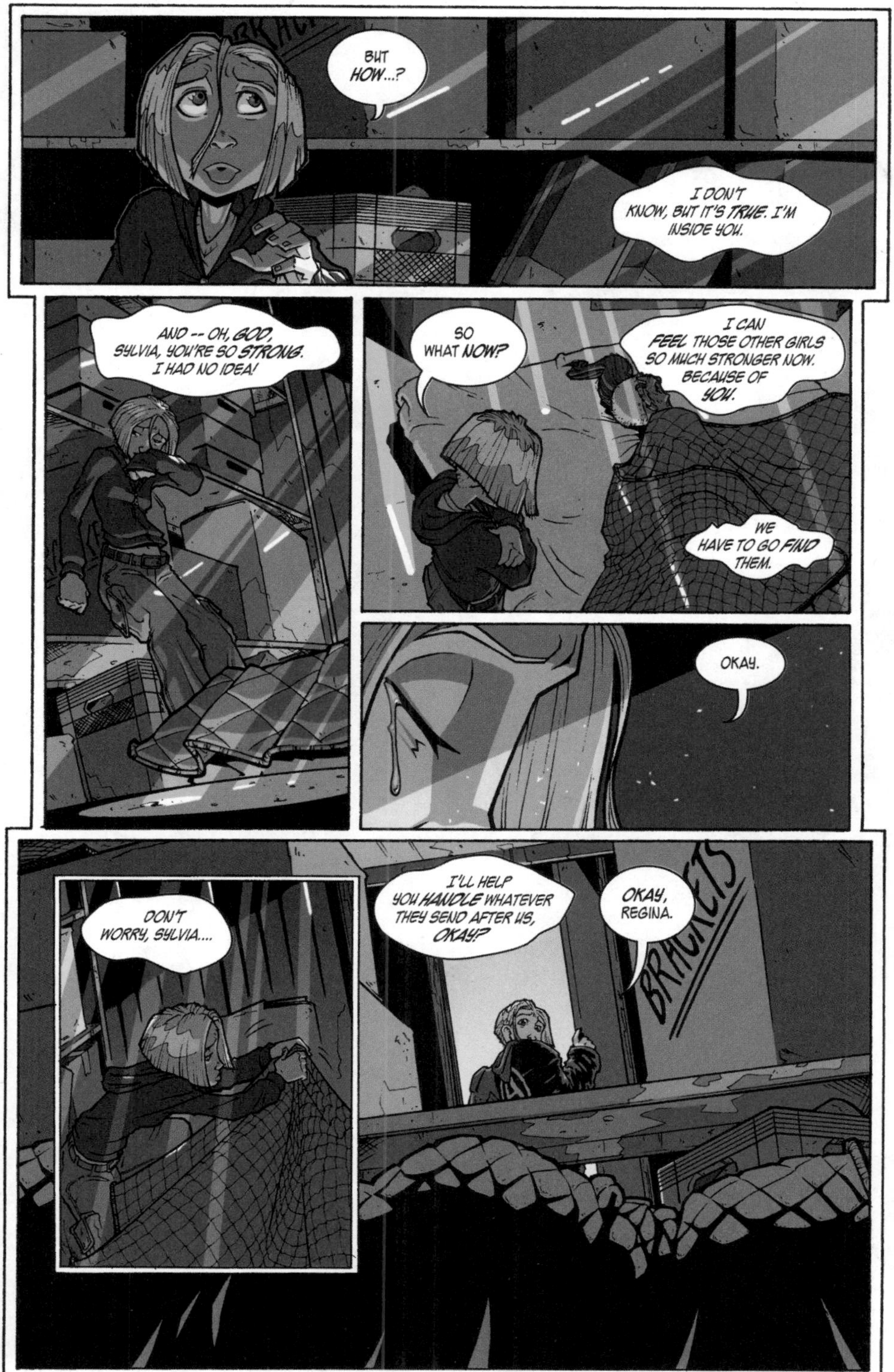
BKACK
BUT HOW...?
I DON'T KNOW, BUT IT'S TRUE. I'M INSIDE YOU.
AND -- OH, GOD, SYLVIA, YOU'RE SO STRONG. I HAD NO IDEA!
SO WHAT NOW?
I CAN FEEL THOSE OTHER GIRLS SO MUCH STRONGER NOW. BECAUSE OF YOU.
WE HAVE TO GO FIND THEM.
OKAY.
DON'T WORRY, SYLVIA....
I'LL HELP YOU HANDLE WHATEVER THEY SEND AFTER US, OKAY?
OKAY, REGINA.
BRACKETS

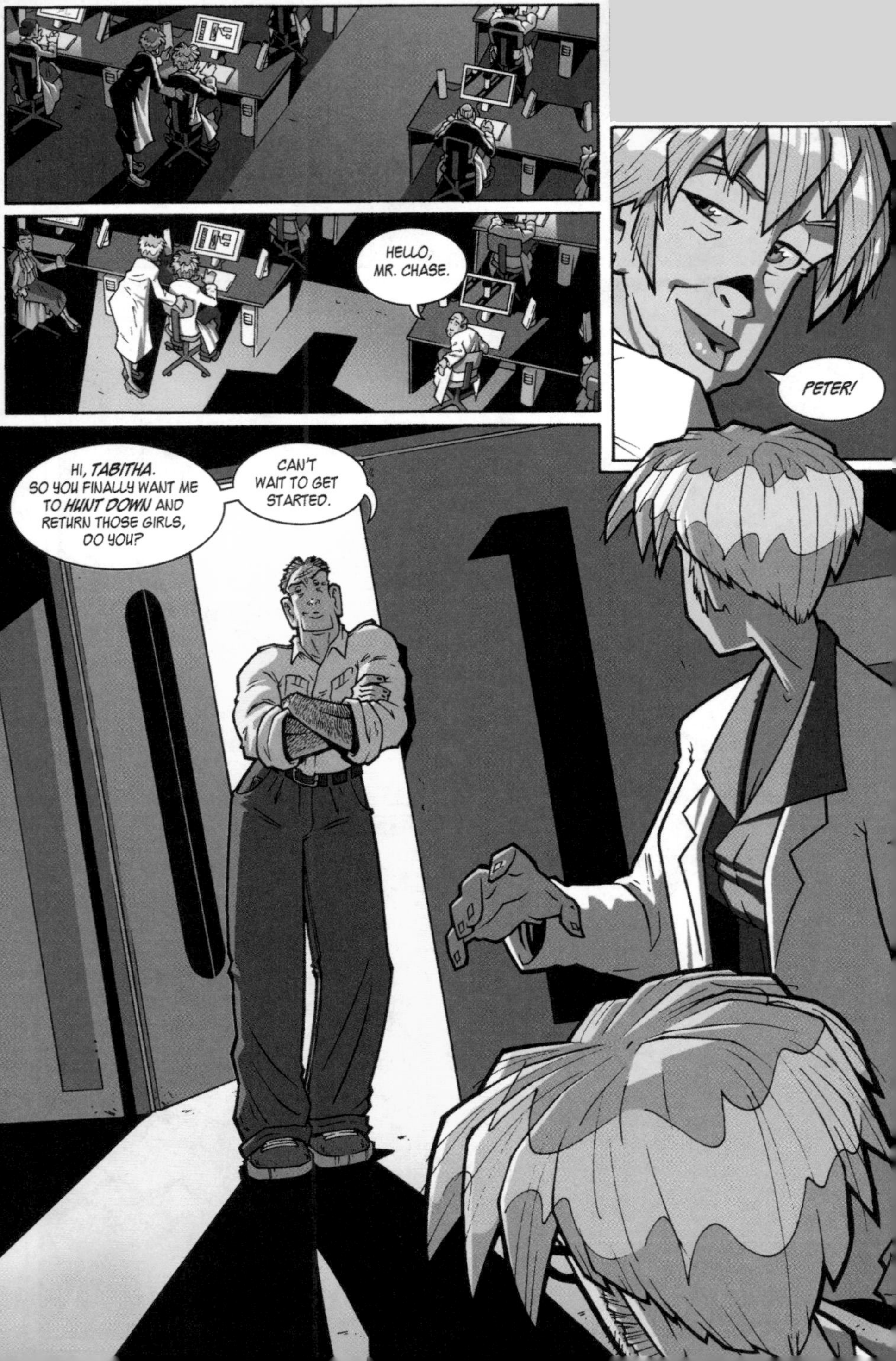
HELLO, MR. CHASE.
PETER!
HI, TABITHA. SO YOU FINALLY WANT ME TO HUNT DOWN AND RETURN THOSE GIRLS, DO YOU?
CAN'T WAIT TO GET STARTED.

CHAPTER three

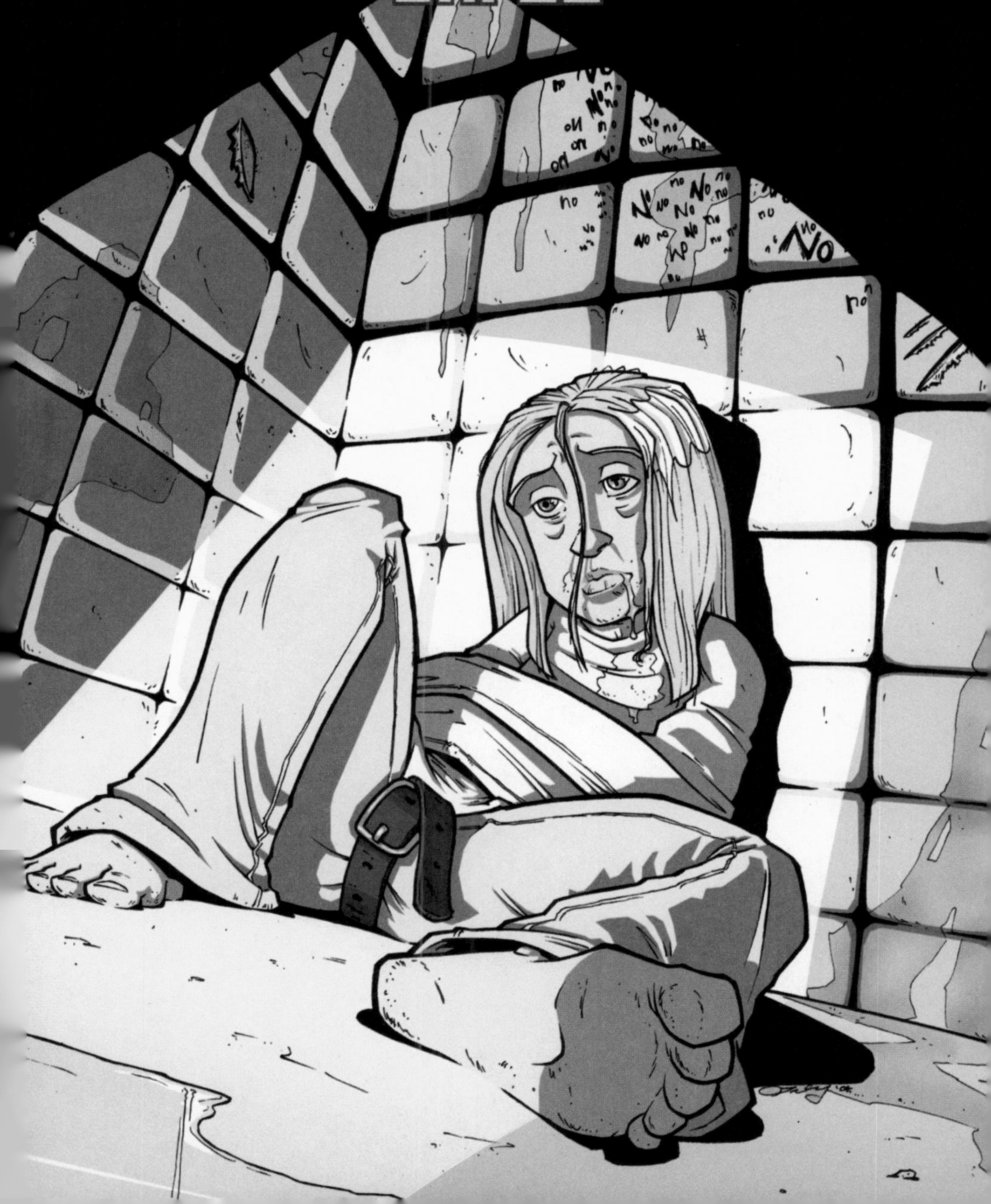

No
No
NO

"I don't think she'll give
you any trouble."

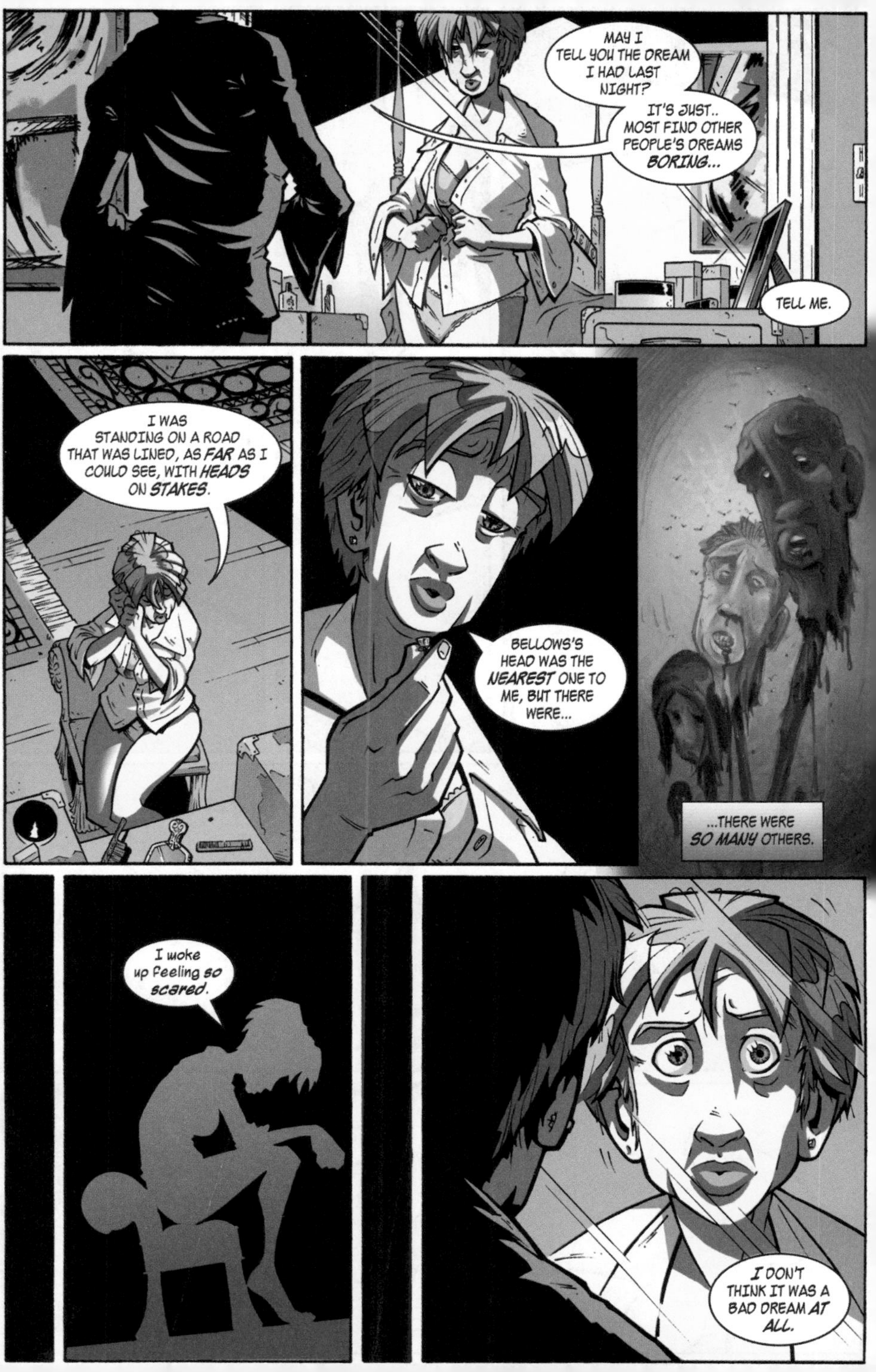

MAY I TELL YOU THE DREAM I HAD LAST NIGHT?
IT'S JUST.. MOST FIND OTHER PEOPLE'S DREAMS BORING...
TELL ME.
I WAS STANDING ON A ROAD THAT WAS LINED, AS FAR AS I COULD SEE, WITH HEADS ON STAKES.
BELLOWS'S HEAD WAS THE NEAREST ONE TO ME, BUT THERE WERE...
...THERE WERE SO MANY OTHERS.
I woke up feeling so scared.
I DON'T THINK IT WAS A BAD DREAM AT ALL.

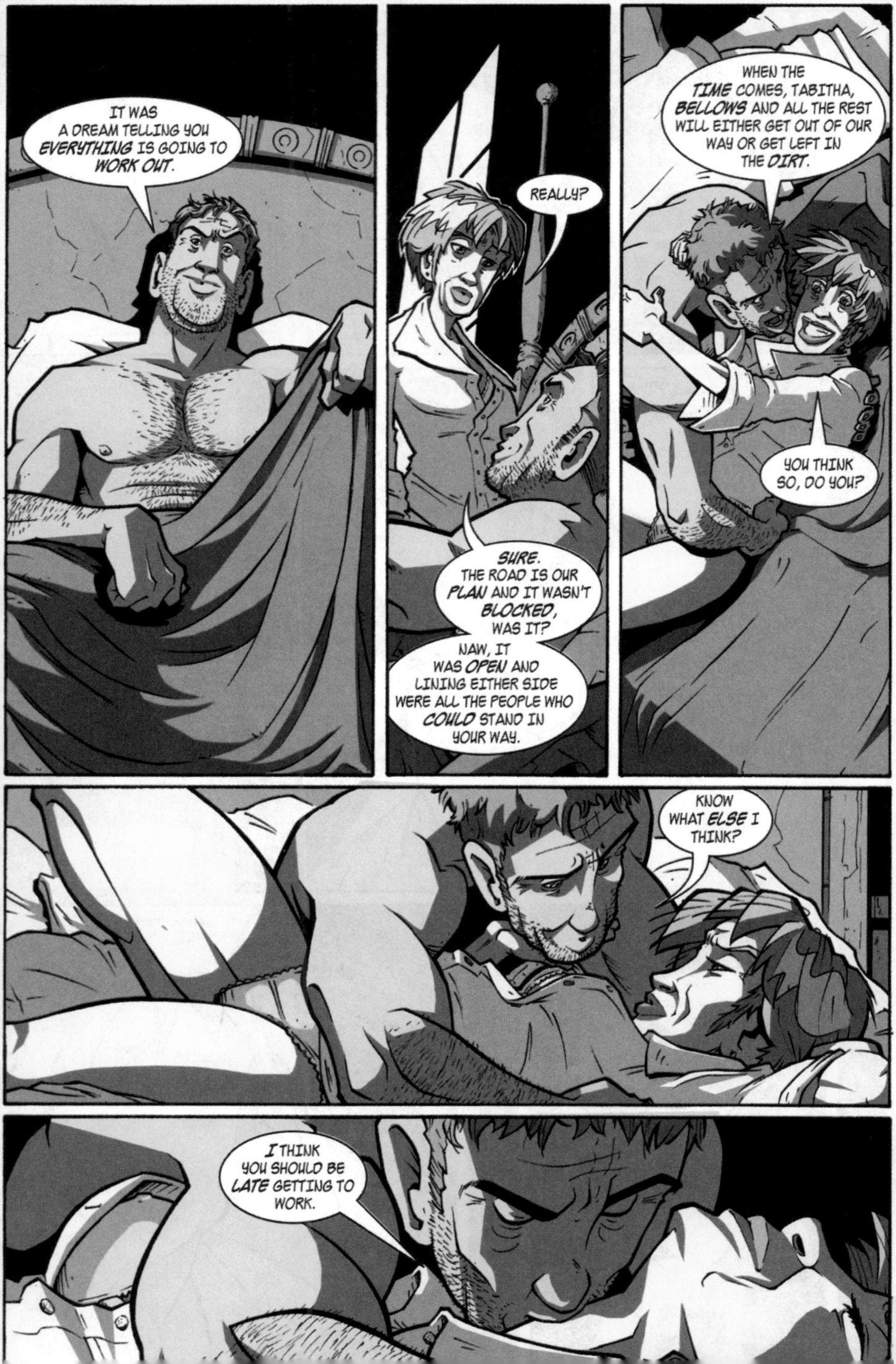
IT WAS A DREAM TELLING YOU EVERYTHING IS GOING TO WORK OUT.
REALLY?
SURE. THE ROAD IS OUR PLAN AND IT WASN'T BLOCKED, WAS IT?
NAW, IT WAS OPEN AND LINING EITHER SIDE WERE ALL THE PEOPLE WHO COULD STAND IN YOUR WAY.
WHEN THE TIME COMES, TABITHA, BELLOWS AND ALL THE REST WILL EITHER GET OUT OF OUR WAY OR GET LEFT IN THE DIRT.
YOU THINK SO, DO YOU?
KNOW WHAT ELSE I THINK?
I THINK YOU SHOULD BE LATE GETTING TO WORK.

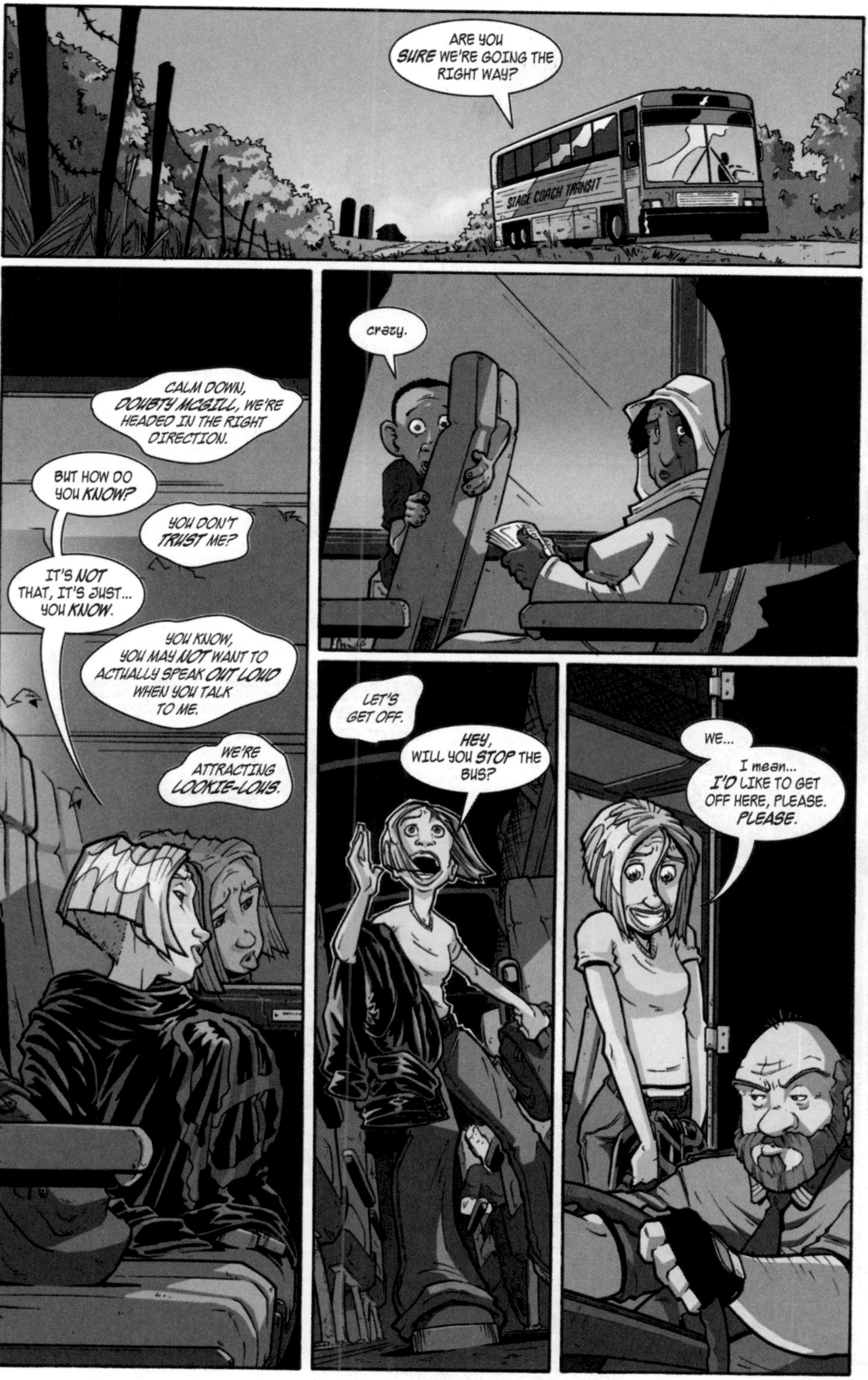
ARE YOU SURE WE'RE GOING THE RIGHT WAY?
STAGE COACH TRANSIT
CALM DOWN, DOUBTY MCGILL, WE'RE HEADED IN THE RIGHT DIRECTION.
BUT HOW DO YOU KNOW?
YOU DON'T TRUST ME?
IT'S NOT THAT, IT'S JUST... YOU KNOW.
YOU KNOW, YOU MAY NOT WANT TO ACTUALLY SPEAK OUT LOUD WHEN YOU TALK TO ME.
WE'RE ATTRACTING LOOKIE-LOUS.
crazy.
LET'S GET OFF.
HEY, WILL YOU STOP THE BUS?
WE...
I mean... I'D LIKE TO GET OFF HERE, PLEASE. PLEASE.

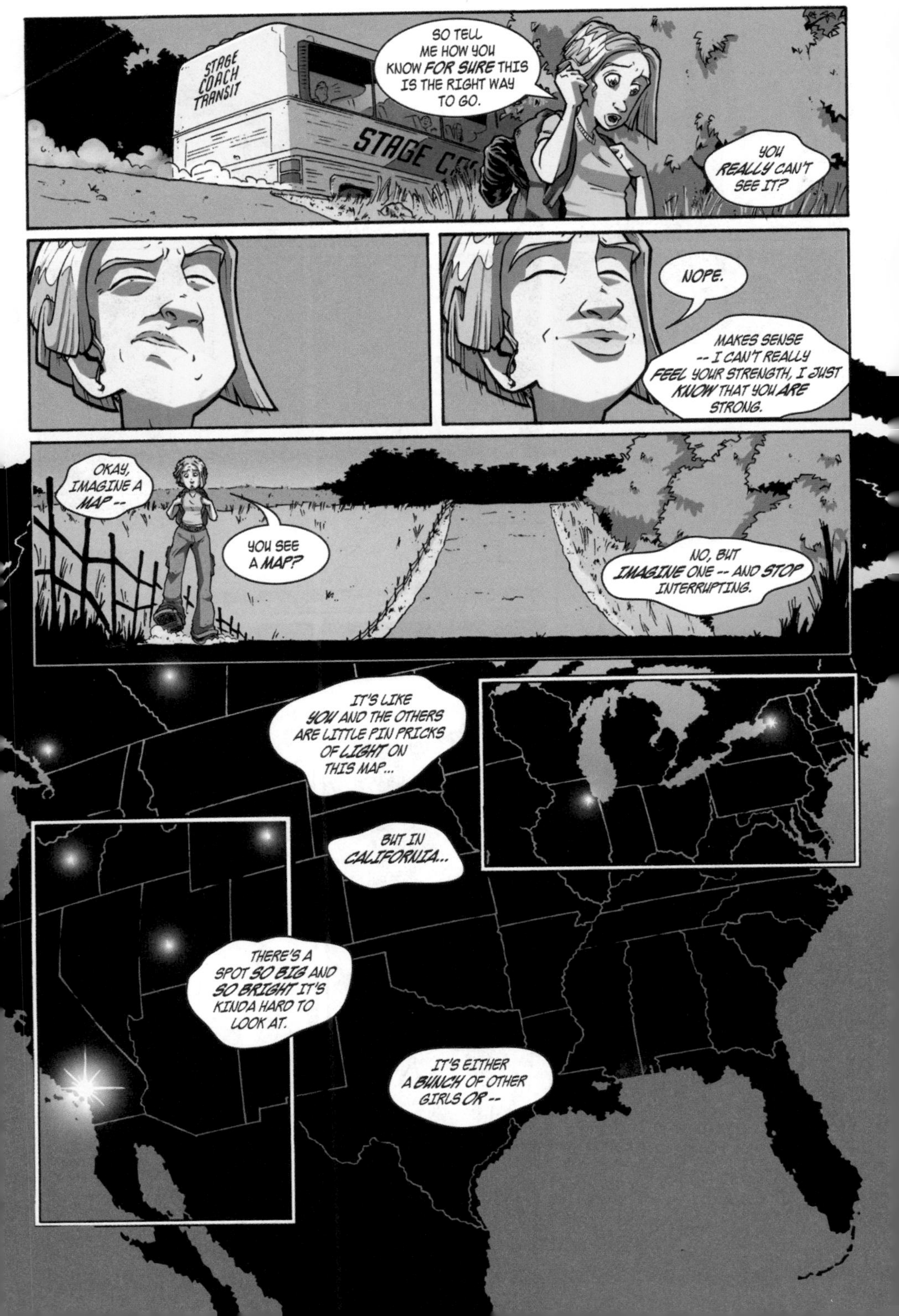
STAGE COACH TRANSIT
STAGE C
SO TELL ME HOW YOU KNOW FOR SURE THIS IS THE RIGHT WAY TO GO.
YOU REALLY CAN'T SEE IT?
NOPE.
MAKES SENSE -- I CAN'T REALLY FEEL YOUR STRENGTH, I JUST KNOW THAT YOU ARE STRONG.
OKAY, IMAGINE A MAP --
YOU SEE A MAP?
NO, BUT IMAGINE ONE -- AND STOP INTERRUPTING.
IT'S LIKE YOU AND THE OTHERS ARE LITTLE PIN PRICKS OF LIGHT ON THIS MAP...
BUT IN CALIFORNIA...
THERE'S A SPOT SO BIG AND SO BRIGHT IT'S KINDA HARD TO LOOK AT.
IT'S EITHER A BUNCH OF OTHER GIRLS OR --

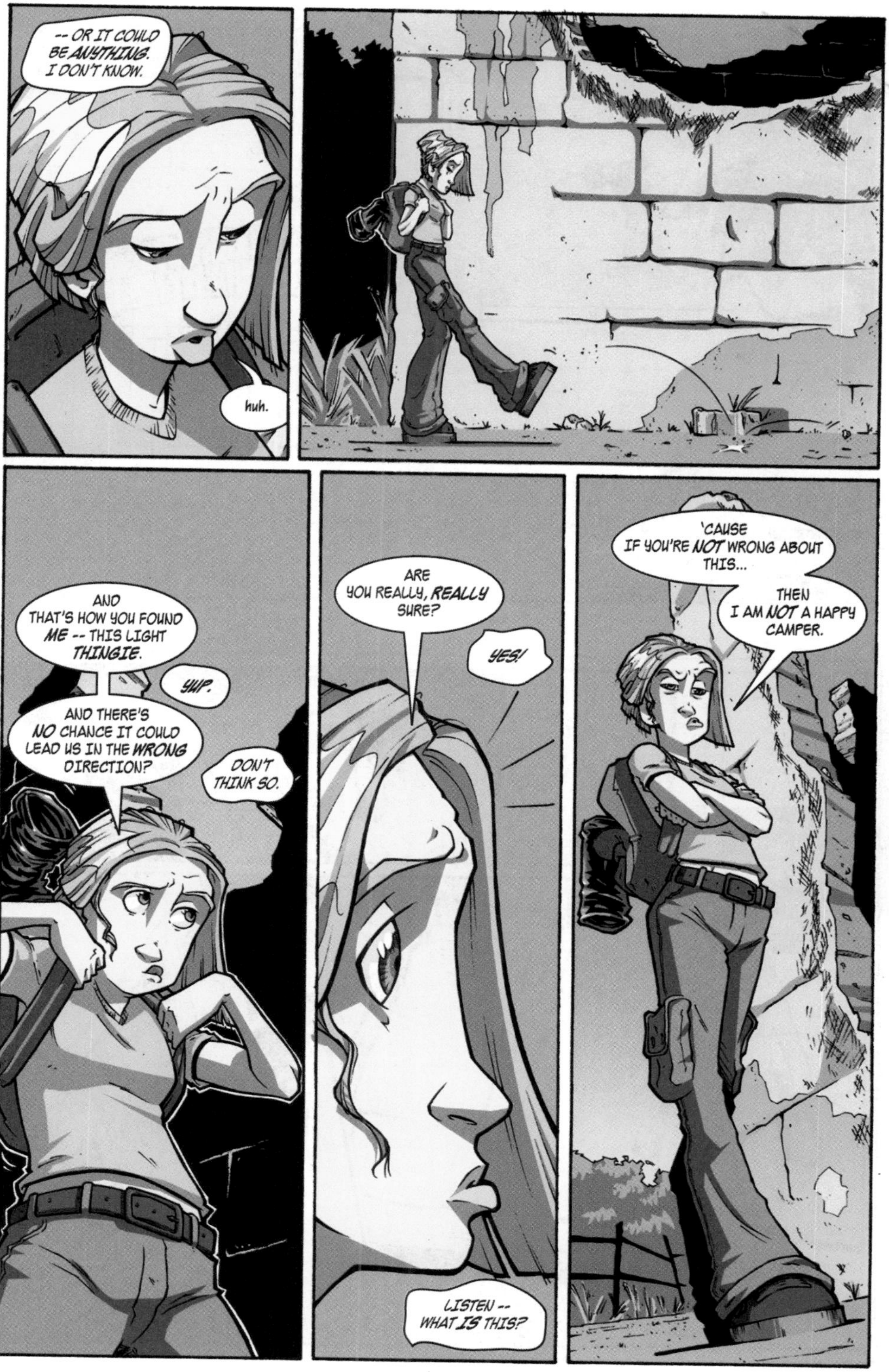
-- OR IT COULD BE ANYTHING. I DON'T KNOW.
huh.
AND THAT'S HOW YOU FOUND ME -- THIS LIGHT THINGIE.
YUP.
AND THERE'S NO CHANCE IT COULD LEAD US IN THE WRONG DIRECTION?
DON'T THINK SO.
ARE YOU REALLY, REALLY SURE?
YES!
LISTEN -- WHAT IS THIS?
'CAUSE IF YOU'RE NOT WRONG ABOUT THIS...
THEN I AM NOT A HAPPY CAMPER.

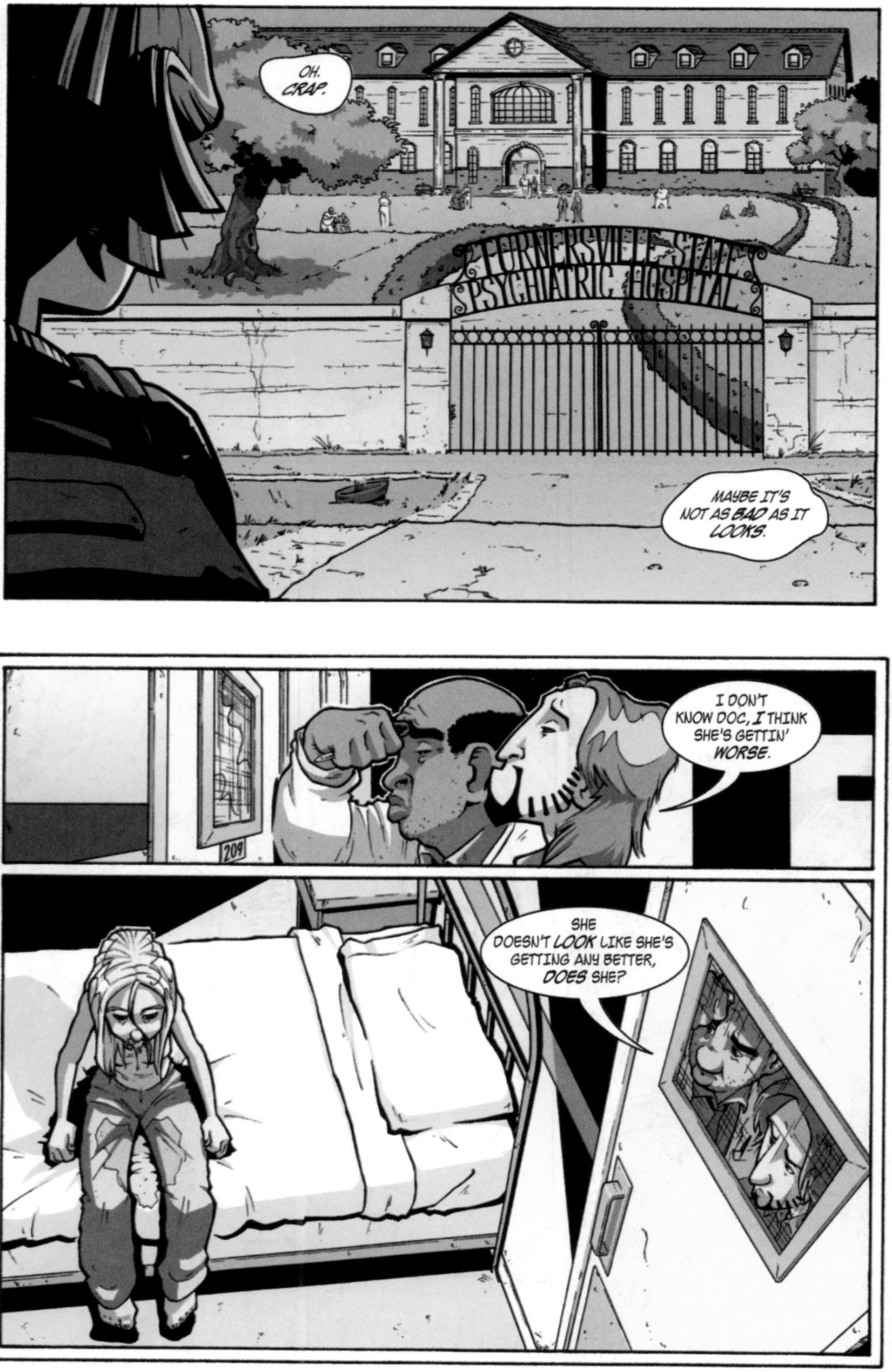
OH. CRAP.
TURNERSVILLE STATE PSYCHIATRIC HOSPITAL
MAYBE IT'S NOT AS BAD AS IT LOOKS.
209
I DON'T KNOW DOC, I THINK SHE'S GETTIN' WORSE.
SHE DOESN'T LOOK LIKE SHE'S GETTING ANY BETTER, DOES SHE?

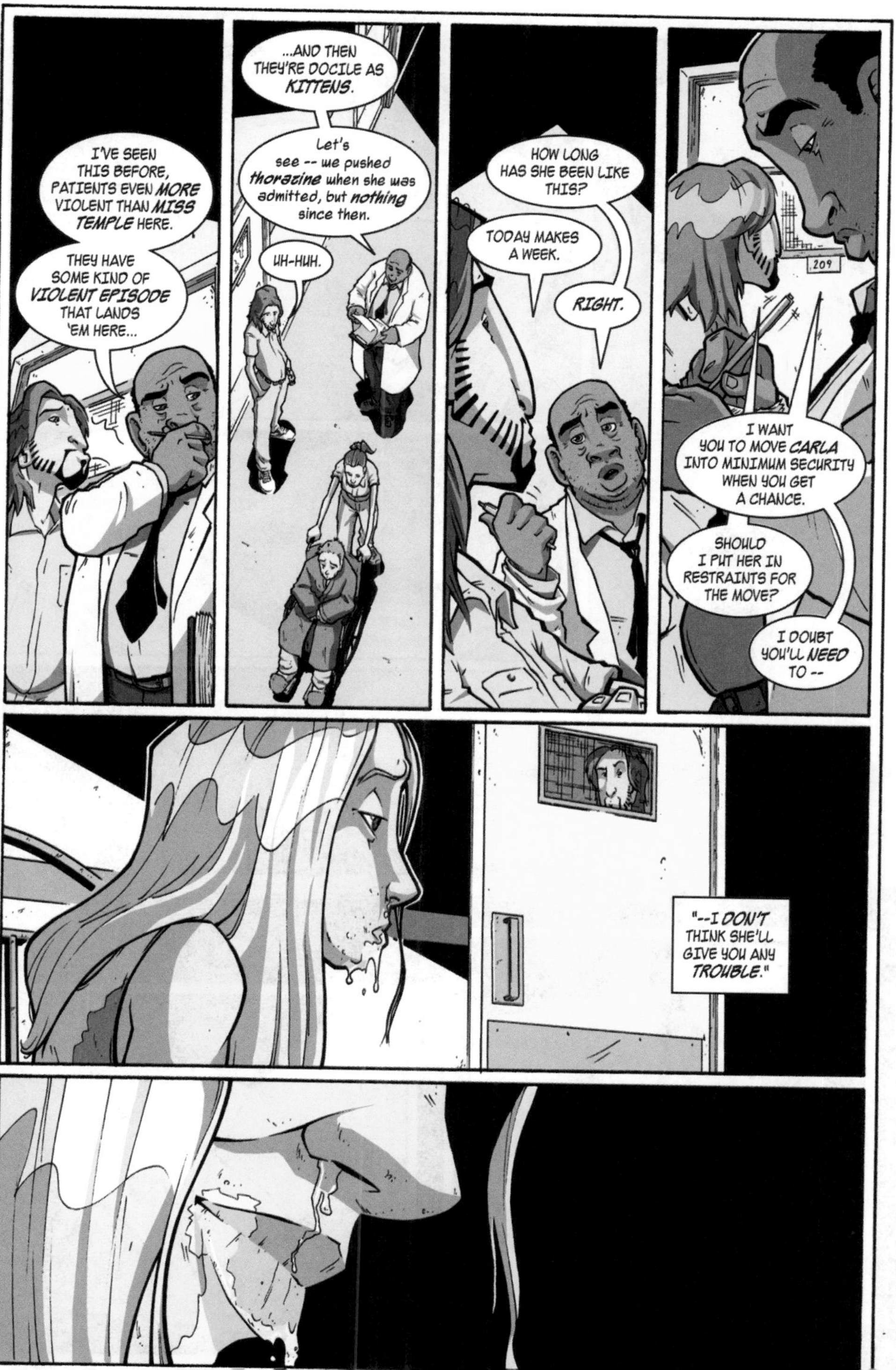
I'VE SEEN THIS BEFORE, PATIENTS EVEN MORE VIOLENT THAN MISS TEMPLE HERE.
THEY HAVE SOME KIND OF VIOLENT EPISODE THAT LANDS 'EM HERE...
...AND THEN THEY'RE DOCILE AS KITTENS.
Let's see -- we pushed thorazine when she was admitted, but nothing since then.
UH-HUH.
HOW LONG HAS SHE BEEN LIKE THIS?
TODAY MAKES A WEEK.
RIGHT.
209
I WANT YOU TO MOVE CARLA INTO MINIMUM SECURITY WHEN YOU GET A CHANCE.
SHOULD I PUT HER IN RESTRAINTS FOR THE MOVE?
I DOUBT YOU'LL NEED TO --
"--I DON'T THINK SHE'LL GIVE YOU ANY TROUBLE."

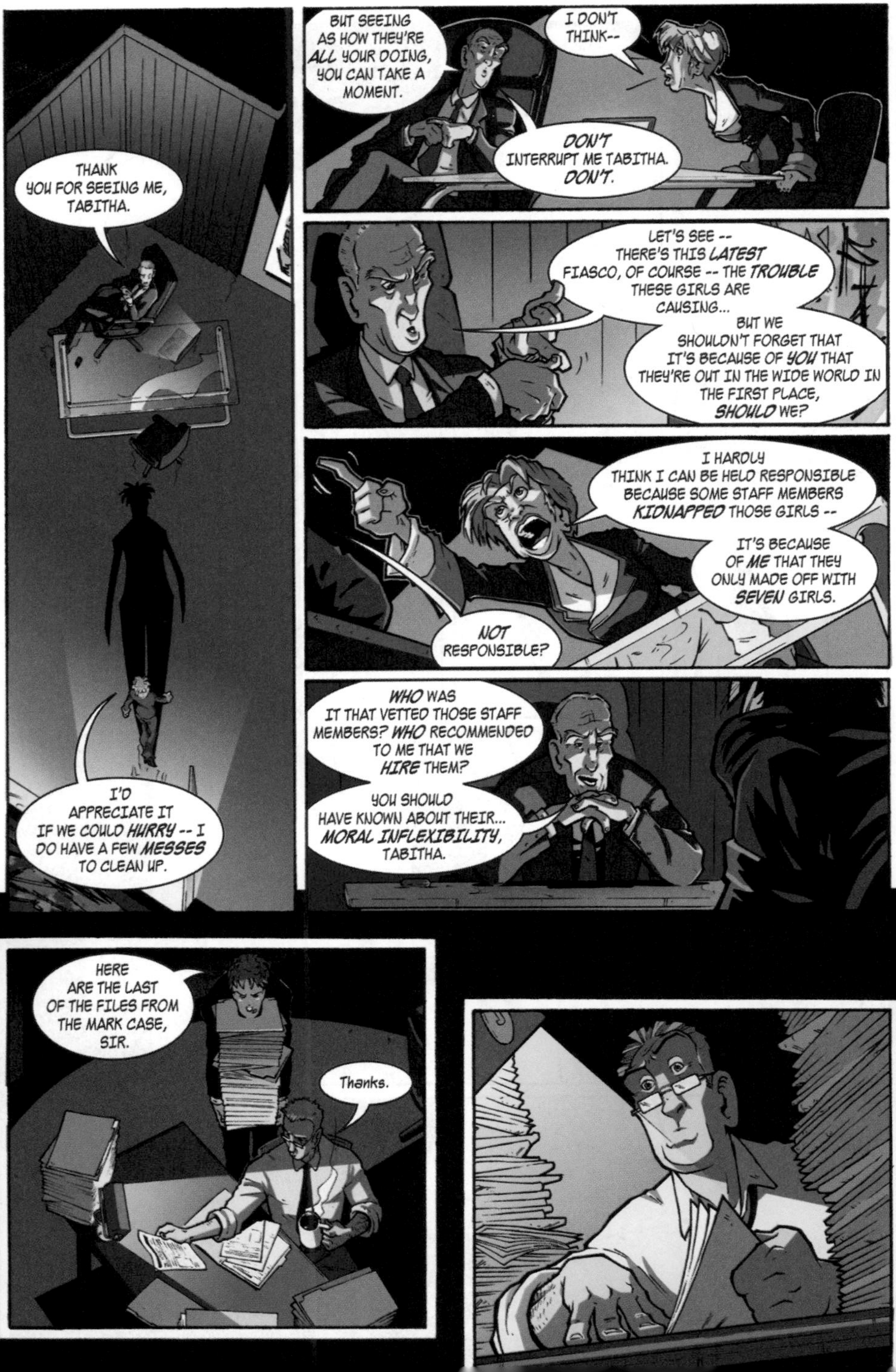
THANK YOU FOR SEEING ME, TABITHA.
I'D APPRECIATE IT IF WE COULD HURRY -- I DO HAVE A FEW MESSES TO CLEAN UP.
BUT SEEING AS HOW THEY'RE ALL YOUR DOING, YOU CAN TAKE A MOMENT.
I DON'T THINK--
DON'T INTERRUPT ME TABITHA. DON'T.
LET'S SEE -- THERE'S THIS LATEST FIASCO, OF COURSE -- THE TROUBLE THESE GIRLS ARE CAUSING...
BUT WE SHOULDN'T FORGET THAT IT'S BECAUSE OF YOU THAT THEY'RE OUT IN THE WIDE WORLD IN THE FIRST PLACE, SHOULD WE?
I HARDLY THINK I CAN BE HELD RESPONSIBLE BECAUSE SOME STAFF MEMBERS KIDNAPPED THOSE GIRLS --
IT'S BECAUSE OF ME THAT THEY ONLY MADE OFF WITH SEVEN GIRLS.
NOT RESPONSIBLE?
WHO WAS IT THAT VETTED THOSE STAFF MEMBERS? WHO RECOMMENDED TO ME THAT WE HIRE THEM?
YOU SHOULD HAVE KNOWN ABOUT THEIR... MORAL INFLEXIBILITY, TABITHA.
HERE ARE THE LAST OF THE FILES FROM THE MARK CASE, SIR.
Thanks.

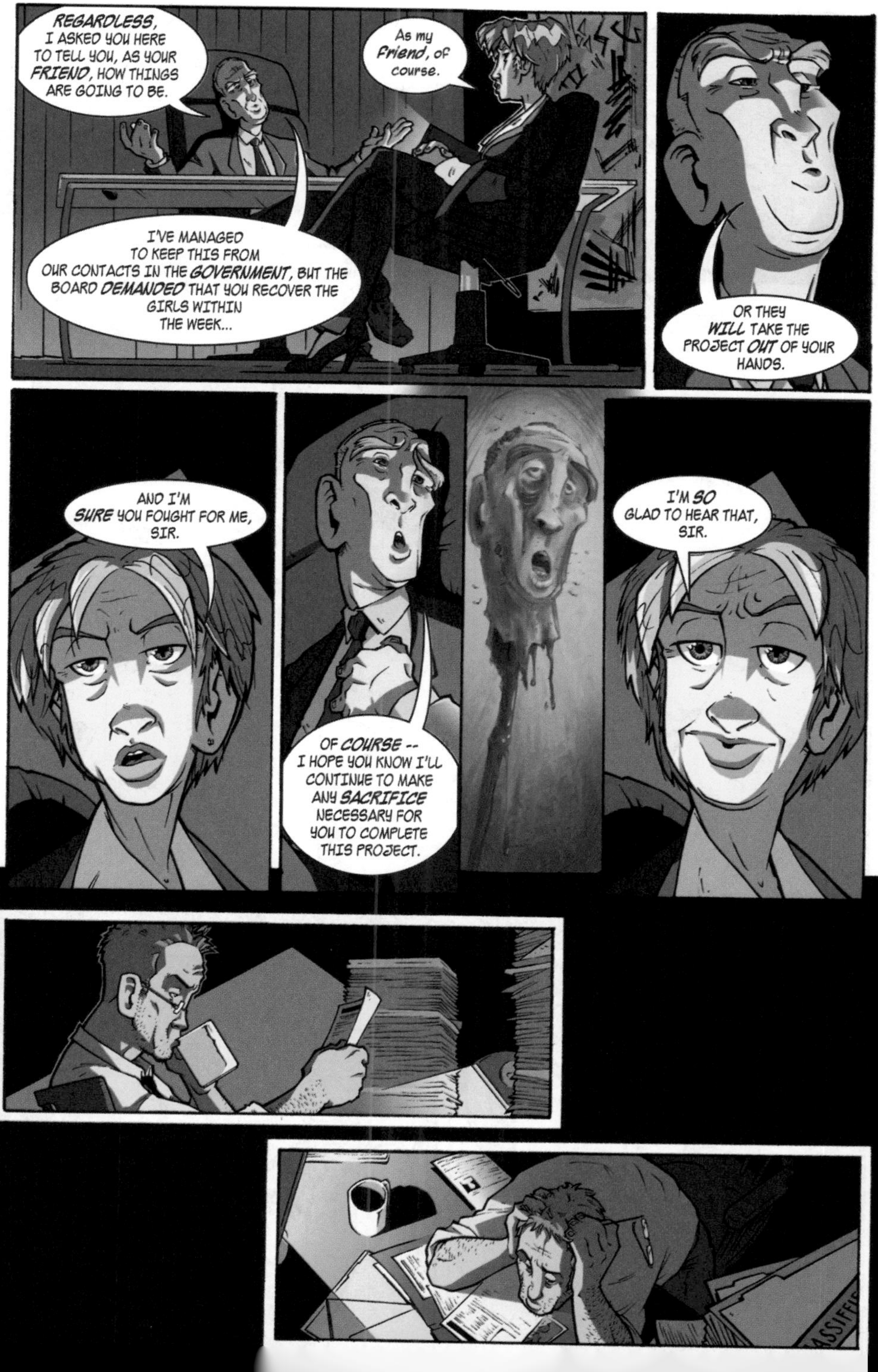

REGARDLESS, I ASKED YOU HERE TO TELL YOU, AS YOUR FRIEND, HOW THINGS ARE GOING TO BE.
As my friend, of course.
I'VE MANAGED TO KEEP THIS FROM OUR CONTACTS IN THE GOVERNMENT, BUT THE BOARD DEMANDED THAT YOU RECOVER THE GIRLS WITHIN THE WEEK...
OR THEY WILL TAKE THE PROJECT OUT OF YOUR HANDS.
AND I'M SURE YOU FOUGHT FOR ME, SIR.
OF COURSE -- I HOPE YOU KNOW I'LL CONTINUE TO MAKE ANY SACRIFICE NECESSARY FOR YOU TO COMPLETE THIS PROJECT.
I'M SO GLAD TO HEAR THAT, SIR.

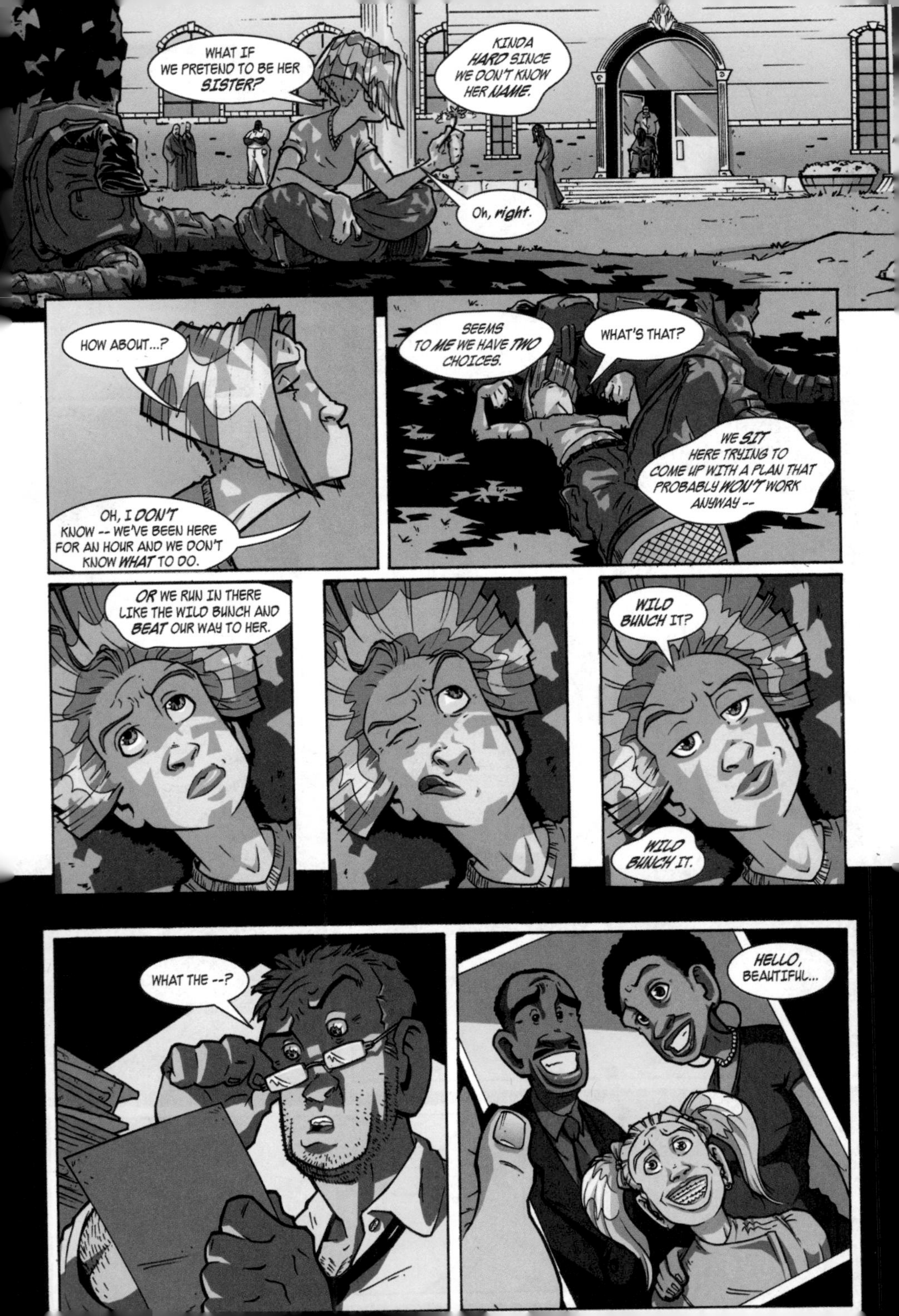
WHAT IF WE PRETEND TO BE HER SISTER?
KINDA HARD SINCE WE DON'T KNOW HER NAME.
Oh, right.
HOW ABOUT...?
OH, I DON'T KNOW -- WE'VE BEEN HERE FOR AN HOUR AND WE DON'T KNOW WHAT TO DO.
SEEMS TO ME WE HAVE TWO CHOICES.
WHAT'S THAT?
WE SIT HERE TRYING TO COME UP WITH A PLAN THAT PROBABLY WON'T WORK ANYWAY --
OR WE RUN IN THERE LIKE THE WILD BUNCH AND BEAT OUR WAY TO HER.
WILD BUNCH IT?
WILD BUNCH IT.
WHAT THE --?
HELLO, BEAUTIFUL...

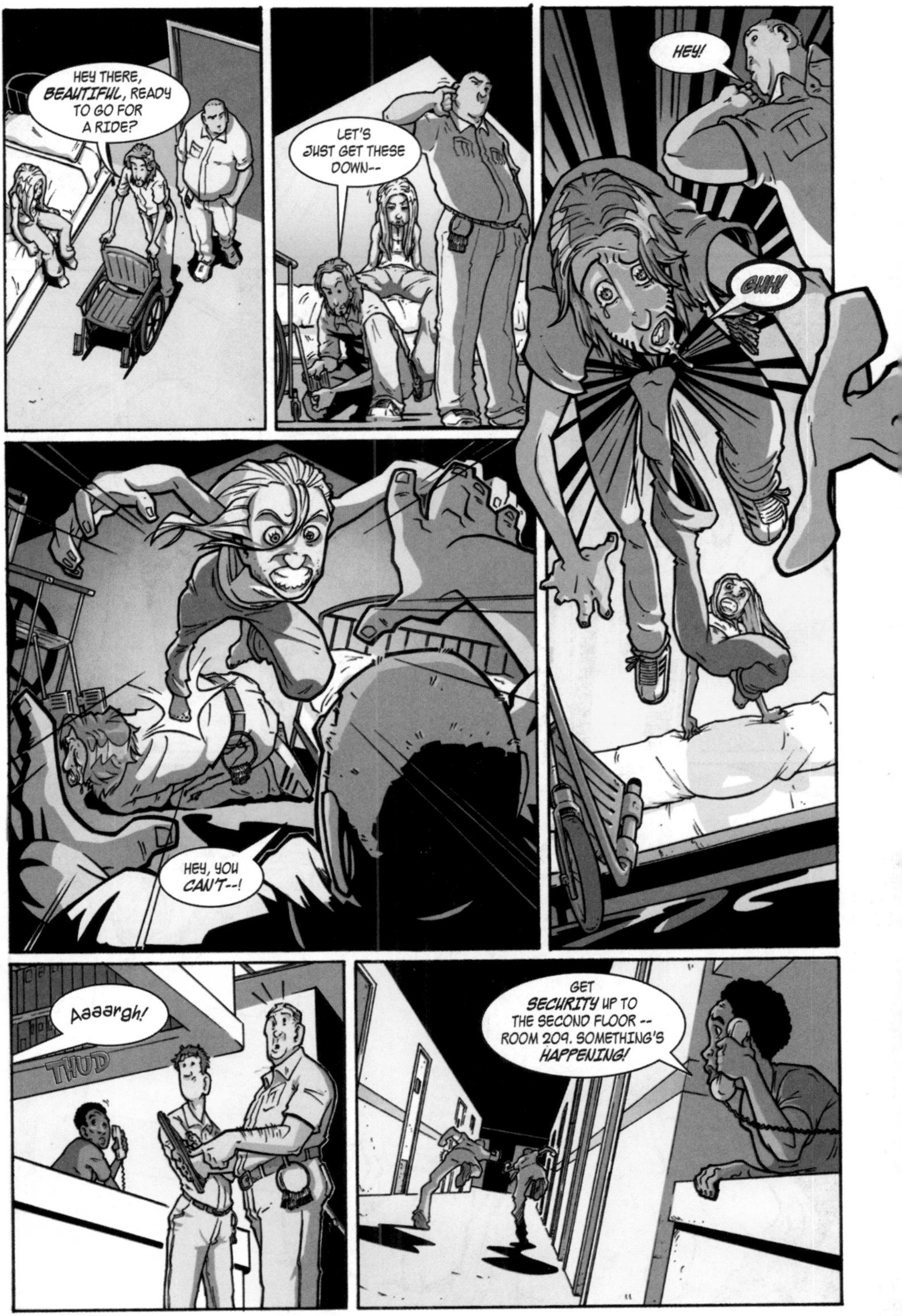

HEY THERE, BEAUTIFUL, READY TO GO FOR A RIDE?
LET'S JUST GET THESE DOWN--
HEY!
GUH!
HEY, YOU CAN'T--!
Aaaargh!
THUD
GET SECURITY UP TO THE SECOND FLOOR -- ROOM 209. SOMETHING'S HAPPENING!

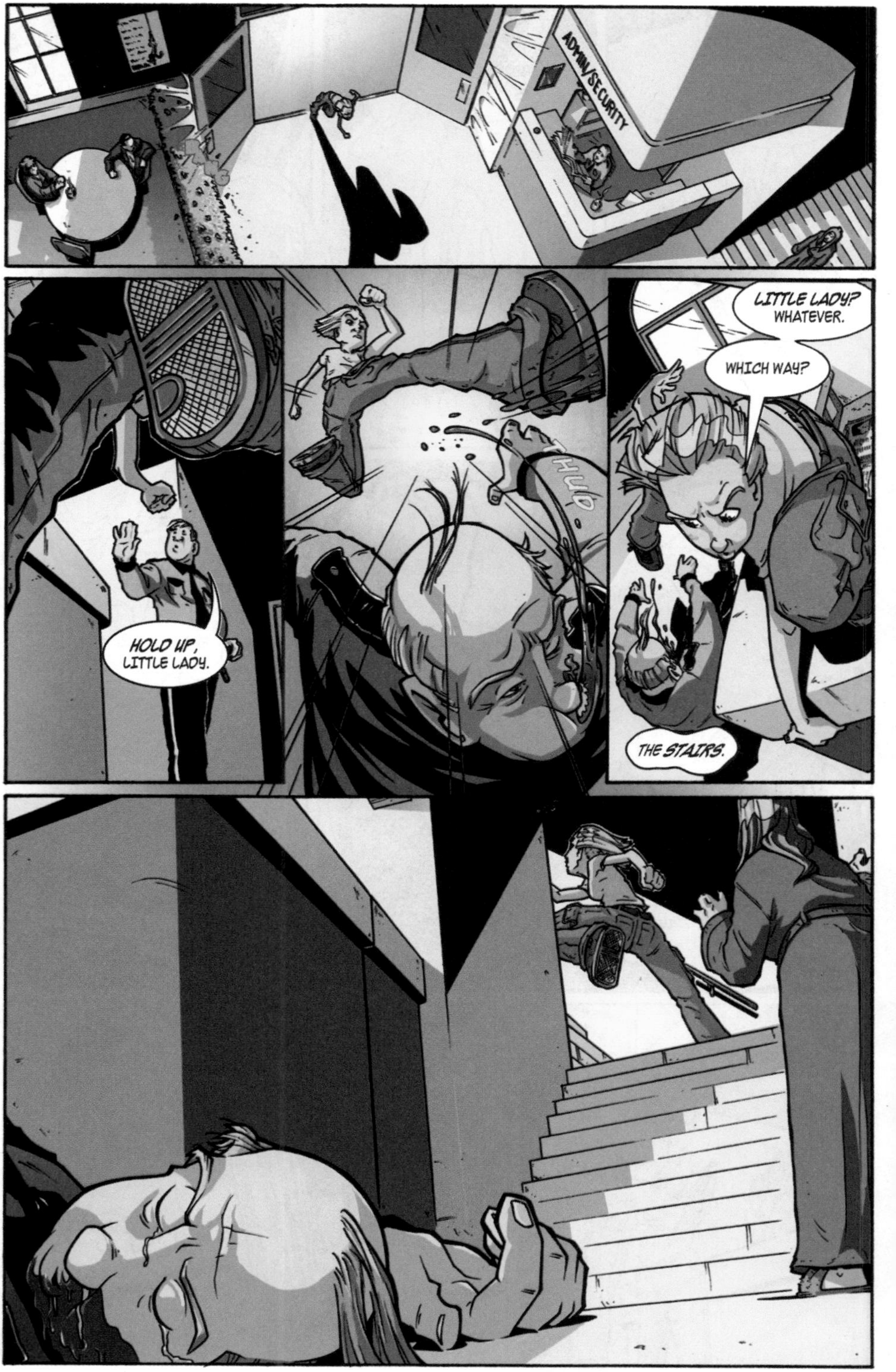
ADMIN/SECURITY
HOLD UP, LITTLE LADY.
THUD
LITTLE LADY? WHATEVER.
WHICH WAY?
THE STAIRS.

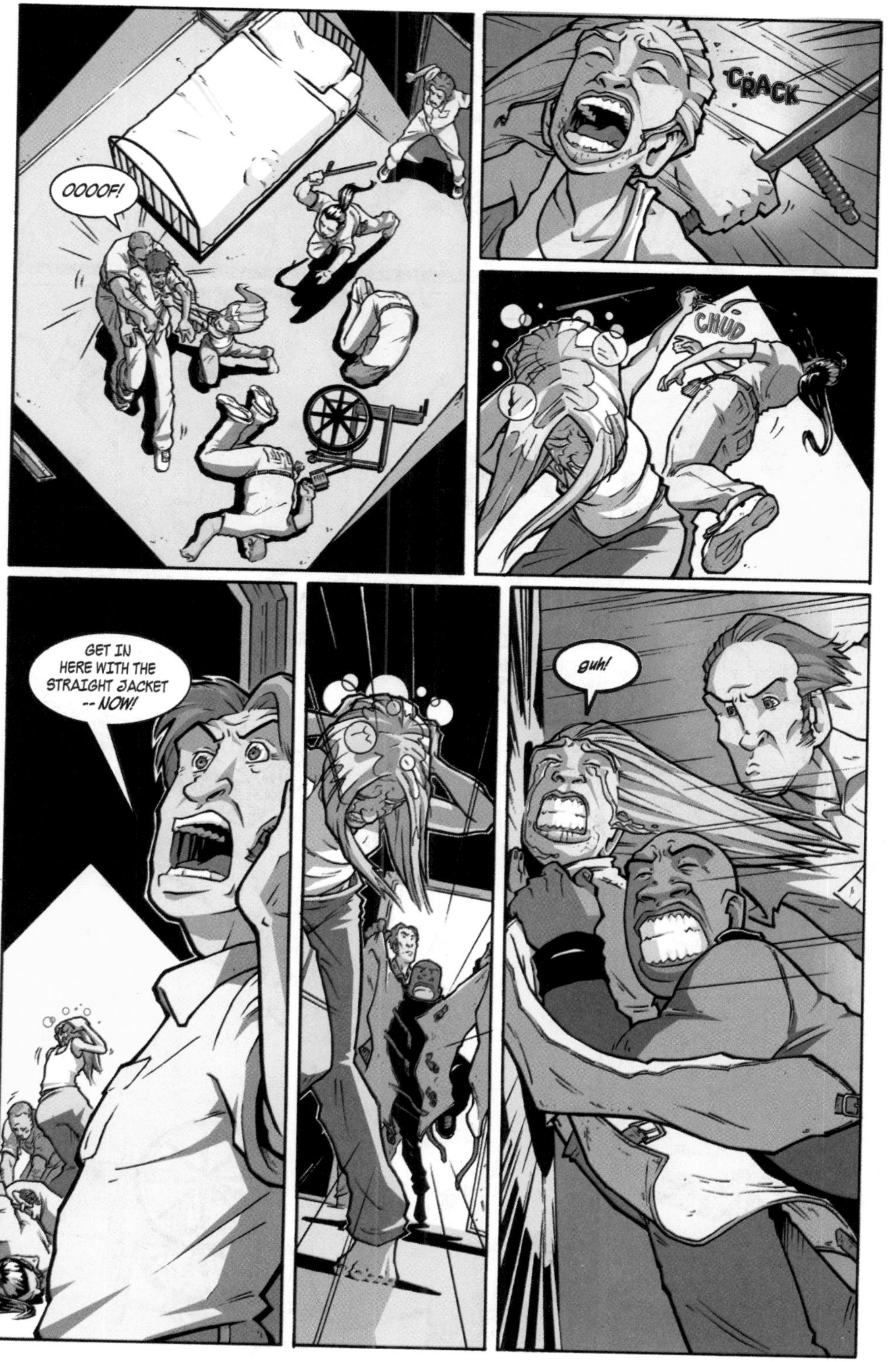
OOOOF!
CRACK
CHUD
GET IN HERE WITH THE STRAIGHT JACKET -- NOW!
guh!

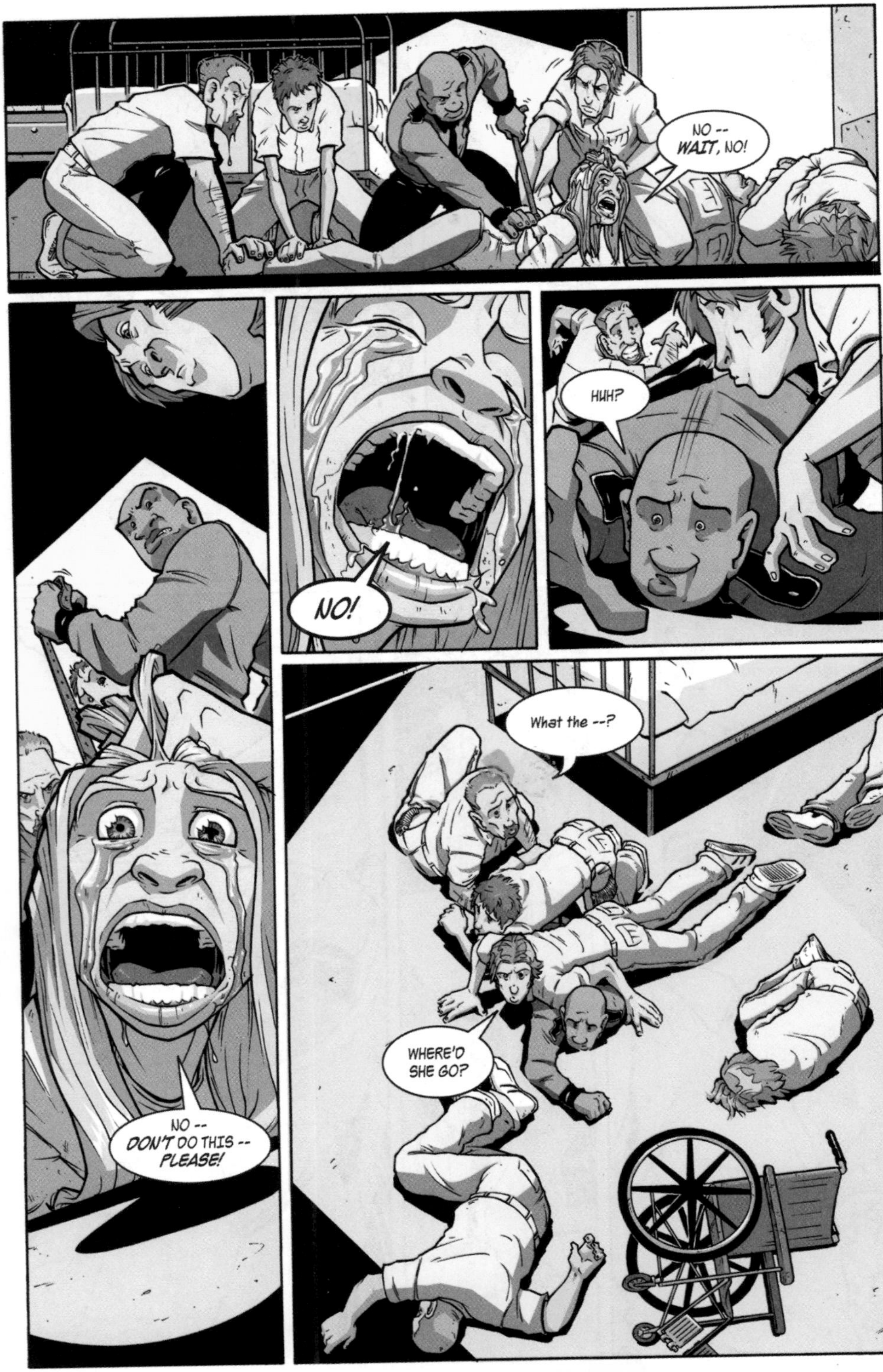
NO -- WAIT, NO!
NO!
HUH?
NO -- DON'T DO THIS -- PLEASE!
What the --?
WHERE'D SHE GO?

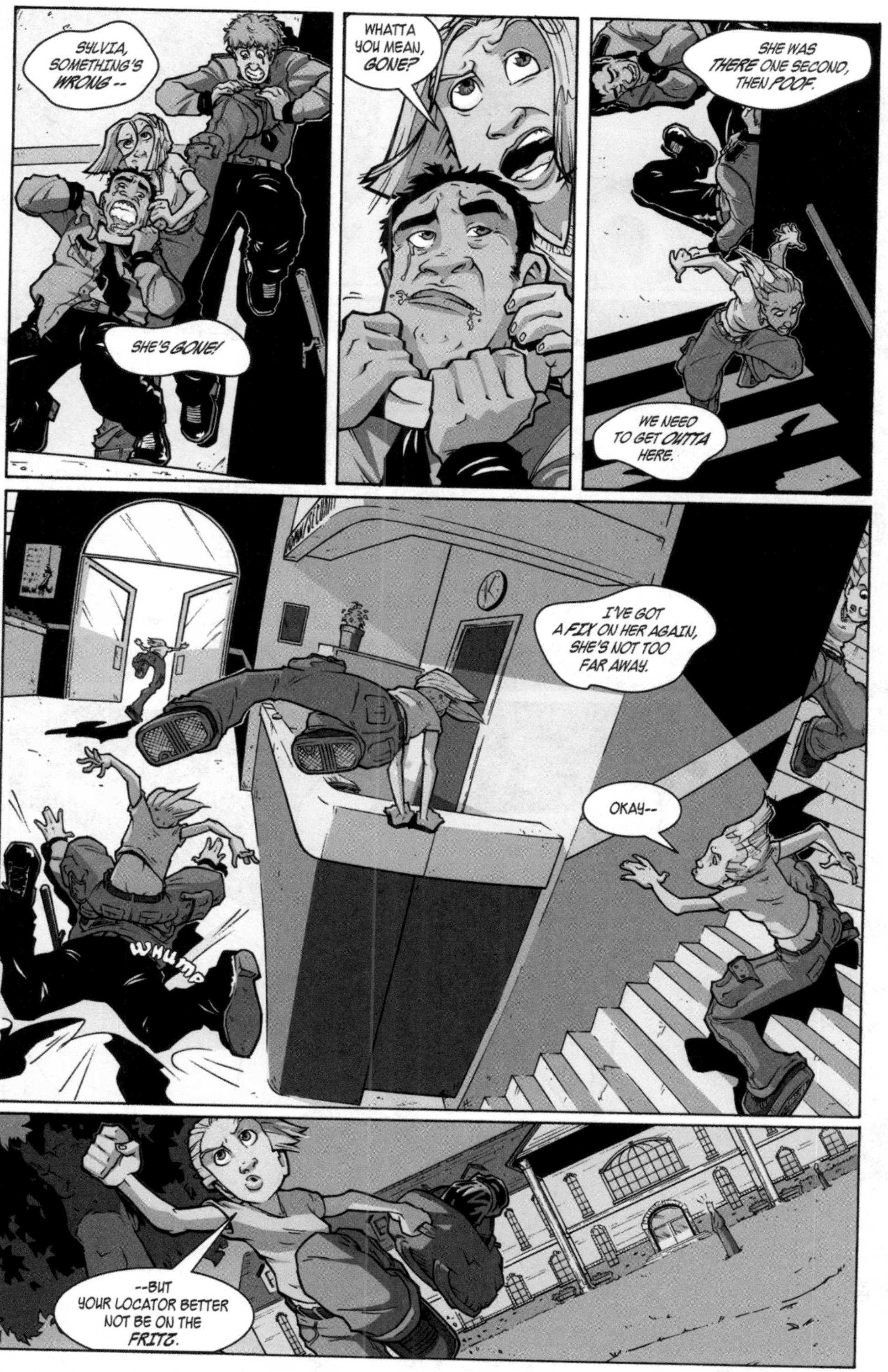
SYLVIA, SOMETHING'S WRONG --
SHE'S GONE!
WHATTA YOU MEAN, GONE?
SHE WAS THERE ONE SECOND, THEN POOF.
WE NEED TO GET OUTTA HERE.
I'VE GOT A FIX ON HER AGAIN, SHE'S NOT TOO FAR AWAY.
OKAY--
WHUMP
--BUT YOUR LOCATOR BETTER NOT BE ON THE FRITZ.

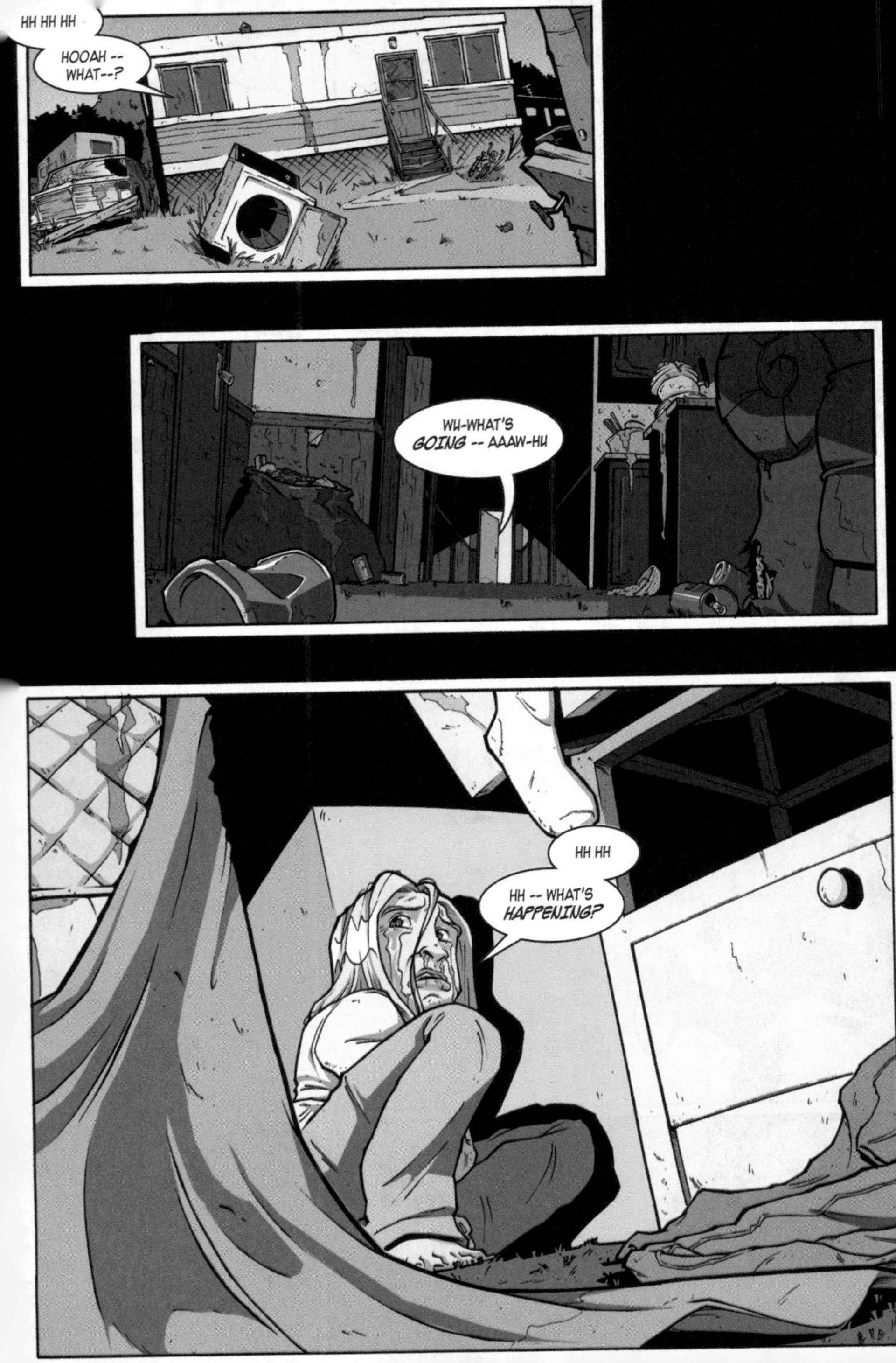
HH HH HH
HOOAH -- WHAT--?
WH-WHAT'S *GOING* -- AAAW-HU
HH HH
HH -- WHAT'S *HAPPENING?*

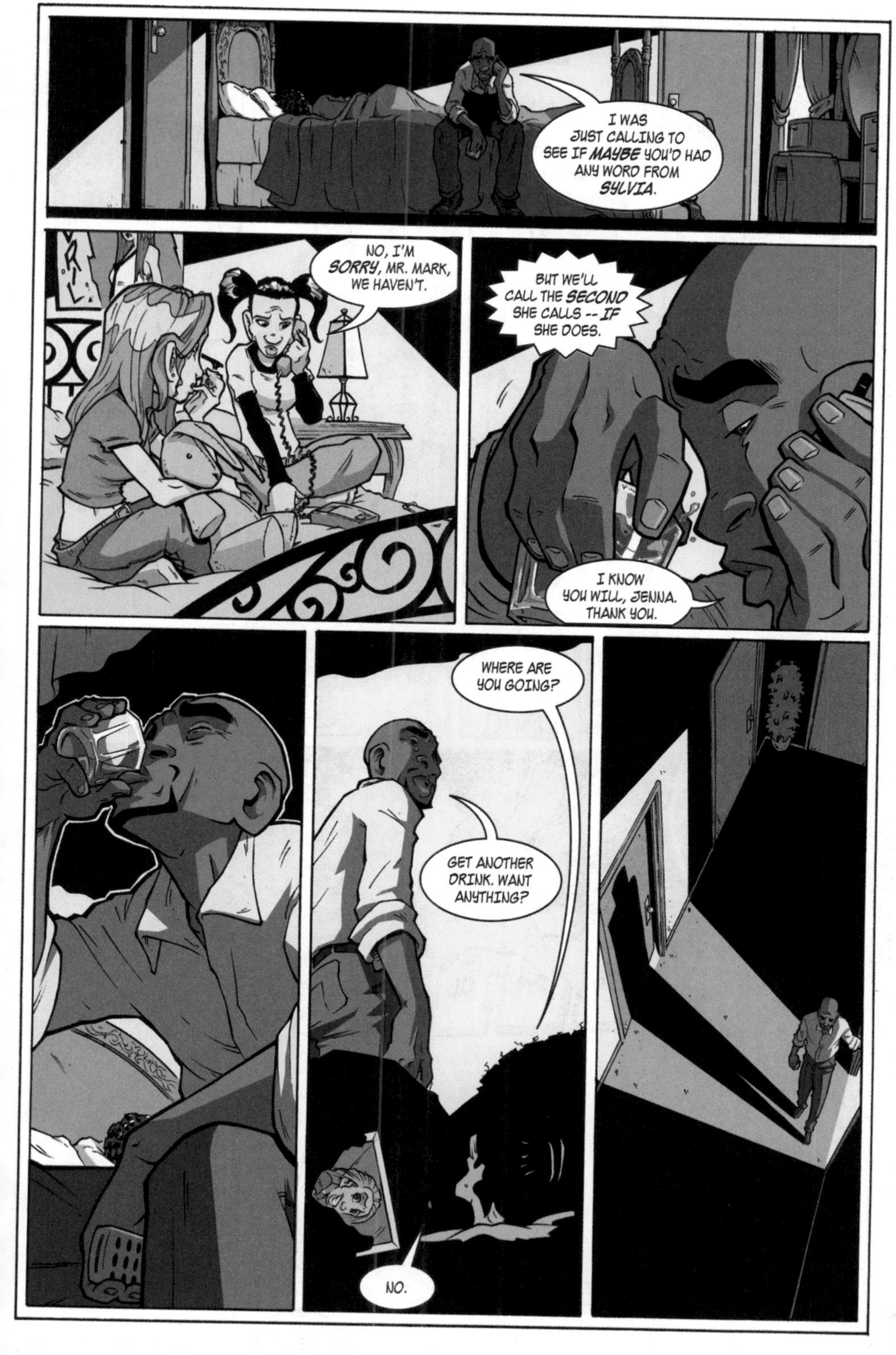
I WAS JUST CALLING TO SEE IF MAYBE YOU'D HAD ANY WORD FROM SYLVIA.
NO, I'M SORRY, MR. MARK, WE HAVEN'T.
BUT WE'LL CALL THE SECOND SHE CALLS -- IF SHE DOES.
I KNOW YOU WILL, JENNA. THANK YOU.
WHERE ARE YOU GOING?
GET ANOTHER DRINK. WANT ANYTHING?
NO.

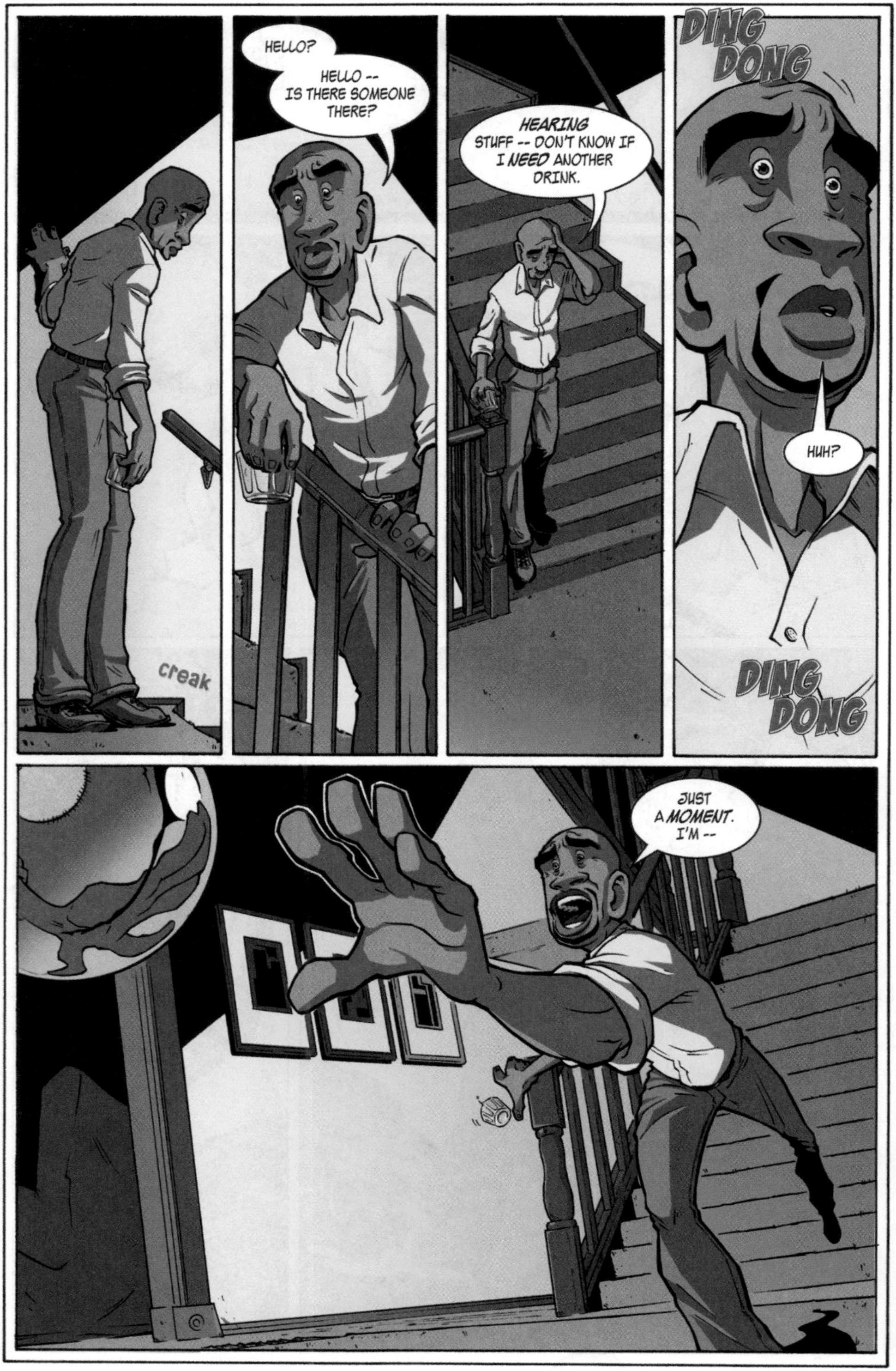
creak
HELLO?
HELLO -- IS THERE SOMEONE THERE?
HEARING STUFF -- DON'T KNOW IF I NEED ANOTHER DRINK.
DING DONG
HUH?
DING DONG
JUST A MOMENT. I'M --

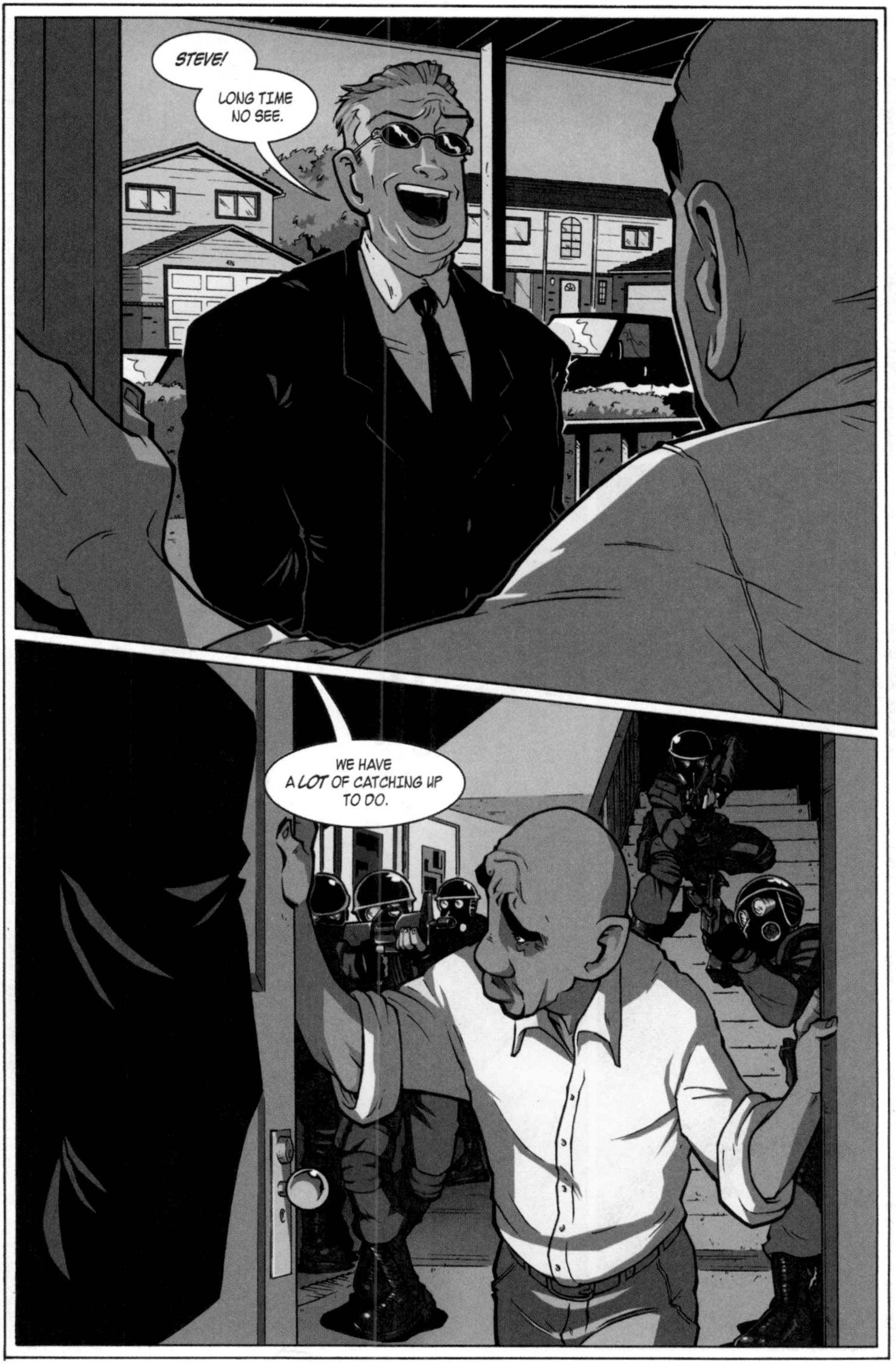
STEVE!
LONG TIME NO SEE.
WE HAVE A LOT OF CATCHING UP TO DO.

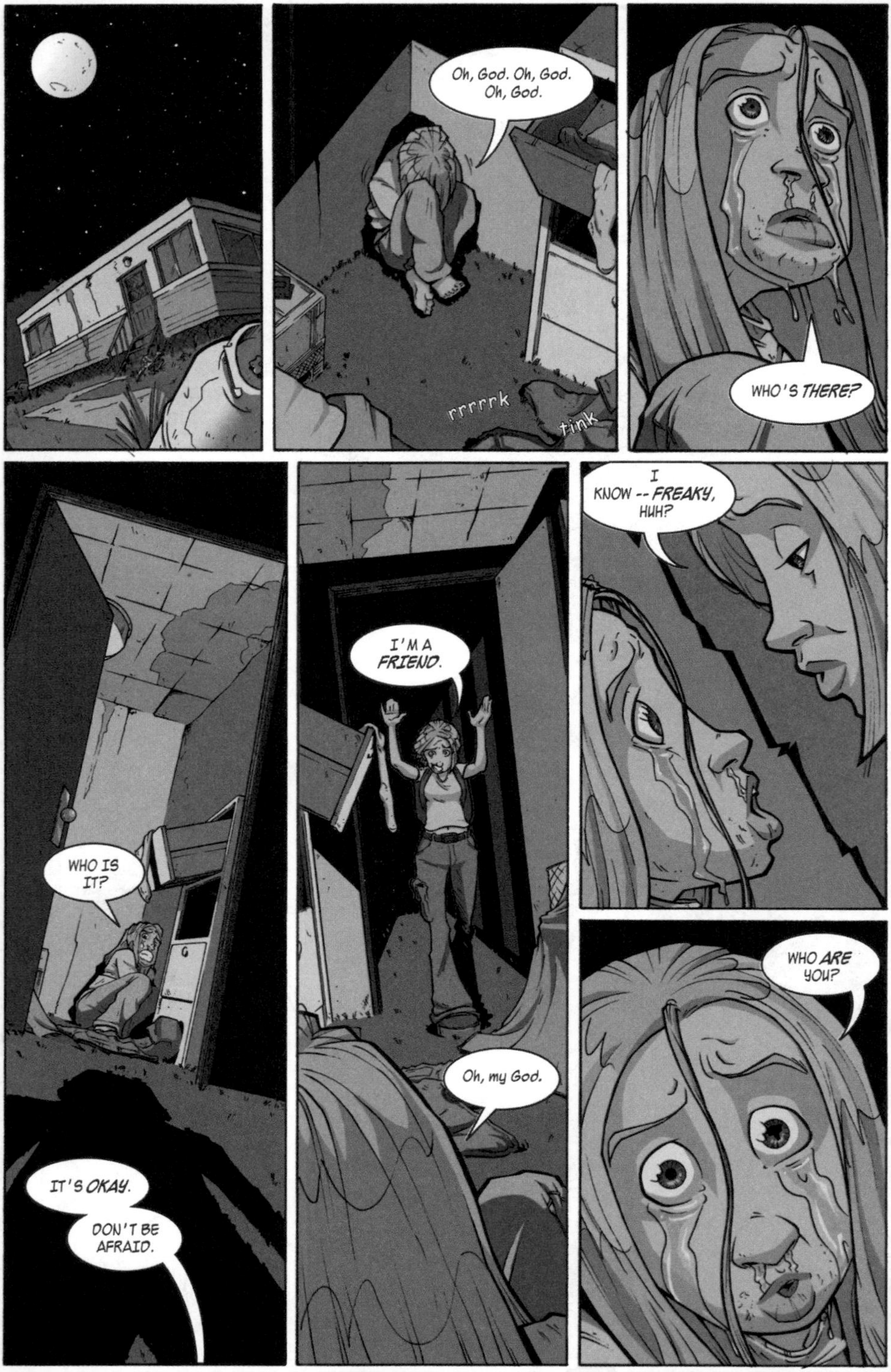
Oh, God. Oh, God. Oh, God.
rrrrrk
tink
WHO'S THERE?
WHO IS IT?
IT'S OKAY.
DON'T BE AFRAID.
I'M A FRIEND.
Oh, my God.
I KNOW -- FREAKY, HUH?
WHO ARE YOU?

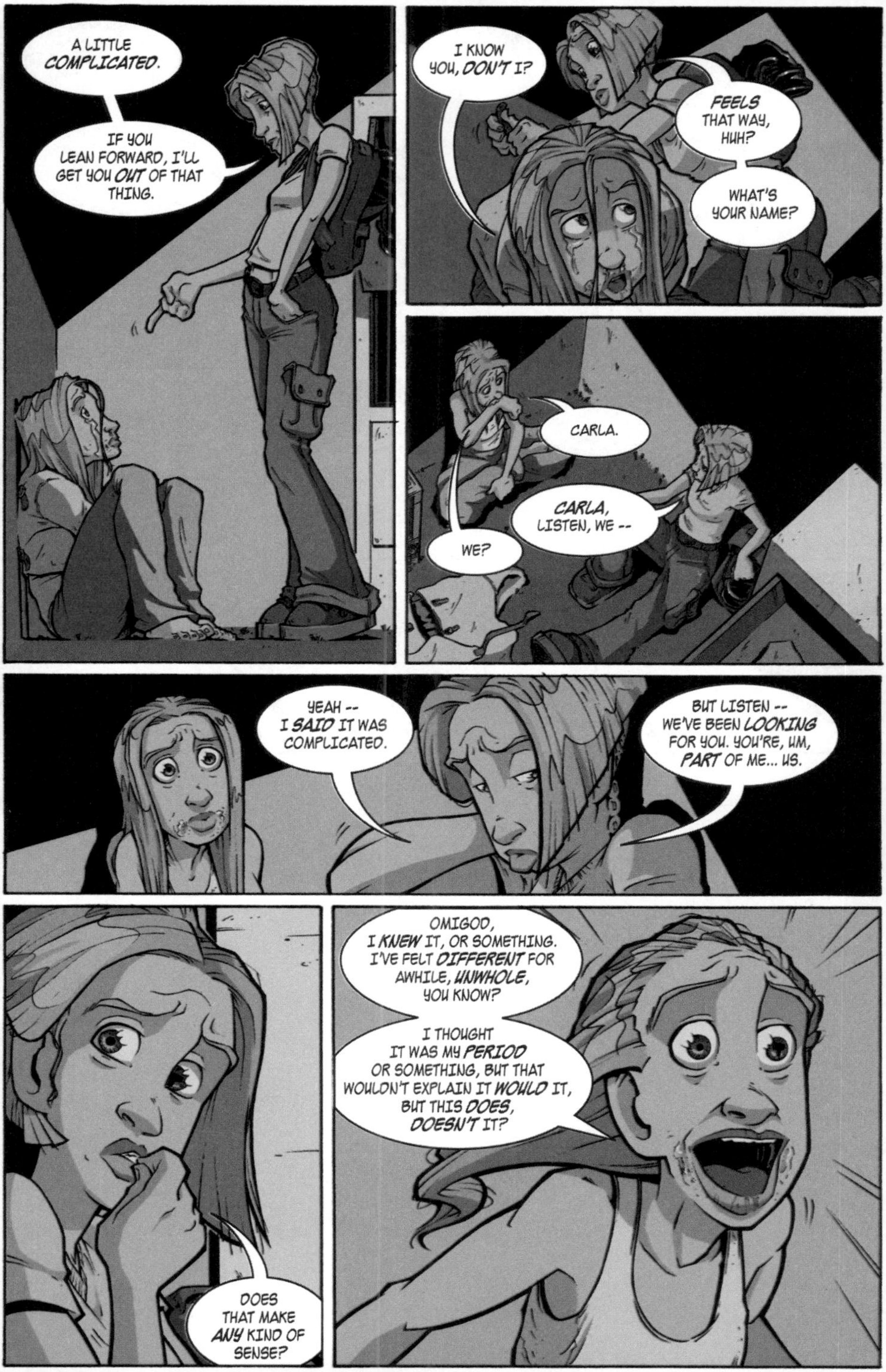
A LITTLE *COMPLICATED*.
IF YOU LEAN FORWARD, I'LL GET YOU *OUT* OF THAT THING.
I KNOW YOU, *DON'T* I?
FEELS THAT WAY, HUH?
WHAT'S YOUR NAME?
CARLA.
CARLA, LISTEN, WE --
WE?
YEAH -- I *SAID* IT WAS COMPLICATED.
BUT LISTEN -- WE'VE BEEN *LOOKING* FOR YOU. YOU'RE, UM, *PART* OF ME... US.
DOES THAT MAKE *ANY* KIND OF SENSE?
OMIGOD, I *KNEW* IT, OR SOMETHING. I'VE FELT *DIFFERENT* FOR AWHILE, *UNWHOLE*, YOU KNOW?
I THOUGHT IT WAS MY *PERIOD* OR SOMETHING, BUT THAT WOULDN'T EXPLAIN IT *WOULD* IT, BUT THIS *DOES*, *DOESN'T* IT?

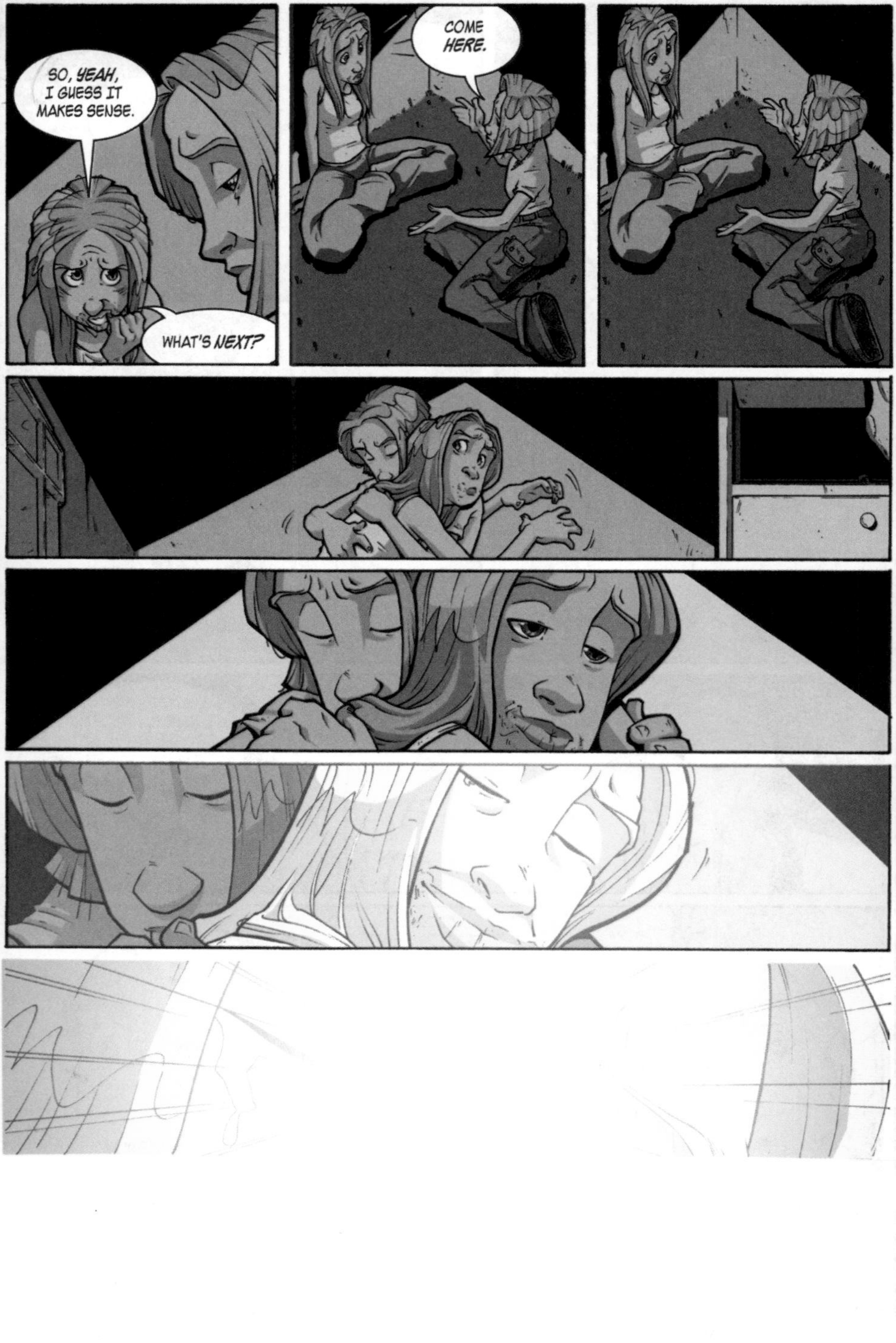
SO, YEAH,
I GUESS IT
MAKES SENSE.
WHAT'S NEXT?
COME
HERE.

CHAPTER FOUR

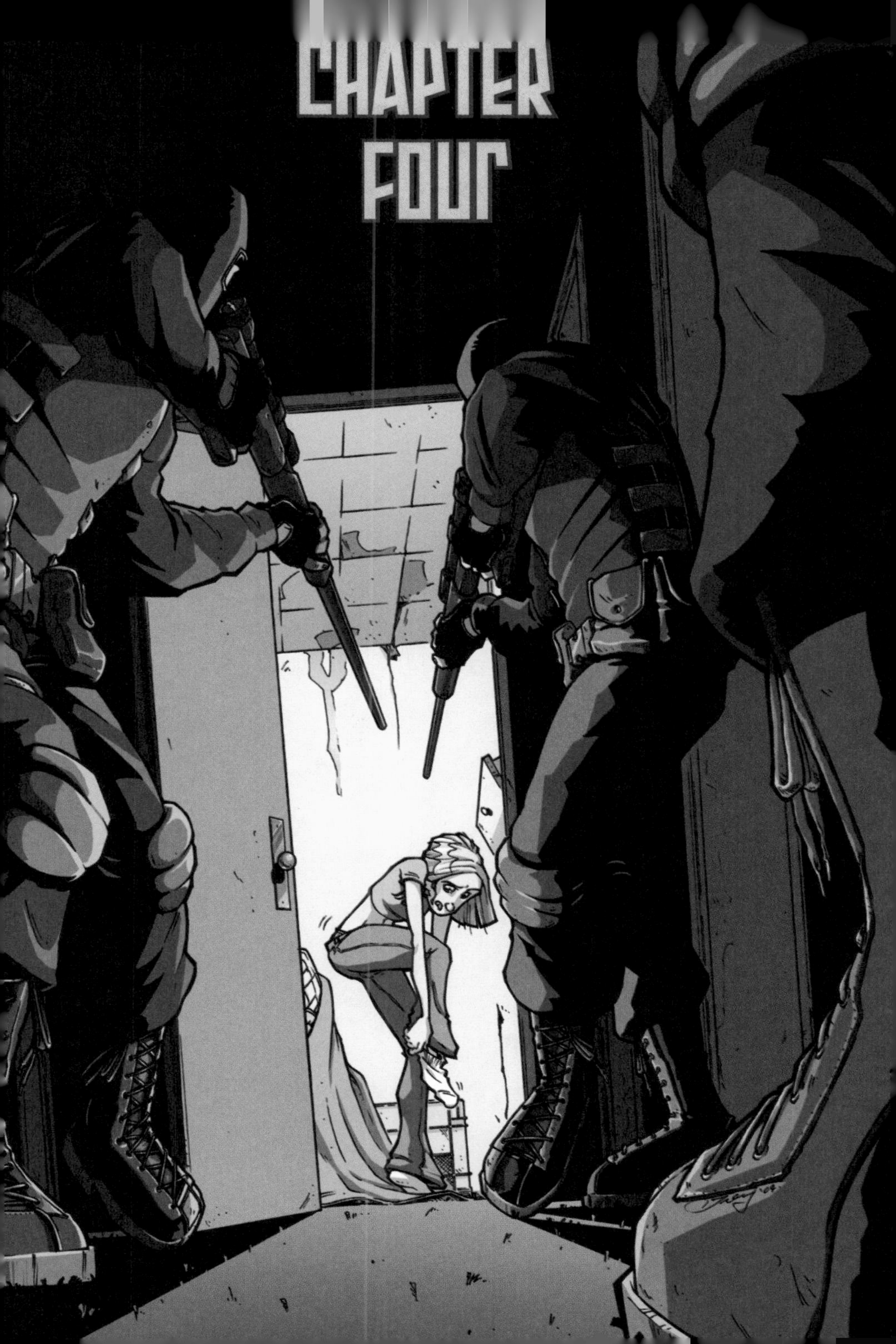

"IF SHE'S ANYTHING LIKE US, SHE'S
PROBABLY ONE SCREWED UP PUPPY."

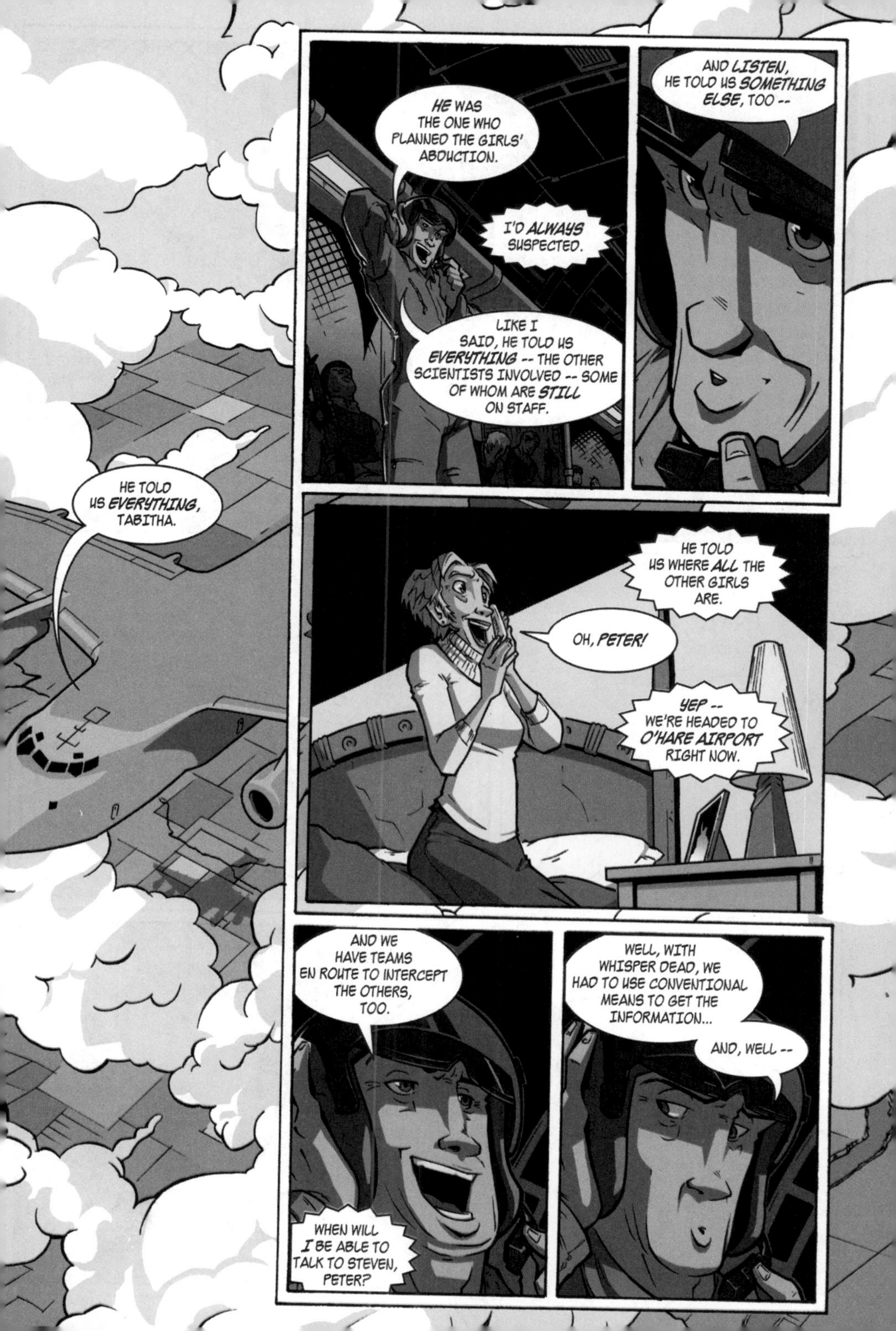
HE TOLD US EVERYTHING, TABITHA.
HE WAS THE ONE WHO PLANNED THE GIRLS' ABDUCTION.
I'D ALWAYS SUSPECTED.
LIKE I SAID, HE TOLD US EVERYTHING -- THE OTHER SCIENTISTS INVOLVED -- SOME OF WHOM ARE STILL ON STAFF.
AND LISTEN, HE TOLD US SOMETHING ELSE, TOO --
HE TOLD US WHERE ALL THE OTHER GIRLS ARE.
OH, PETER!
YEP -- WE'RE HEADED TO O'HARE AIRPORT RIGHT NOW.
AND WE HAVE TEAMS EN ROUTE TO INTERCEPT THE OTHERS, TOO.
WHEN WILL I BE ABLE TO TALK TO STEVEN, PETER?
WELL, WITH WHISPER DEAD, WE HAD TO USE CONVENTIONAL MEANS TO GET THE INFORMATION...
AND, WELL --

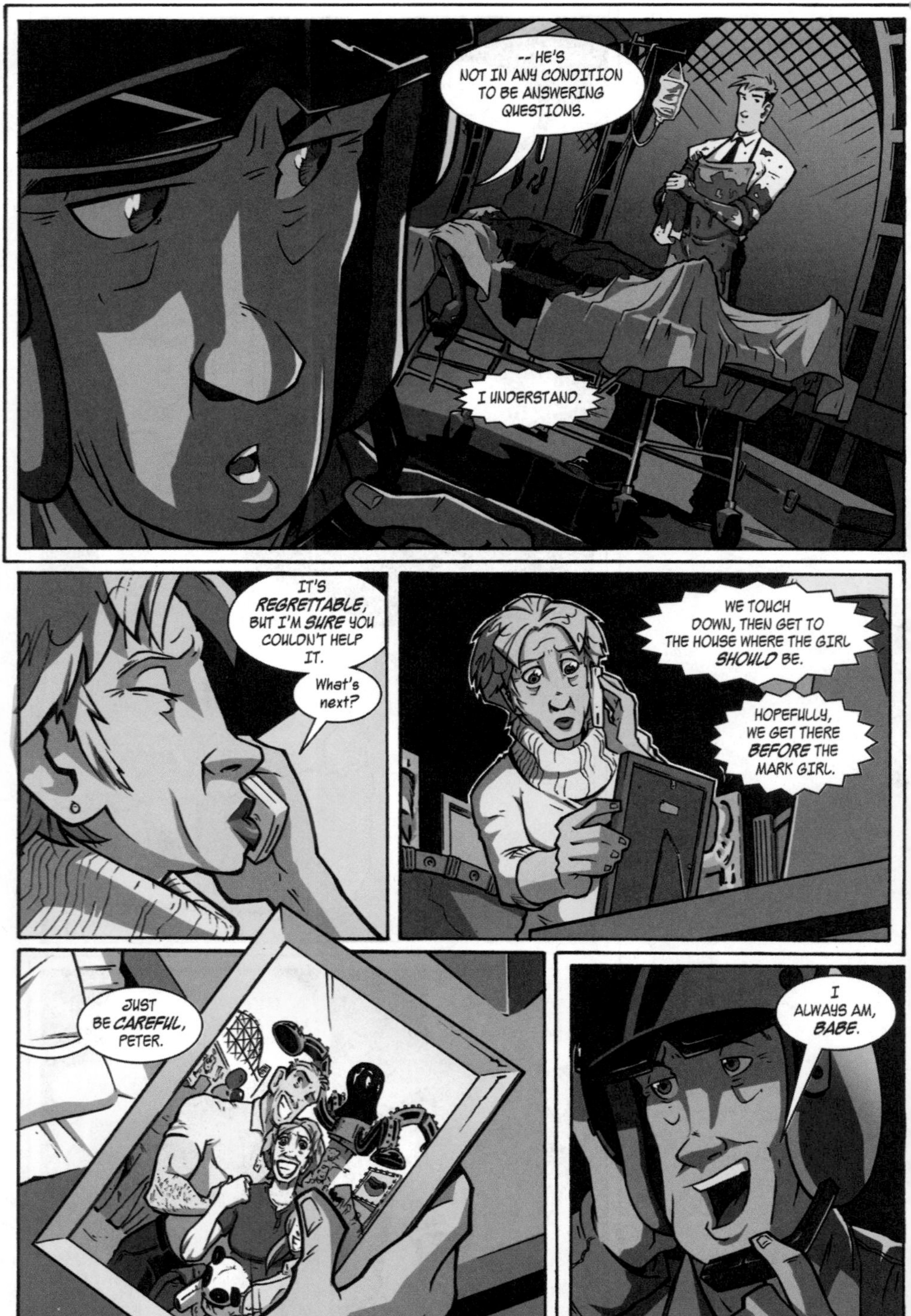
-- HE'S NOT IN ANY CONDITION TO BE ANSWERING QUESTIONS.
I UNDERSTAND.
IT'S REGRETTABLE, BUT I'M SURE YOU COULDN'T HELP IT.
What's next?
WE TOUCH DOWN, THEN GET TO THE HOUSE WHERE THE GIRL SHOULD BE.
HOPEFULLY, WE GET THERE BEFORE THE MARK GIRL.
JUST BE CAREFUL, PETER.
I ALWAYS AM, BABE.

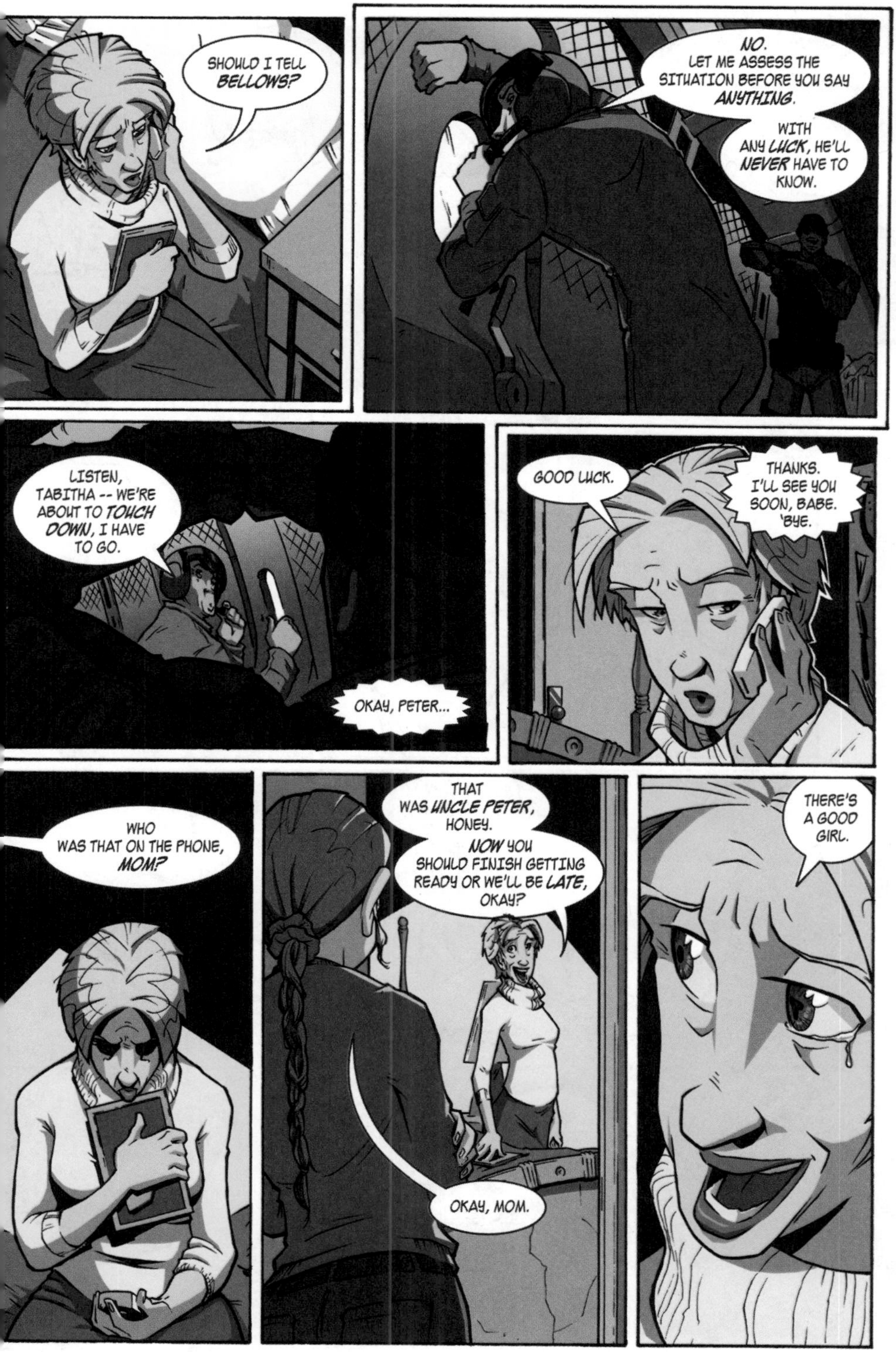
SHOULD I TELL BELLOWS?
NO. LET ME ASSESS THE SITUATION BEFORE YOU SAY ANYTHING.
WITH ANY LUCK, HE'LL NEVER HAVE TO KNOW.
LISTEN, TABITHA -- WE'RE ABOUT TO TOUCH DOWN, I HAVE TO GO.
OKAY, PETER...
GOOD LUCK.
THANKS. I'LL SEE YOU SOON, BABE. 'BYE.
WHO WAS THAT ON THE PHONE, MOM?
THAT WAS UNCLE PETER, HONEY.
NOW YOU SHOULD FINISH GETTING READY OR WE'LL BE LATE, OKAY?
OKAY, MOM.
THERE'S A GOOD GIRL.

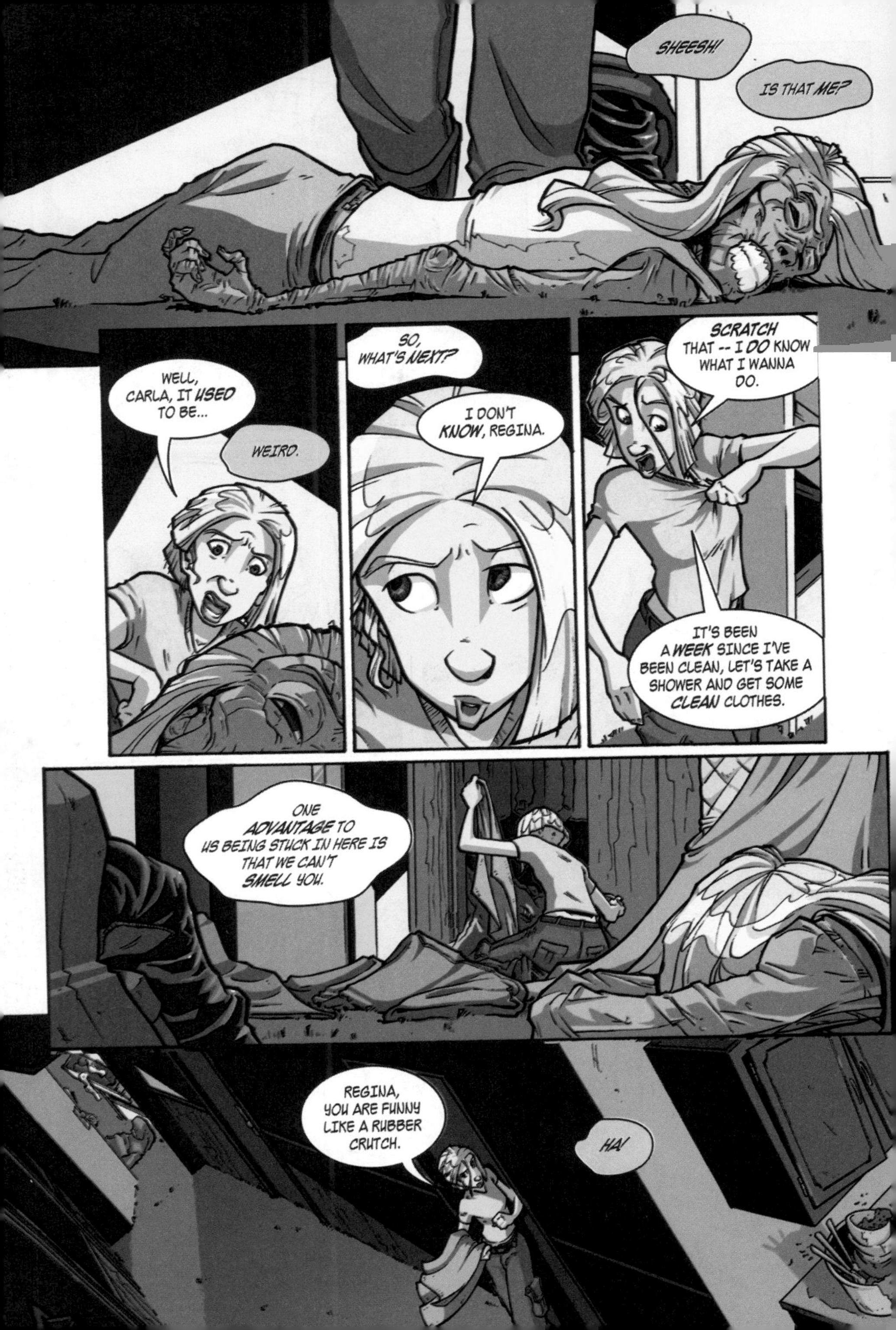
SHEESH!
IS THAT ME?
WELL, CARLA, IT USED TO BE...
WEIRD.
SO, WHAT'S NEXT?
I DON'T KNOW, REGINA.
SCRATCH THAT -- I DO KNOW WHAT I WANNA DO.
IT'S BEEN A WEEK SINCE I'VE BEEN CLEAN, LET'S TAKE A SHOWER AND GET SOME CLEAN CLOTHES.
ONE ADVANTAGE TO US BEING STUCK IN HERE IS THAT WE CAN'T SMELL YOU.
REGINA, YOU ARE FUNNY LIKE A RUBBER CRUTCH.
HA!

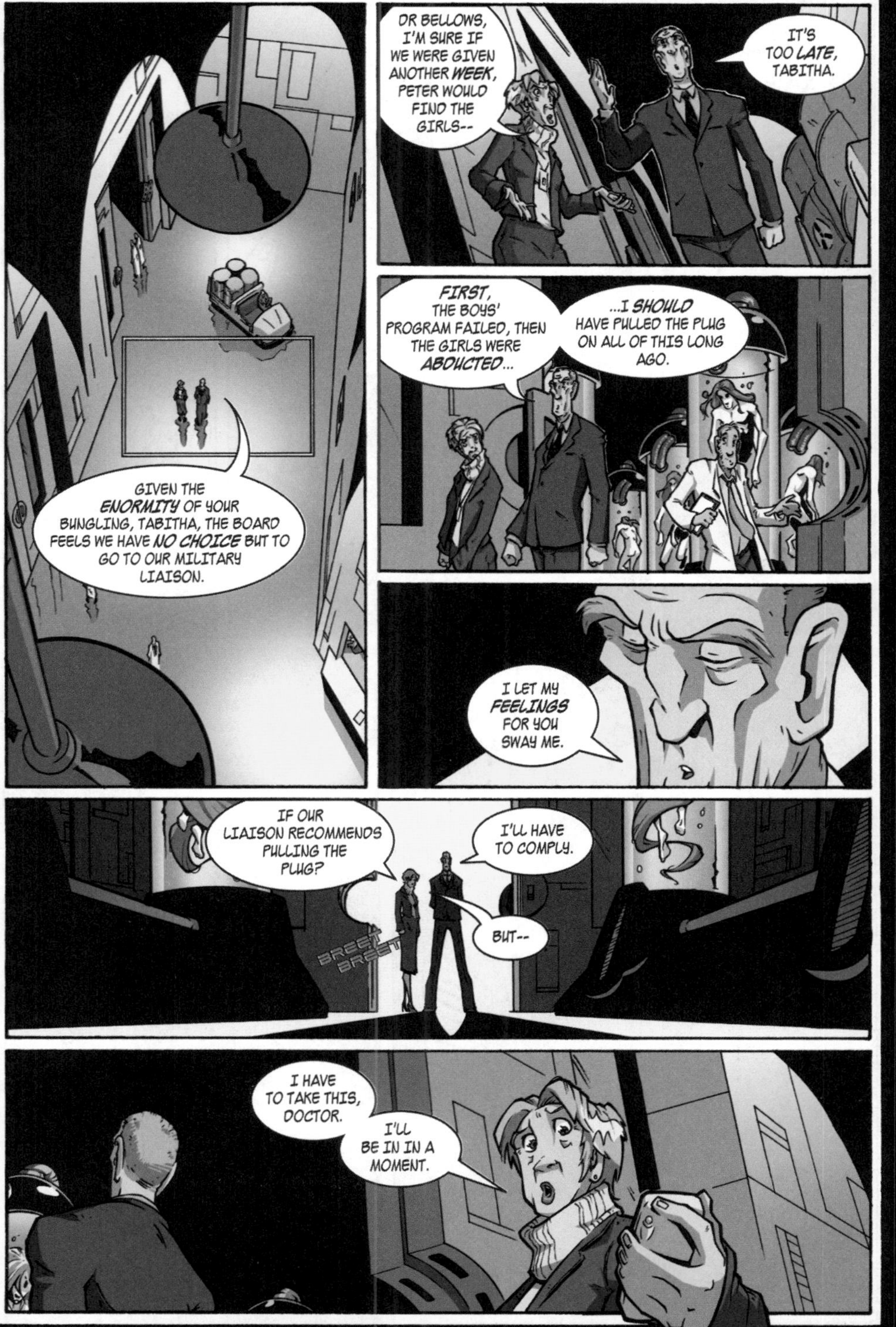
GIVEN THE ENORMITY OF YOUR BUNGLING, TABITHA, THE BOARD FEELS WE HAVE NO CHOICE BUT TO GO TO OUR MILITARY LIAISON.
DR BELLOWS, I'M SURE IF WE WERE GIVEN ANOTHER WEEK, PETER WOULD FIND THE GIRLS--
IT'S TOO LATE, TABITHA.
FIRST, THE BOYS' PROGRAM FAILED, THEN THE GIRLS WERE ABDUCTED...
...I SHOULD HAVE PULLED THE PLUG ON ALL OF THIS LONG AGO.
I LET MY FEELINGS FOR YOU SWAY ME.
IF OUR LIAISON RECOMMENDS PULLING THE PLUG?
I'LL HAVE TO COMPLY.
BUT--
BREET BREET
I HAVE TO TAKE THIS, DOCTOR.
I'LL BE IN IN A MOMENT.

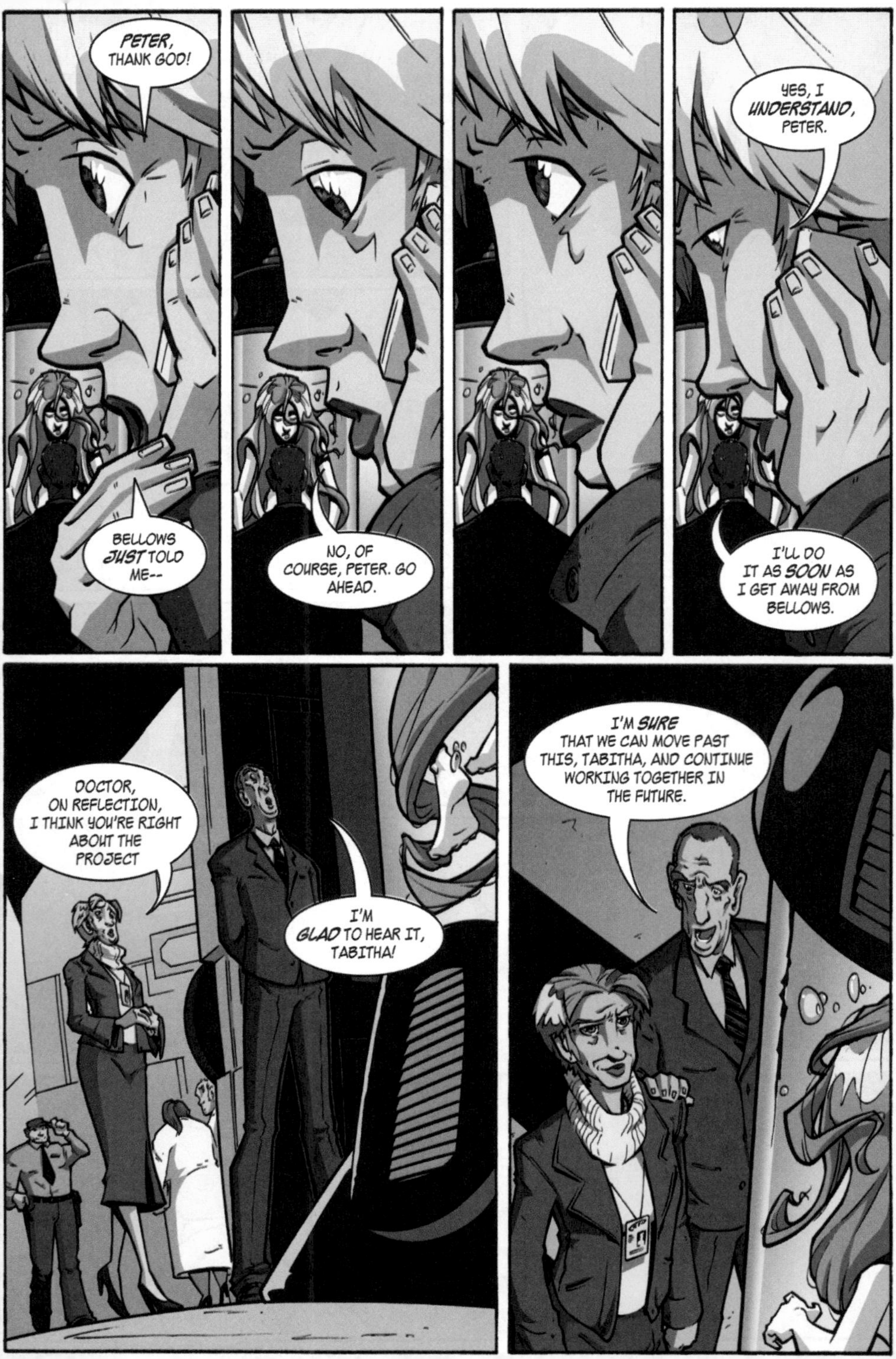
PETER, THANK GOD!
BELLOWS JUST TOLD ME--
NO, OF COURSE, PETER. GO AHEAD.
YES, I UNDERSTAND, PETER.
I'LL DO IT AS SOON AS I GET AWAY FROM BELLOWS.
DOCTOR, ON REFLECTION, I THINK YOU'RE RIGHT ABOUT THE PROJECT
I'M GLAD TO HEAR IT, TABITHA!
I'M SURE THAT WE CAN MOVE PAST THIS, TABITHA, AND CONTINUE WORKING TOGETHER IN THE FUTURE.

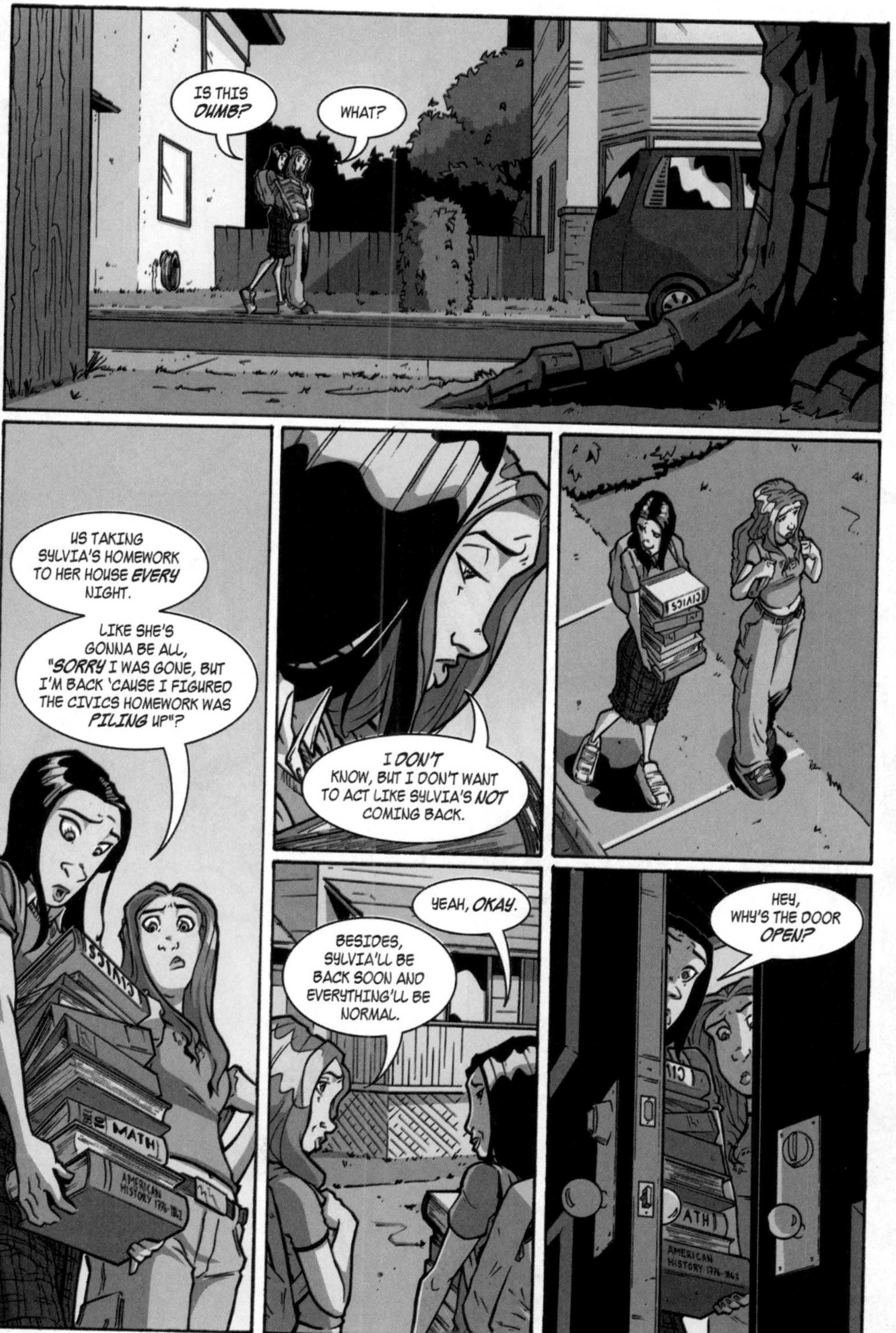
IS THIS DUMB?
WHAT?
US TAKING SYLVIA'S HOMEWORK TO HER HOUSE EVERY NIGHT.
LIKE SHE'S GONNA BE ALL, "SORRY I WAS GONE, BUT I'M BACK 'CAUSE I FIGURED THE CIVICS HOMEWORK WAS PILING UP"?
CIVICS
MATH
AMERICAN HISTORY 1776-1862
I DON'T KNOW, BUT I DON'T WANT TO ACT LIKE SYLVIA'S NOT COMING BACK.
CIVICS
BESIDES, SYLVIA'LL BE BACK SOON AND EVERYTHING'LL BE NORMAL.
YEAH, OKAY.
HEY, WHY'S THE DOOR OPEN?

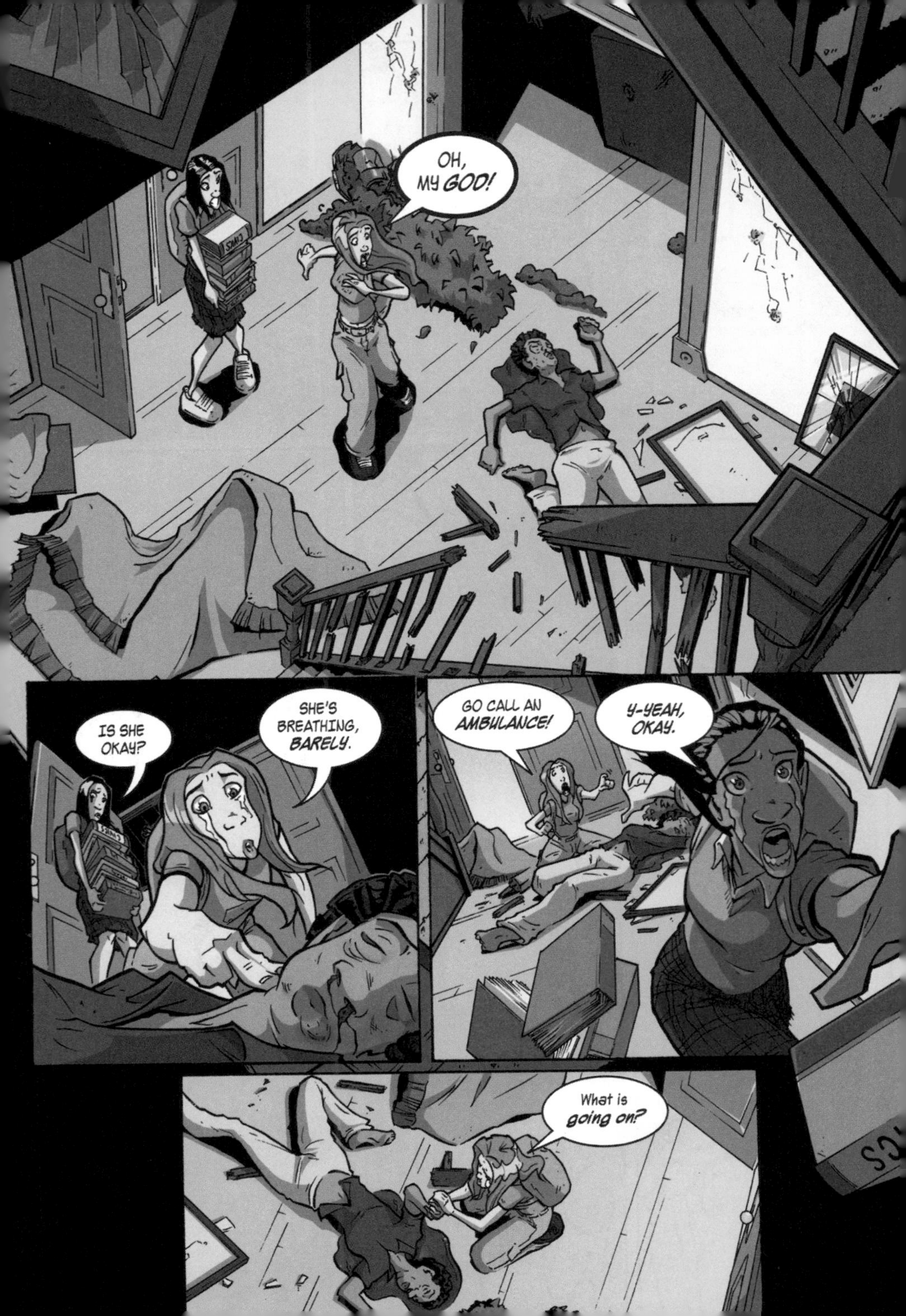

OH, MY GOD!
IS SHE OKAY?
SHE'S BREATHING, BARELY.
GO CALL AN AMBULANCE!
Y-YEAH, OKAY.
What is going on?

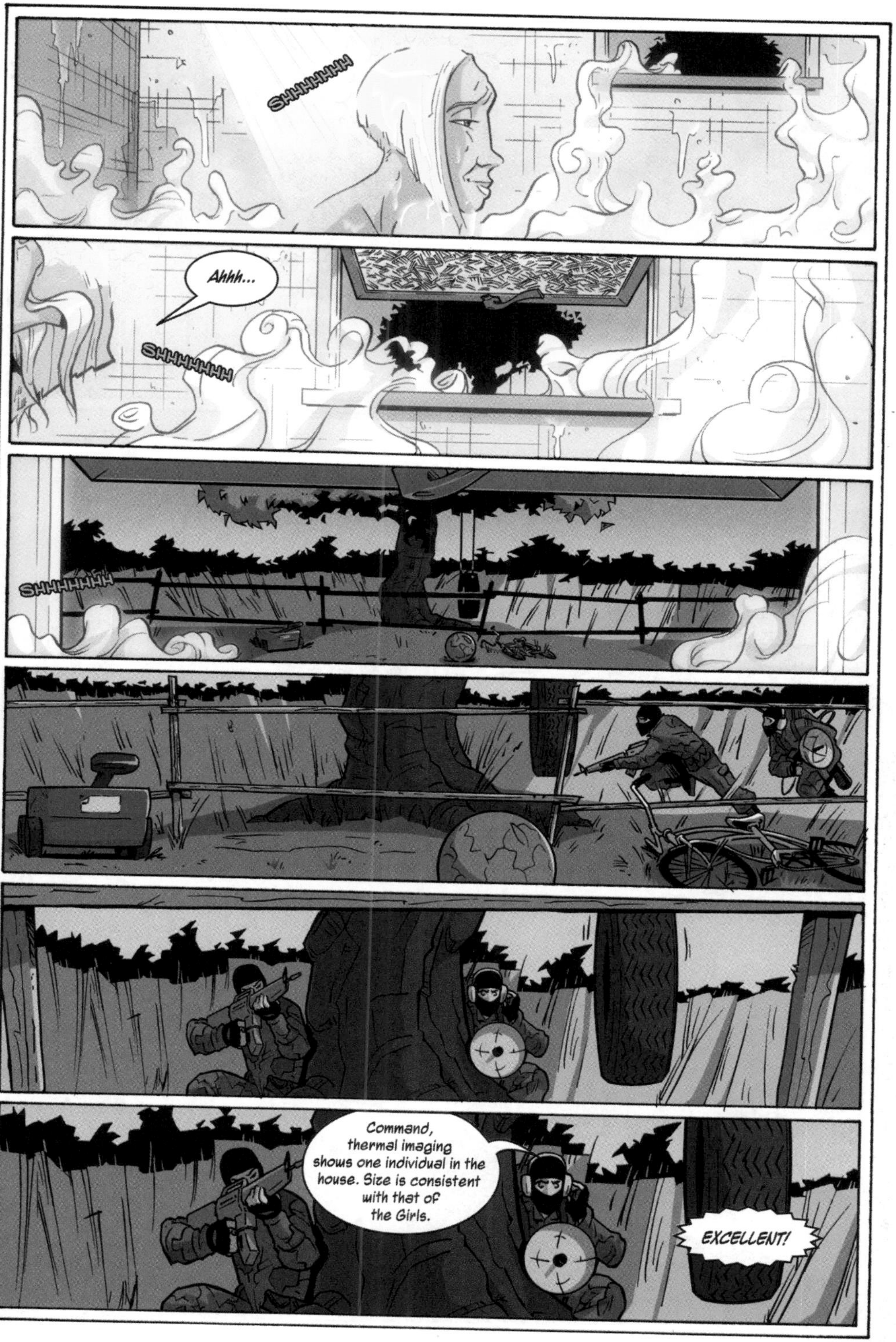
SHHHHHHH
Ahhh...
SHHHHHHH
SHHHHHHH
Command, thermal imaging shows one individual in the house. Size is consistent with that of the Girls.
EXCELLENT!

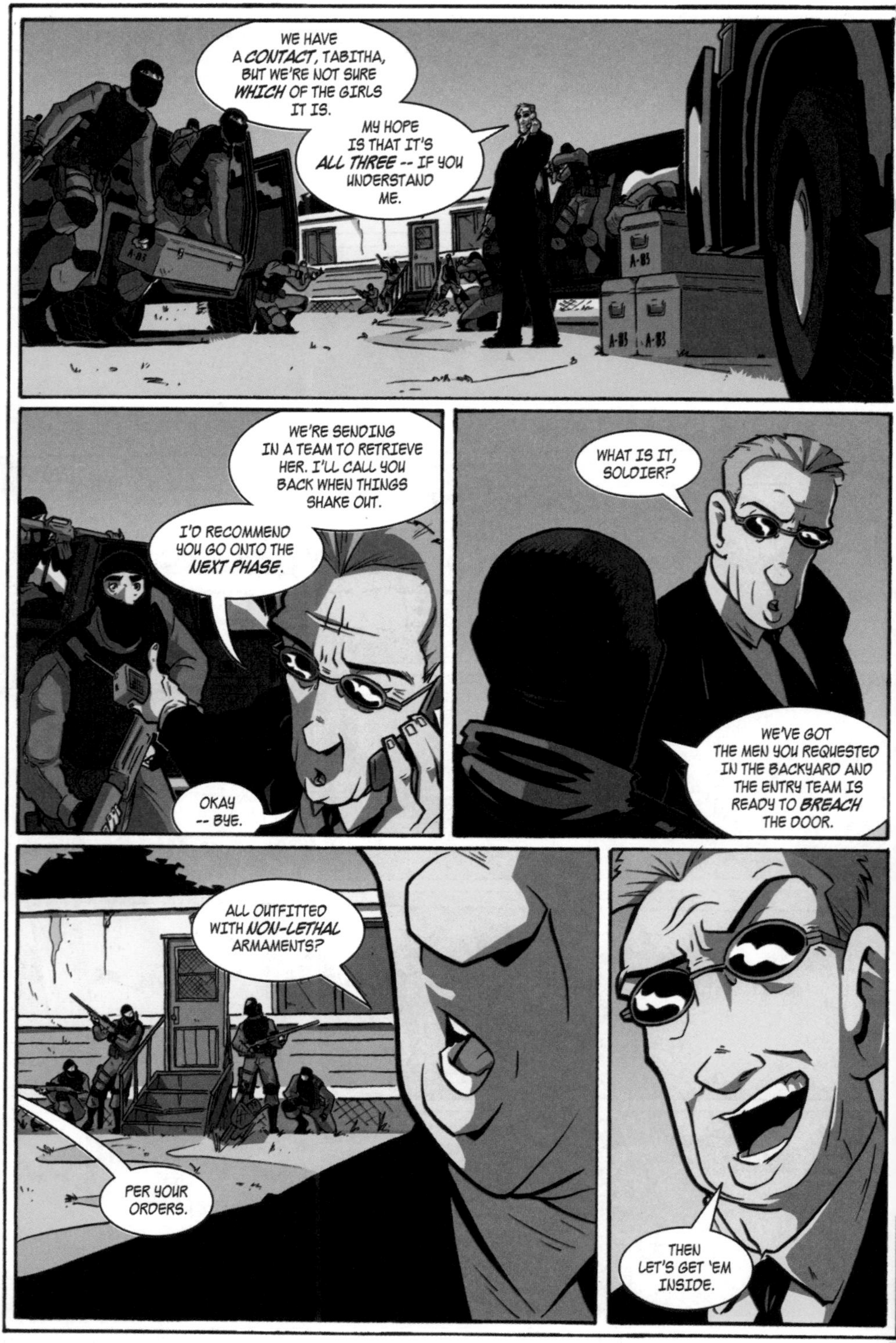
WE HAVE A *CONTACT*, TABITHA, BUT WE'RE NOT SURE *WHICH* OF THE GIRLS IT IS.
MY HOPE IS THAT IT'S *ALL THREE* -- IF YOU UNDERSTAND ME.
WE'RE SENDING IN A TEAM TO RETRIEVE HER. I'LL CALL YOU BACK WHEN THINGS SHAKE OUT.
I'D RECOMMEND YOU GO ONTO THE *NEXT PHASE*.
OKAY -- BYE.
WHAT IS IT, SOLDIER?
WE'VE GOT THE MEN YOU REQUESTED IN THE BACKYARD AND THE ENTRY TEAM IS READY TO *BREACH* THE DOOR.
ALL OUTFITTED WITH *NON-LETHAL* ARMAMENTS?
PER YOUR ORDERS.
THEN LET'S GET 'EM INSIDE.

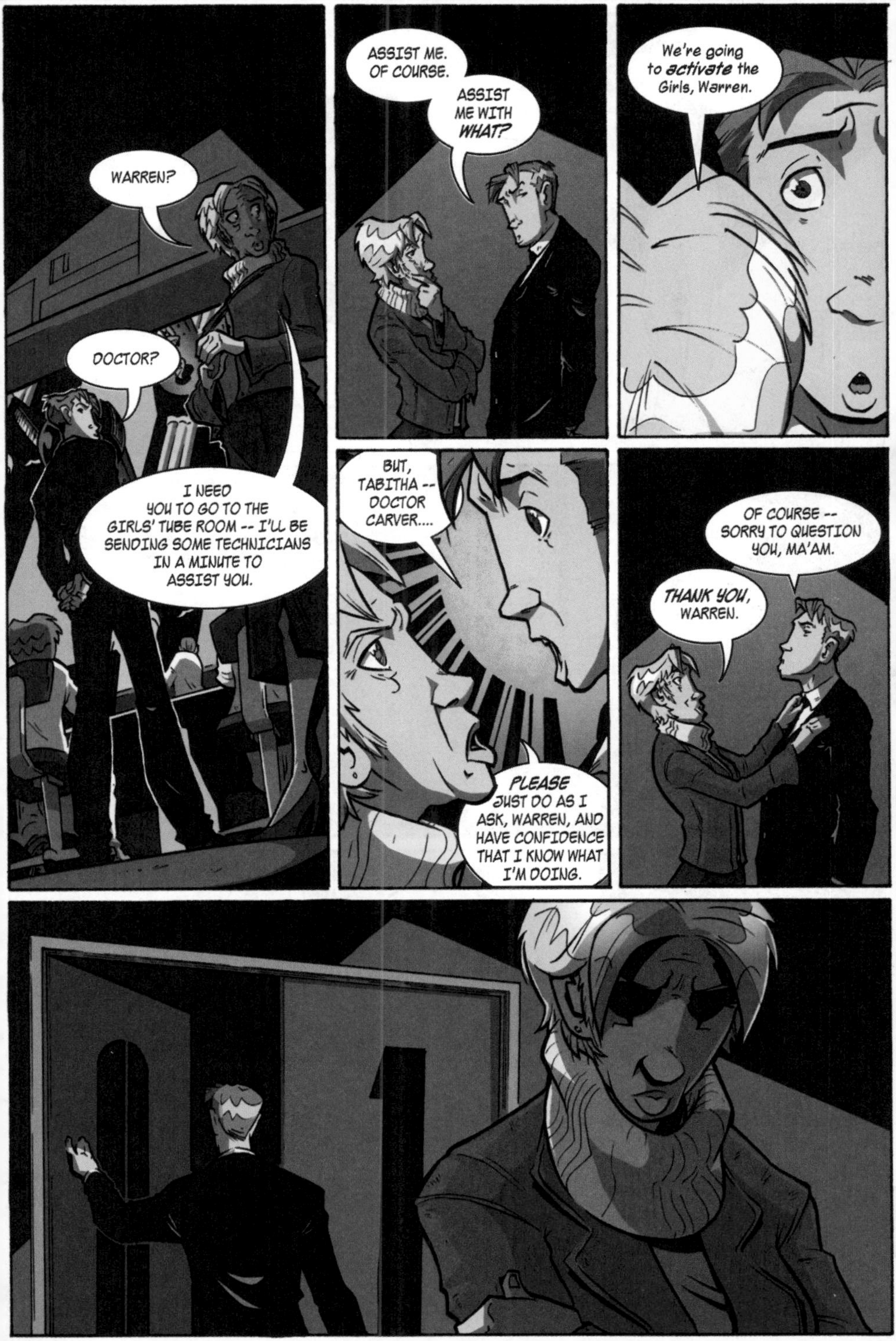
WARREN?
DOCTOR?
I NEED YOU TO GO TO THE GIRLS' TUBE ROOM -- I'LL BE SENDING SOME TECHNICIANS IN A MINUTE TO ASSIST YOU.
ASSIST ME. OF COURSE.
ASSIST ME WITH *WHAT?*
We're going to *activate* the Girls, Warren.
BUT, TABITHA -- DOCTOR CARVER....
PLEASE JUST DO AS I ASK, WARREN, AND HAVE CONFIDENCE THAT I KNOW WHAT I'M DOING.
OF COURSE -- SORRY TO QUESTION YOU, MA'AM.
THANK YOU, WARREN.

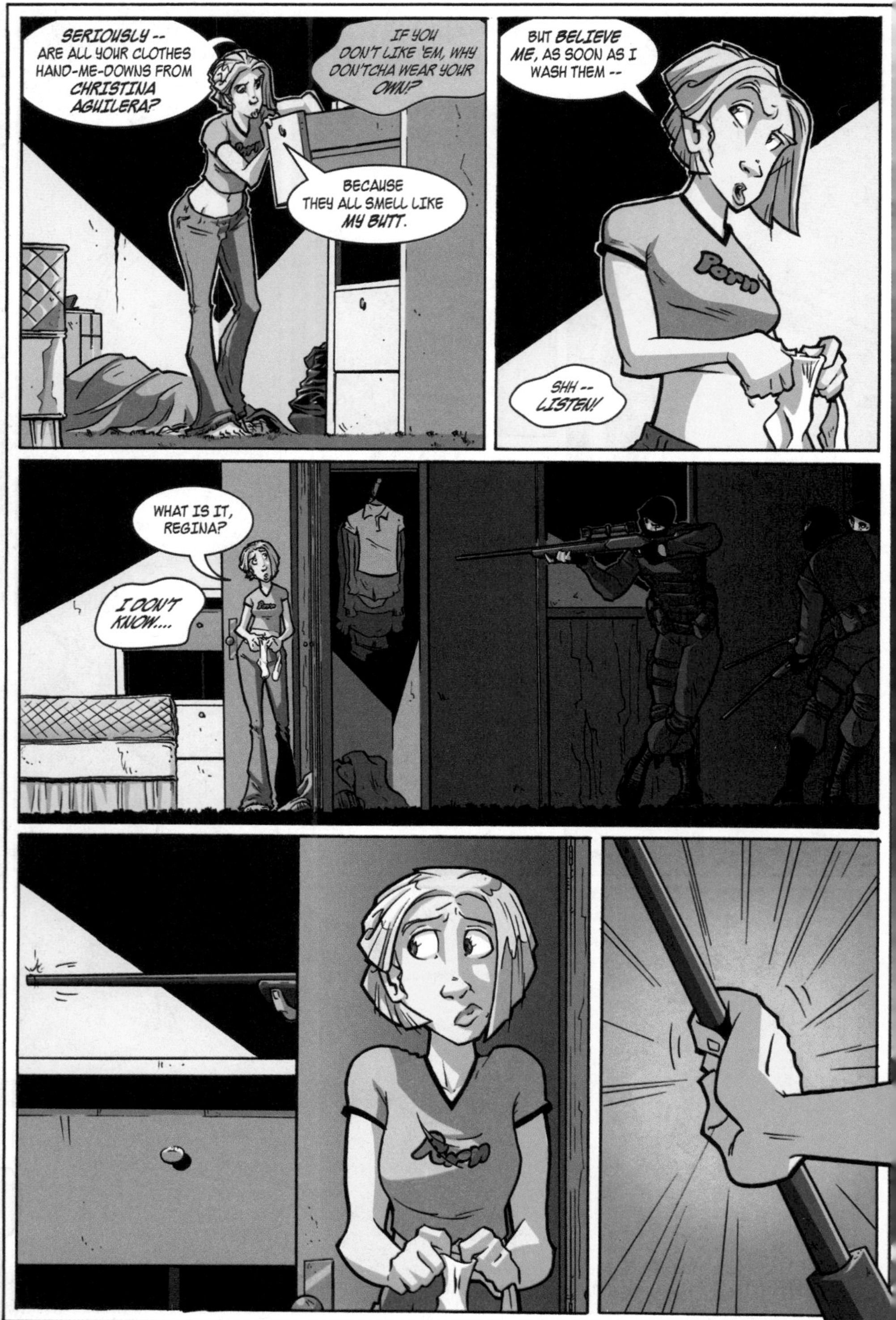
SERIOUSLY -- ARE ALL YOUR CLOTHES HAND-ME-DOWNS FROM CHRISTINA AGUILERA?
IF YOU DON'T LIKE 'EM, WHY DON'TCHA WEAR YOUR OWN?
BECAUSE THEY ALL SMELL LIKE MY BUTT.
BUT BELIEVE ME, AS SOON AS I WASH THEM --
SHH -- LISTEN!
WHAT IS IT, REGINA?
I DON'T KNOW....

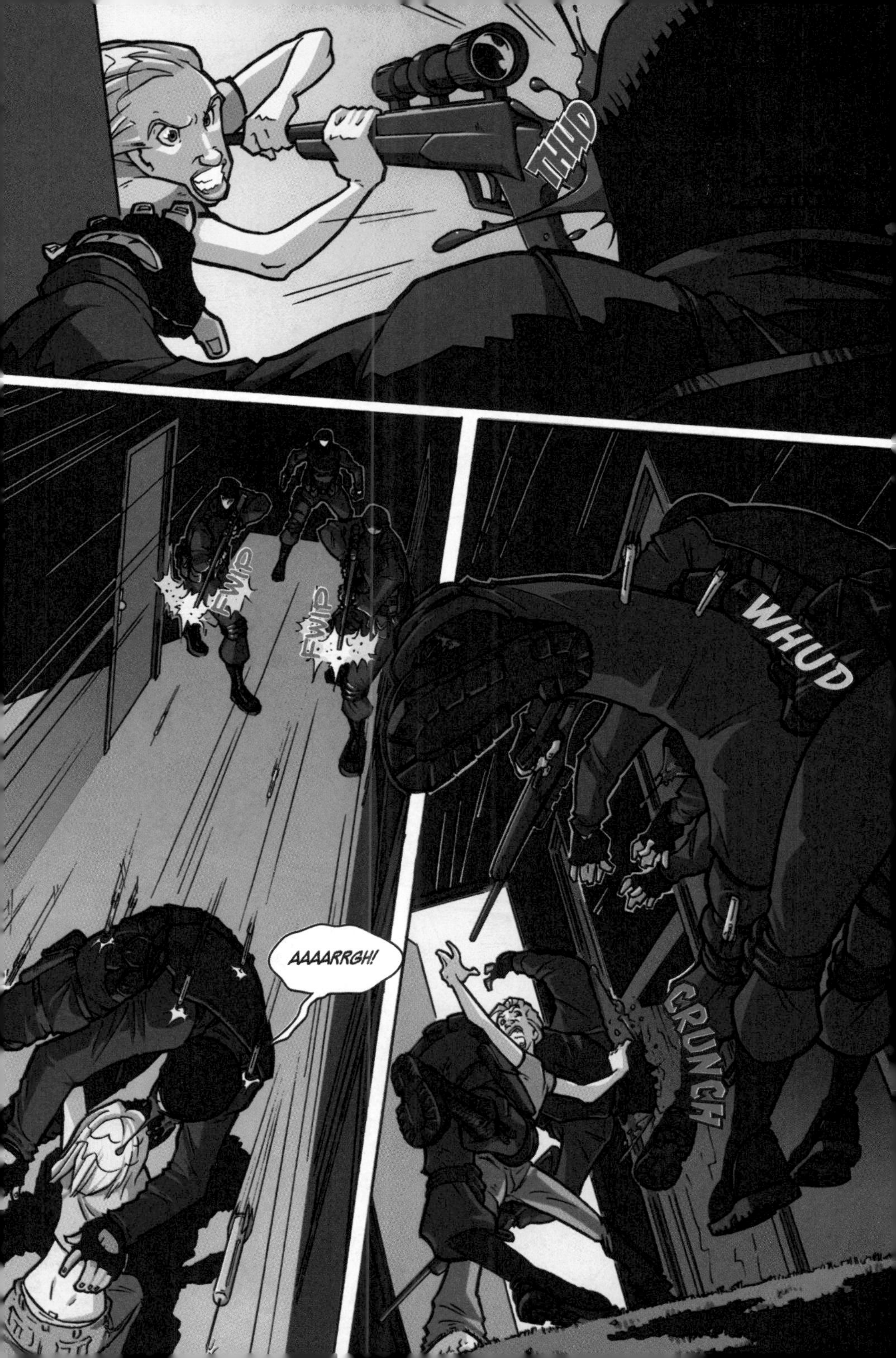
THUD
FWIP
FWIP
WHUD
AAAARRGH!
CRUNCH

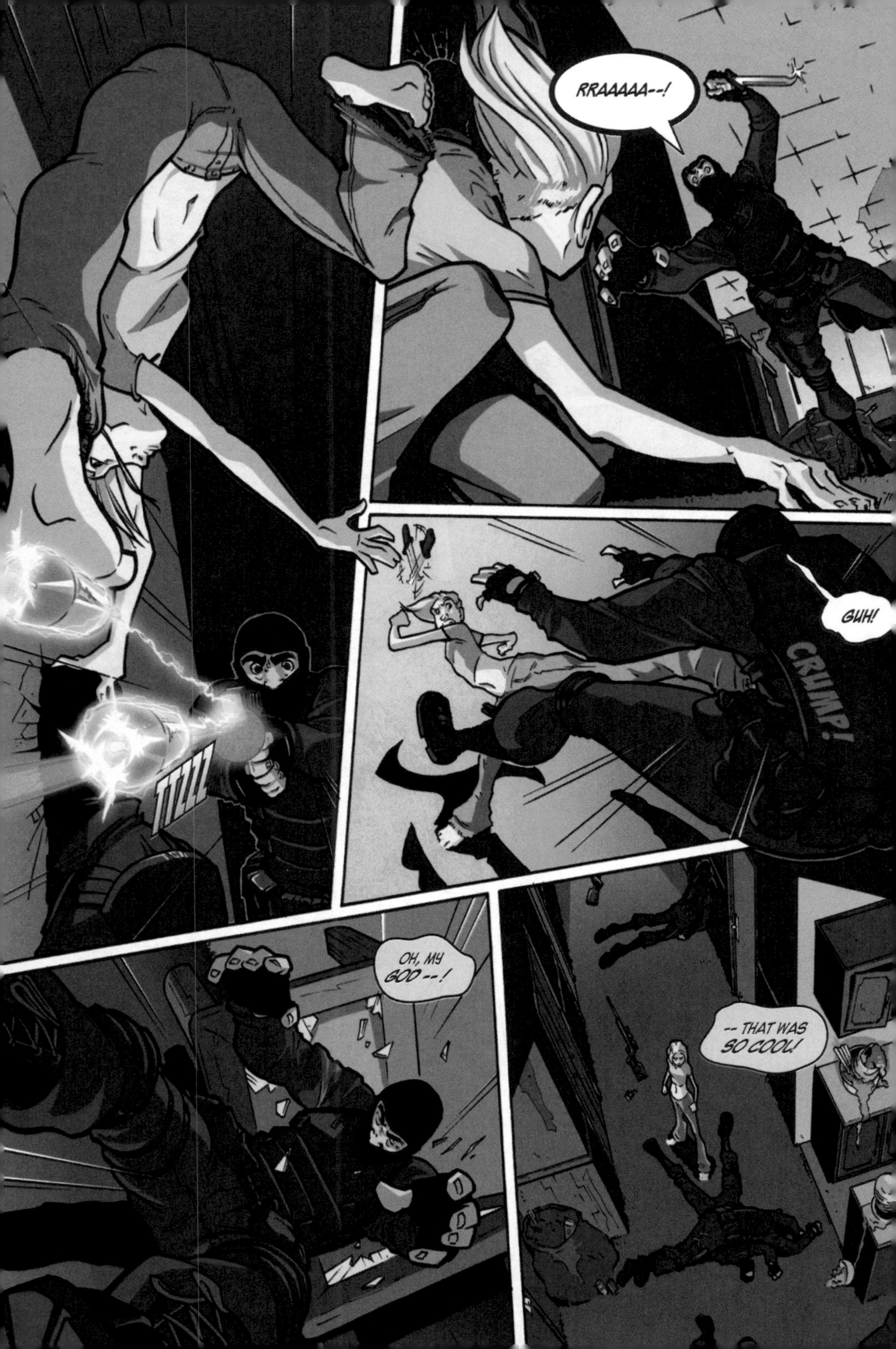
RRAAAAA--!
TTZZZ
GUH!
CRUMP!
OH, MY GOD--!
-- THAT WAS SO COOL!

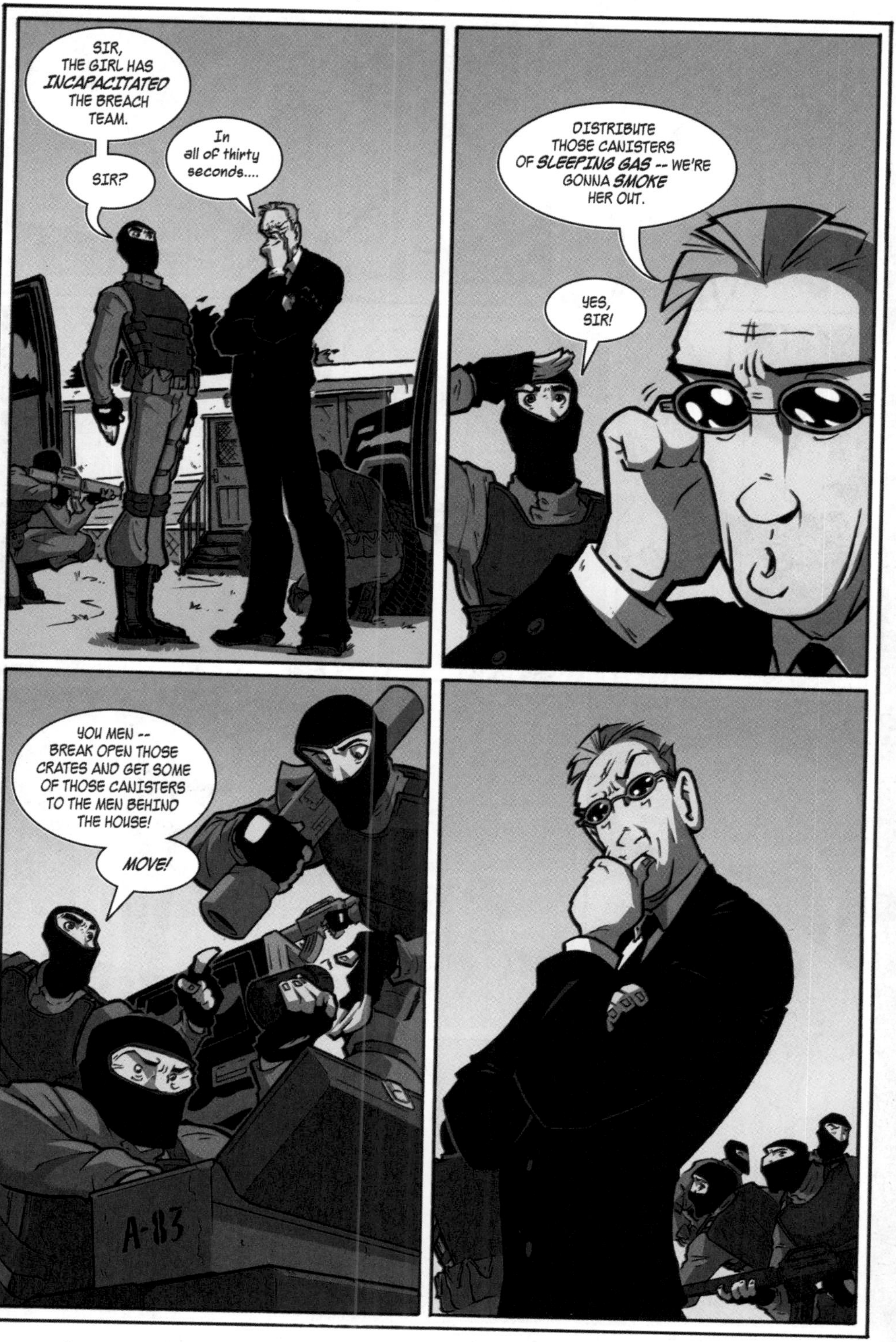
SIR, THE GIRL HAS *INCAPACITATED* THE BREACH TEAM.
SIR?
In all of thirty seconds....
DISTRIBUTE THOSE CANISTERS OF *SLEEPING GAS* -- WE'RE GONNA *SMOKE* HER OUT.
YES, SIR!
YOU MEN -- BREAK OPEN THOSE CRATES AND GET SOME OF THOSE CANISTERS TO THE MEN BEHIND THE HOUSE!
MOVE!
A-83

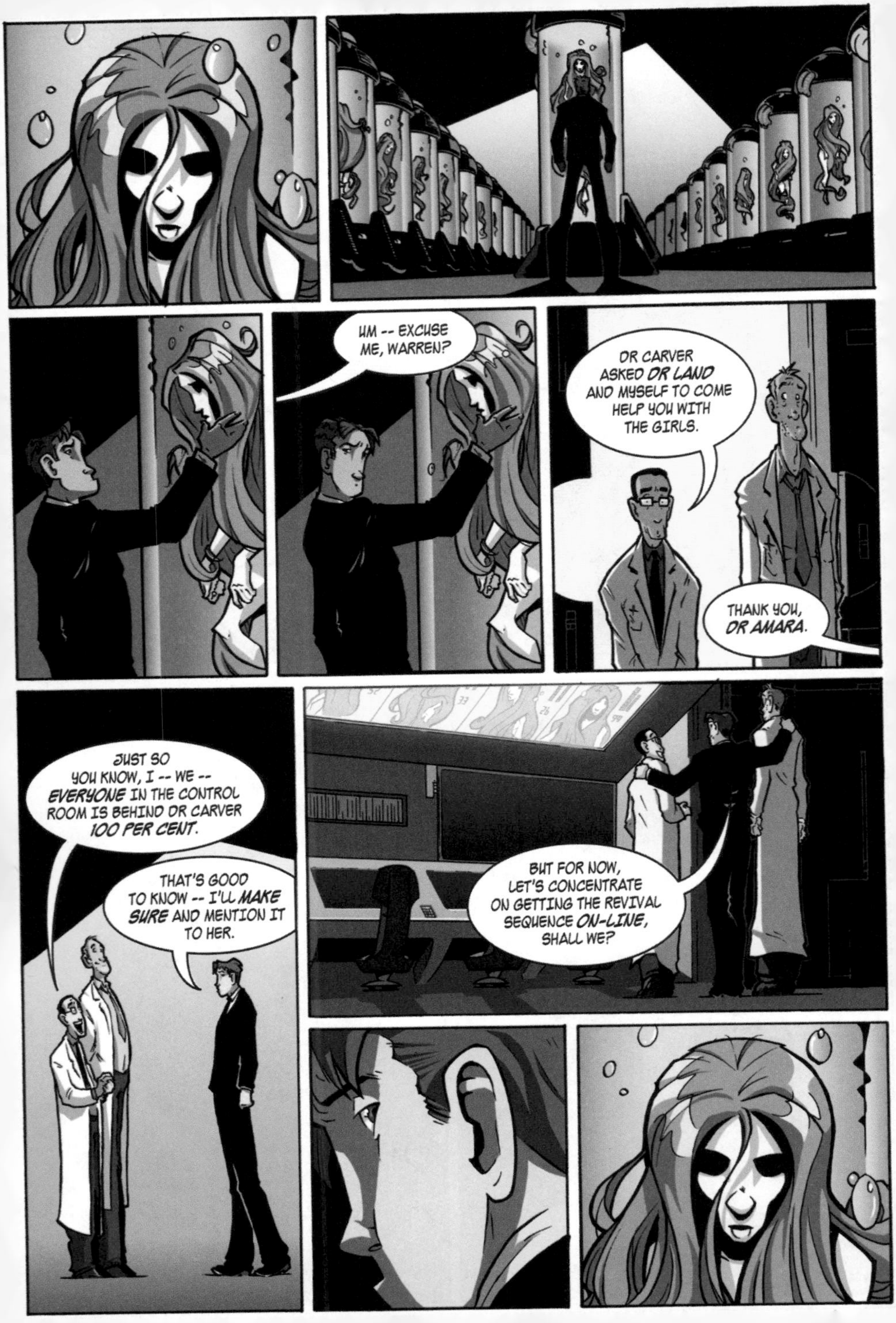
UM -- EXCUSE ME, WARREN?
DR CARVER ASKED DR LAND AND MYSELF TO COME HELP YOU WITH THE GIRLS.
THANK YOU, DR AMARA.
JUST SO YOU KNOW, I -- WE -- EVERYONE IN THE CONTROL ROOM IS BEHIND DR CARVER 100 PER CENT.
THAT'S GOOD TO KNOW -- I'LL MAKE SURE AND MENTION IT TO HER.
BUT FOR NOW, LET'S CONCENTRATE ON GETTING THE REVIVAL SEQUENCE ON-LINE, SHALL WE?

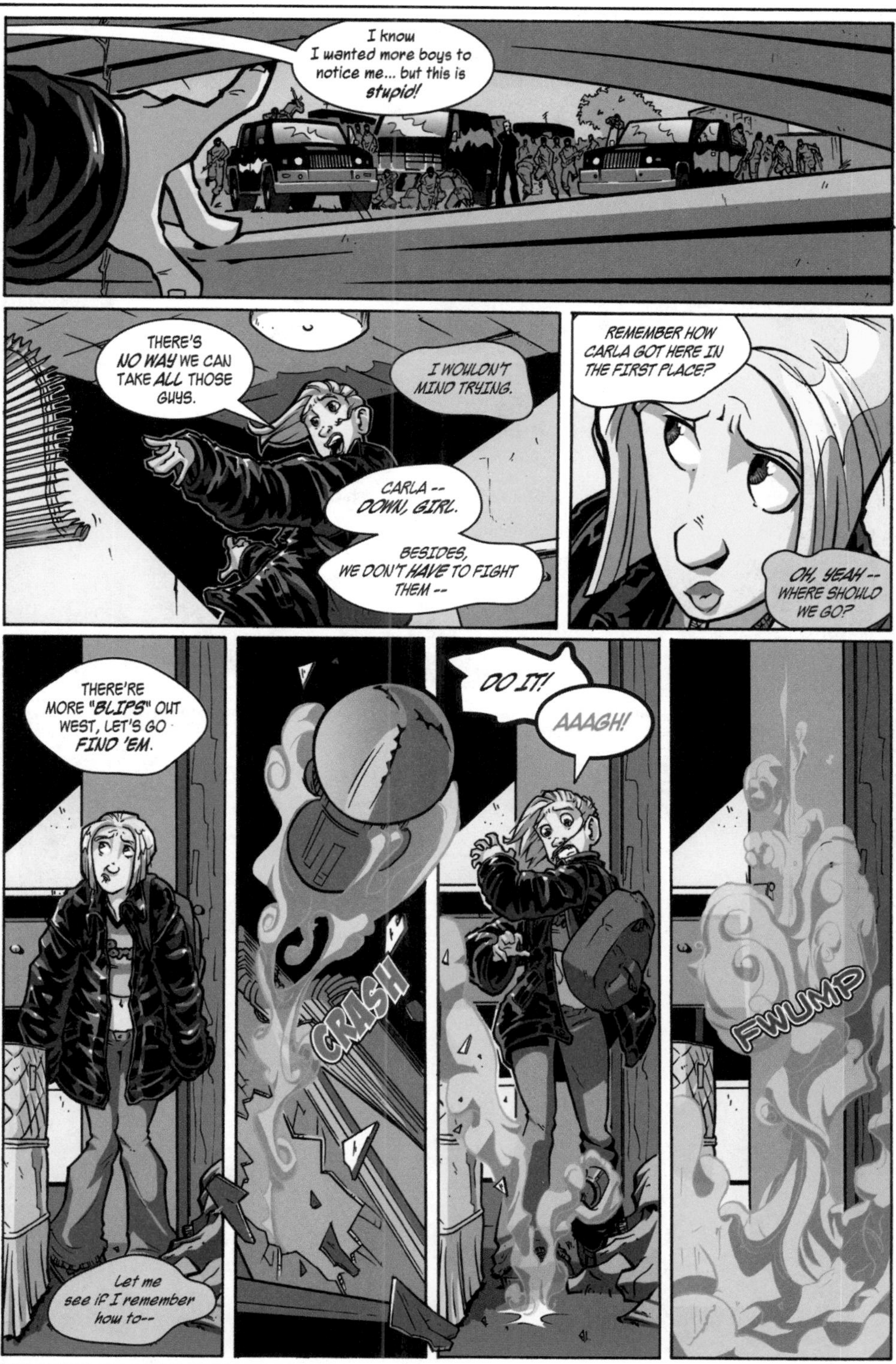
I know I wanted more boys to notice me... but this is stupid!
THERE'S NO WAY WE CAN TAKE ALL THOSE GUYS.
I WOULDN'T MIND TRYING.
CARLA -- DOWN, GIRL.
BESIDES, WE DON'T HAVE TO FIGHT THEM --
REMEMBER HOW CARLA GOT HERE IN THE FIRST PLACE?
OH, YEAH -- WHERE SHOULD WE GO?
THERE'RE MORE "BLIPS" OUT WEST, LET'S GO FIND 'EM.
Let me see if I remember how to--
CRASH
DO IT!
AAAGH!
FWUMP

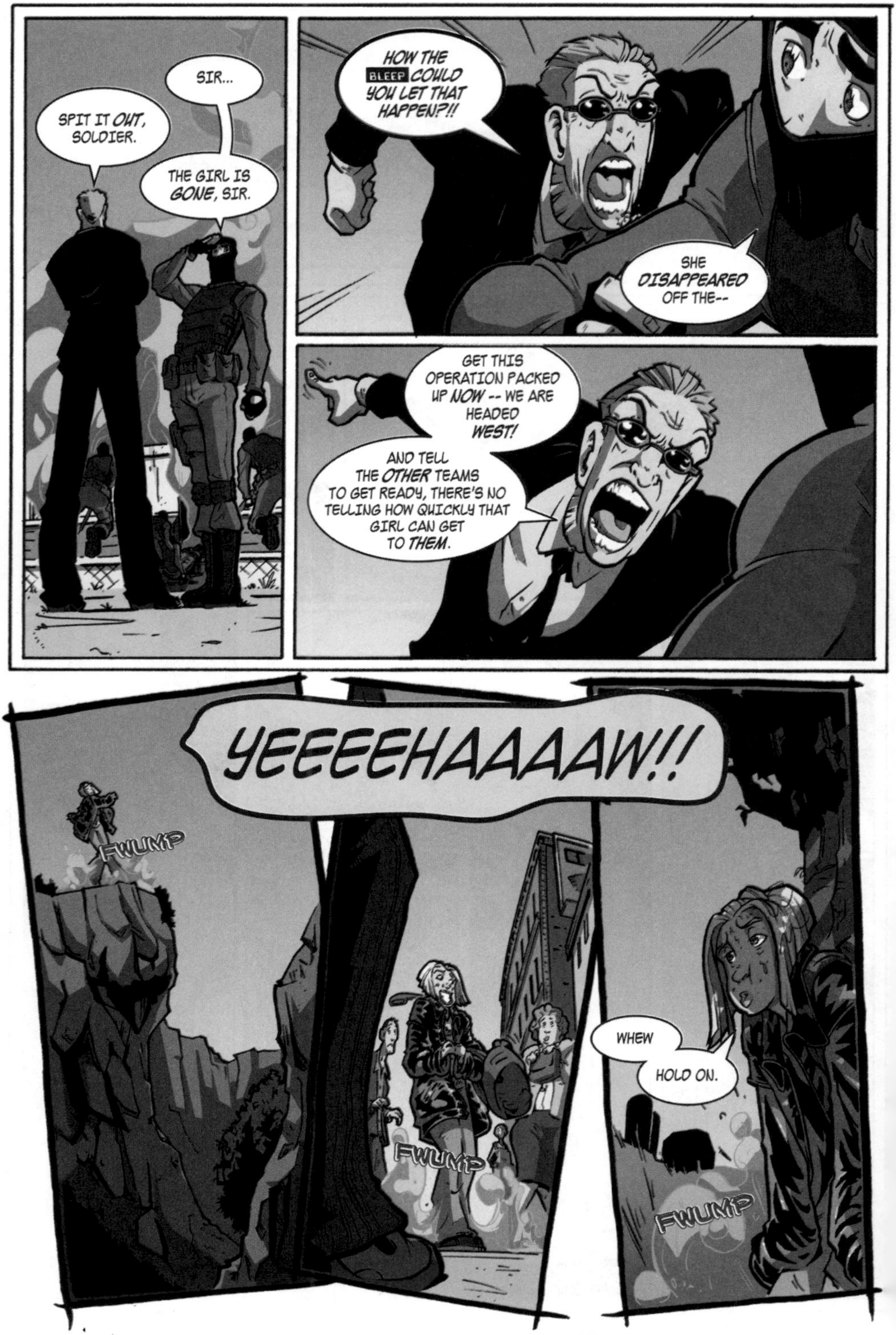
SIR...
SPIT IT OUT, SOLDIER.
THE GIRL IS GONE, SIR.
HOW THE BLEEP COULD YOU LET THAT HAPPEN?!!
SHE DISAPPEARED OFF THE--
GET THIS OPERATION PACKED UP NOW -- WE ARE HEADED WEST!
AND TELL THE OTHER TEAMS TO GET READY, THERE'S NO TELLING HOW QUICKLY THAT GIRL CAN GET TO THEM.
YEEEEHAAAAAW!!
FWUMP
FWUMP
WHEW
HOLD ON.
FWUMP

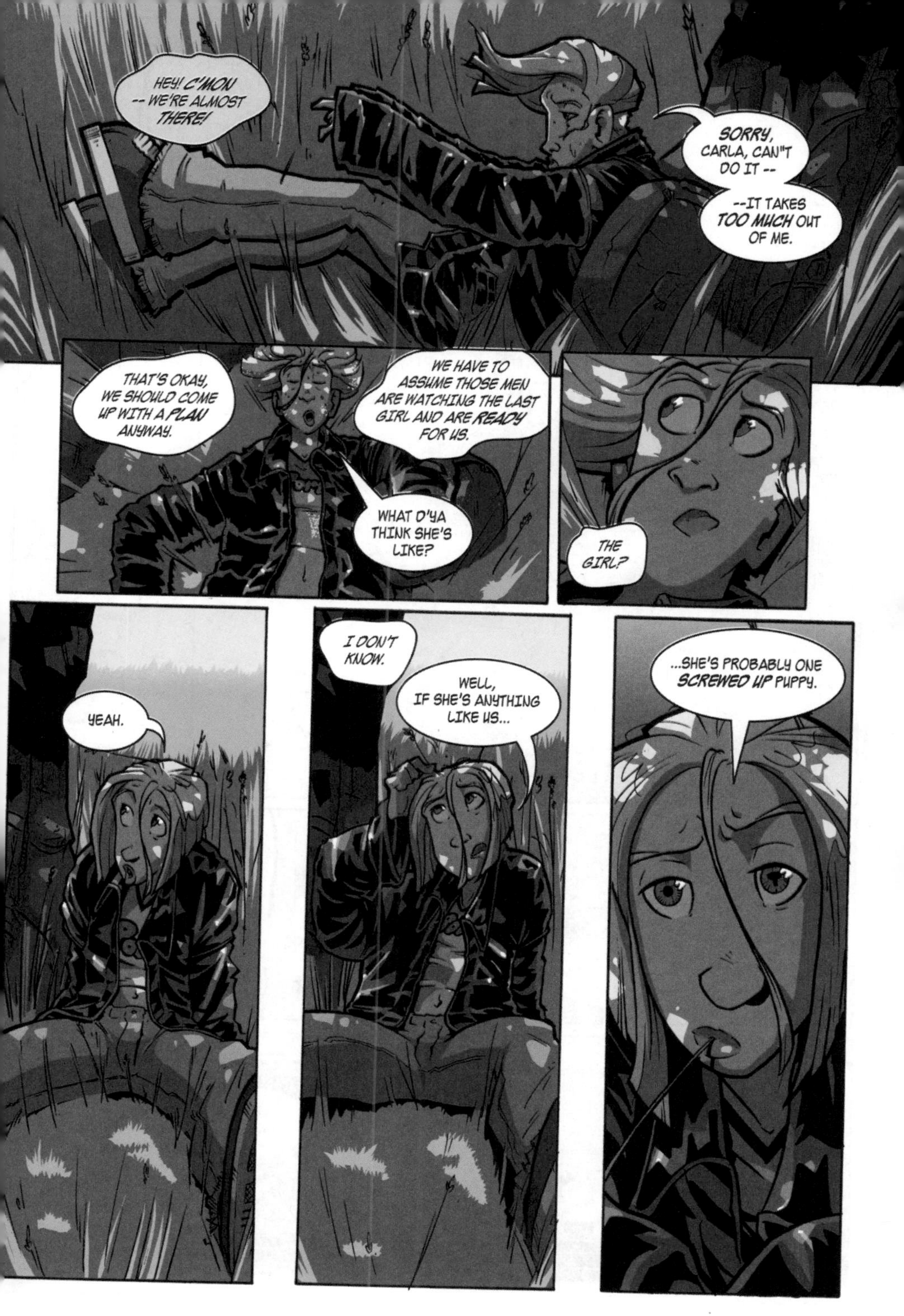
HEY! C'MON -- WE'RE ALMOST THERE!
SORRY, CARLA, CAN"T DO IT --
--IT TAKES TOO MUCH OUT OF ME.
THAT'S OKAY, WE SHOULD COME UP WITH A PLAN ANYWAY.
WE HAVE TO ASSUME THOSE MEN ARE WATCHING THE LAST GIRL AND ARE READY FOR US.
WHAT D'YA THINK SHE'S LIKE?
THE GIRL?
YEAH.
I DON'T KNOW.
WELL, IF SHE'S ANYTHING LIKE US...
...SHE'S PROBABLY ONE SCREWED UP PUPPY.

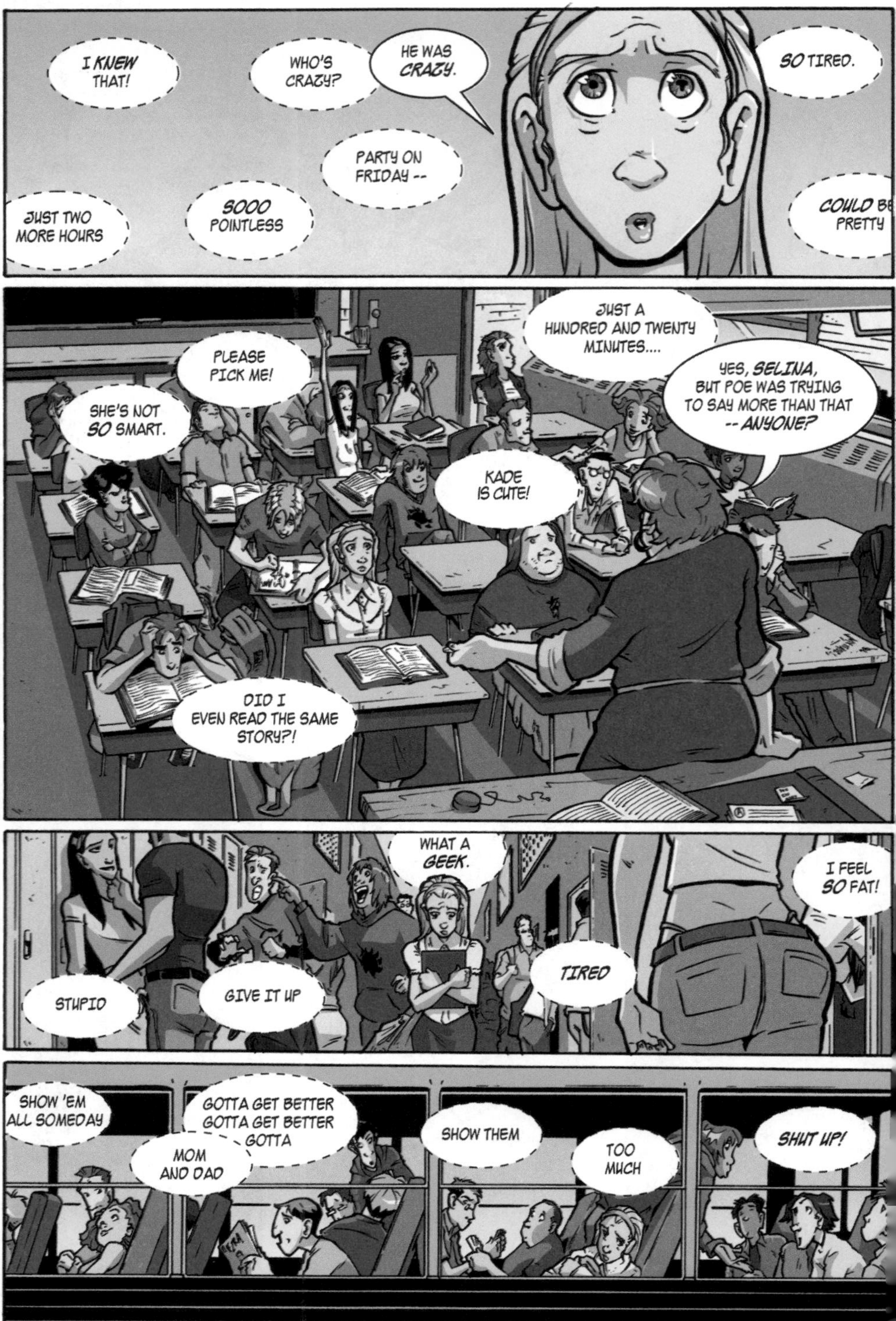
I KNEW THAT!
WHO'S CRAZY?
HE WAS CRAZY.
SO TIRED.
PARTY ON FRIDAY --
JUST TWO MORE HOURS
SOOO POINTLESS
COULD BE PRETTY
JUST A HUNDRED AND TWENTY MINUTES....
PLEASE PICK ME!
SHE'S NOT SO SMART.
YES, SELINA, BUT POE WAS TRYING TO SAY MORE THAN THAT -- ANYONE?
KADE IS CUTE!
DID I EVEN READ THE SAME STORY?!
WHAT A GEEK.
I FEEL SO FAT!
STUPID
GIVE IT UP
TIRED
SHOW 'EM ALL SOMEDAY
GOTTA GET BETTER GOTTA GET BETTER GOTTA
MOM AND DAD
SHOW THEM
TOO MUCH
SHUT UP!

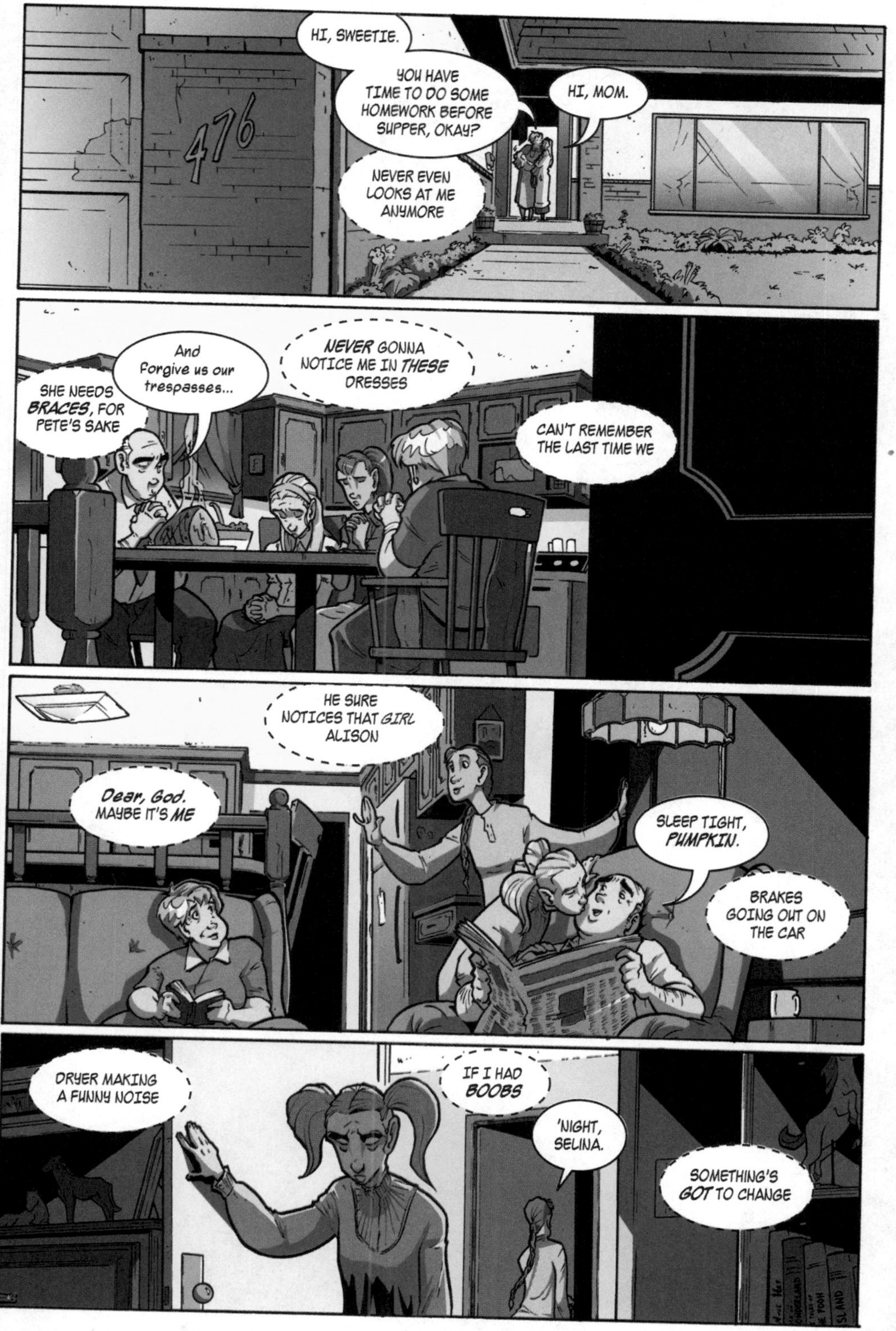
HI, SWEETIE.
YOU HAVE TIME TO DO SOME HOMEWORK BEFORE SUPPER, OKAY?
HI, MOM.
NEVER EVEN LOOKS AT ME ANYMORE
476
SHE NEEDS BRACES, FOR PETE'S SAKE
And forgive us our trespasses...
NEVER GONNA NOTICE ME IN THESE DRESSES
CAN'T REMEMBER THE LAST TIME WE
HE SURE NOTICES THAT GIRL ALISON
Dear, God. MAYBE IT'S ME
SLEEP TIGHT, PUMPKIN.
BRAKES GOING OUT ON THE CAR
DRYER MAKING A FUNNY NOISE
IF I HAD BOOBS
'NIGHT, SELINA.
SOMETHING'S GOT TO CHANGE

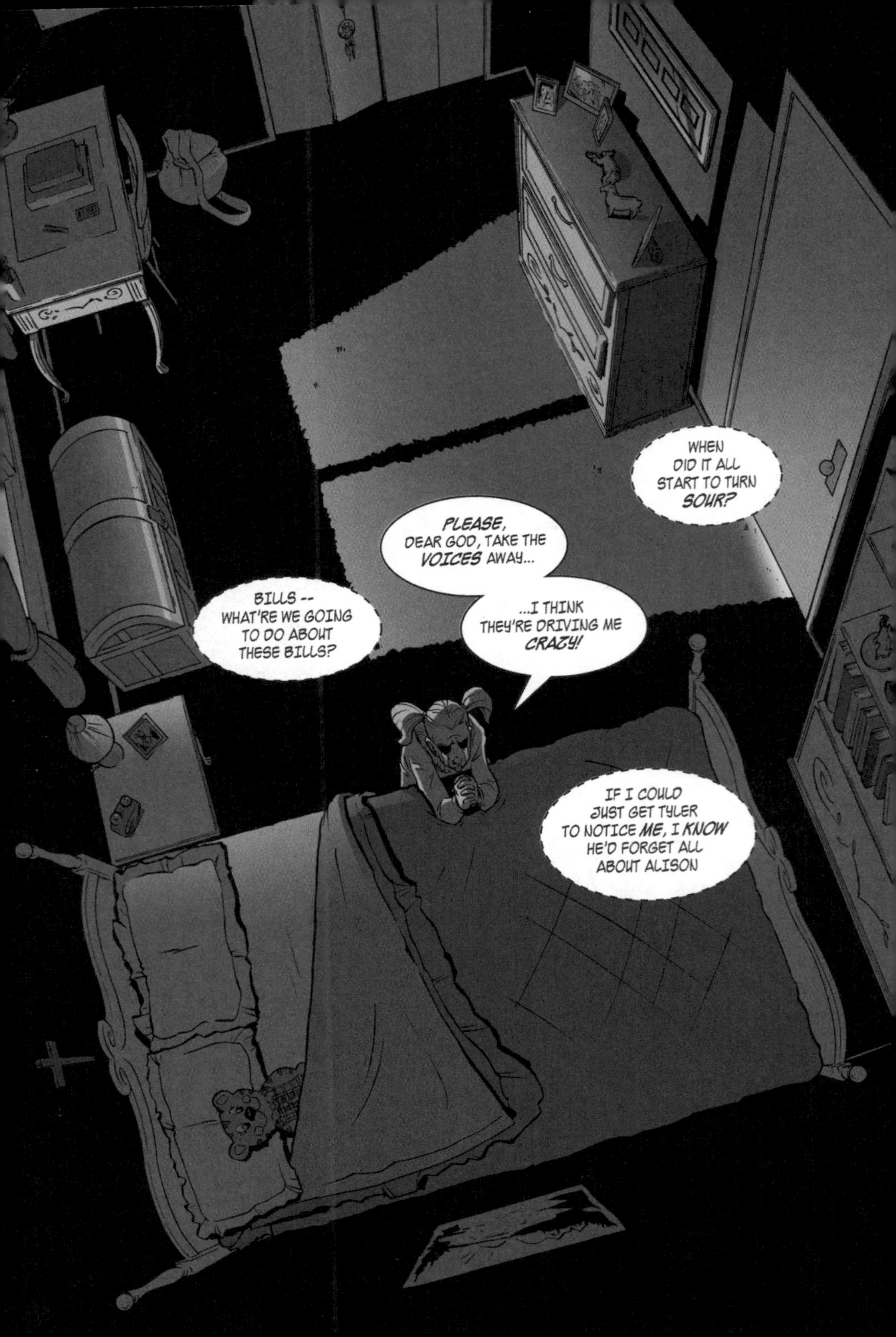
WHEN DID IT ALL START TO TURN SOUR?
PLEASE, DEAR GOD, TAKE THE VOICES AWAY...
BILLS -- WHAT'RE WE GOING TO DO ABOUT THESE BILLS?
...I THINK THEY'RE DRIVING ME CRAZY!
IF I COULD JUST GET TYLER TO NOTICE ME, I KNOW HE'D FORGET ALL ABOUT ALISON

CHAPTER FIVE

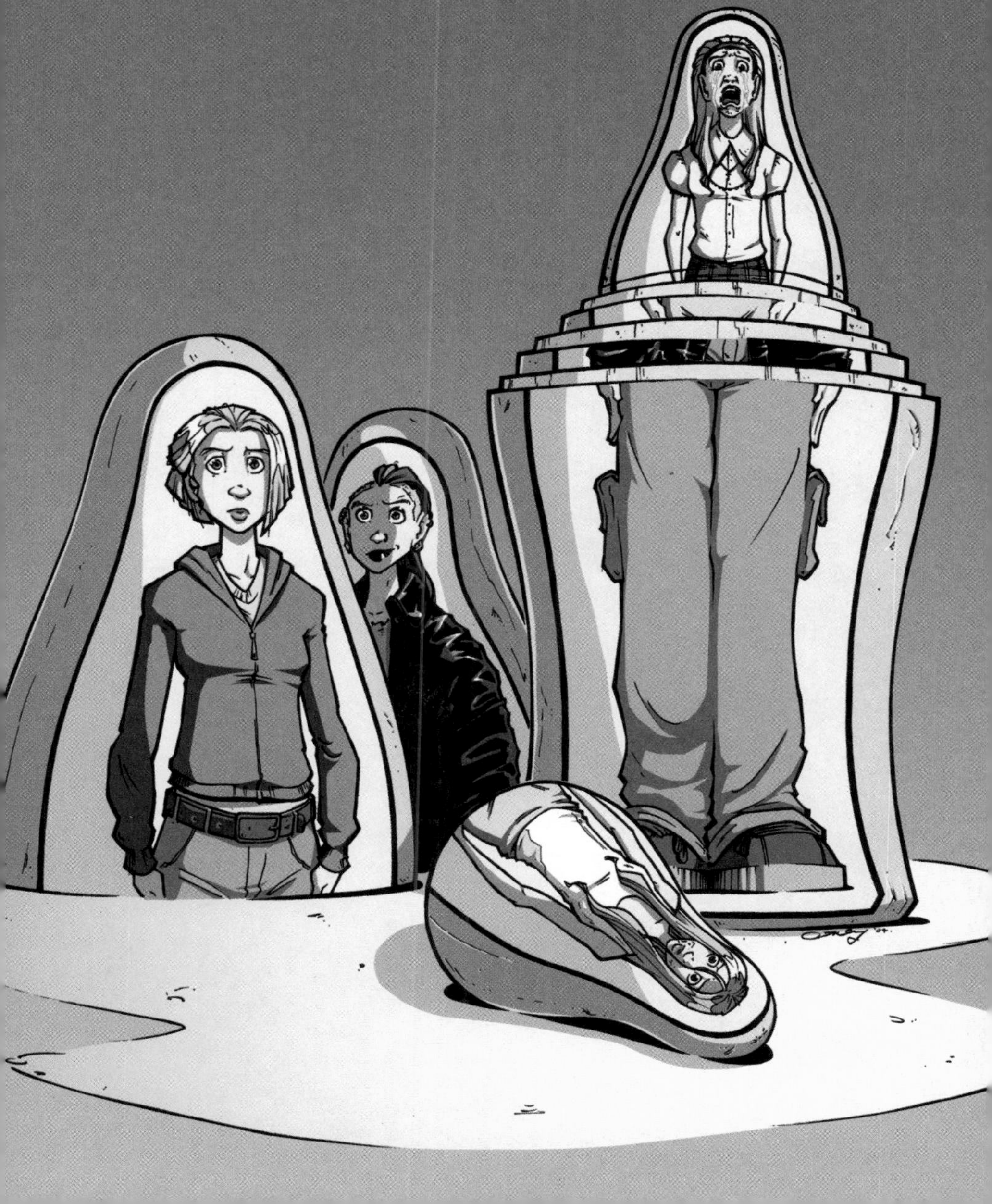

"we decided that plans are for wussies."

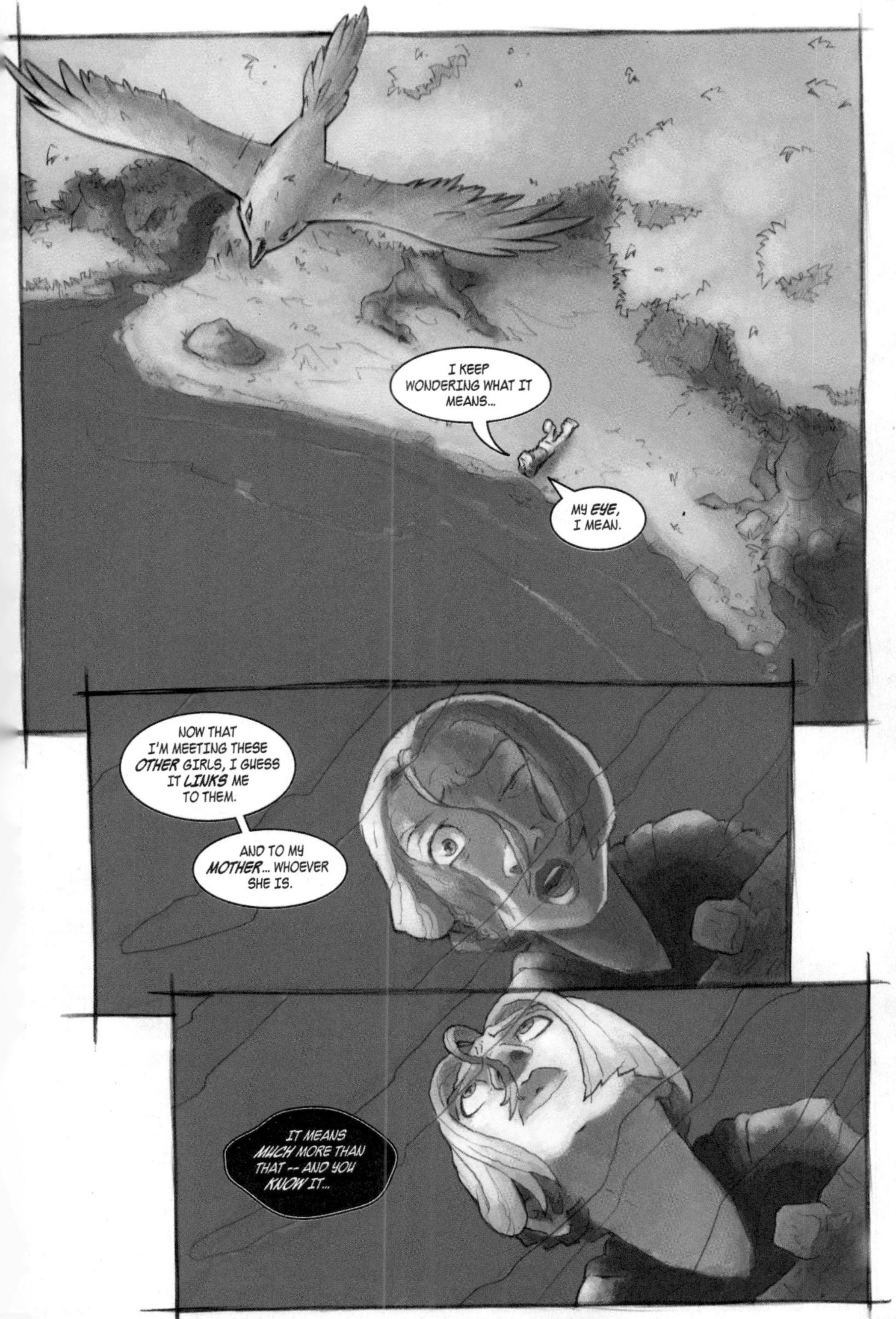
I KEEP WONDERING WHAT IT MEANS...
MY EYE, I MEAN.
NOW THAT I'M MEETING THESE OTHER GIRLS, I GUESS IT LINKS ME TO THEM.
AND TO MY MOTHER... WHOEVER SHE IS.
IT MEANS MUCH MORE THAN THAT -- AND YOU KNOW IT...

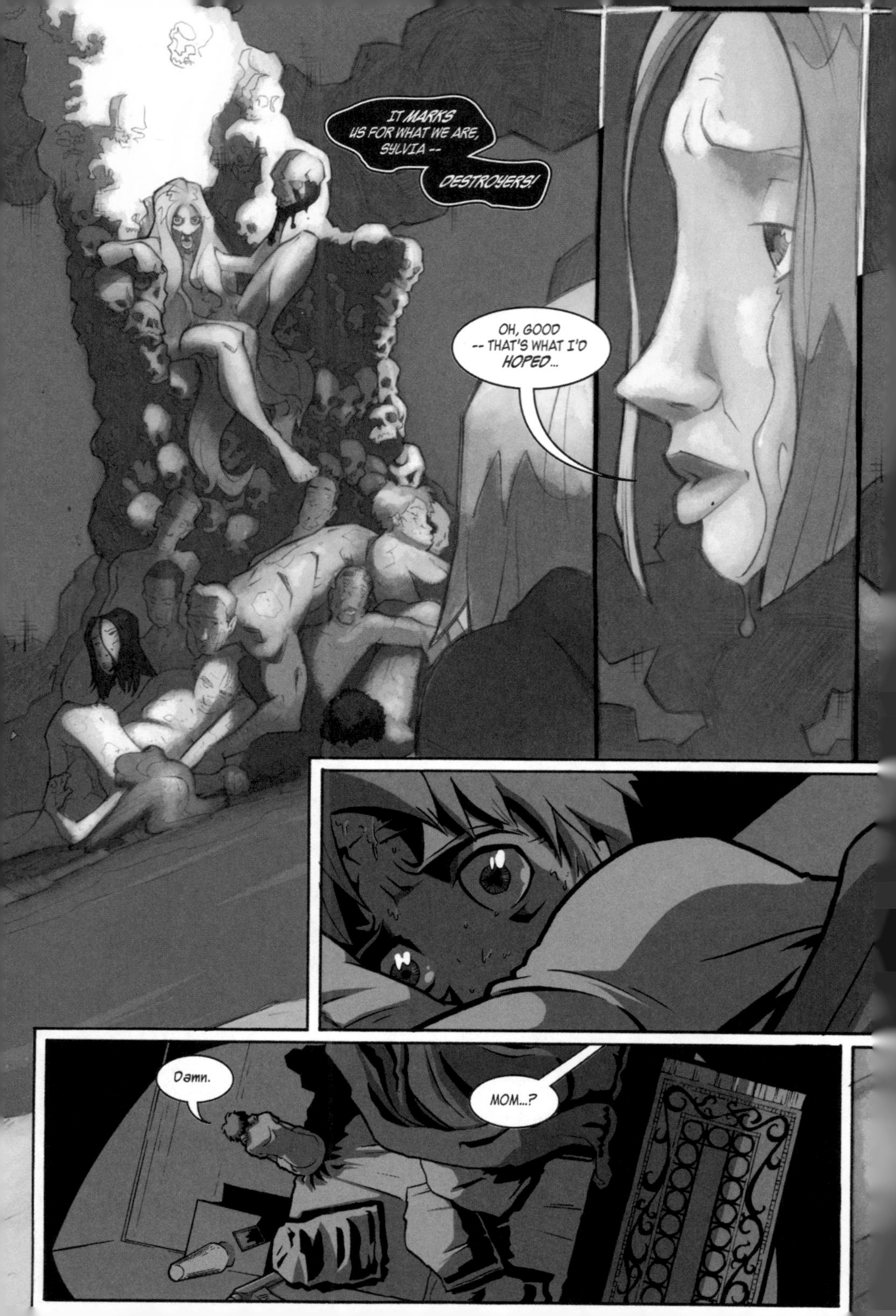
IT MARKS US FOR WHAT WE ARE, SYLVIA --
DESTROYERS!
OH, GOOD -- THAT'S WHAT I'D HOPED...
Damn.
MOM...?

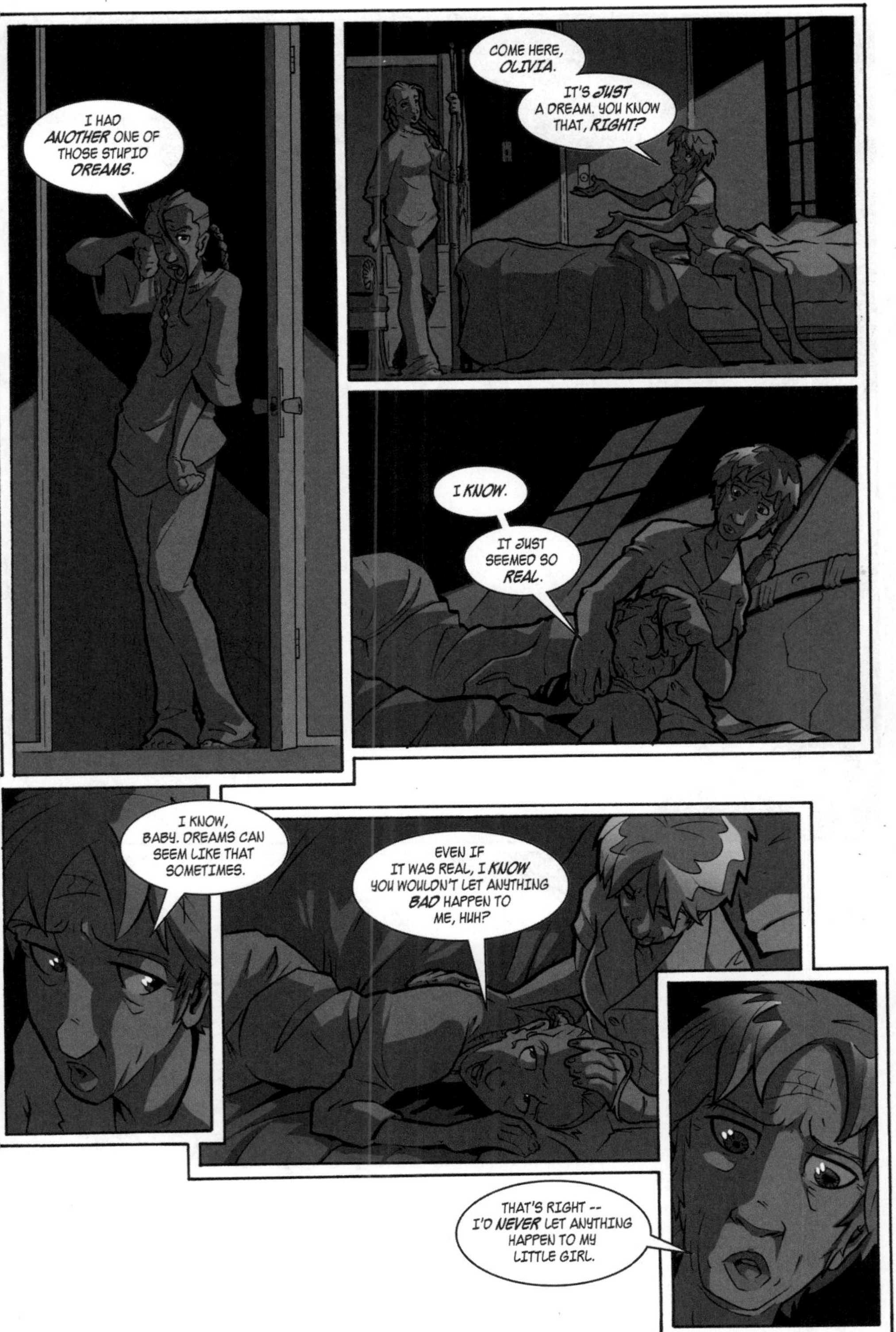
I HAD ANOTHER ONE OF THOSE STUPID DREAMS.
COME HERE, OLIVIA.
IT'S JUST A DREAM. YOU KNOW THAT, RIGHT?
I KNOW.
IT JUST SEEMED SO REAL.
I KNOW, BABY. DREAMS CAN SEEM LIKE THAT SOMETIMES.
EVEN IF IT WAS REAL, I KNOW YOU WOULDN'T LET ANYTHING BAD HAPPEN TO ME, HUH?
THAT'S RIGHT -- I'D NEVER LET ANYTHING HAPPEN TO MY LITTLE GIRL.

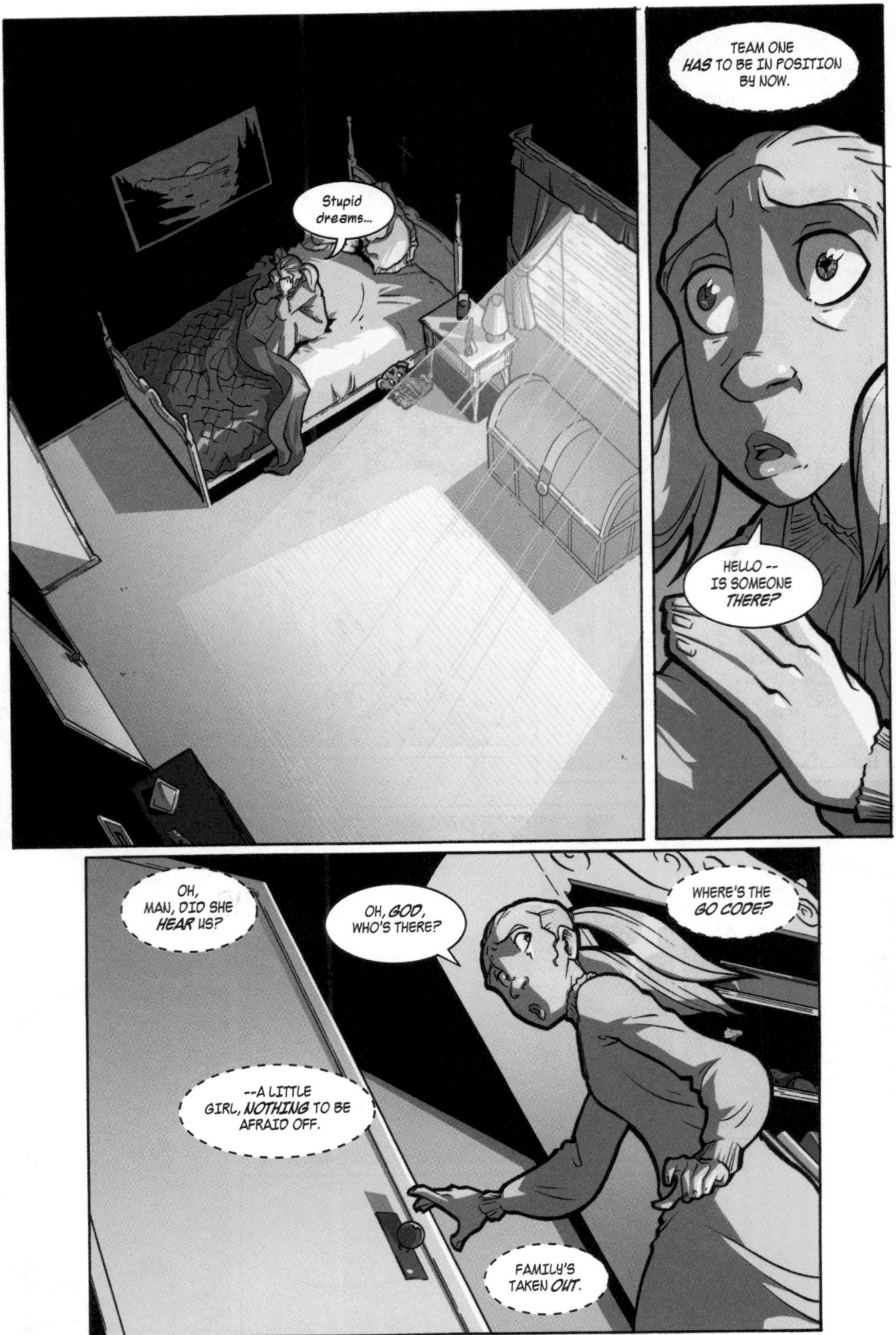
Stupid dreams...
TEAM ONE HAS TO BE IN POSITION BY NOW.
HELLO -- IS SOMEONE THERE?
OH, MAN, DID SHE HEAR US?
OH, GOD, WHO'S THERE?
WHERE'S THE GO CODE?
--A LITTLE GIRL, NOTHING TO BE AFRAID OFF.
FAMILY'S TAKEN OUT.

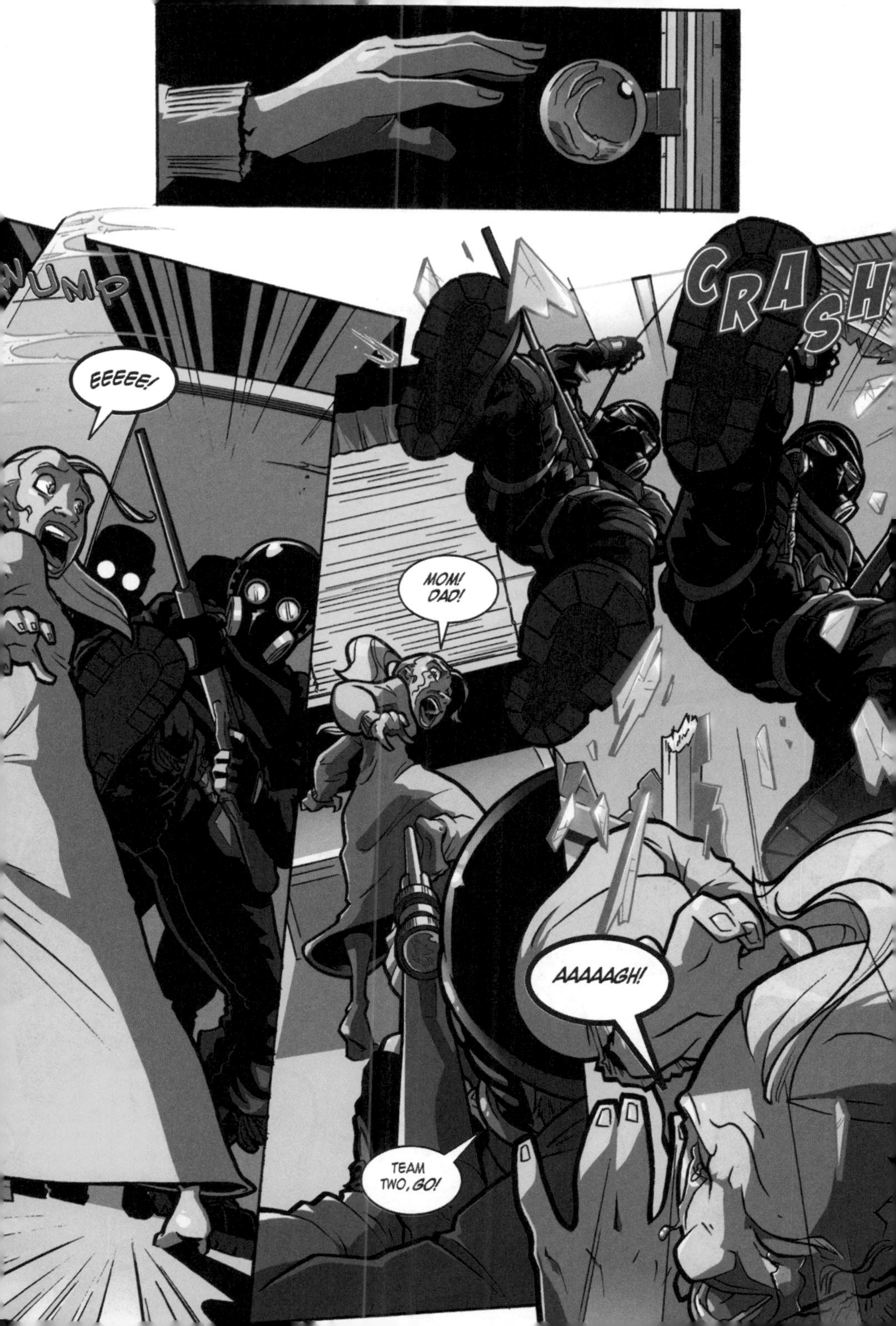
WUMP
EEEEEE!
CRASH
MOM! DAD!
AAAAAGH!
TEAM TWO, GO!

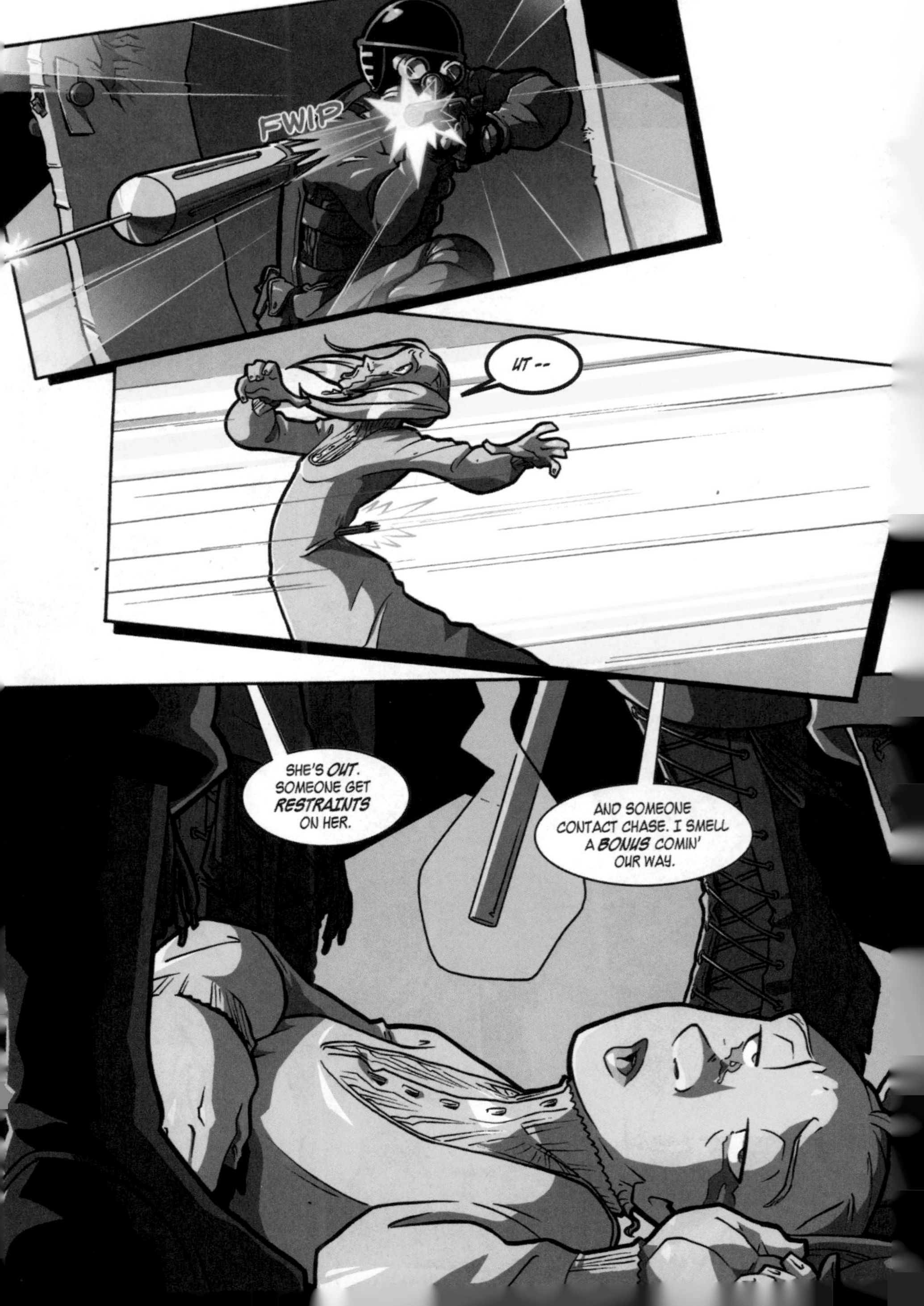
FWIP
UT --
SHE'S OUT. SOMEONE GET RESTRAINTS ON HER.
AND SOMEONE CONTACT CHASE. I SMELL A BONUS COMIN' OUR WAY.

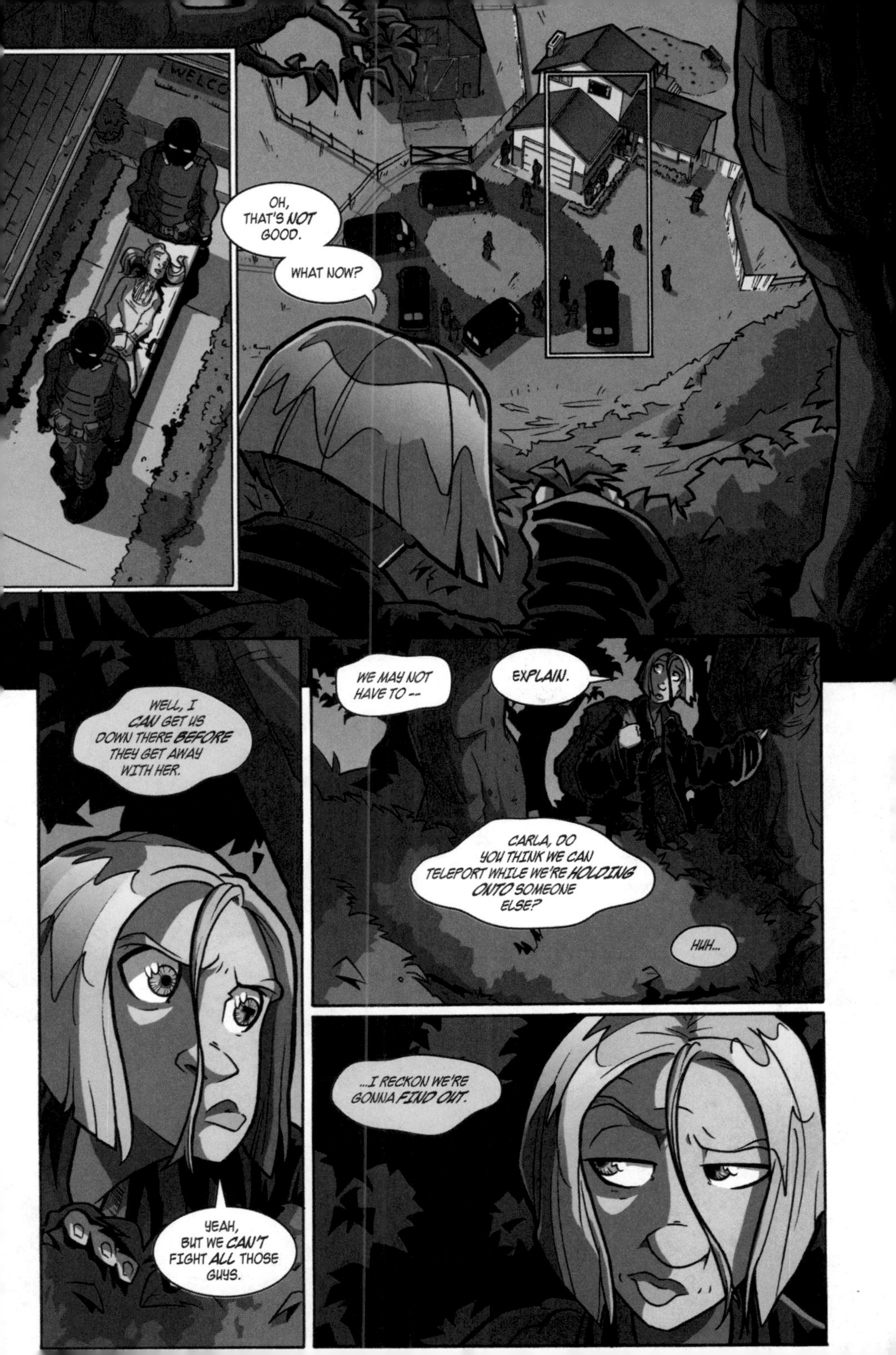
WELCO
OH, THAT'S NOT GOOD.
WHAT NOW?
WELL, I CAN GET US DOWN THERE BEFORE THEY GET AWAY WITH HER.
YEAH, BUT WE CAN'T FIGHT ALL THOSE GUYS.
WE MAY NOT HAVE TO --
EXPLAIN.
CARLA, DO YOU THINK WE CAN TELEPORT WHILE WE'RE HOLDING ONTO SOMEONE ELSE?
HUH...
...I RECKON WE'RE GONNA FIND OUT.

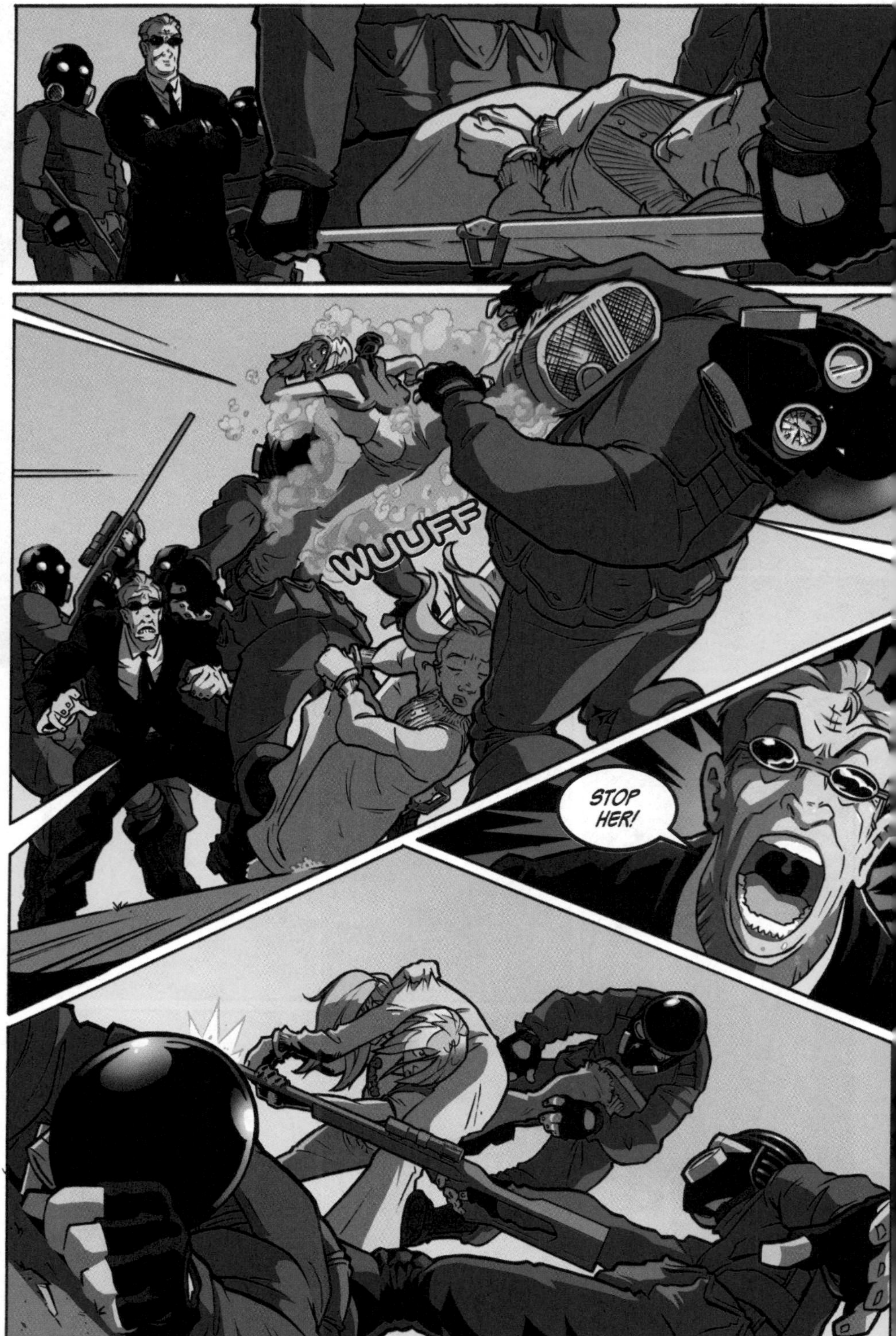
WUUFF
STOP
HER!

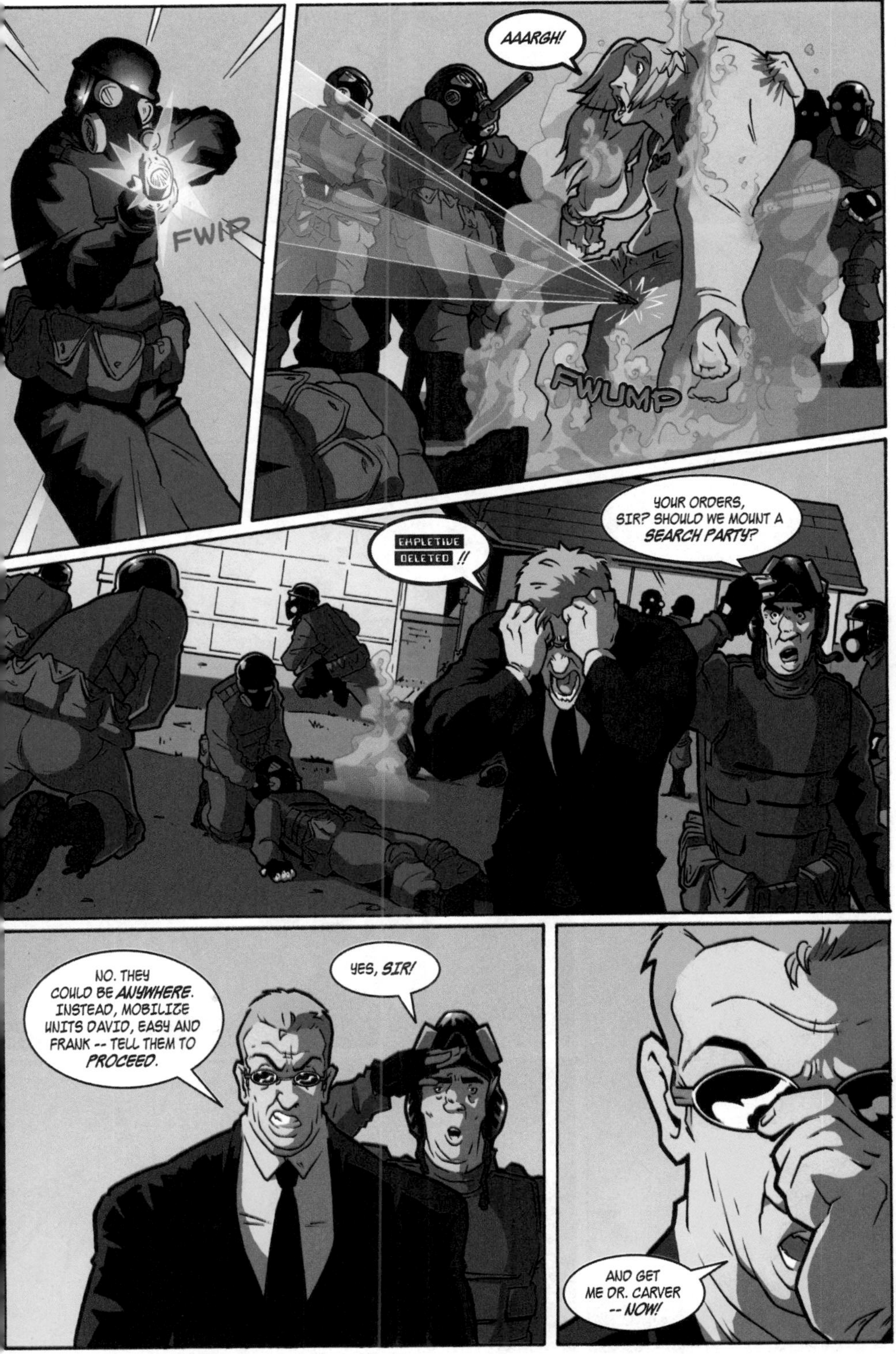
FWIP
AAARGH!
FWUMP
EXPLETIVE DELETED !!
YOUR ORDERS, SIR? SHOULD WE MOUNT A SEARCH PARTY?
NO. THEY COULD BE ANYWHERE. INSTEAD, MOBILIZE UNITS DAVID, EASY AND FRANK -- TELL THEM TO PROCEED.
YES, SIR!
AND GET ME DR. CARVER -- NOW!

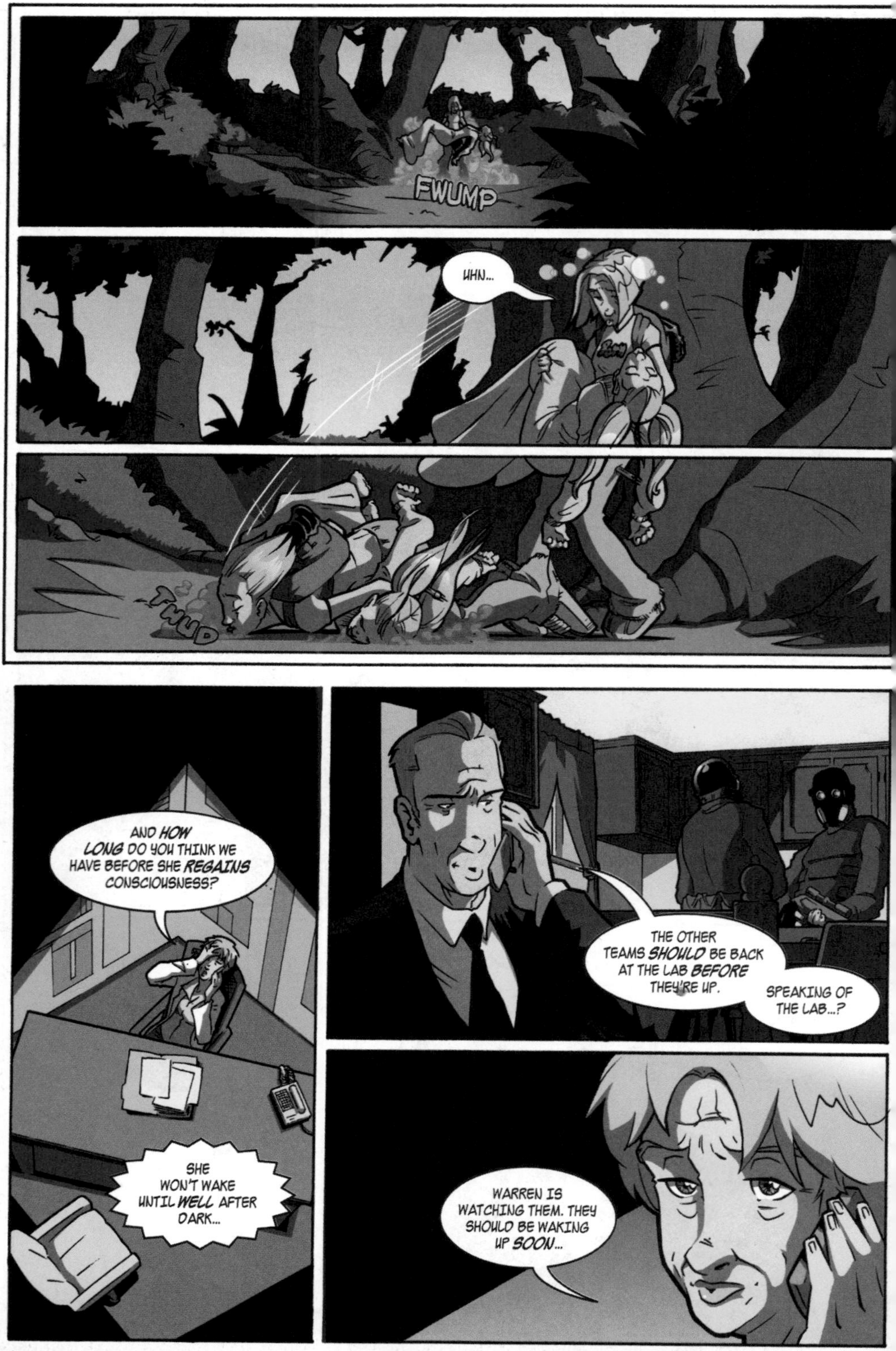
FWUMP
UHN...
THUD
AND HOW LONG DO YOU THINK WE HAVE BEFORE SHE REGAINS CONSCIOUSNESS?
THE OTHER TEAMS SHOULD BE BACK AT THE LAB BEFORE THEY'RE UP.
SPEAKING OF THE LAB...?
SHE WON'T WAKE UNTIL WELL AFTER DARK...
WARREN IS WATCHING THEM. THEY SHOULD BE WAKING UP SOON...

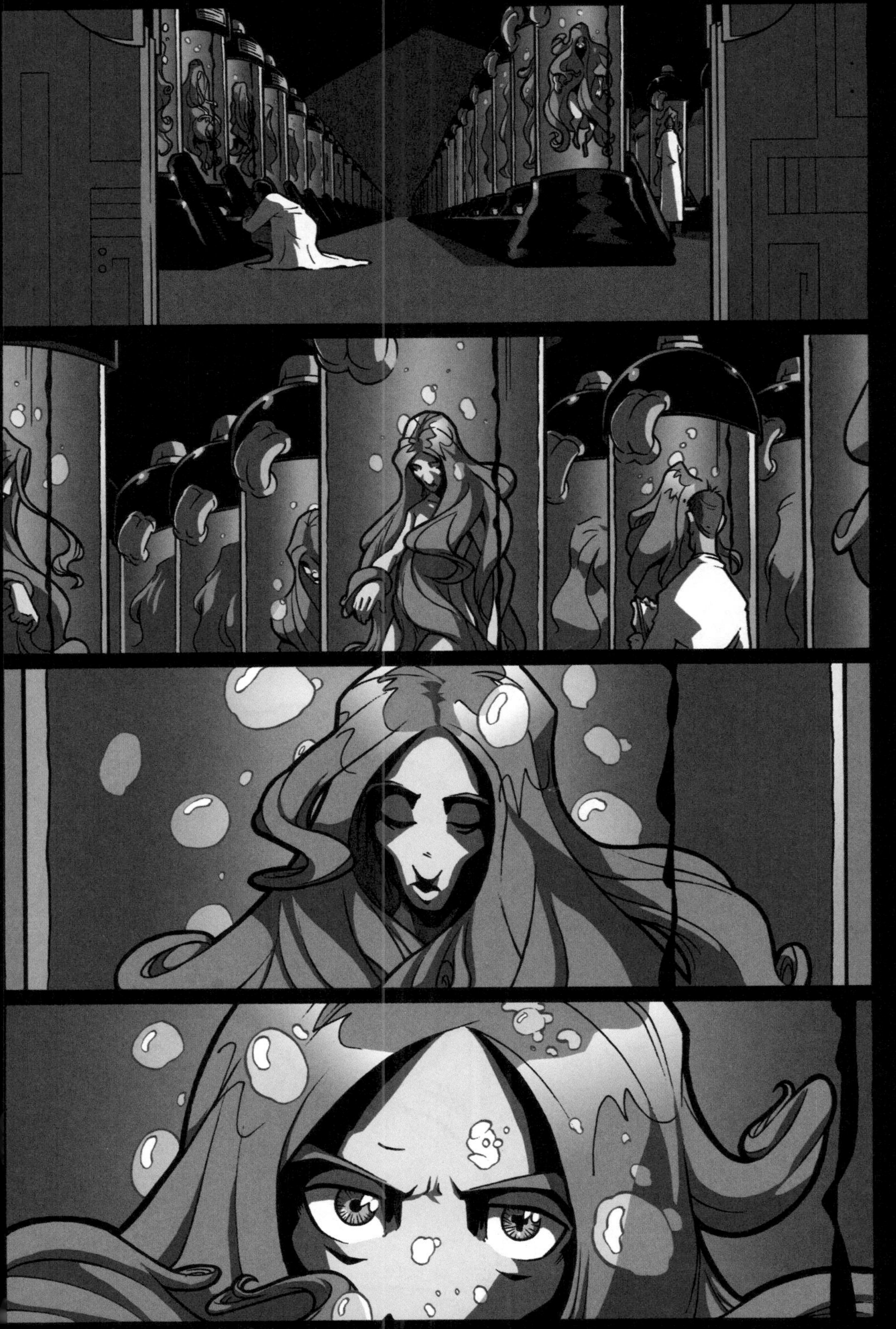

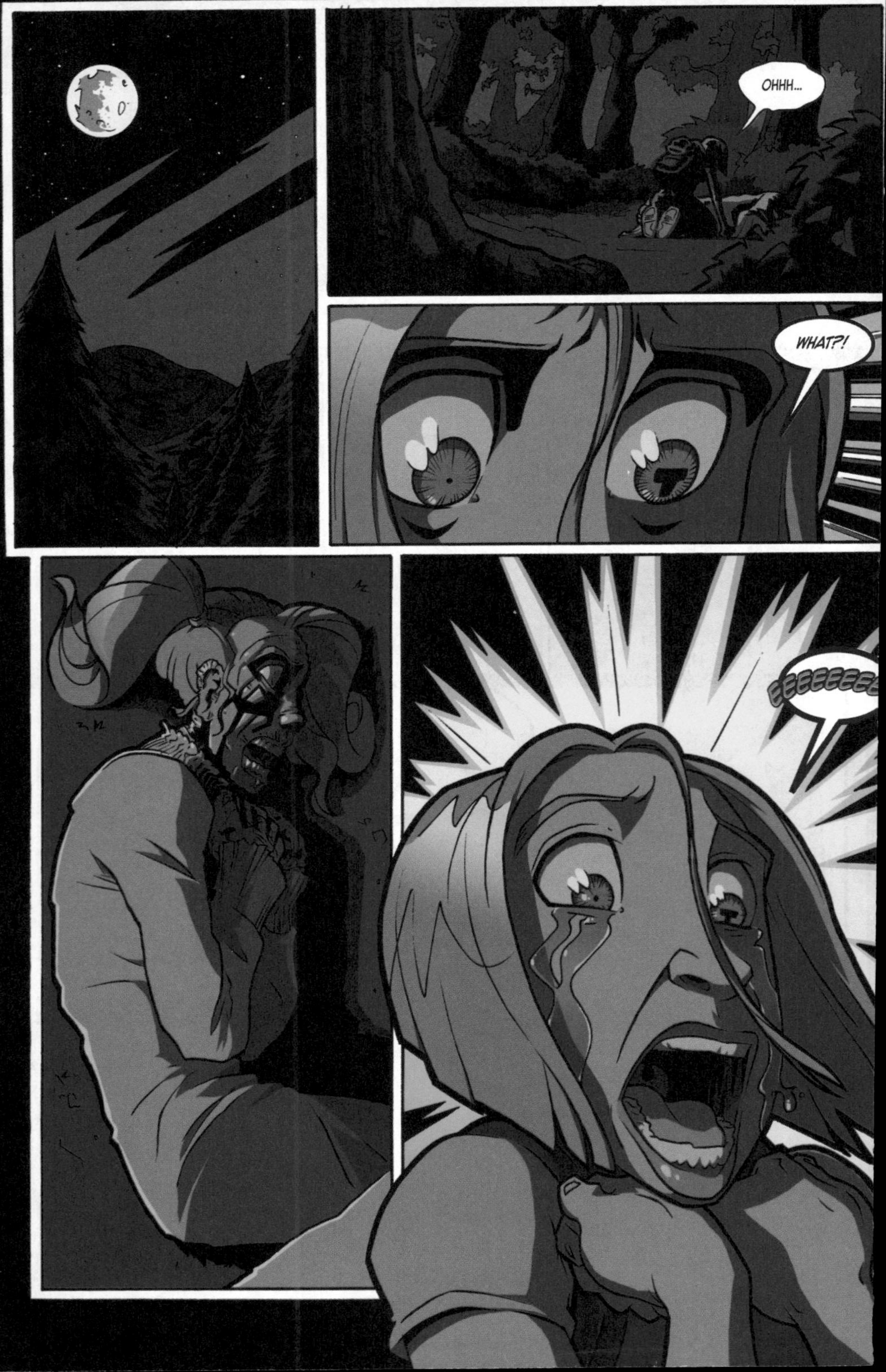
OHHH...
WHAT?!
EEEEEEEEE

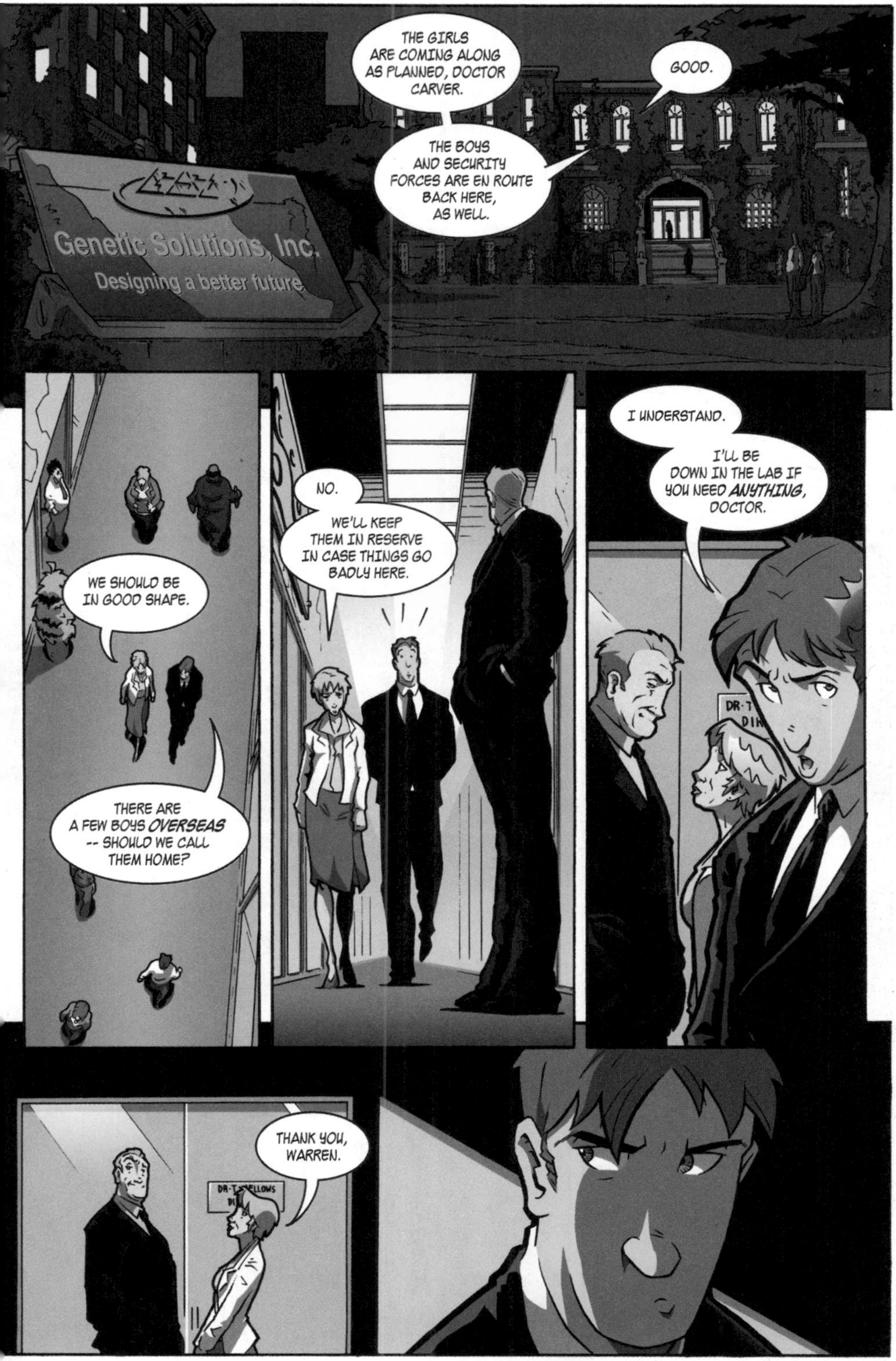
Genetic Solutions, Inc.
Designing a better future
THE GIRLS ARE COMING ALONG AS PLANNED, DOCTOR CARVER.
GOOD.
THE BOYS AND SECURITY FORCES ARE EN ROUTE BACK HERE, AS WELL.
WE SHOULD BE IN GOOD SHAPE.
THERE ARE A FEW BOYS OVERSEAS -- SHOULD WE CALL THEM HOME?
NO.
WE'LL KEEP THEM IN RESERVE IN CASE THINGS GO BADLY HERE.
I UNDERSTAND.
I'LL BE DOWN IN THE LAB IF YOU NEED ANYTHING, DOCTOR.
THANK YOU, WARREN.

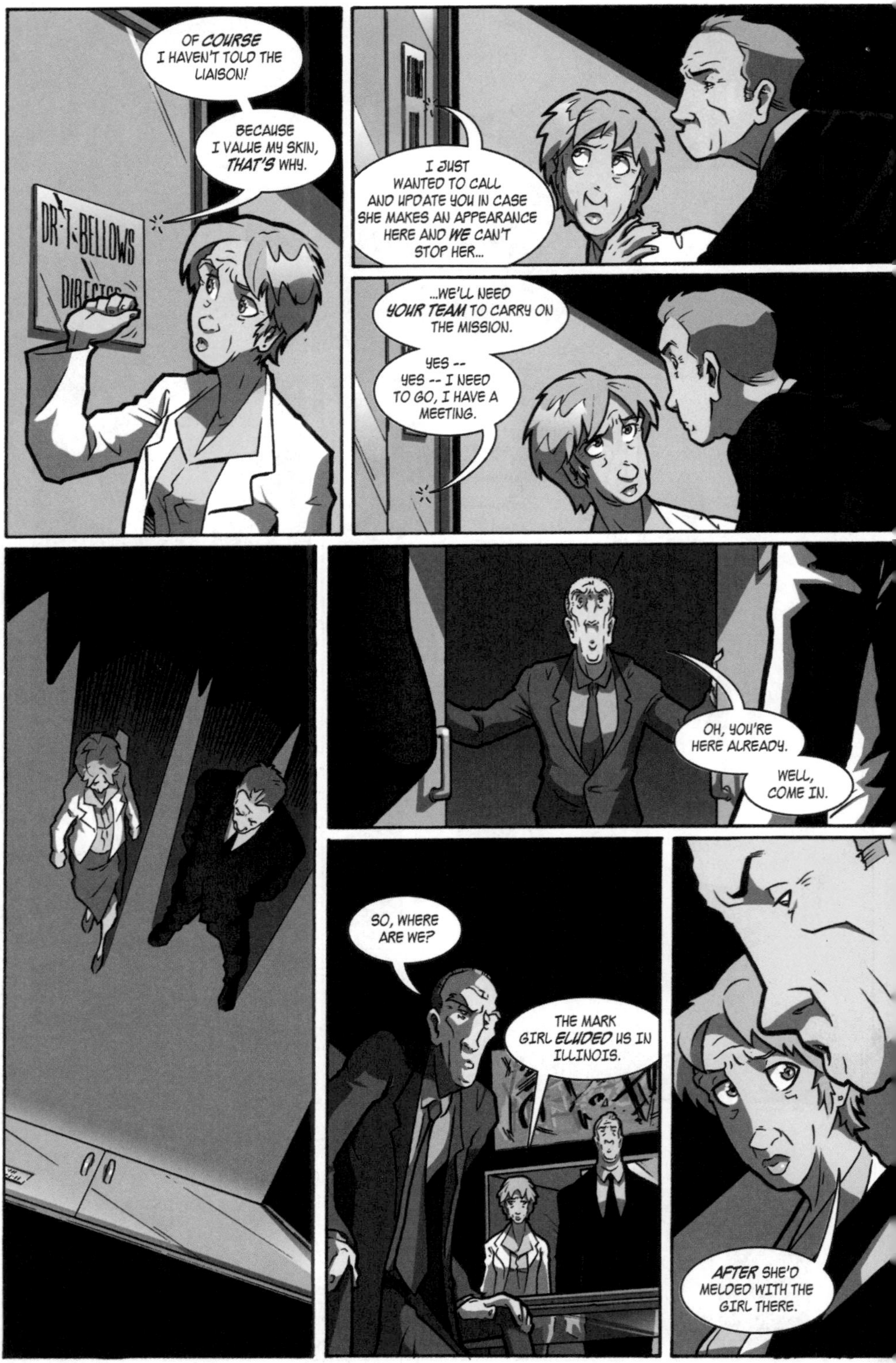
OF COURSE I HAVEN'T TOLD THE LIAISON!
BECAUSE I VALUE MY SKIN, THAT'S WHY.
DR. T. BELLOWS
I JUST WANTED TO CALL AND UPDATE YOU IN CASE SHE MAKES AN APPEARANCE HERE AND WE CAN'T STOP HER...
...WE'LL NEED YOUR TEAM TO CARRY ON THE MISSION.
YES -- YES -- I NEED TO GO, I HAVE A MEETING.
OH, YOU'RE HERE ALREADY.
WELL, COME IN.
SO, WHERE ARE WE?
THE MARK GIRL ELUDED US IN ILLINOIS.
AFTER SHE'D MELDED WITH THE GIRL THERE.

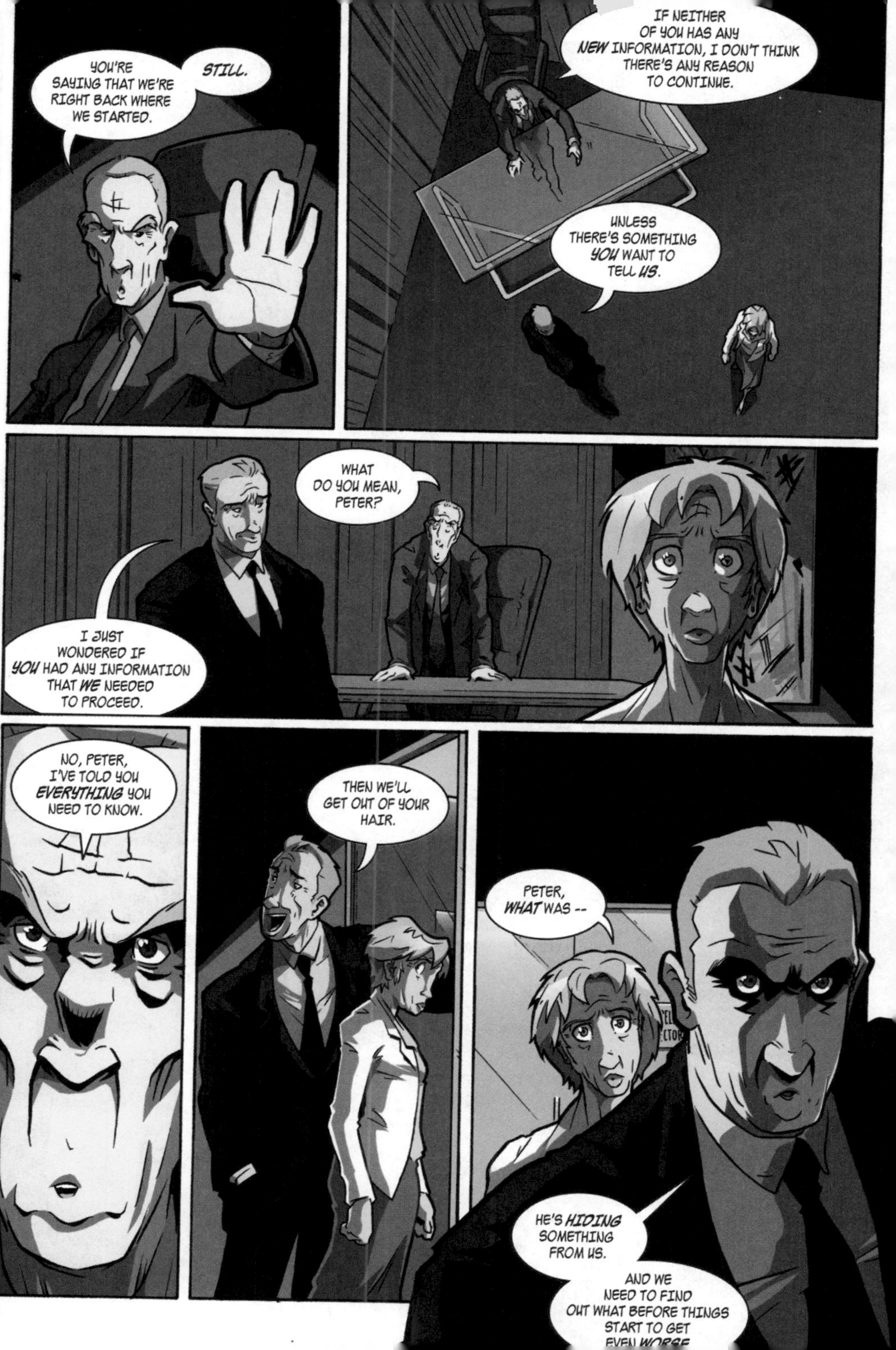
YOU'RE SAYING THAT WE'RE RIGHT BACK WHERE WE STARTED.
STILL.
IF NEITHER OF YOU HAS ANY NEW INFORMATION, I DON'T THINK THERE'S ANY REASON TO CONTINUE.
UNLESS THERE'S SOMETHING YOU WANT TO TELL US.
WHAT DO YOU MEAN, PETER?
I JUST WONDERED IF YOU HAD ANY INFORMATION THAT WE NEEDED TO PROCEED.
NO, PETER, I'VE TOLD YOU EVERYTHING YOU NEED TO KNOW.
THEN WE'LL GET OUT OF YOUR HAIR.
PETER, WHAT WAS --
HE'S HIDING SOMETHING FROM US.
AND WE NEED TO FIND OUT WHAT BEFORE THINGS START TO GET

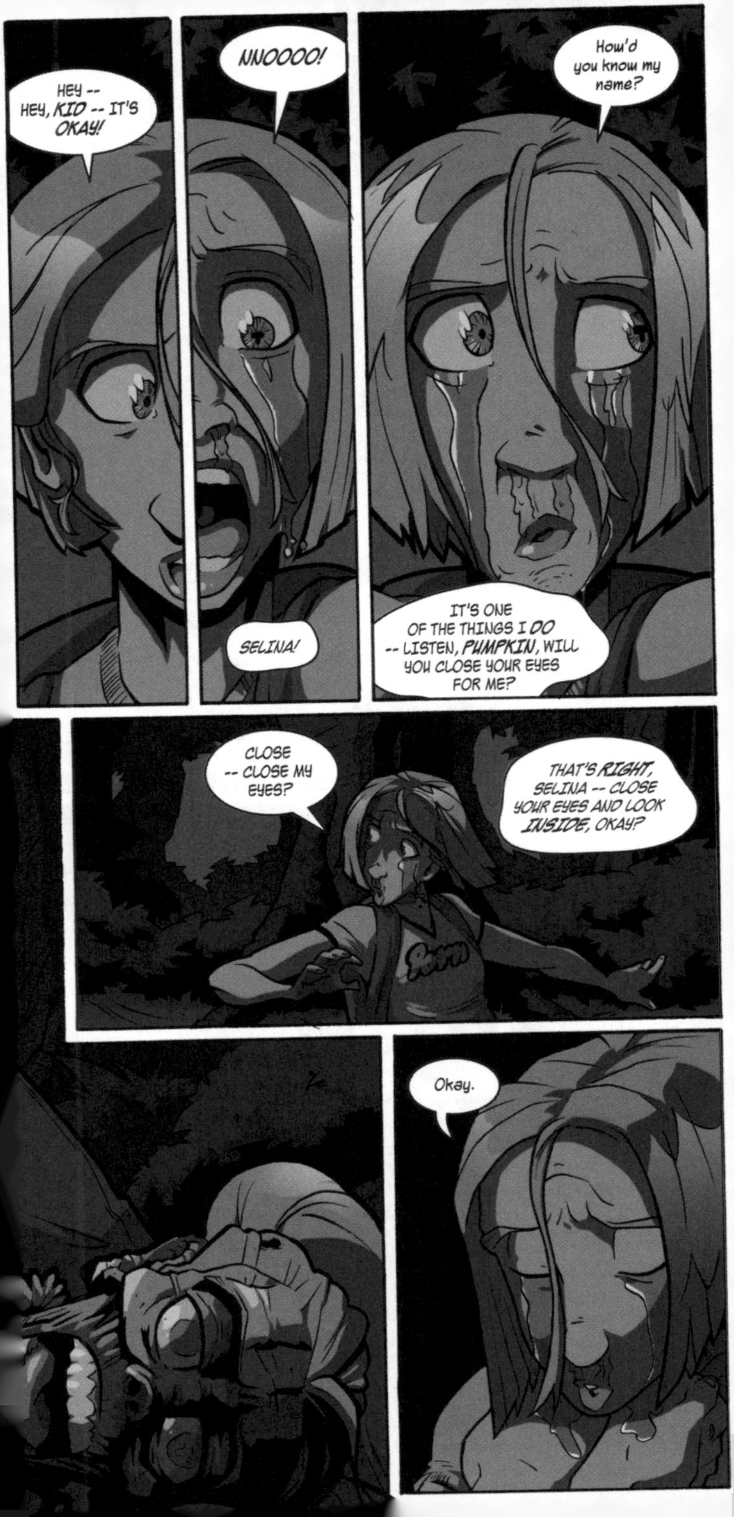
HEY -- HEY, KID -- IT'S OKAY!
NNOOOO!
SELINA!
How'd you know my name?
IT'S ONE OF THE THINGS I DO -- LISTEN, PUMPKIN, WILL YOU CLOSE YOUR EYES FOR ME?
CLOSE -- CLOSE MY EYES?
THAT'S RIGHT, SELINA -- CLOSE YOUR EYES AND LOOK INSIDE, OKAY?
Okay.

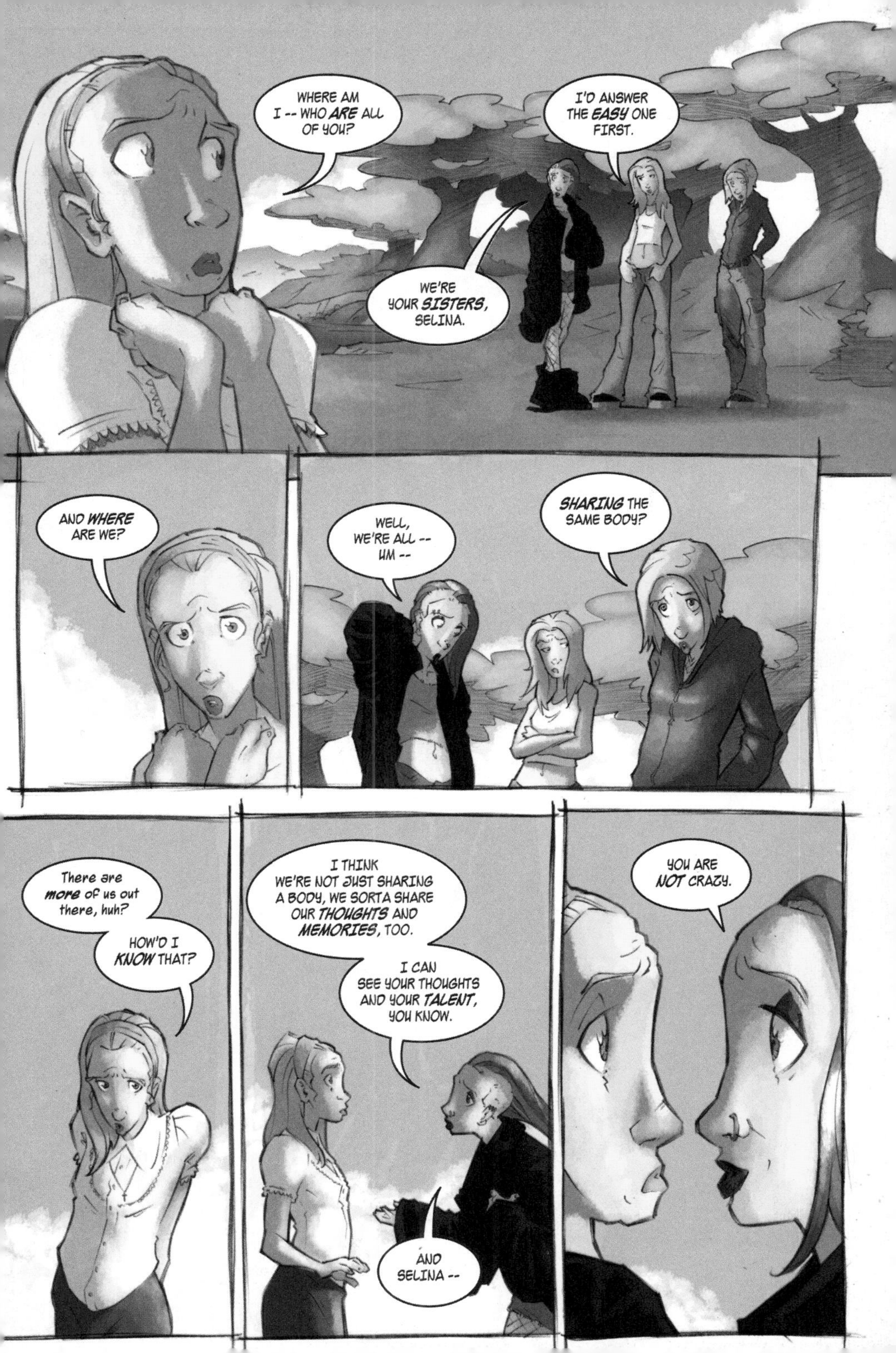
WHERE AM I -- WHO ARE ALL OF YOU?
I'D ANSWER THE EASY ONE FIRST.
WE'RE YOUR SISTERS, SELINA.
AND WHERE ARE WE?
WELL, WE'RE ALL -- UM --
SHARING THE SAME BODY?
There are more of us out there, huh?
HOW'D I KNOW THAT?
I THINK WE'RE NOT JUST SHARING A BODY, WE SORTA SHARE OUR THOUGHTS AND MEMORIES, TOO.
I CAN SEE YOUR THOUGHTS AND YOUR TALENT, YOU KNOW.
AND SELINA --
YOU ARE NOT CRAZY.

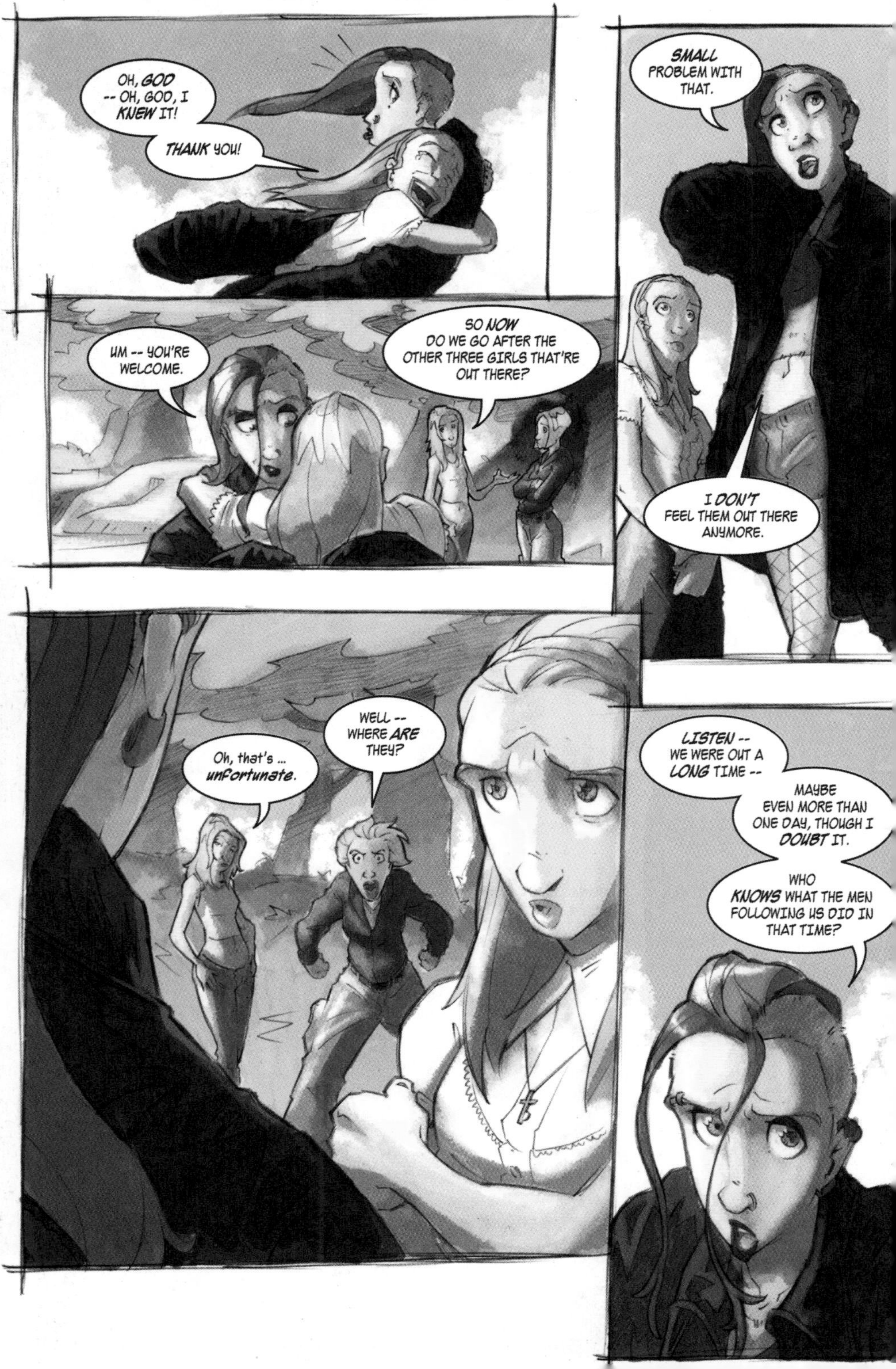
OH, GOD -- OH, GOD, I KNEW IT!
THANK YOU!
SMALL PROBLEM WITH THAT.
UM -- YOU'RE WELCOME.
SO NOW DO WE GO AFTER THE OTHER THREE GIRLS THAT'RE OUT THERE?
I DON'T FEEL THEM OUT THERE ANYMORE.
Oh, that's ... unfortunate.
WELL -- WHERE ARE THEY?
LISTEN -- WE WERE OUT A LONG TIME --
MAYBE EVEN MORE THAN ONE DAY, THOUGH I DOUBT IT.
WHO KNOWS WHAT THE MEN FOLLOWING US DID IN THAT TIME?

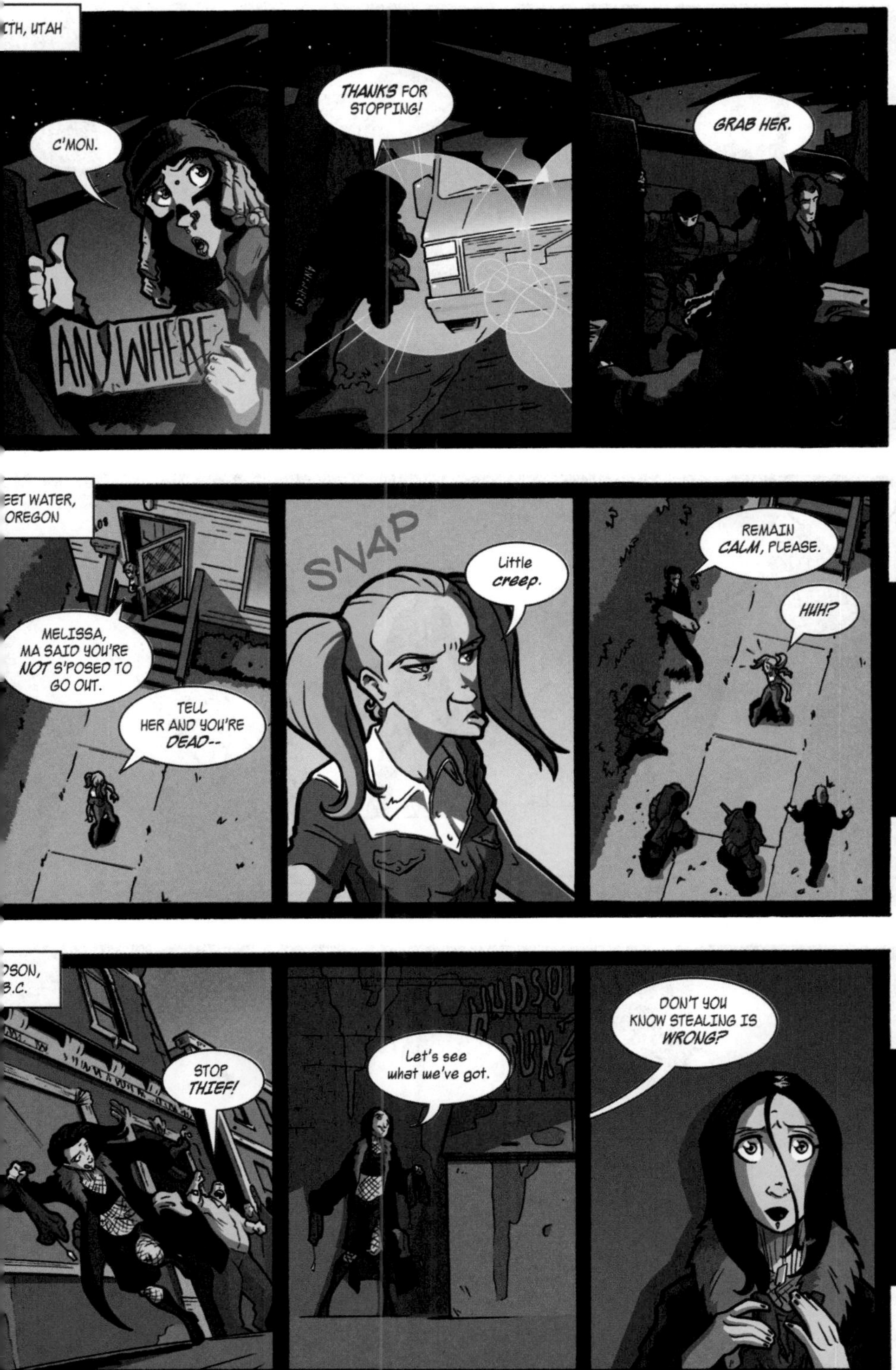

CTH, UTAH
C'MON.
ANYWHERE
THANKS FOR STOPPING!
GRAB HER.
EET WATER, OREGON
MELISSA, MA SAID YOU'RE NOT S'POSED TO GO OUT.
TELL HER AND YOU'RE DEAD--
SNAP
Little creep.
REMAIN CALM, PLEASE.
HUH?
DSON, B.C.
STOP THIEF!
Let's see what we've got.
DON'T YOU KNOW STEALING IS WRONG?

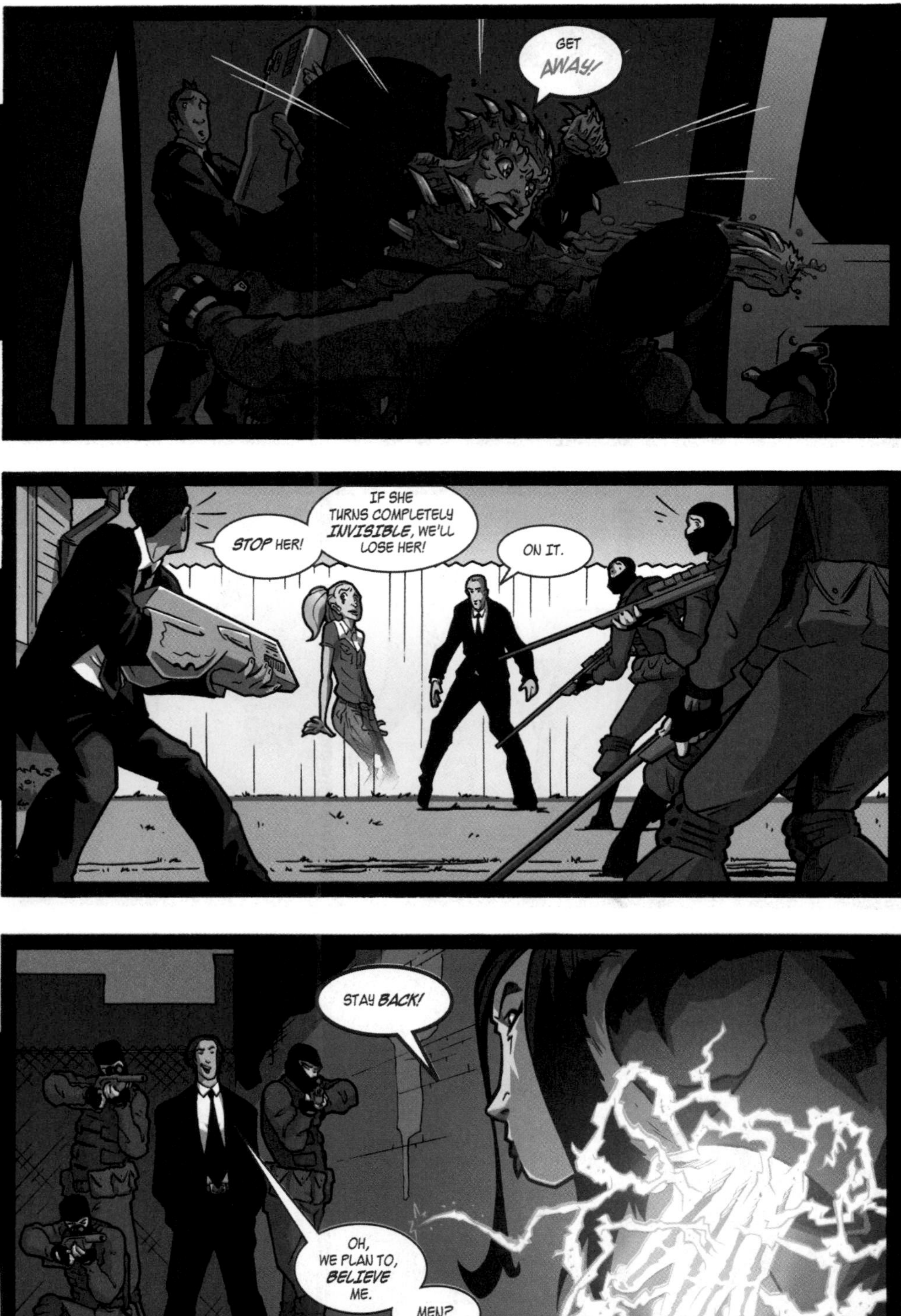
GET AWAY!
STOP HER!
IF SHE TURNS COMPLETELY INVISIBLE, WE'LL LOSE HER!
ON IT.
STAY BACK!
OH, WE PLAN TO, BELIEVE ME.
MEN?

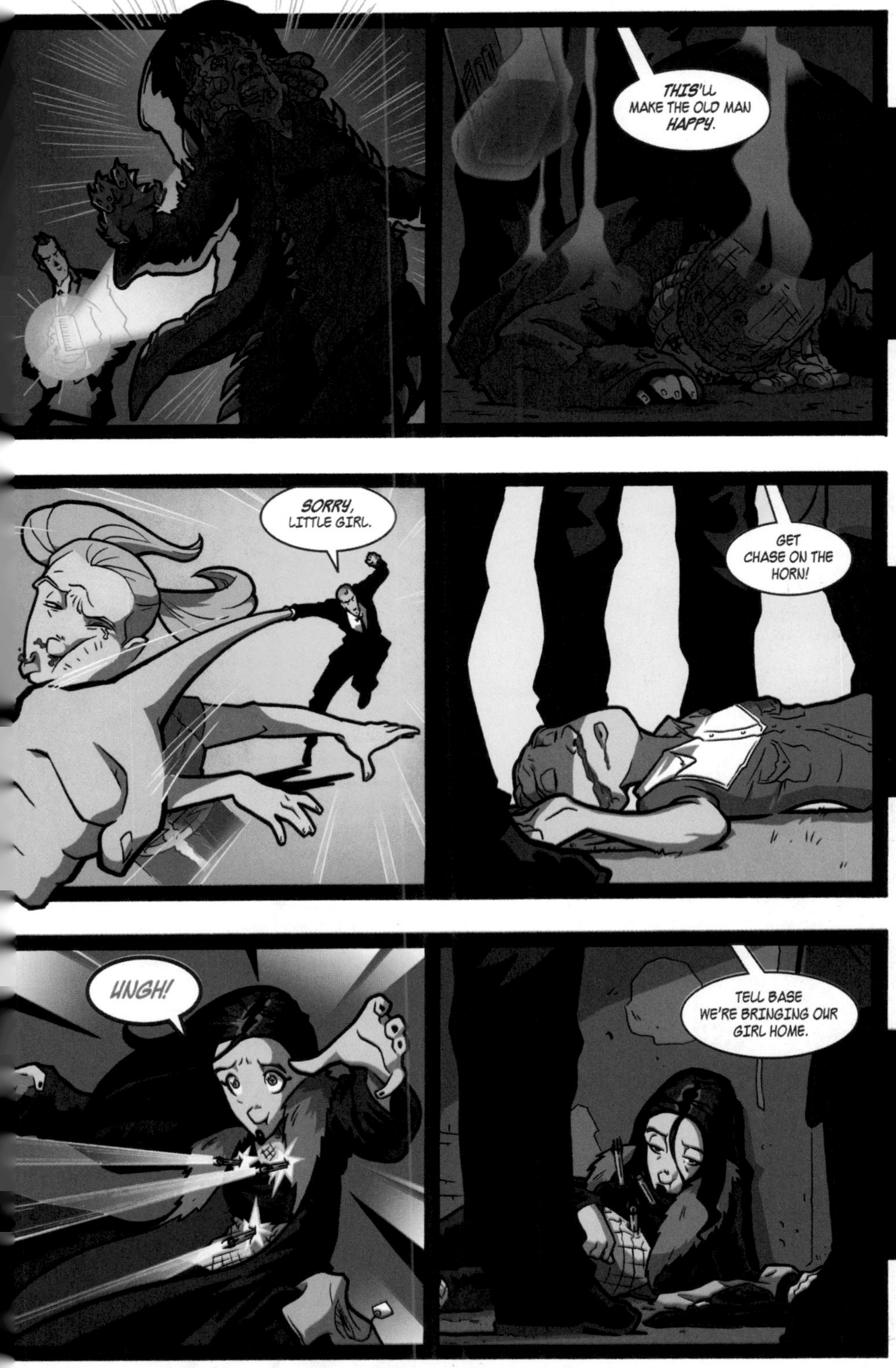
THIS'LL MAKE THE OLD MAN HAPPY.
SORRY, LITTLE GIRL.
GET CHASE ON THE HORN!
UNGH!
TELL BASE WE'RE BRINGING OUR GIRL HOME.

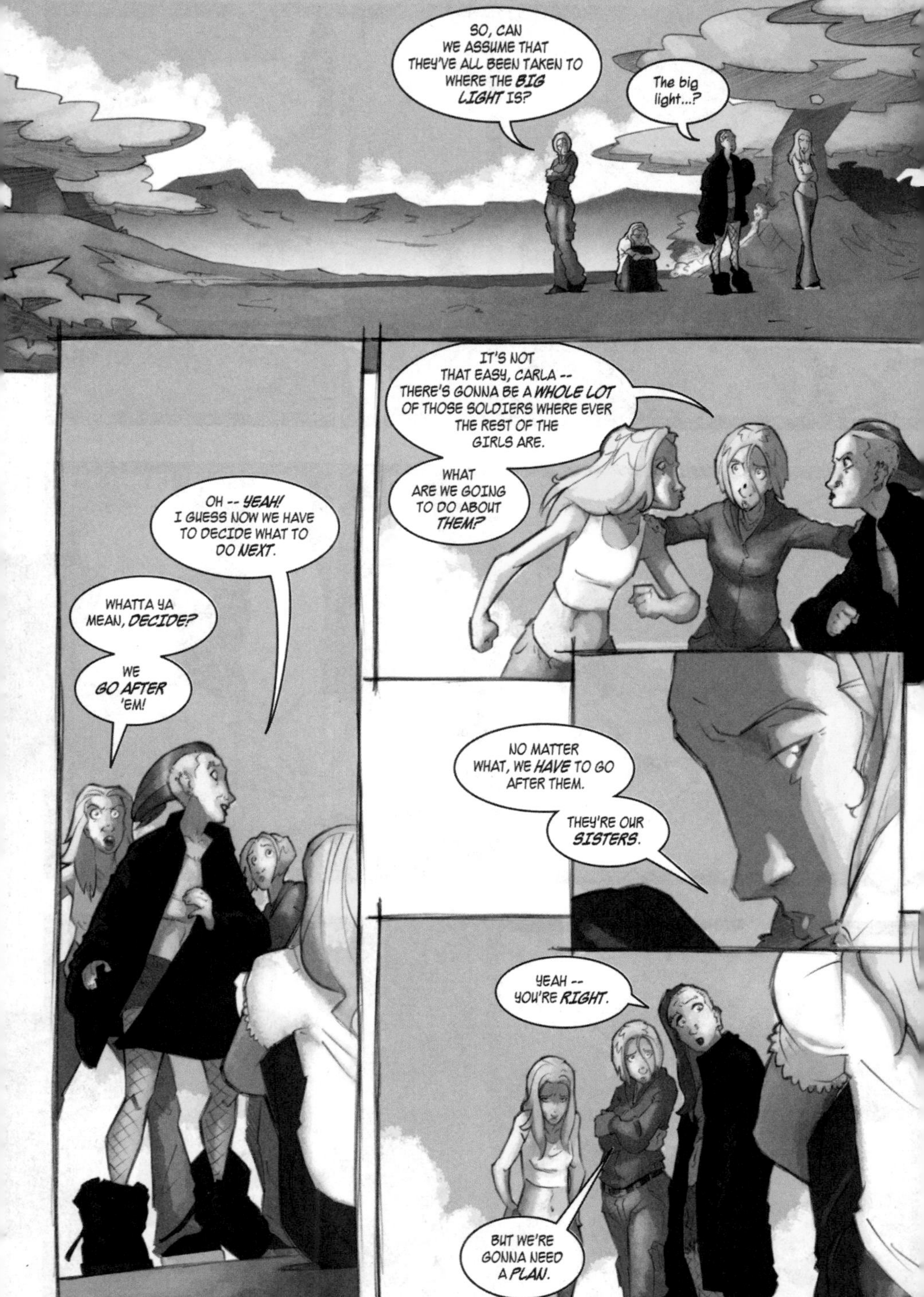
SO, CAN WE ASSUME THAT THEY'VE ALL BEEN TAKEN TO WHERE THE BIG LIGHT IS?
The big light...?
OH -- YEAH! I GUESS NOW WE HAVE TO DECIDE WHAT TO DO NEXT.
WHATTA YA MEAN, DECIDE?
WE GO AFTER 'EM!
IT'S NOT THAT EASY, CARLA -- THERE'S GONNA BE A WHOLE LOT OF THOSE SOLDIERS WHERE EVER THE REST OF THE GIRLS ARE.
WHAT ARE WE GOING TO DO ABOUT THEM?
NO MATTER WHAT, WE HAVE TO GO AFTER THEM.
THEY'RE OUR SISTERS.
YEAH -- YOU'RE RIGHT.
BUT WE'RE GONNA NEED A PLAN.

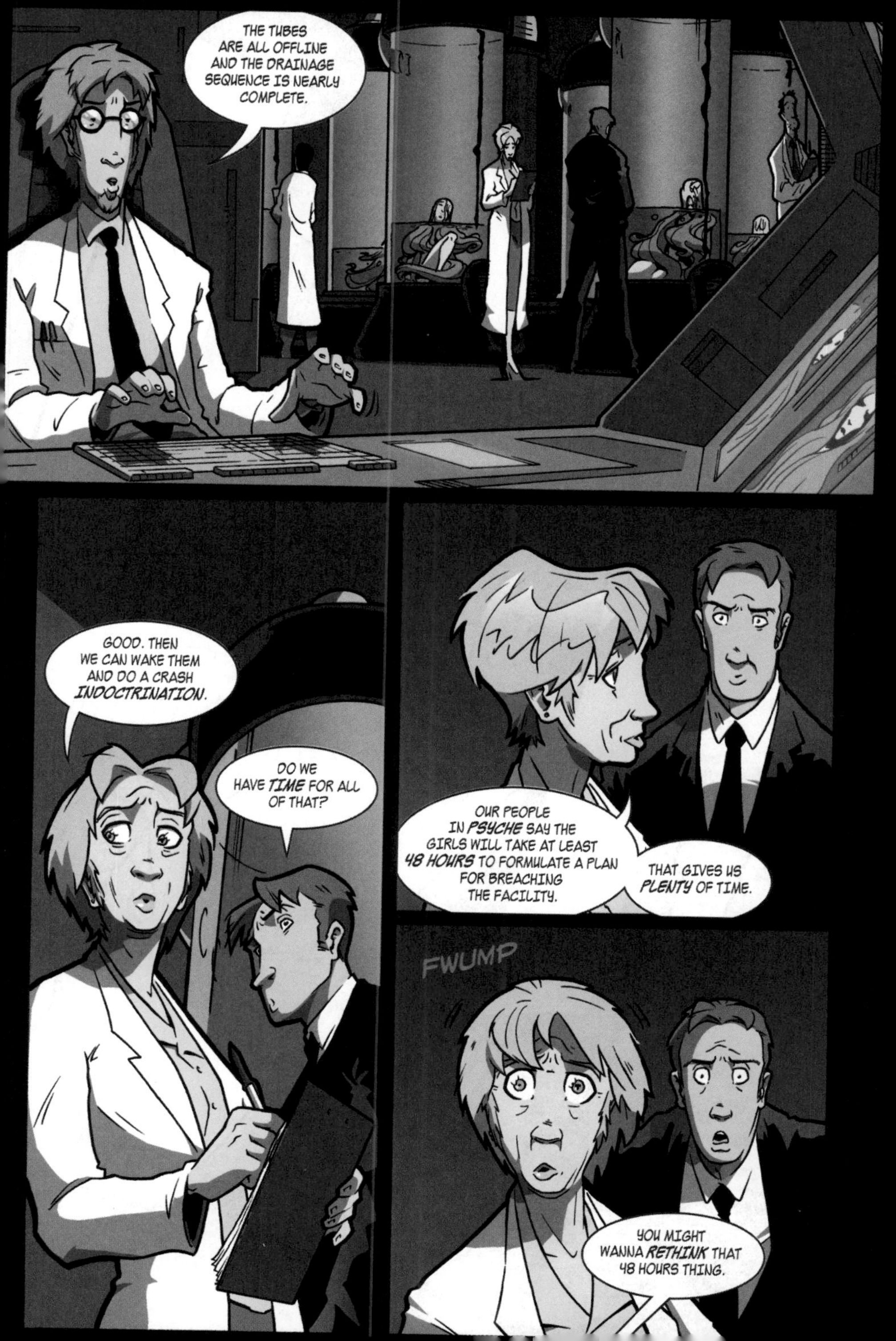
THE TUBES ARE ALL OFFLINE AND THE DRAINAGE SEQUENCE IS NEARLY COMPLETE.
GOOD. THEN WE CAN WAKE THEM AND DO A CRASH INDOCTRINATION.
DO WE HAVE TIME FOR ALL OF THAT?
OUR PEOPLE IN PSYCHE SAY THE GIRLS WILL TAKE AT LEAST 48 HOURS TO FORMULATE A PLAN FOR BREACHING THE FACILITY.
THAT GIVES US PLENTY OF TIME.
FWUMP
YOU MIGHT WANNA RETHINK THAT 48 HOURS THING.

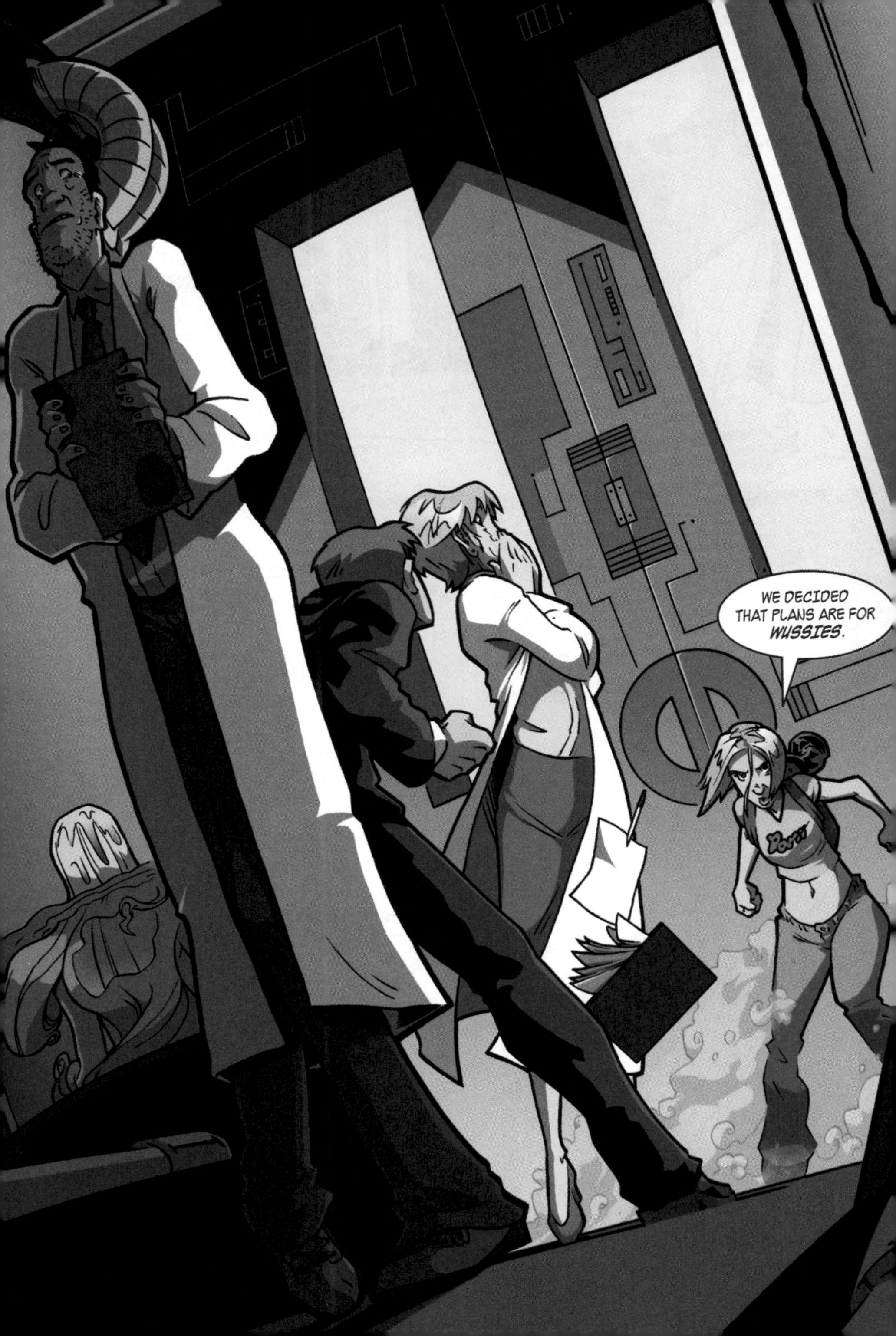
WE DECIDED
THAT PLANS ARE FOR
WUSSIES.

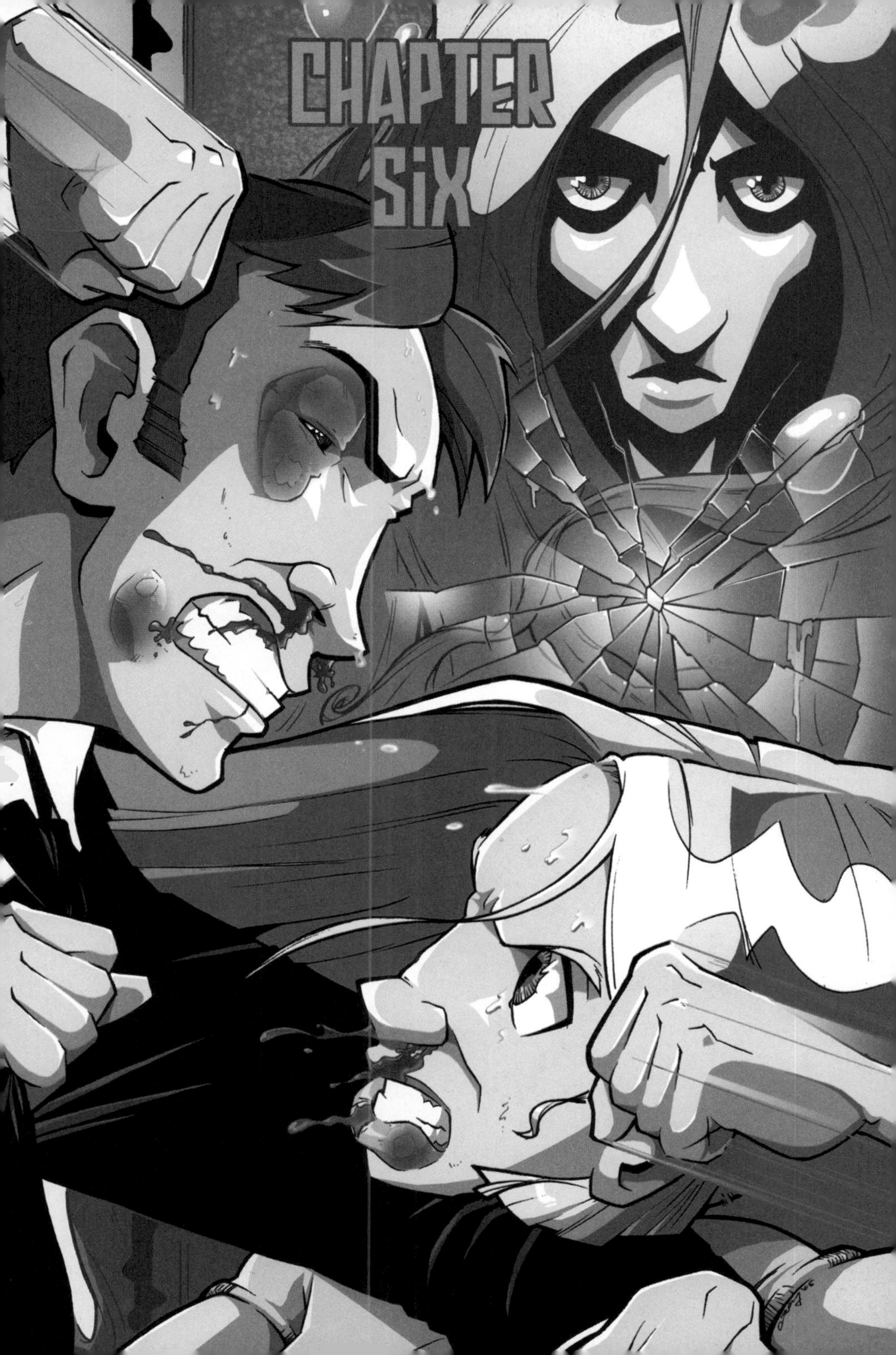
CHAPTER
SIX

"okay -- here we go, sweetheart."

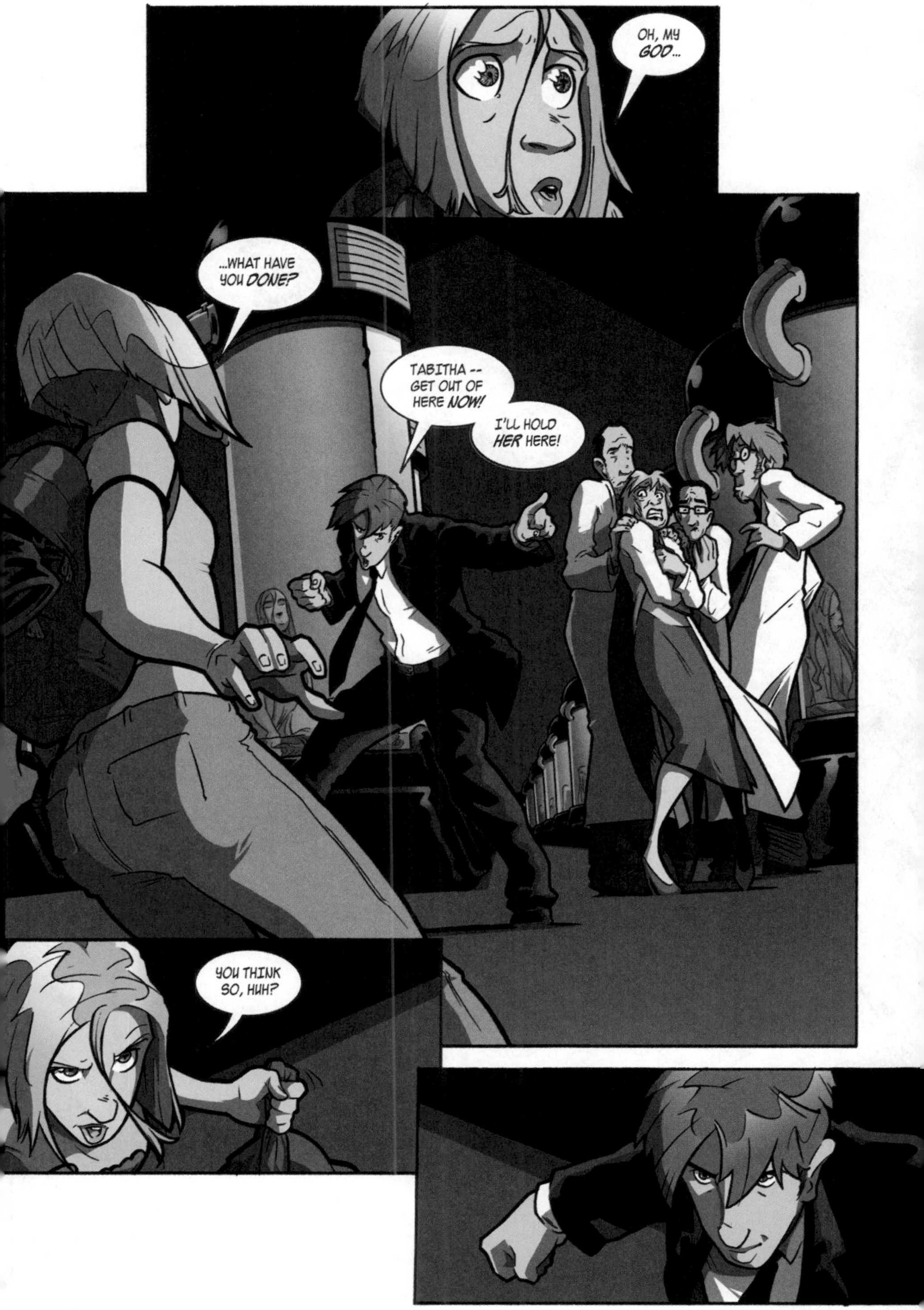
OH, MY GOD...
...WHAT HAVE YOU DONE?
TABITHA -- GET OUT OF HERE NOW!
I'LL HOLD HER HERE!
YOU THINK SO, HUH?

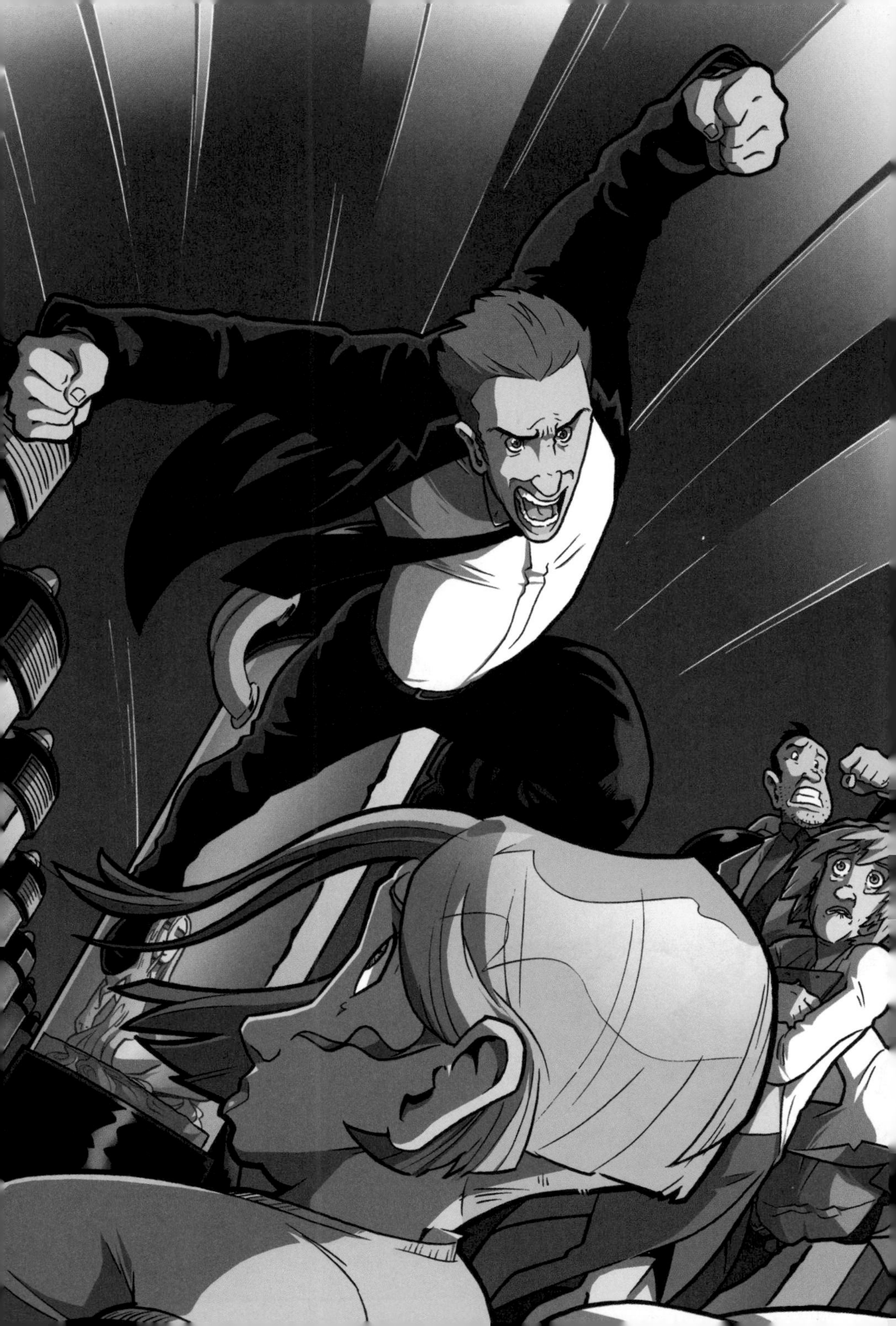

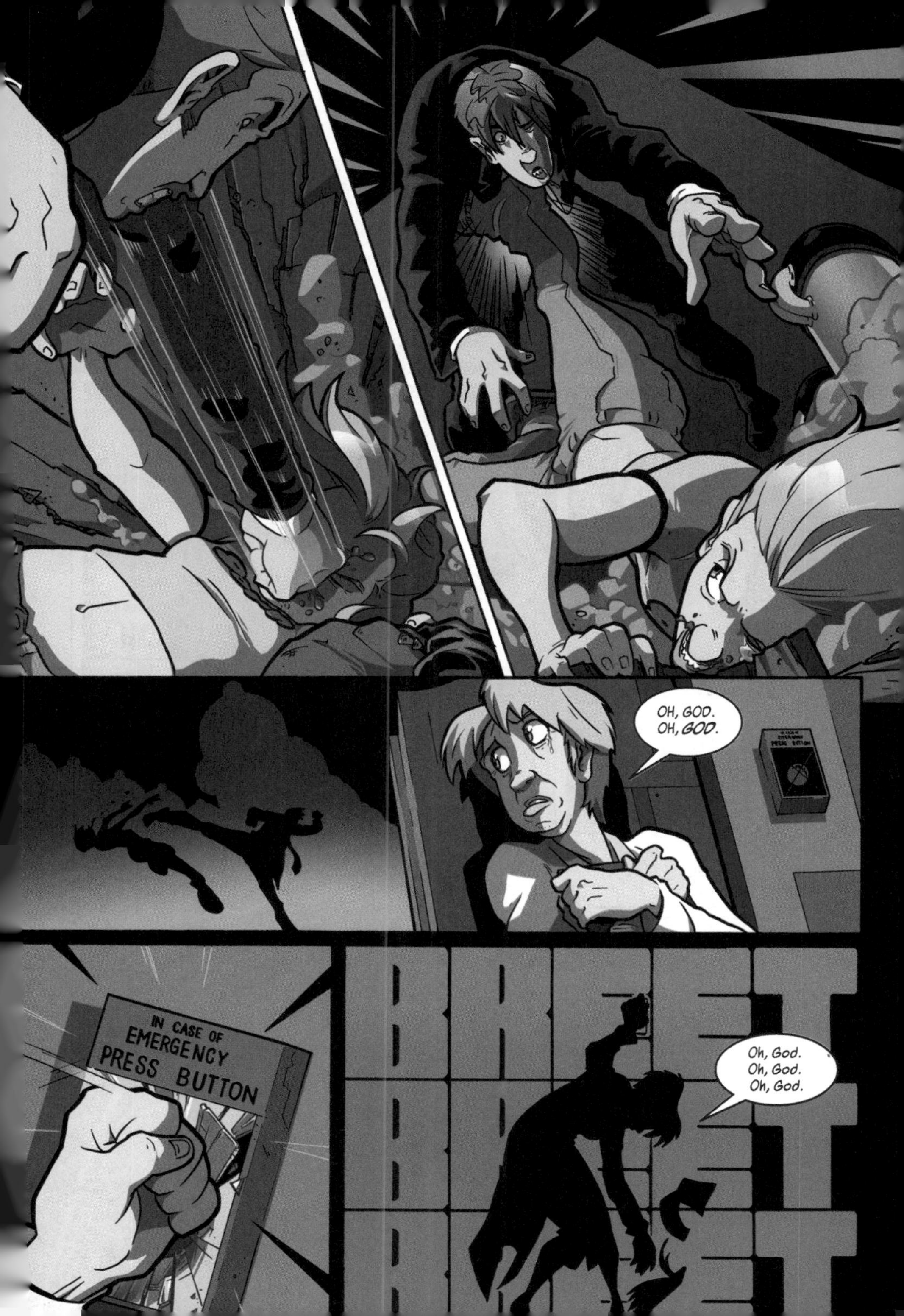
OH, GOD.
OH, *GOD*.
IN CASE OF EMERGENCY PRESS BUTTON
BREET
Oh, God.
Oh, God.
Oh, God.

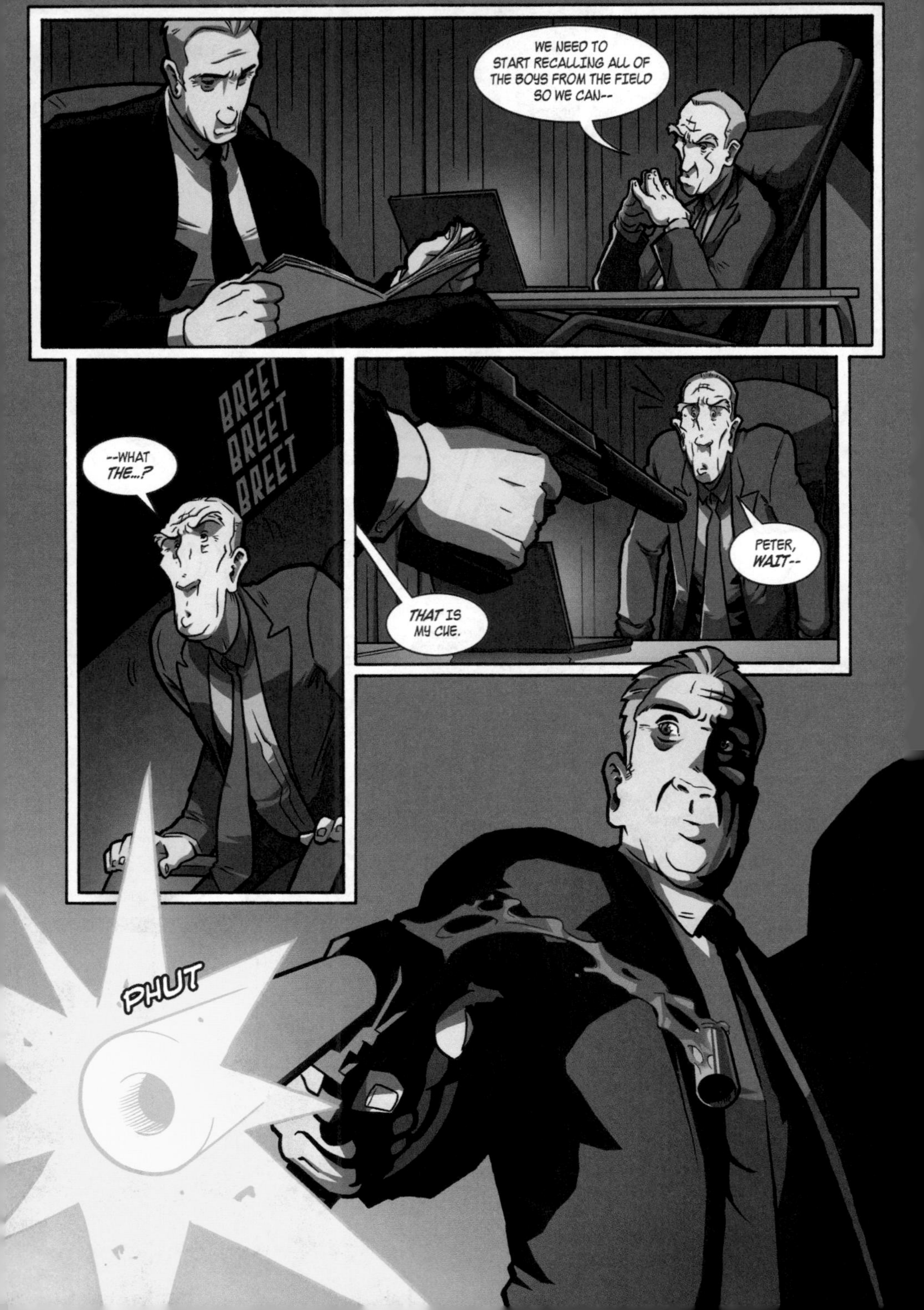
WE NEED TO START RECALLING ALL OF THE BOYS FROM THE FIELD SO WE CAN--
BREET BREET BREET
--WHAT THE...?
PETER, WAIT--
THAT IS MY CUE.
PHUT

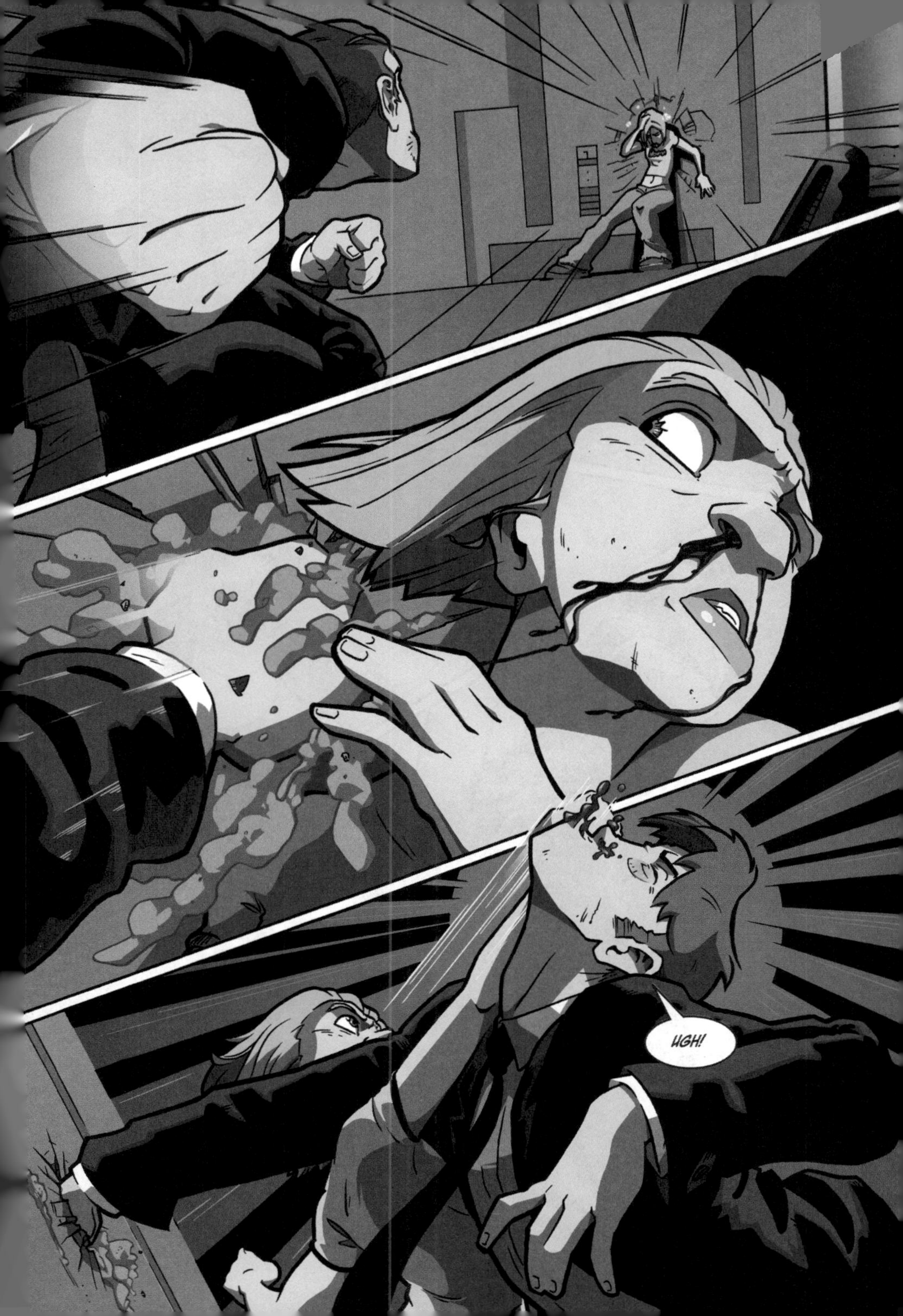
UGH!

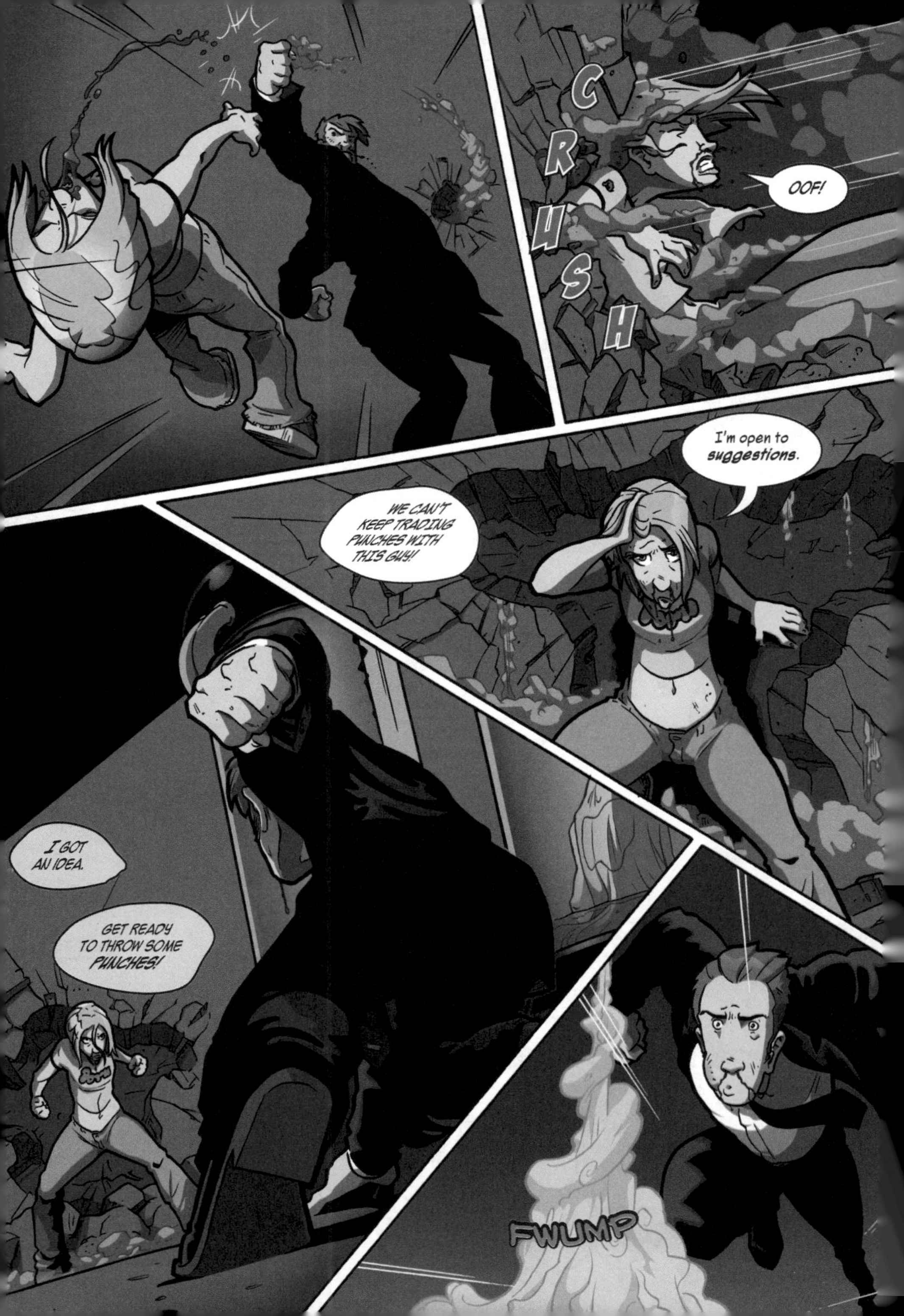
CRUSH
OOF!
I'm open to suggestions.
WE CAN'T KEEP TRADING PUNCHES WITH THIS GUY!
I GOT AN IDEA.
GET READY TO THROW SOME PUNCHES!
FWUMP

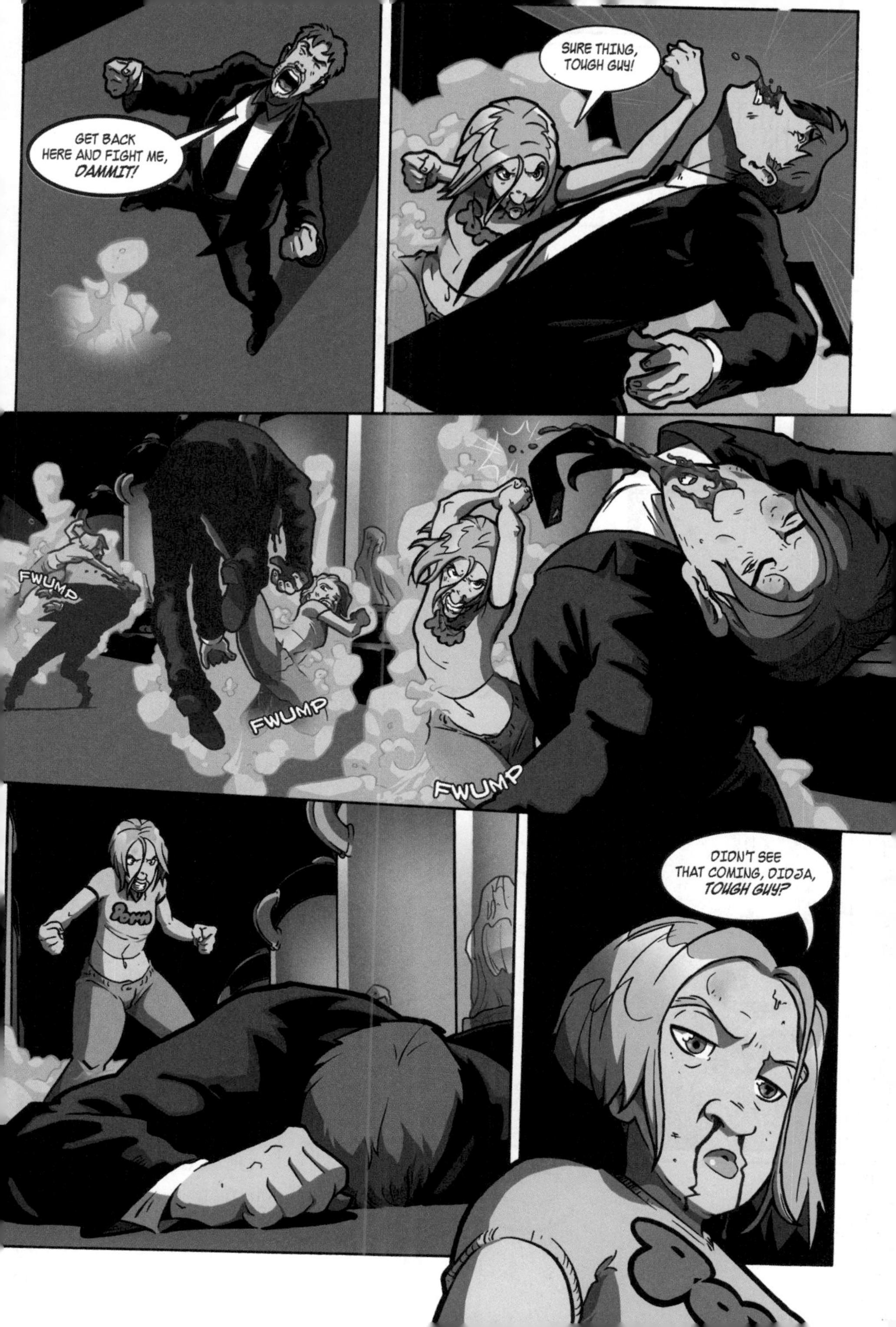
GET BACK HERE AND FIGHT ME, *DAMMIT!*
SURE THING, TOUGH GUY!
FWUMP
FWUMP
FWUMP
DIDN'T SEE THAT COMING, DIDJA, *TOUGH GUY?*

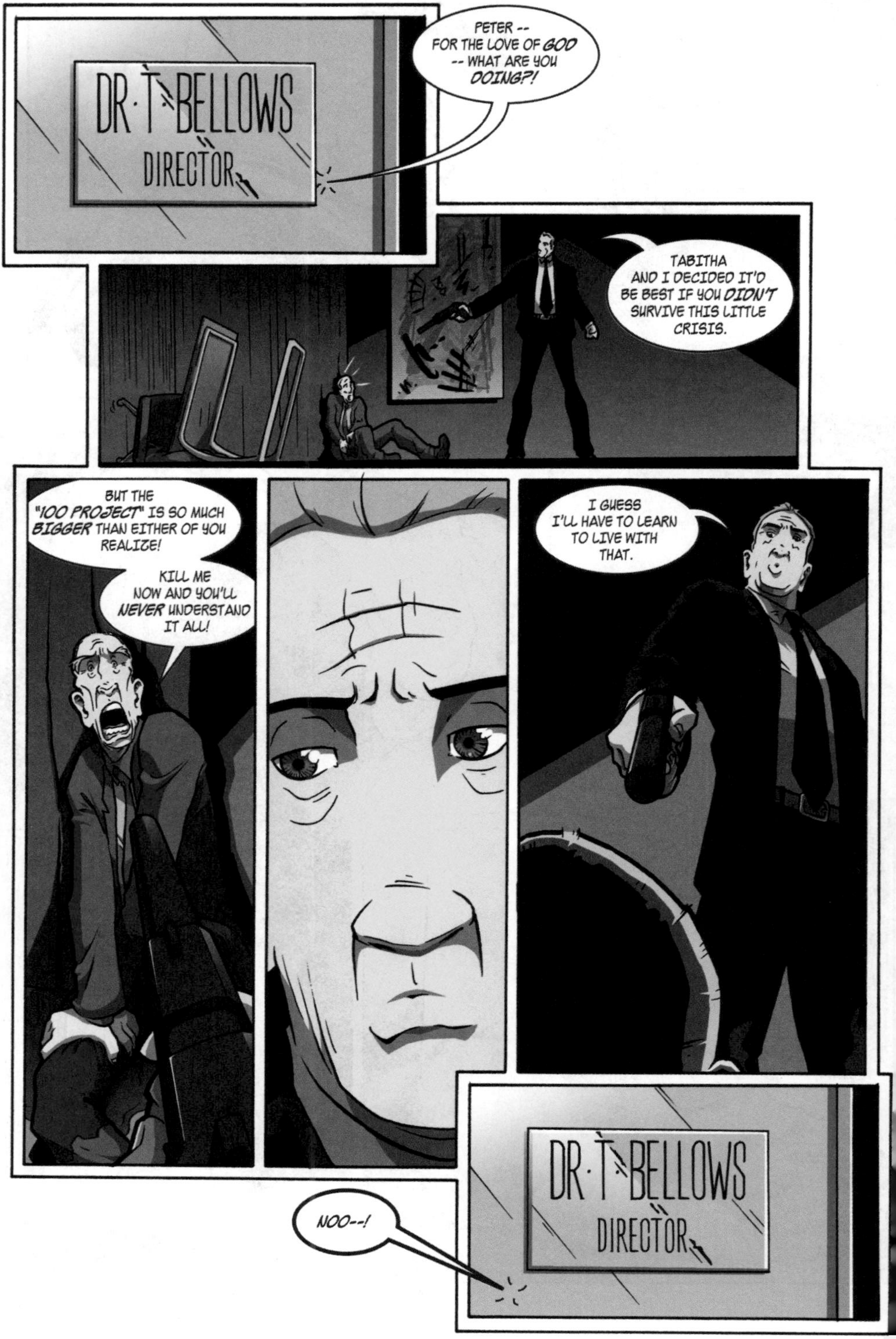
DR · T · BELLOWS
DIRECTOR
PETER -- FOR THE LOVE OF GOD -- WHAT ARE YOU DOING?!
TABITHA AND I DECIDED IT'D BE BEST IF YOU DIDN'T SURVIVE THIS LITTLE CRISIS.
BUT THE "100 PROJECT" IS SO MUCH BIGGER THAN EITHER OF YOU REALIZE!
KILL ME NOW AND YOU'LL NEVER UNDERSTAND IT ALL!
I GUESS I'LL HAVE TO LEARN TO LIVE WITH THAT.
DR · T · BELLOWS
DIRECTOR
NOO--!

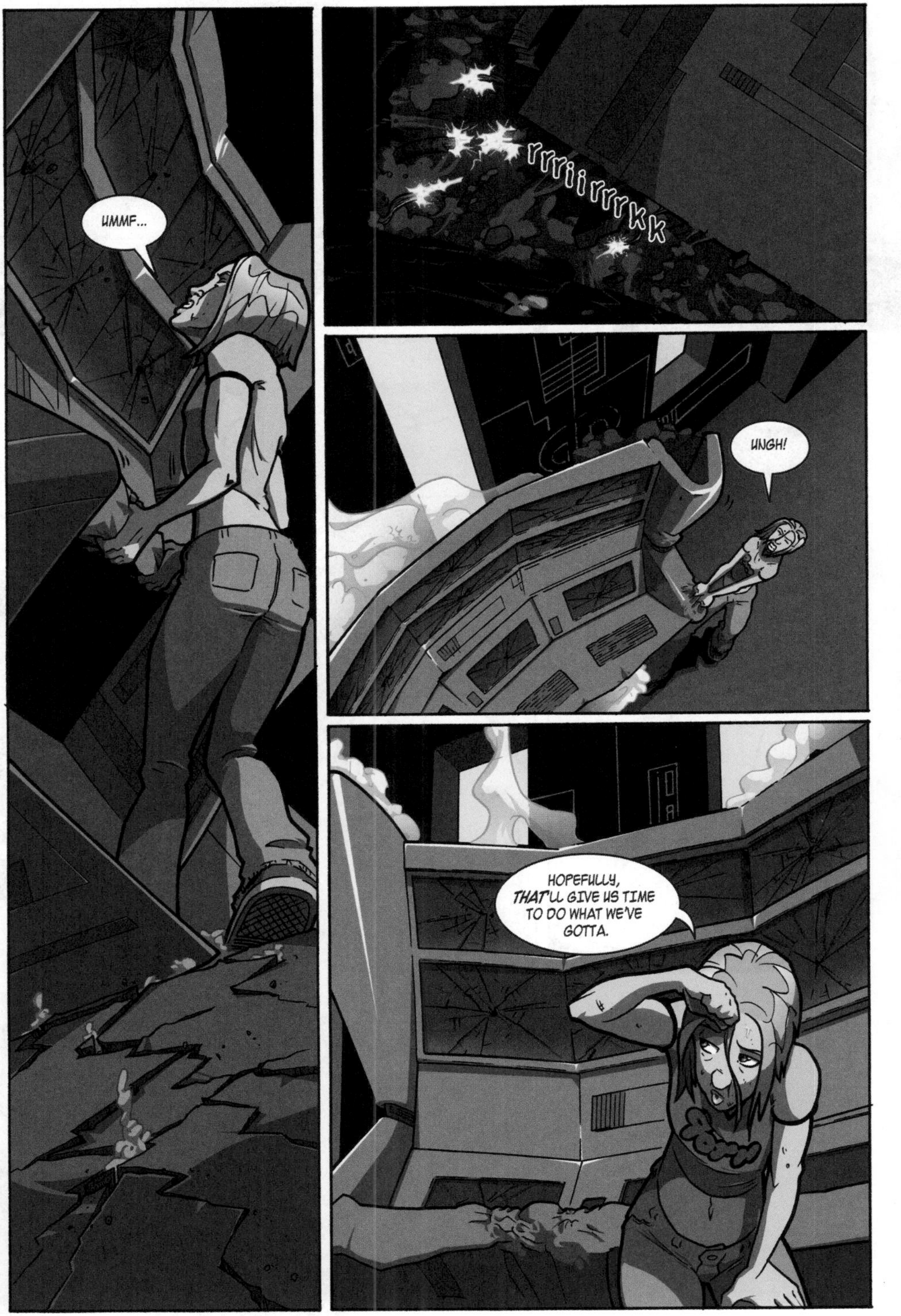
UMMF...
rrriirrrkk
UNGH!
HOPEFULLY, *THAT*'LL GIVE US TIME TO DO WHAT WE'VE GOTTA.

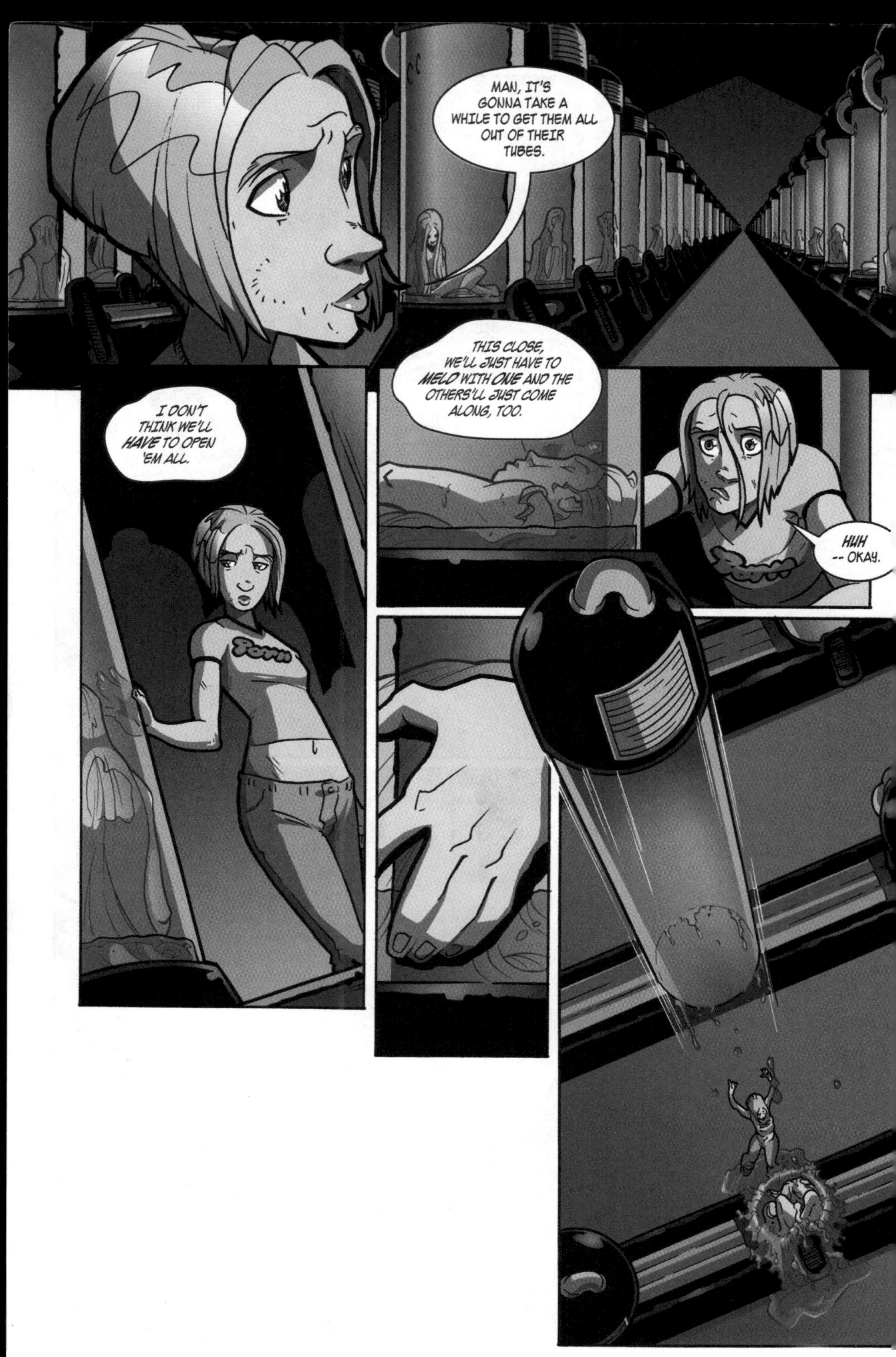

MAN, IT'S GONNA TAKE A WHILE TO GET THEM ALL OUT OF THEIR TUBES.
I DON'T THINK WE'LL HAVE TO OPEN 'EM ALL.
THIS CLOSE, WE'LL JUST HAVE TO MELD WITH ONE AND THE OTHERS'LL JUST COME ALONG, TOO.
HUH -- OKAY.

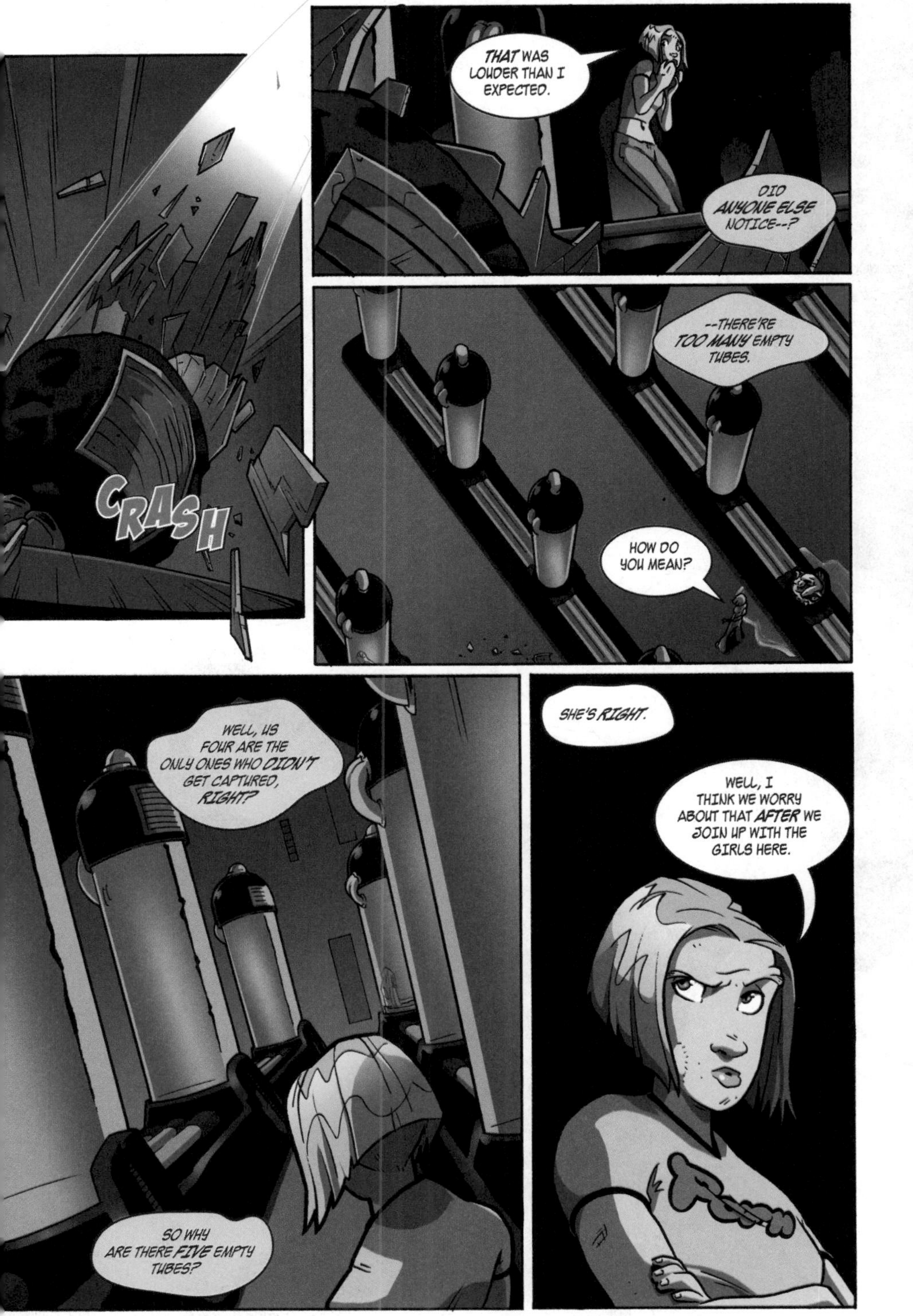
CRASH
THAT WAS LOUDER THAN I EXPECTED.
DID ANYONE ELSE NOTICE--?
--THERE'RE TOO MANY EMPTY TUBES.
HOW DO YOU MEAN?
WELL, US FOUR ARE THE ONLY ONES WHO DIDN'T GET CAPTURED, RIGHT?
SO WHY ARE THERE FIVE EMPTY TUBES?
SHE'S RIGHT.
WELL, I THINK WE WORRY ABOUT THAT AFTER WE JOIN UP WITH THE GIRLS HERE.

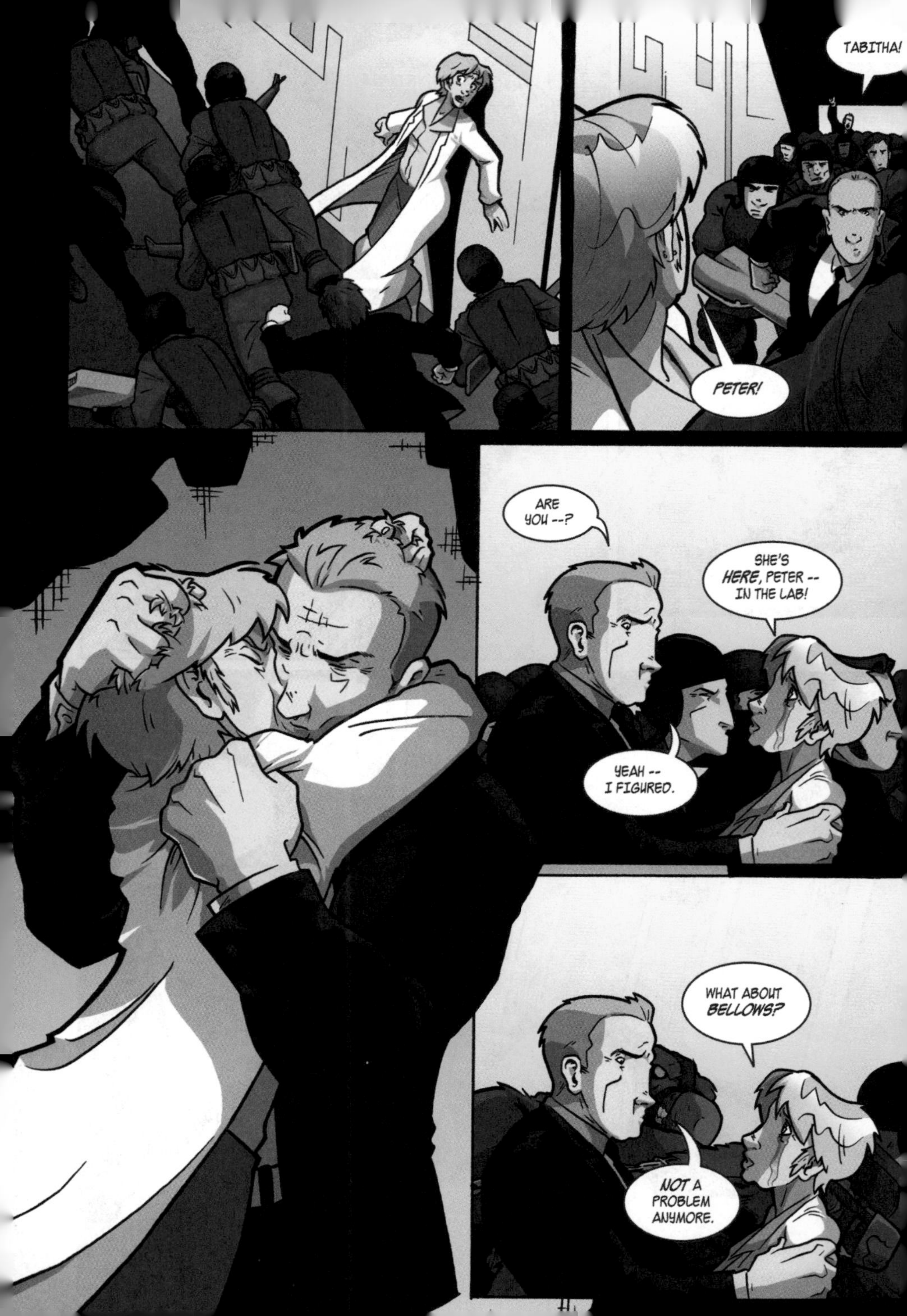
TABITHA!
PETER!
ARE YOU --?
SHE'S HERE, PETER -- IN THE LAB!
YEAH -- I FIGURED.
WHAT ABOUT BELLOWS?
NOT A PROBLEM ANYMORE.

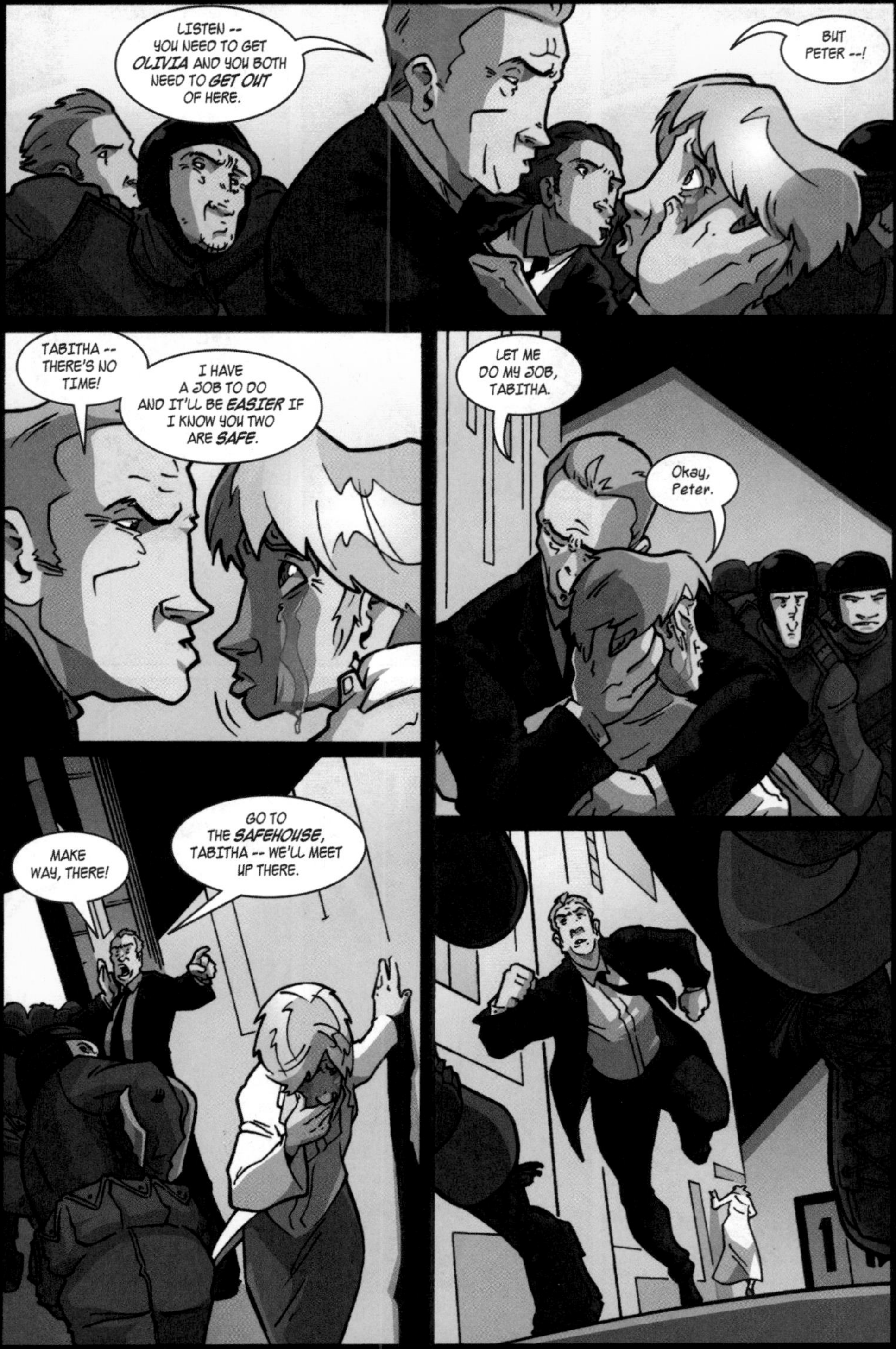
LISTEN -- YOU NEED TO GET OLIVIA AND YOU BOTH NEED TO GET OUT OF HERE.
BUT PETER --!
TABITHA -- THERE'S NO TIME!
I HAVE A JOB TO DO AND IT'LL BE EASIER IF I KNOW YOU TWO ARE SAFE.
LET ME DO MY JOB, TABITHA.
Okay, Peter.
MAKE WAY, THERE!
GO TO THE SAFEHOUSE, TABITHA -- WE'LL MEET UP THERE.

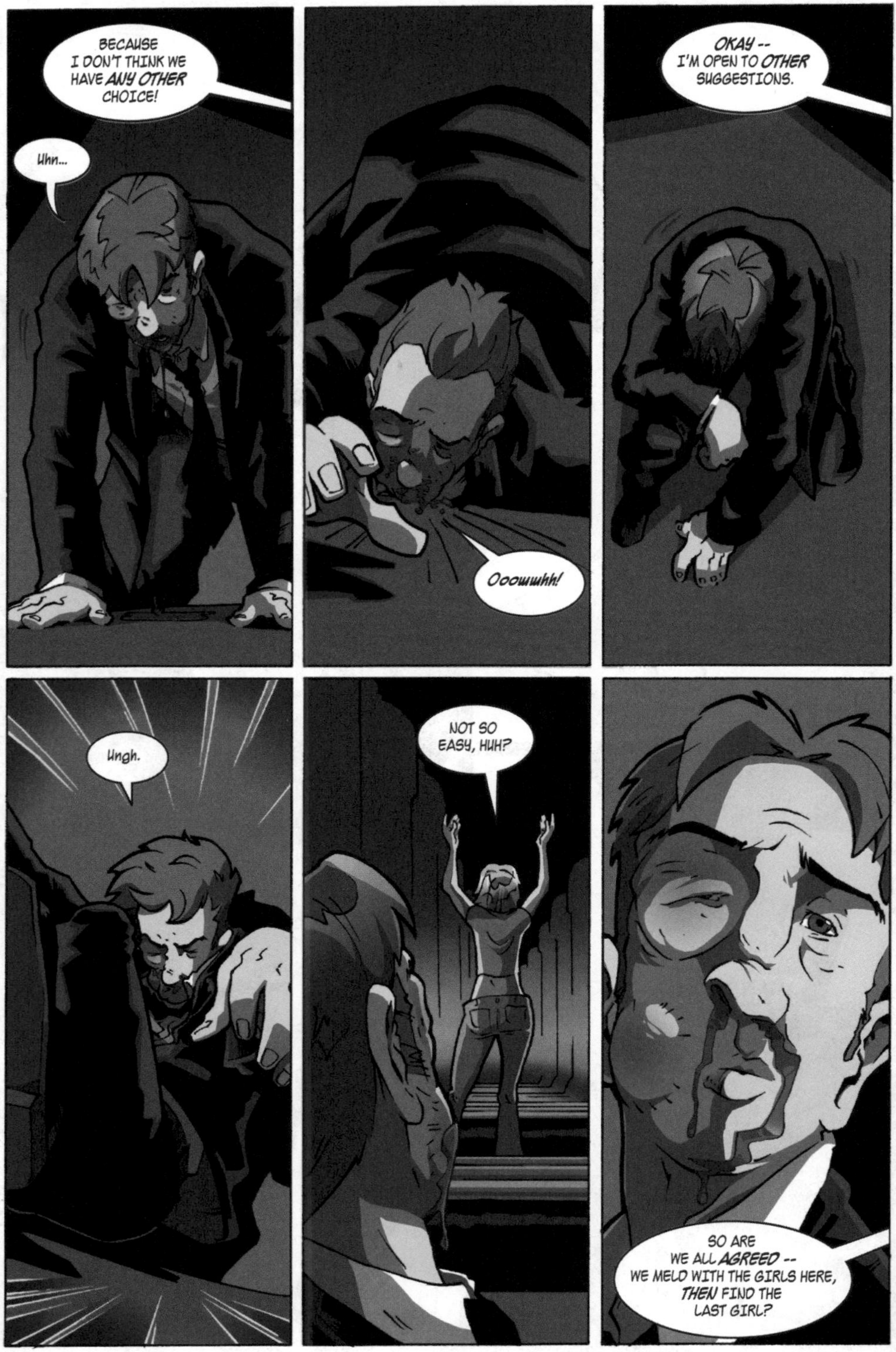
BECAUSE I DON'T THINK WE HAVE ANY OTHER CHOICE!
Uhn...
Ooowuhh!
OKAY -- I'M OPEN TO OTHER SUGGESTIONS.
Ungh.
NOT SO EASY, HUH?
SO ARE WE ALL AGREED -- WE MELD WITH THE GIRLS HERE, THEN FIND THE LAST GIRL?

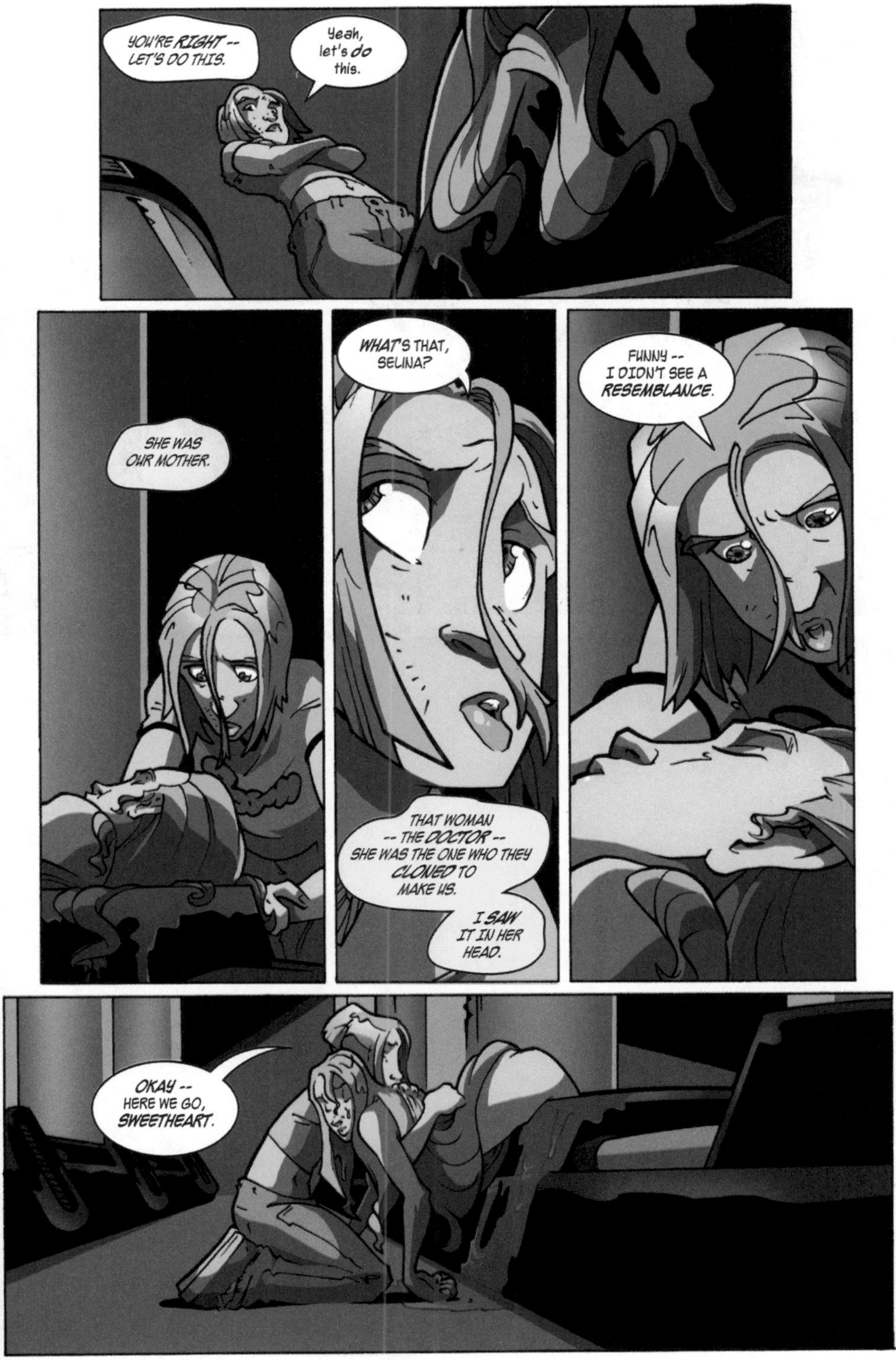
YOU'RE RIGHT -- LET'S DO THIS.
Yeah, let's do this.
SHE WAS OUR MOTHER.
WHAT'S THAT, SELINA?
THAT WOMAN -- THE DOCTOR -- SHE WAS THE ONE WHO THEY CLONED TO MAKE US.
I SAW IT IN HER HEAD.
FUNNY -- I DIDN'T SEE A RESEMBLANCE.
OKAY -- HERE WE GO, SWEETHEART.

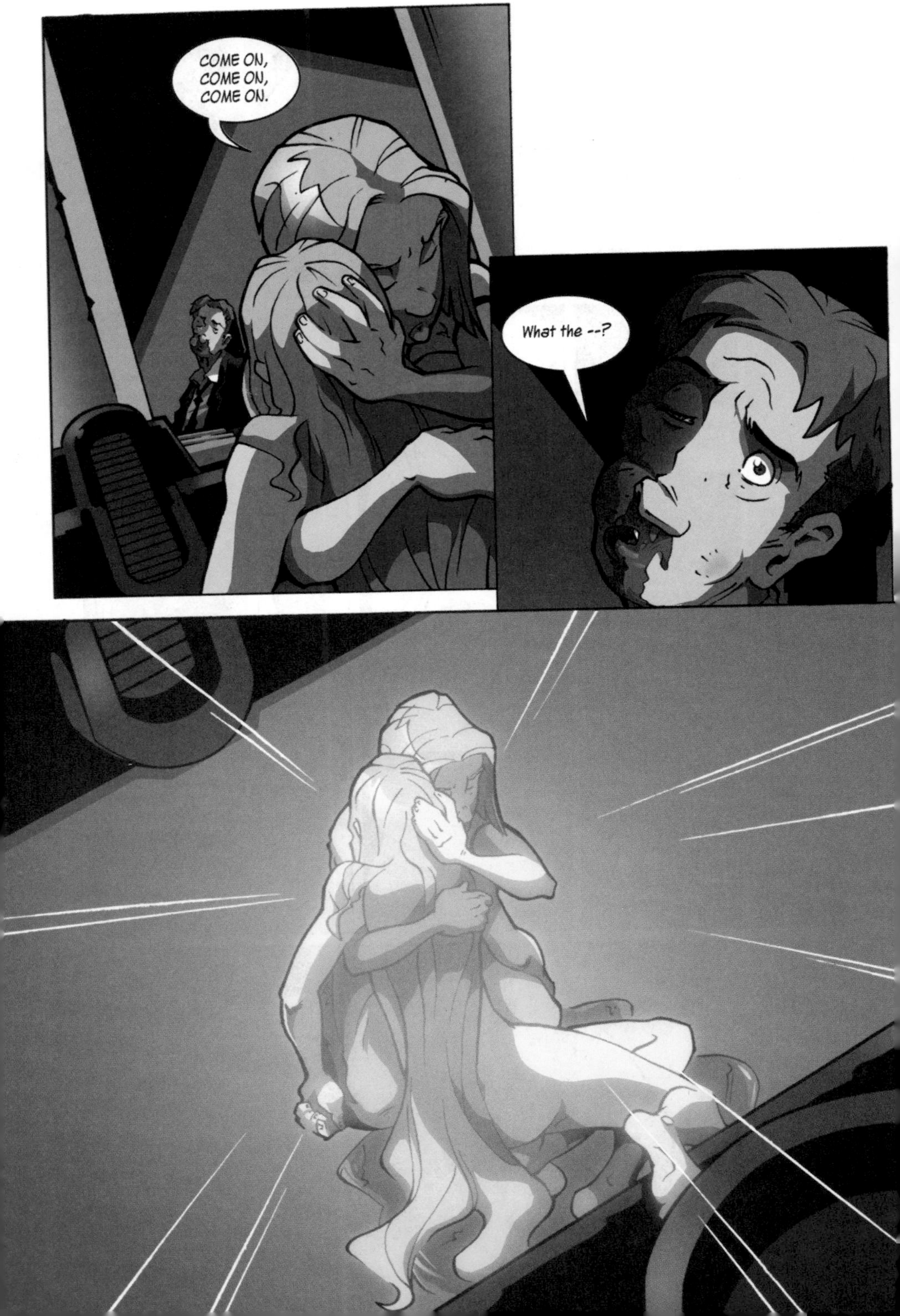
COME ON,
COME ON,
COME ON.
What the --?

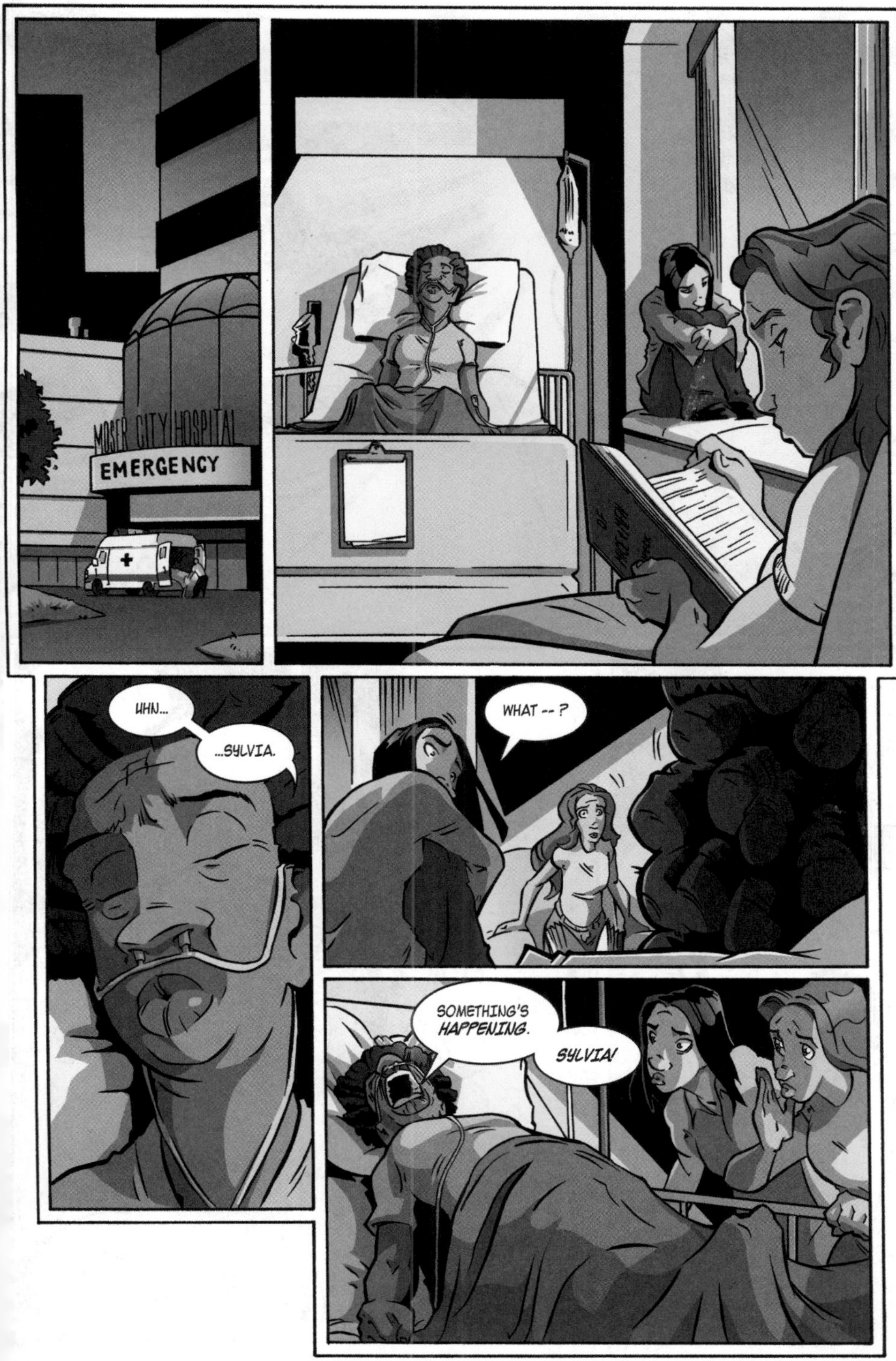
MOSER CITY HOSPITAL
EMERGENCY
UHN...
...SYLVIA.
WHAT -- ?
SOMETHING'S *HAPPENING*.
SYLVIA!

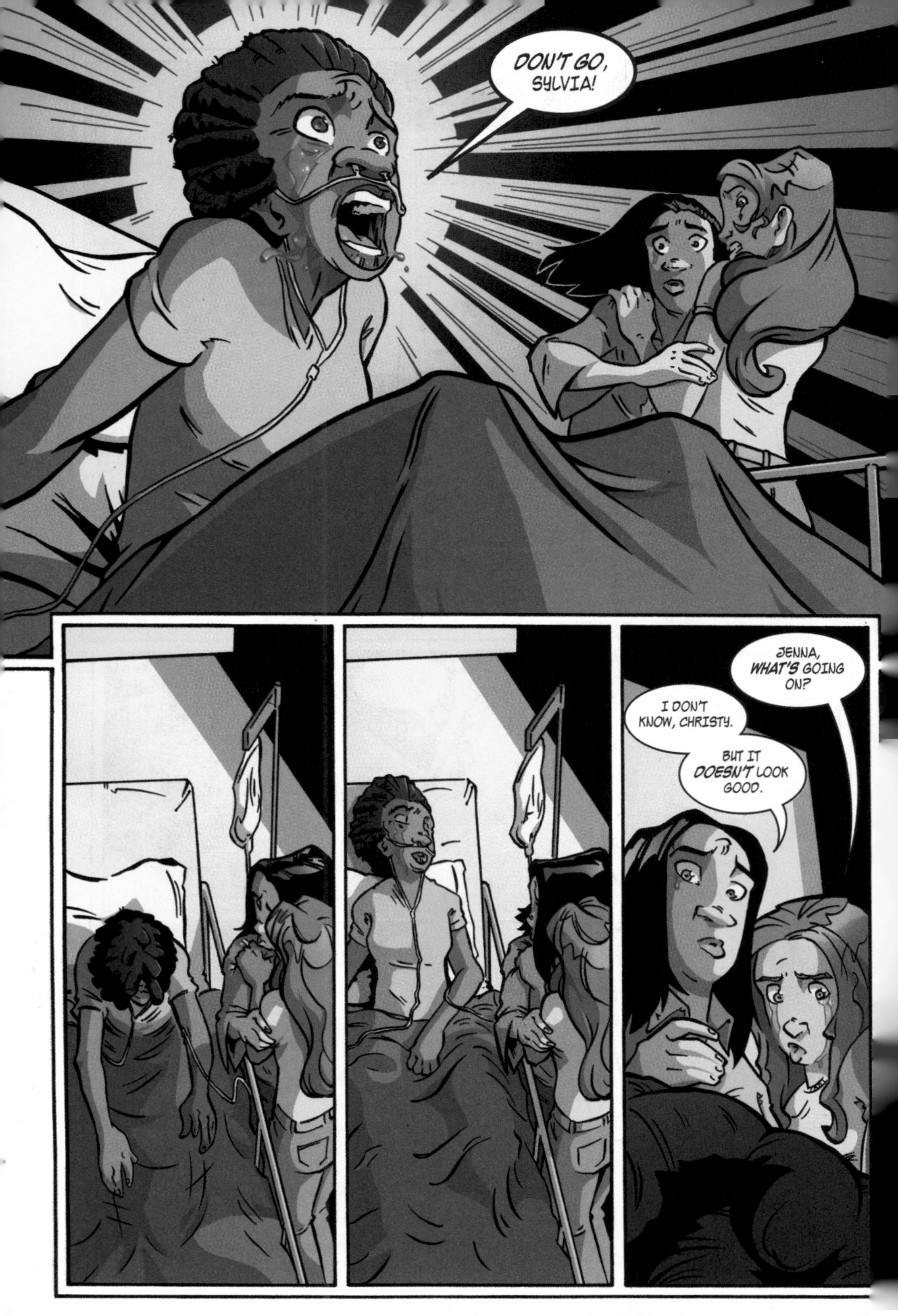
DON'T GO, SYLVIA!
JENNA, WHAT'S GOING ON?
I DON'T KNOW, CHRISTY.
BUT IT DOESN'T LOOK GOOD.

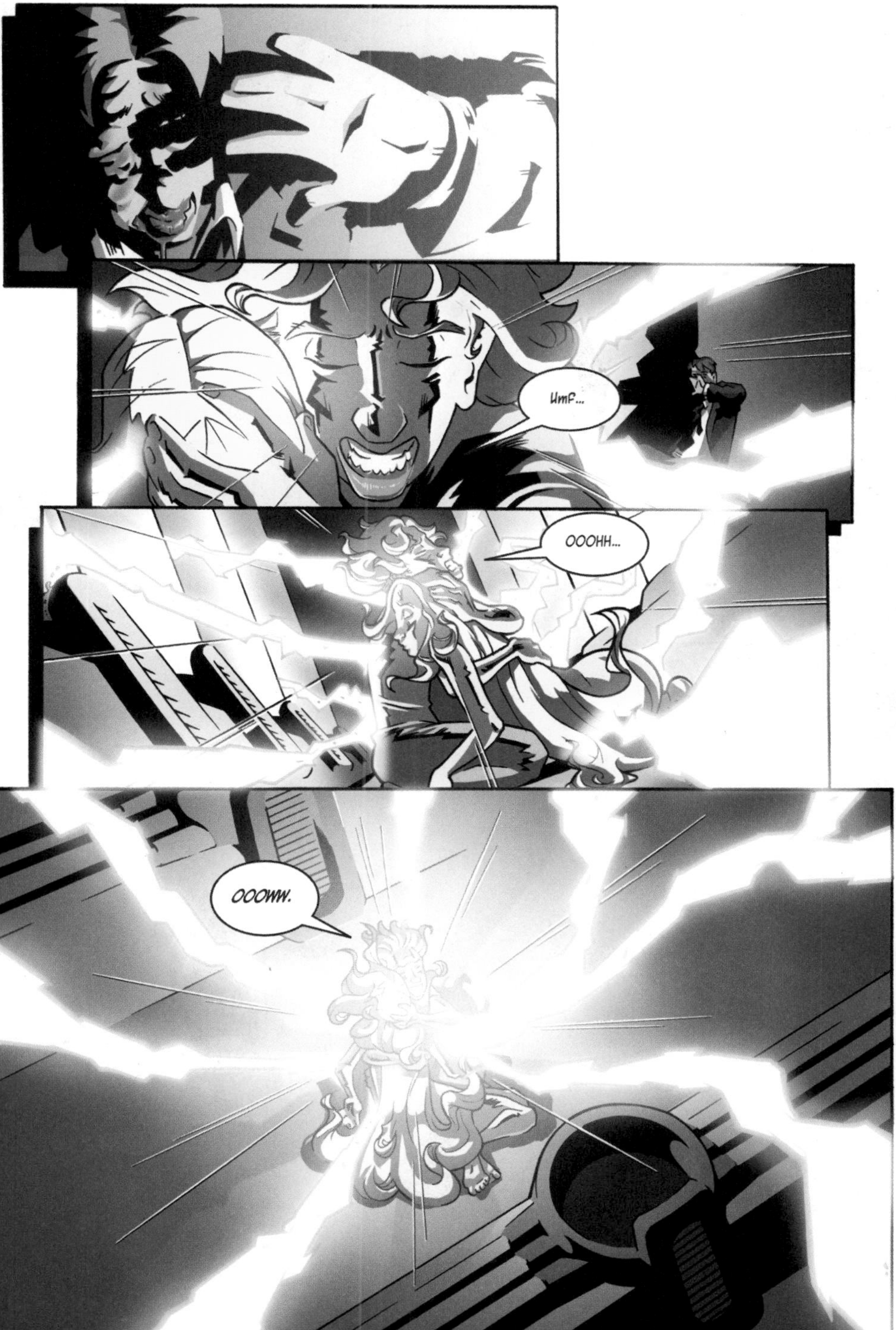
UMF...
OOOHH...
OOOWW.

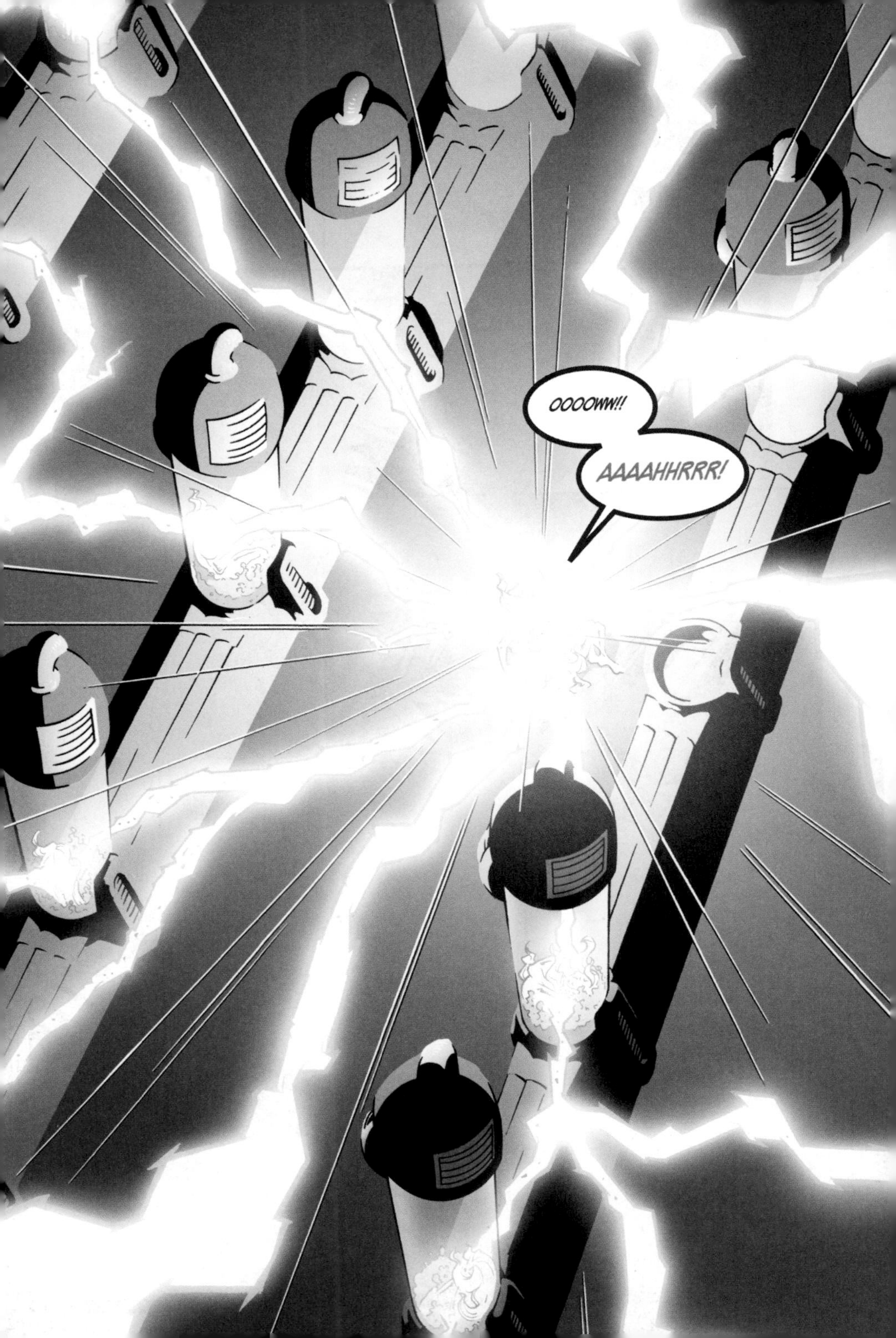
OOOOWW!!
AAAAHHRRR!

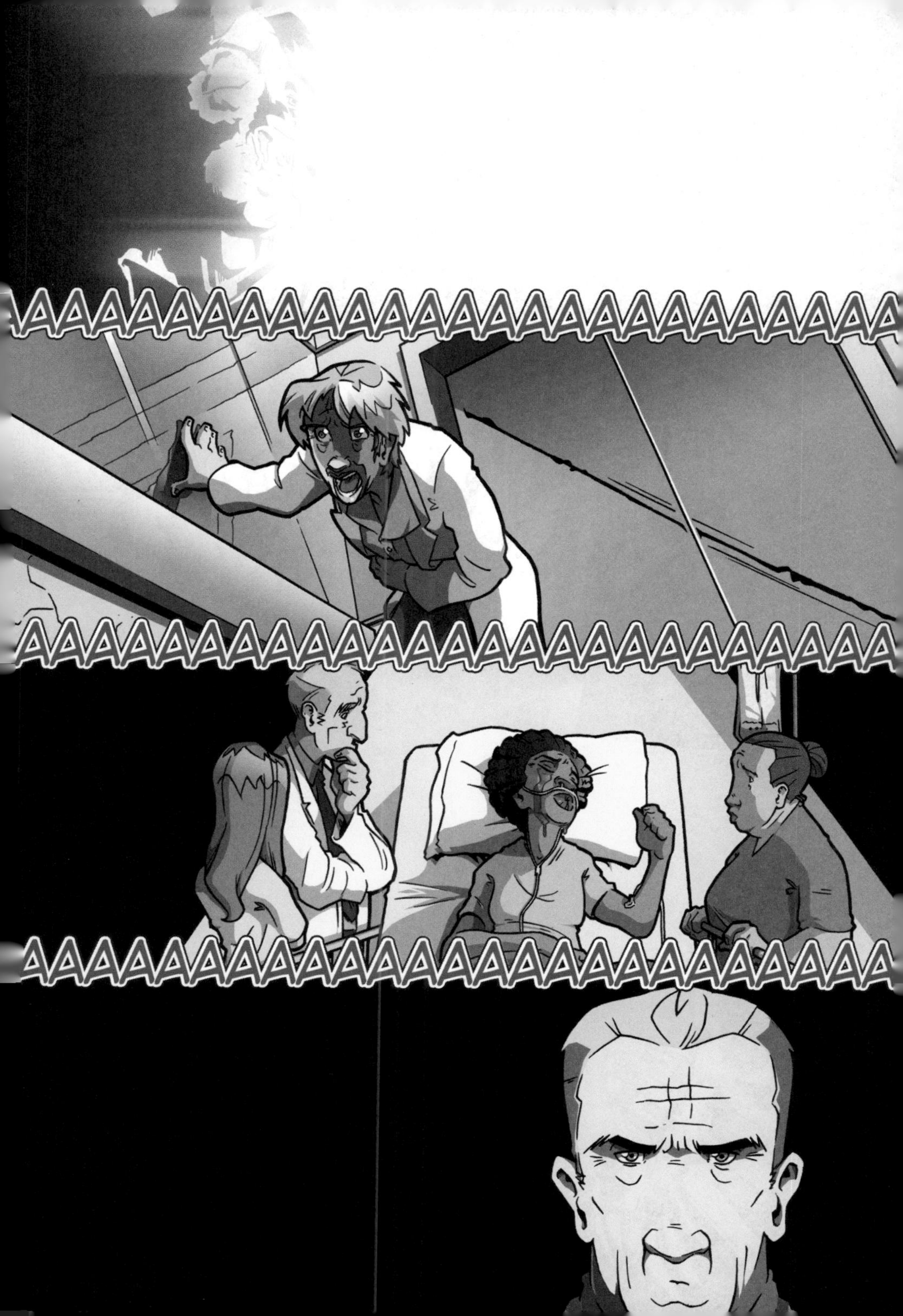
AAAAAAAAAAAAAAAAAAAAAAAAA
AAAAAAAAAAAAAAAAAAAAAAAAA
AAAAAAAAAAAAAAAAAAAAAAAAA
AAAAAAAAAAAAAAAAAAAAAAAAA

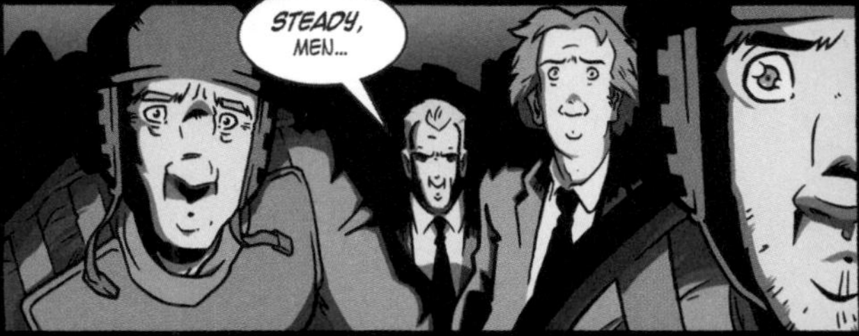
STEADY, MEN...

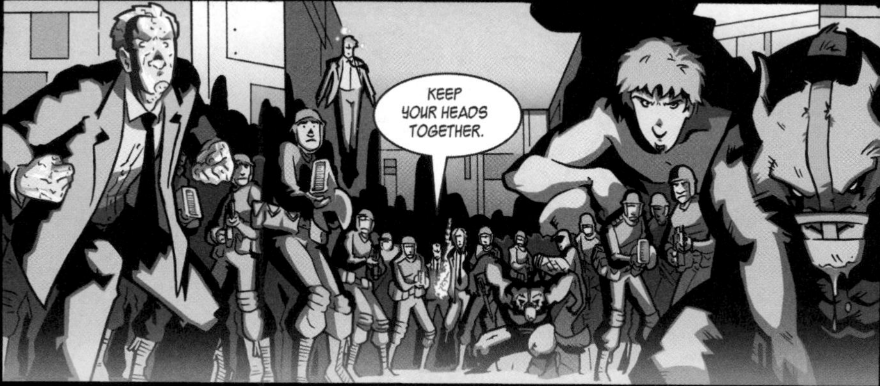
KEEP YOUR HEADS TOGETHER.

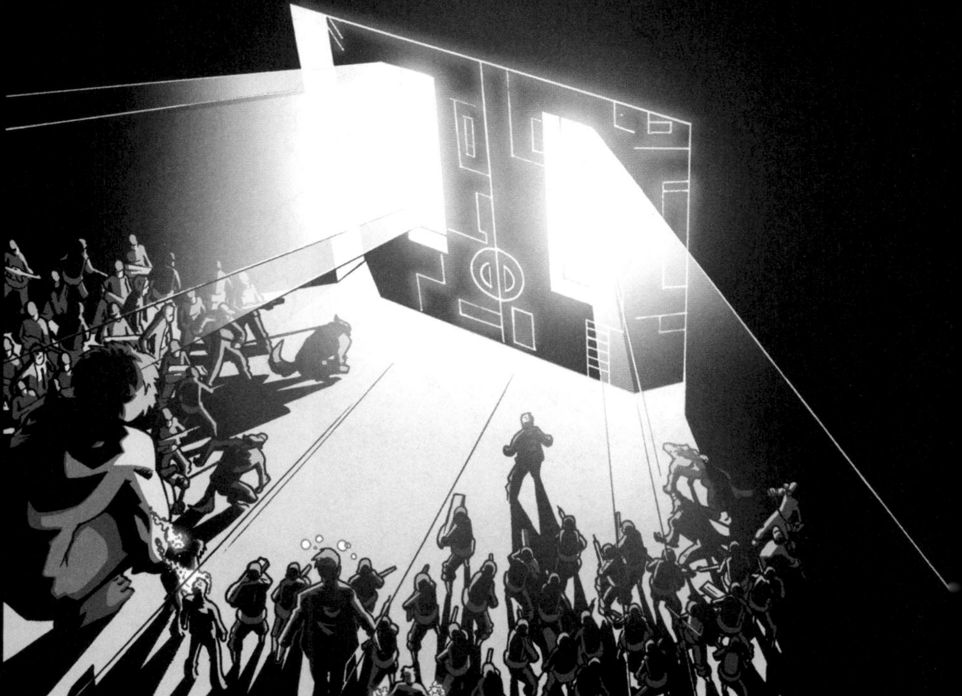

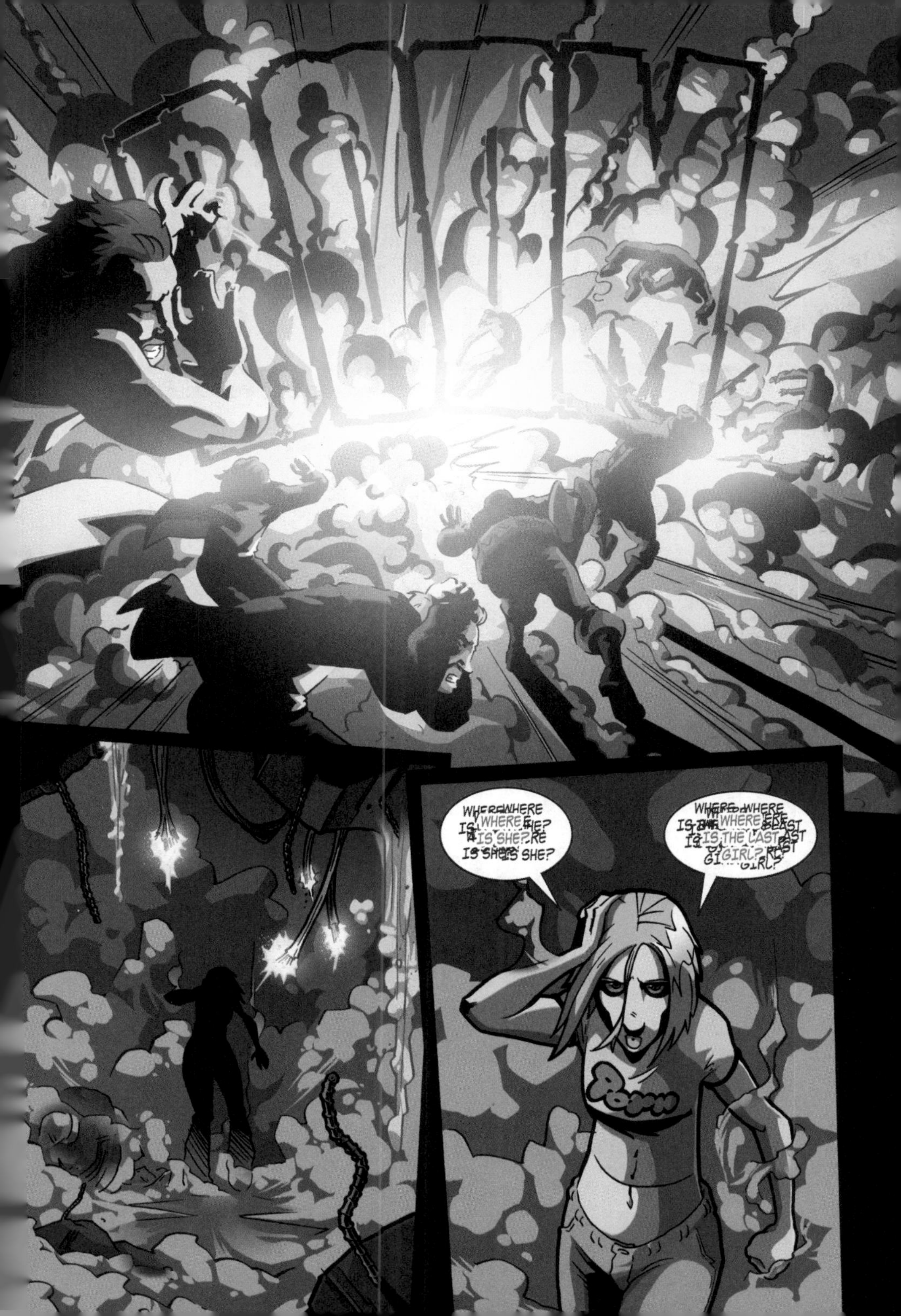
WHERE IS SHE?
WHERE IS THE LAST GIRL?

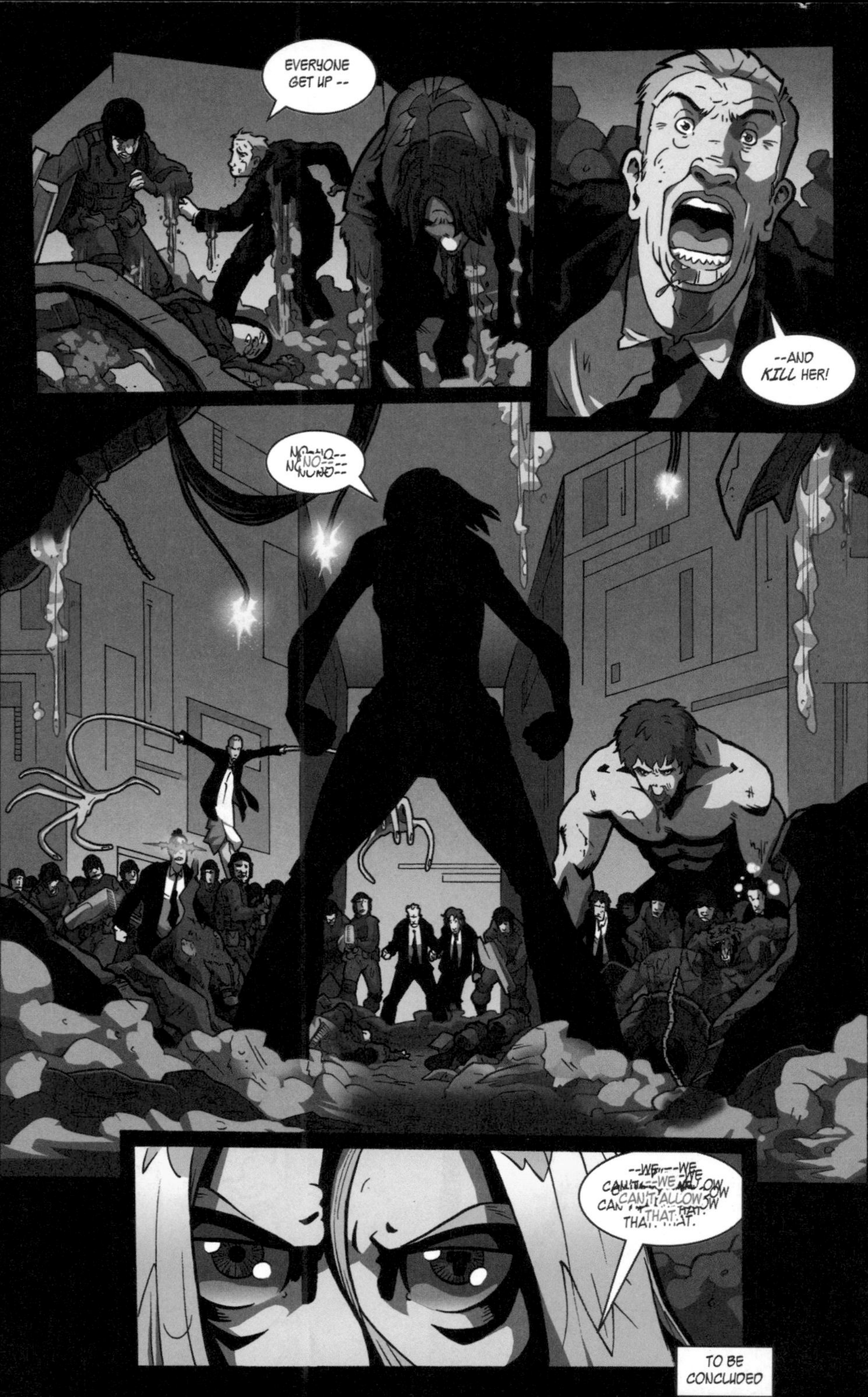
EVERYONE GET UP --
--AND KILL HER!
NO-- NO-- NO--
--WE CAN'T ALLOW THAT.
TO BE CONCLUDED

CHAPTER SEVEN

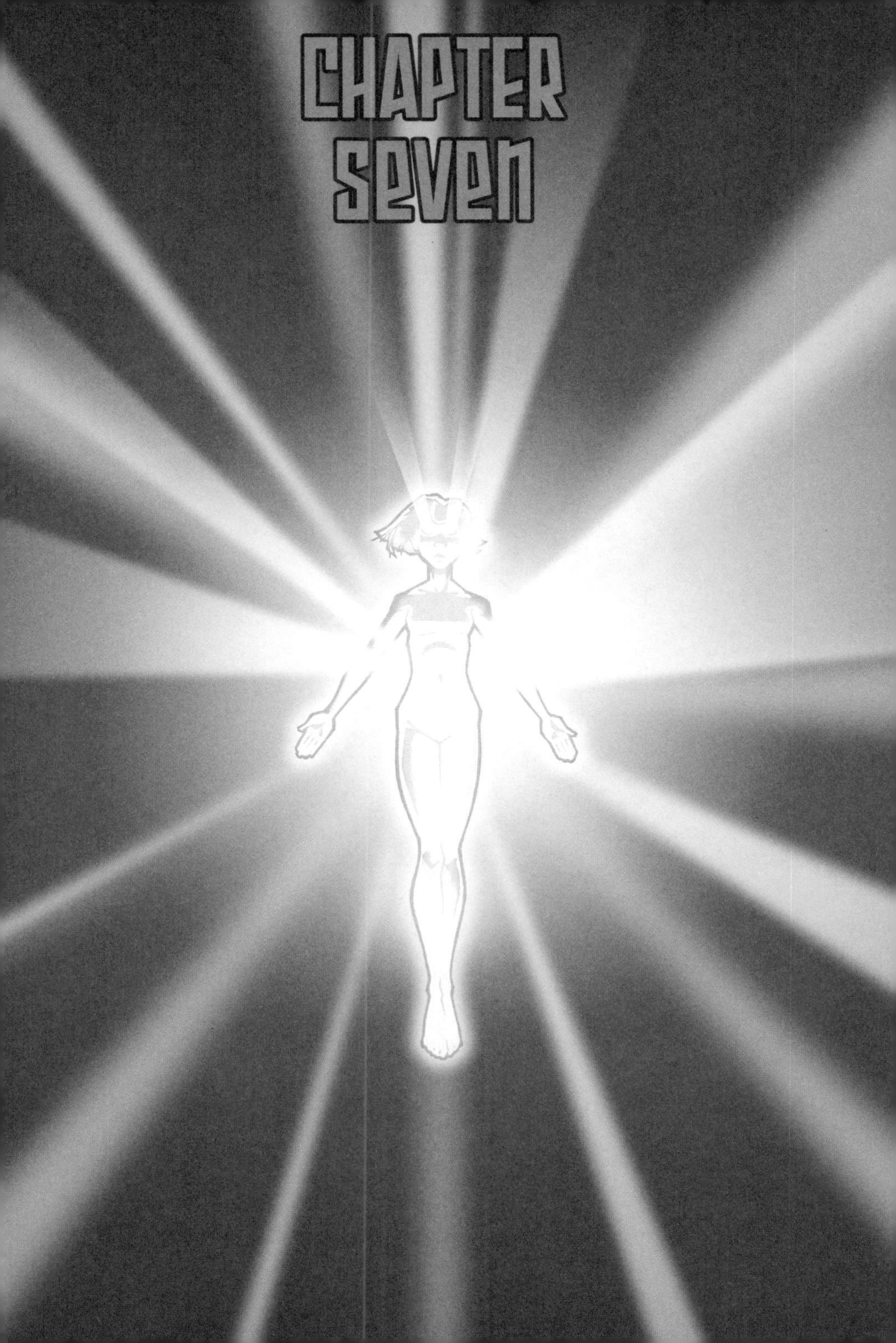

"Are you ready?"

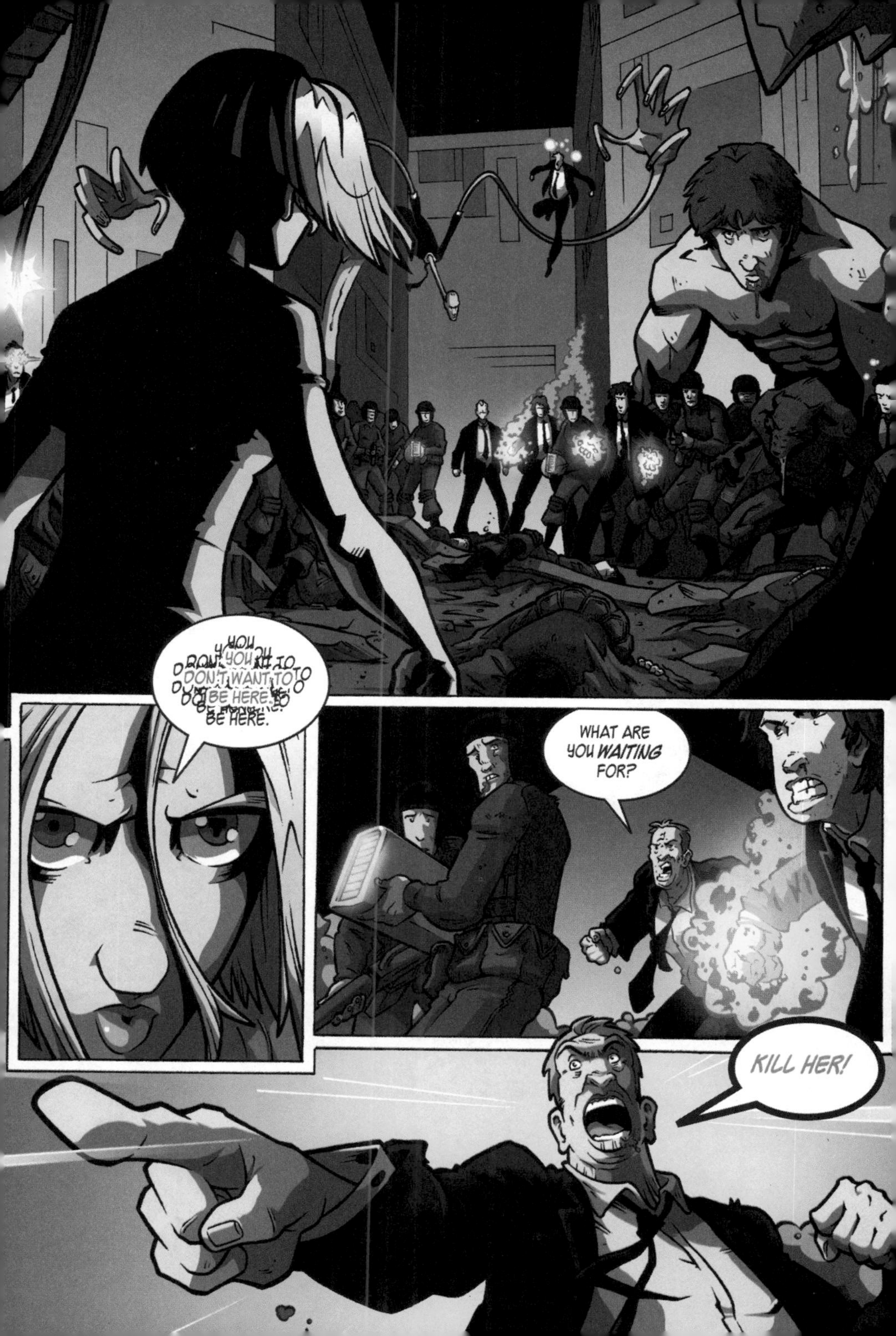
YOU DON'T WANT TO BE HERE.
WHAT ARE YOU WAITING FOR?
KILL HER!

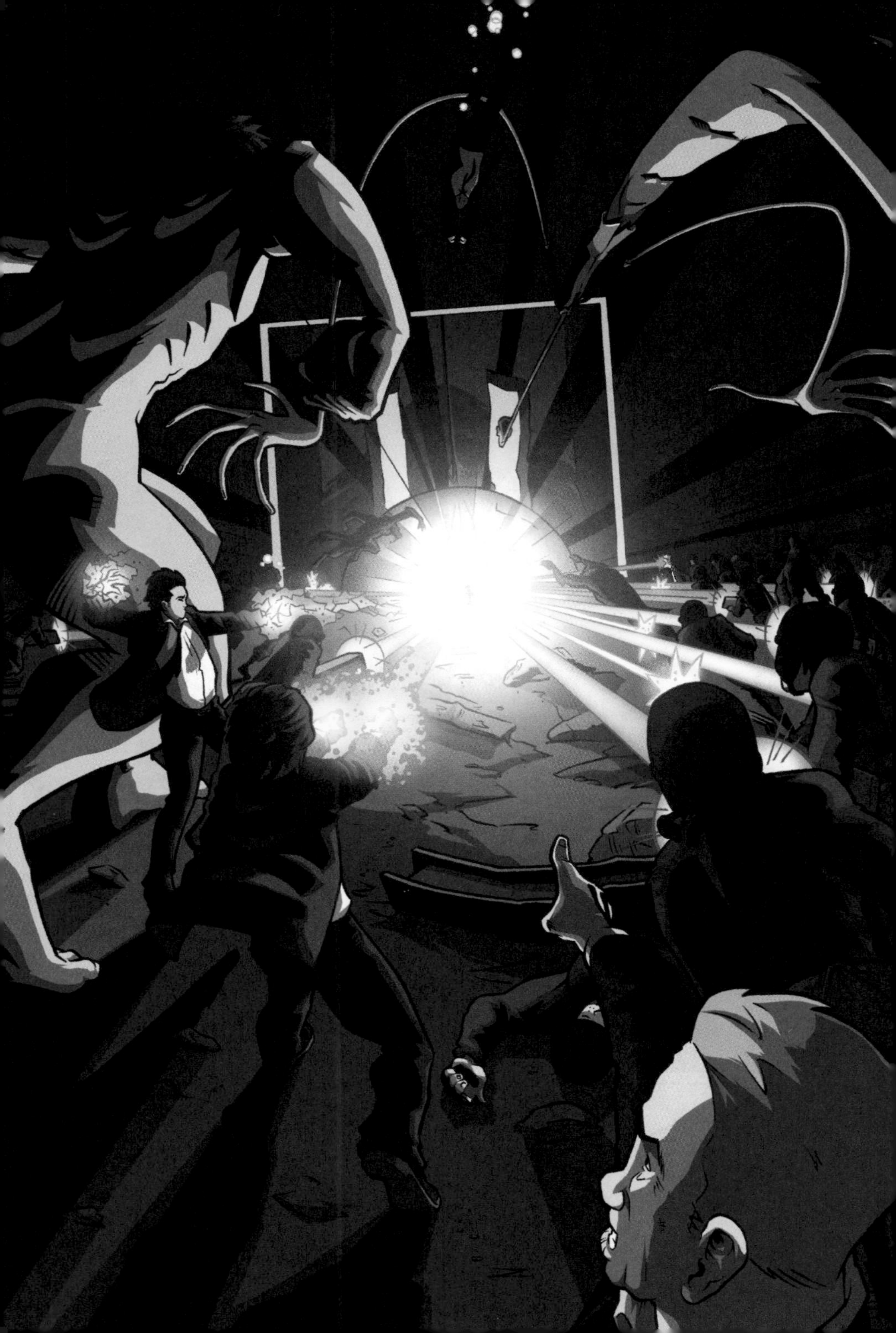

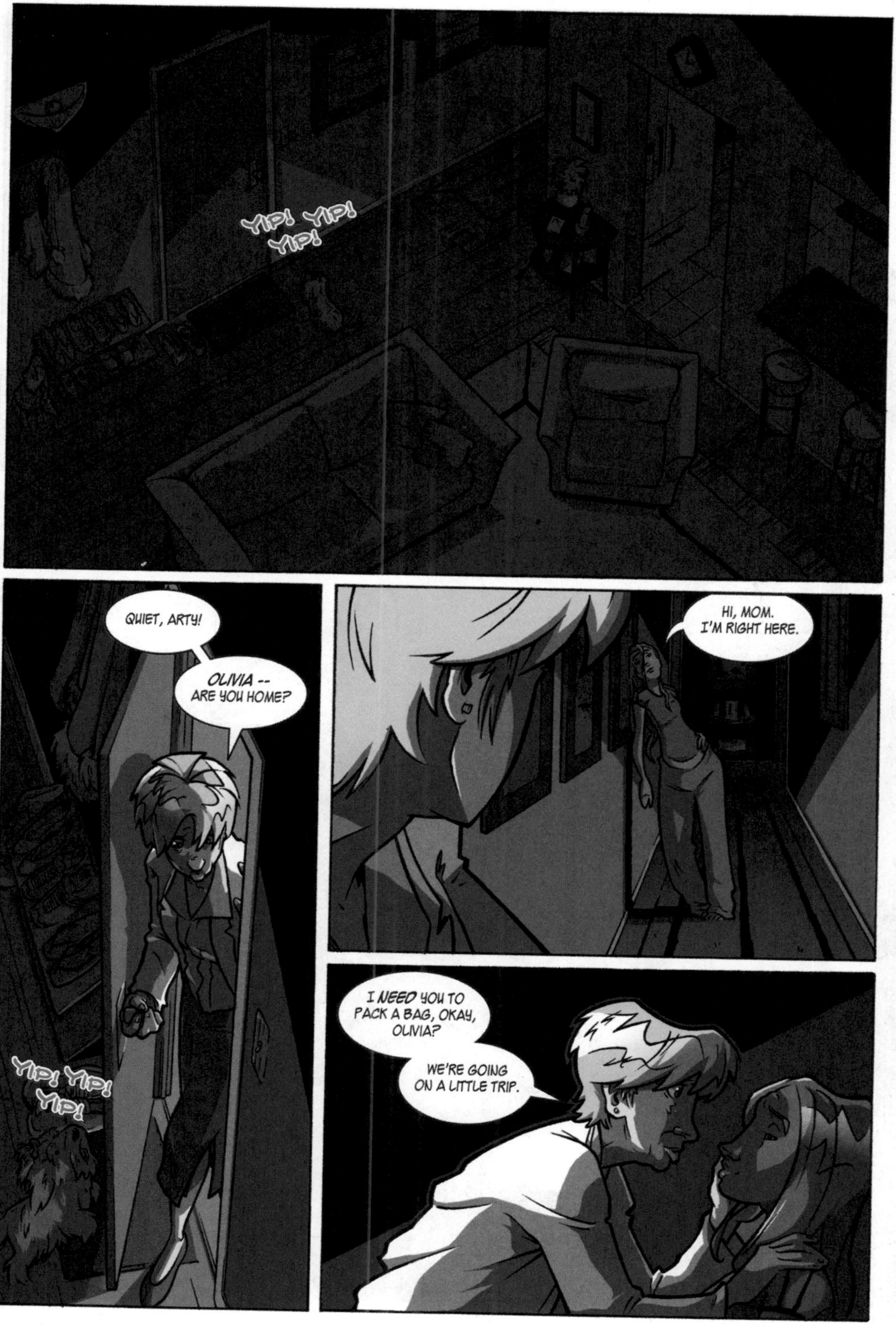
YIP! YIP!
YIP!
QUIET, ARTY!
OLIVIA --
ARE YOU HOME?
YIP! YIP!
YIP!
HI, MOM.
I'M RIGHT HERE.
I NEED YOU TO
PACK A BAG, OKAY,
OLIVIA?
WE'RE GOING
ON A LITTLE TRIP.

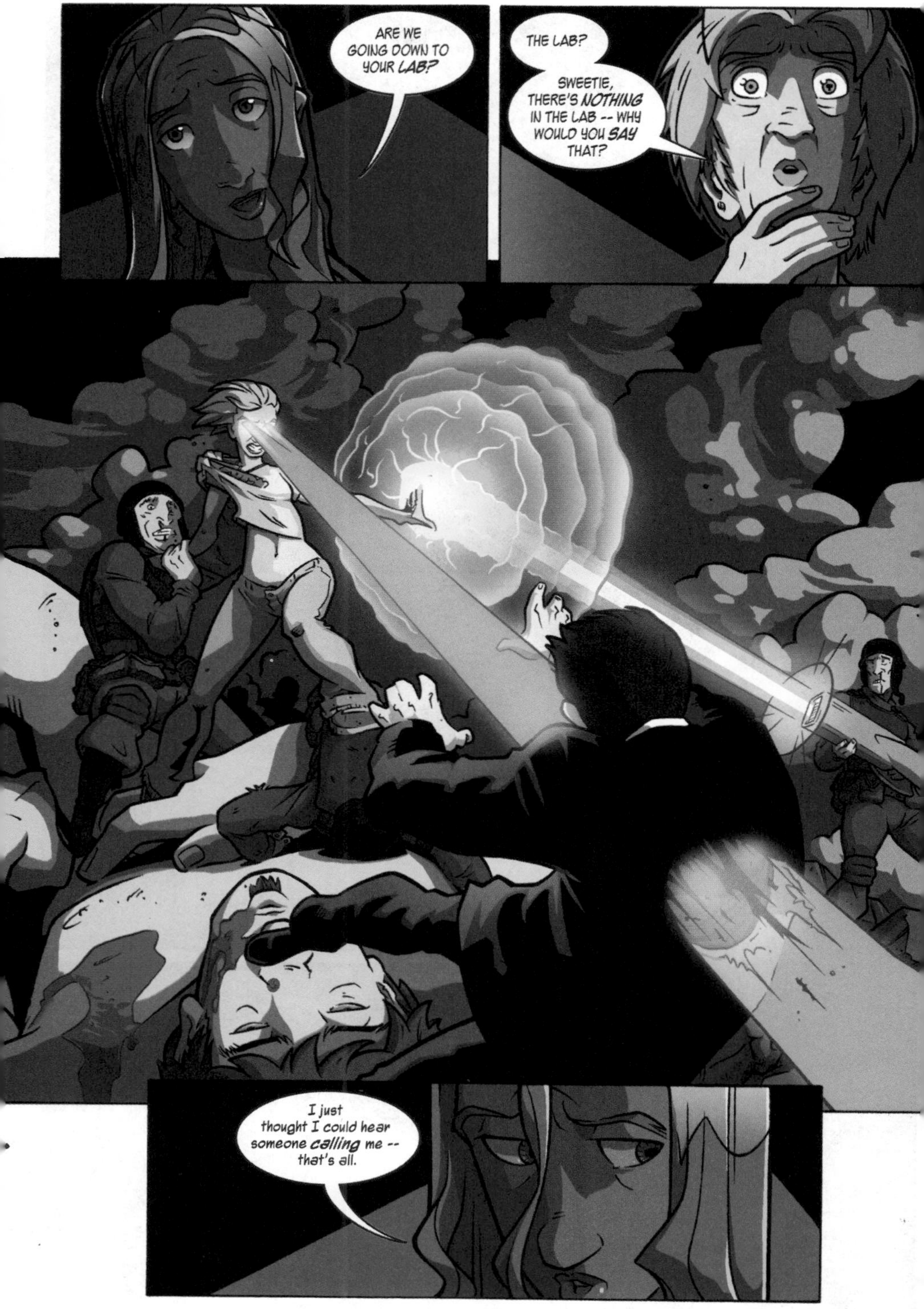
ARE WE GOING DOWN TO YOUR LAB?
THE LAB?
SWEETIE, THERE'S NOTHING IN THE LAB -- WHY WOULD YOU SAY THAT?
I just thought I could hear someone calling me -- that's all.

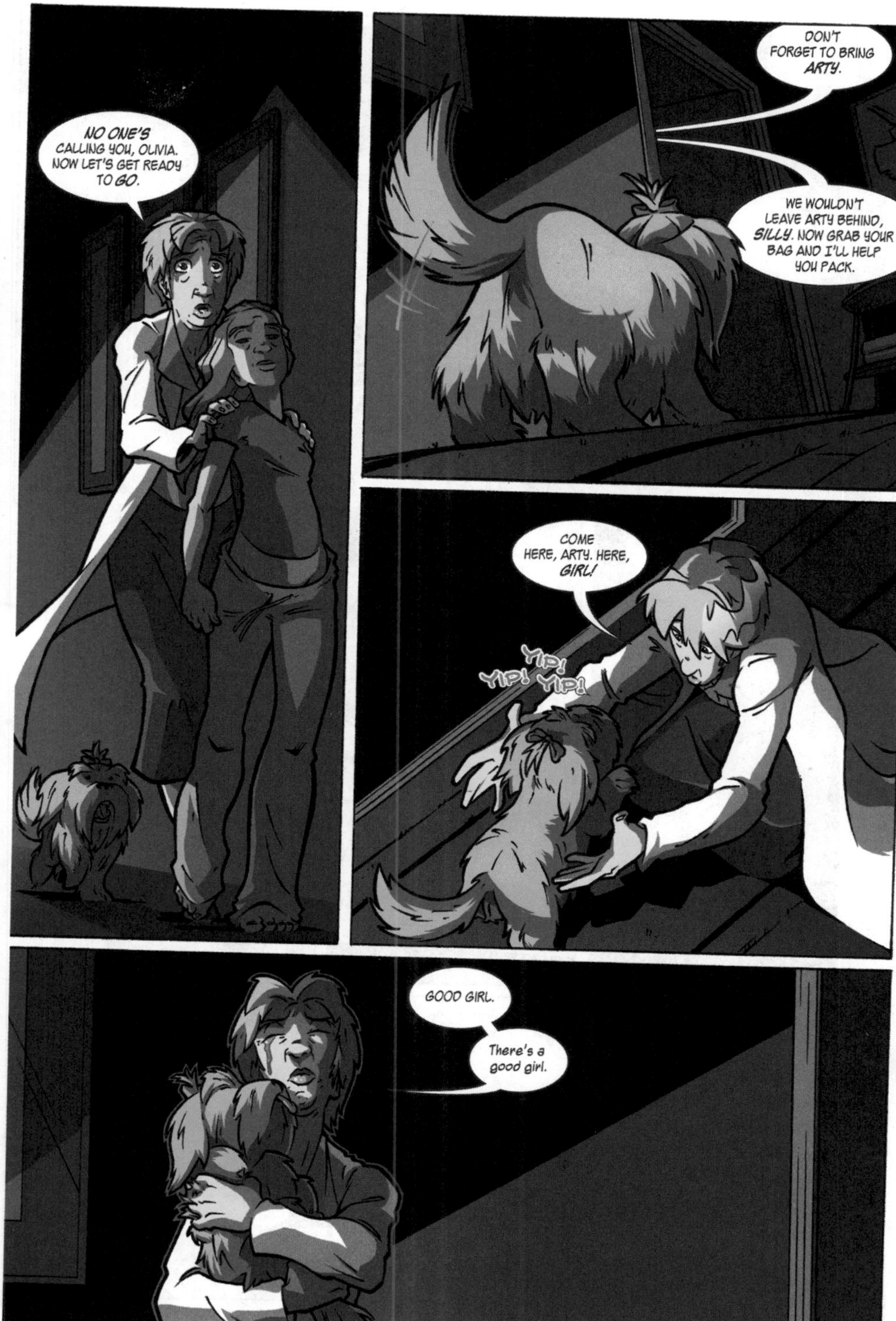
NO ONE'S CALLING YOU, OLIVIA. NOW LET'S GET READY TO GO.
DON'T FORGET TO BRING ARTY.
WE WOULDN'T LEAVE ARTY BEHIND, SILLY. NOW GRAB YOUR BAG AND I'LL HELP YOU PACK.
COME HERE, ARTY. HERE, GIRL!
YIP! YIP! YIP!
GOOD GIRL.
There's a good girl.

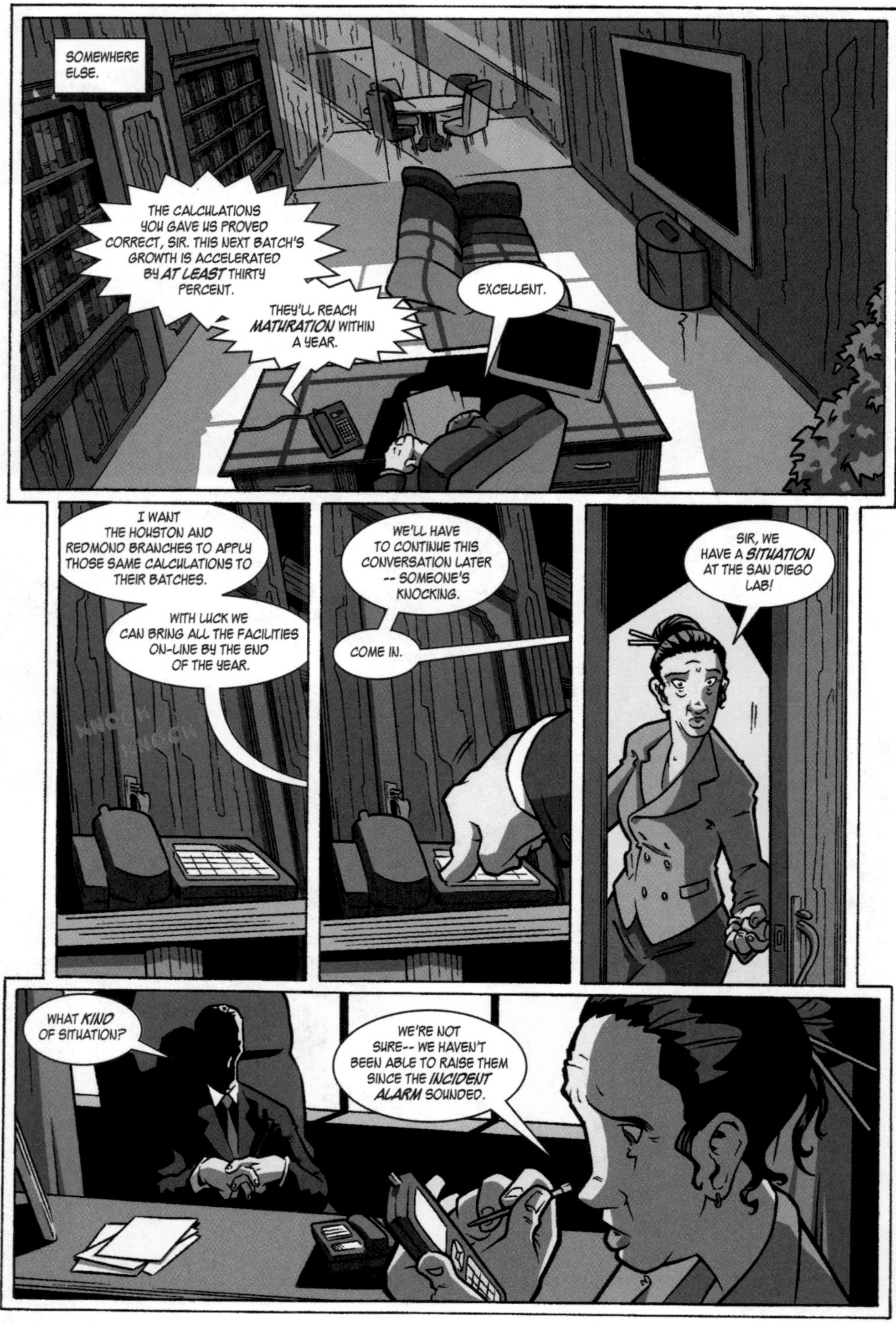
SOMEWHERE ELSE.
THE CALCULATIONS YOU GAVE US PROVED CORRECT, SIR. THIS NEXT BATCH'S GROWTH IS ACCELERATED BY *AT LEAST* THIRTY PERCENT.
THEY'LL REACH *MATURATION* WITHIN A YEAR.
EXCELLENT.
I WANT THE HOUSTON AND REDMOND BRANCHES TO APPLY THOSE SAME CALCULATIONS TO THEIR BATCHES.
WITH LUCK WE CAN BRING ALL THE FACILITIES ON-LINE BY THE END OF THE YEAR.
KNOCK KNOCK
WE'LL HAVE TO CONTINUE THIS CONVERSATION LATER -- SOMEONE'S KNOCKING.
COME IN.
SIR, WE HAVE A *SITUATION* AT THE SAN DIEGO LAB!
WHAT *KIND* OF SITUATION?
WE'RE NOT SURE-- WE HAVEN'T BEEN ABLE TO RAISE THEM SINCE THE *INCIDENT ALARM* SOUNDED.

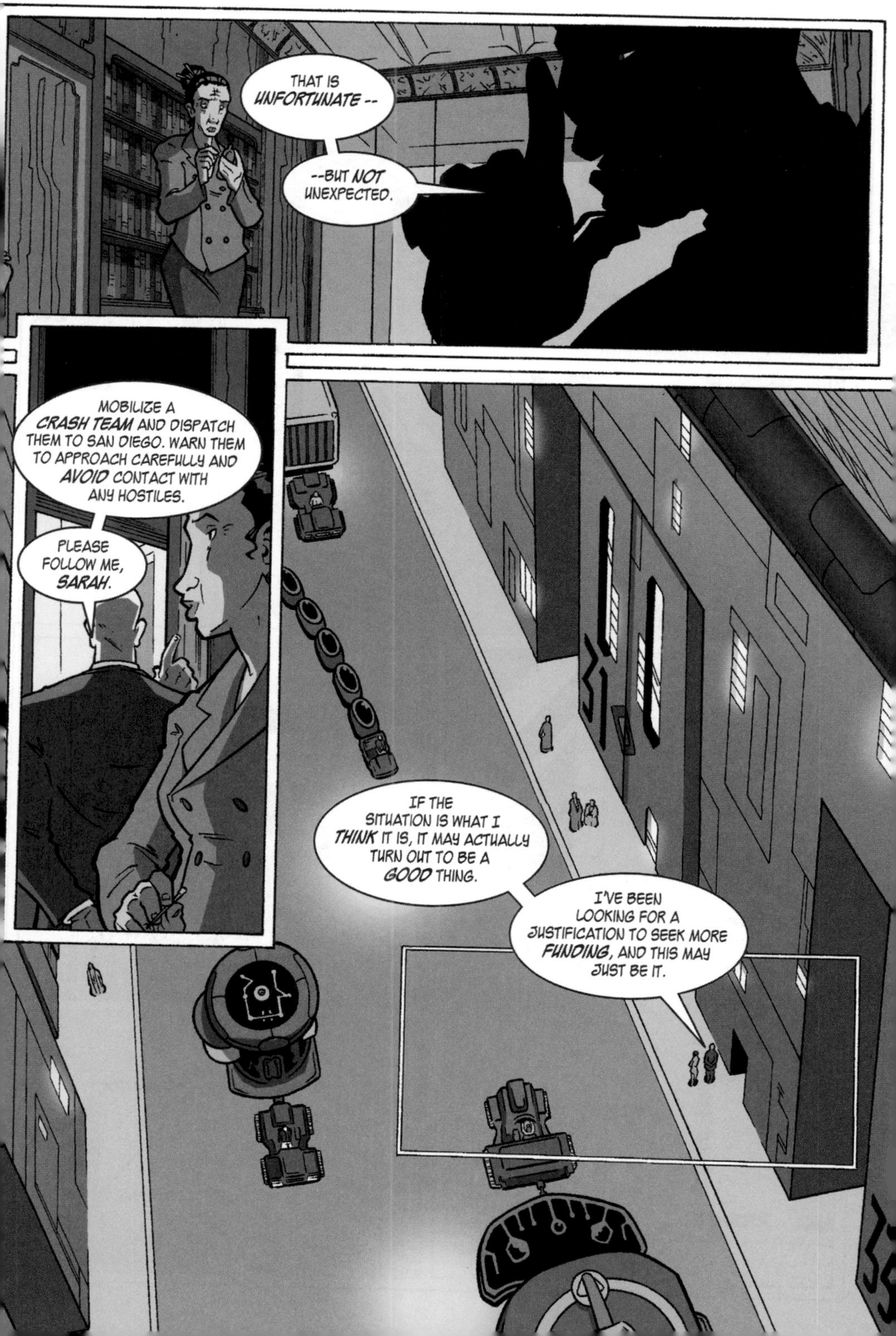
THAT IS UNFORTUNATE --
--BUT NOT UNEXPECTED.
MOBILIZE A CRASH TEAM AND DISPATCH THEM TO SAN DIEGO. WARN THEM TO APPROACH CAREFULLY AND AVOID CONTACT WITH ANY HOSTILES.
PLEASE FOLLOW ME, SARAH.
IF THE SITUATION IS WHAT I THINK IT IS, IT MAY ACTUALLY TURN OUT TO BE A GOOD THING.
I'VE BEEN LOOKING FOR A JUSTIFICATION TO SEEK MORE FUNDING, AND THIS MAY JUST BE IT.

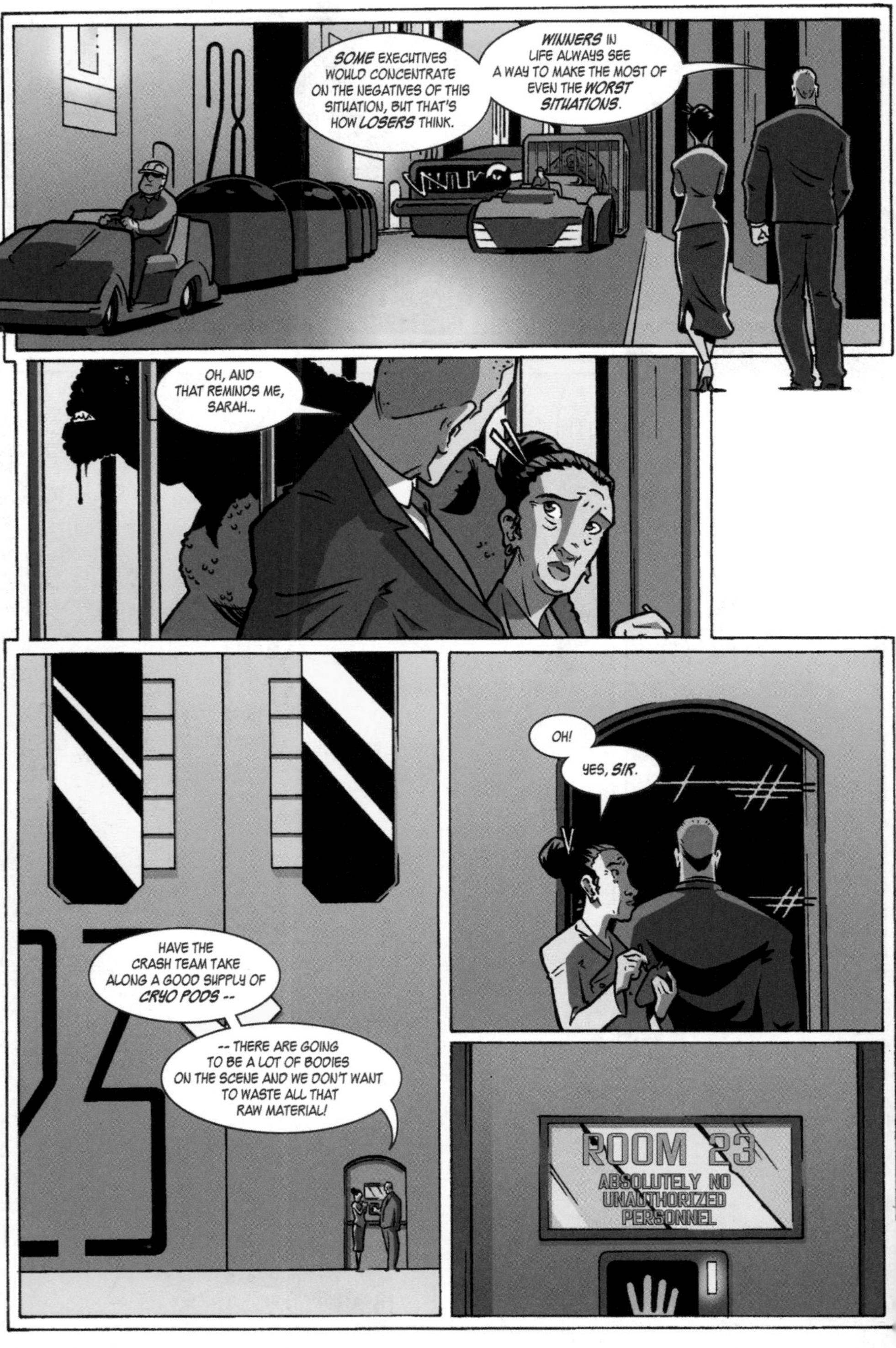

SOME EXECUTIVES WOULD CONCENTRATE ON THE NEGATIVES OF THIS SITUATION, BUT THAT'S HOW LOSERS THINK.
WINNERS IN LIFE ALWAYS SEE A WAY TO MAKE THE MOST OF EVEN THE WORST SITUATIONS.
OH, AND THAT REMINDS ME, SARAH...
HAVE THE CRASH TEAM TAKE ALONG A GOOD SUPPLY OF CRYO PODS --
-- THERE ARE GOING TO BE A LOT OF BODIES ON THE SCENE AND WE DON'T WANT TO WASTE ALL THAT RAW MATERIAL!
OH!
YES, SIR.
ROOM 23
ABSOLUTELY NO UNAUTHORIZED PERSONNEL

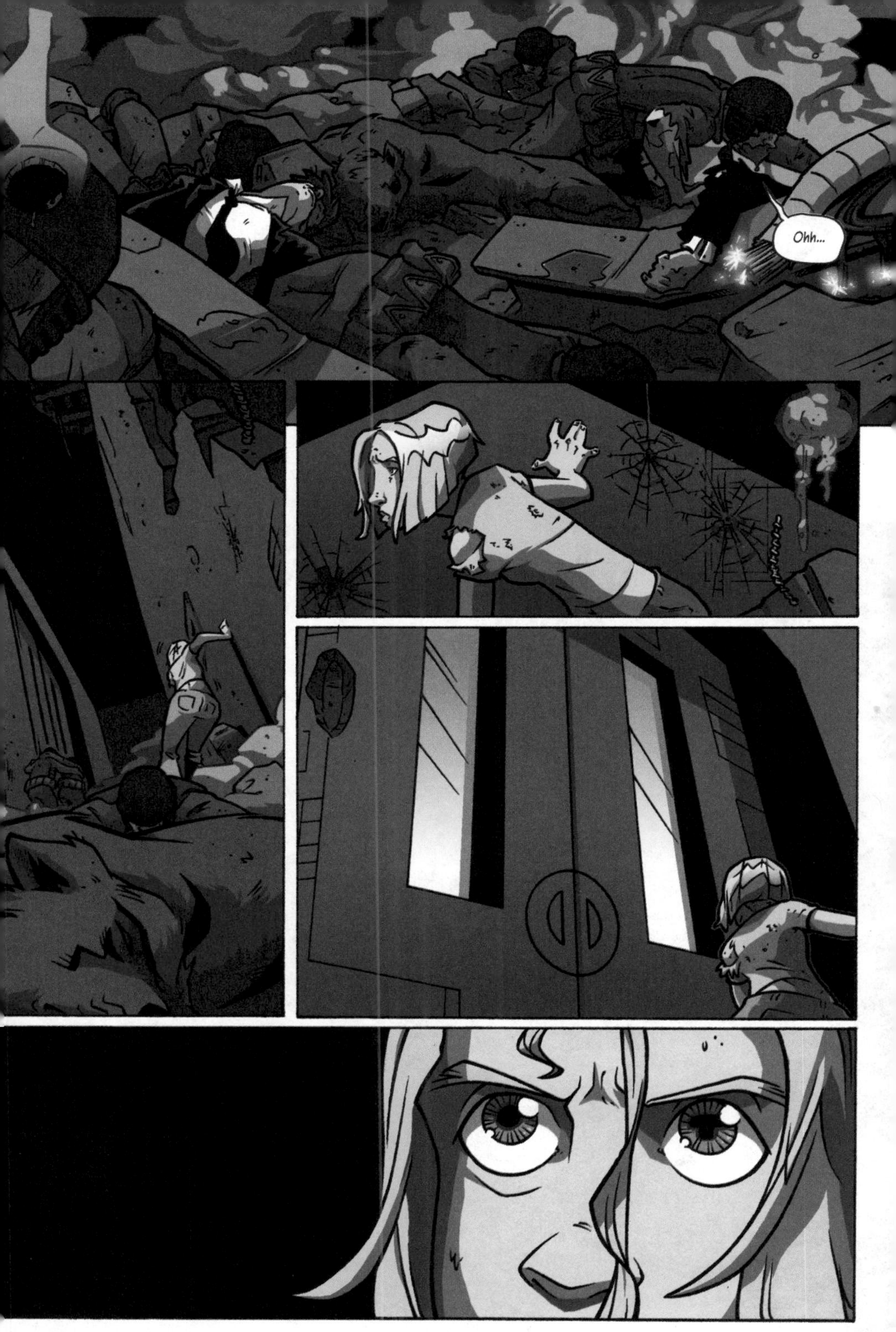
Ohh...

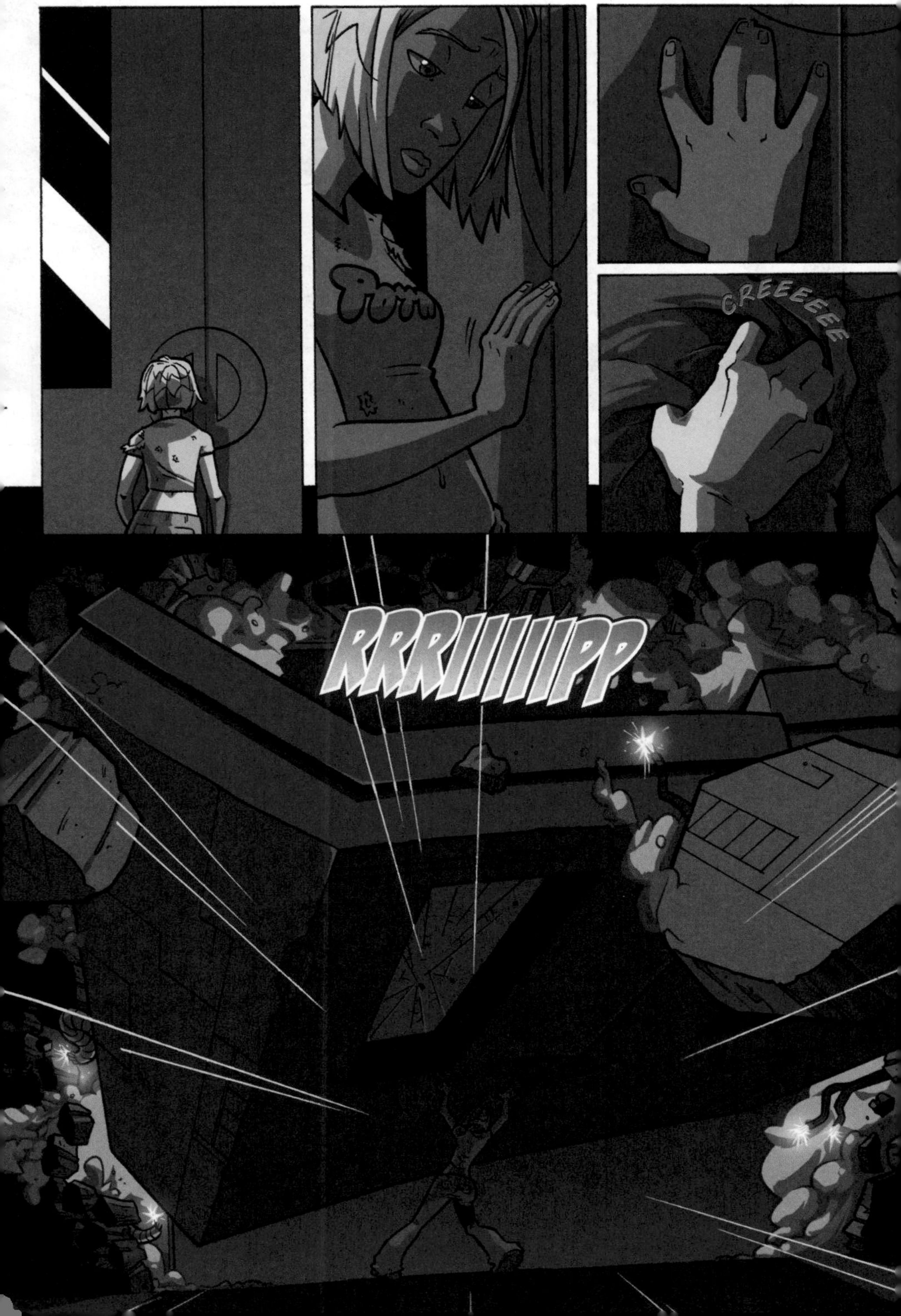
CREEEEEEE
RRRIIIIIIPP

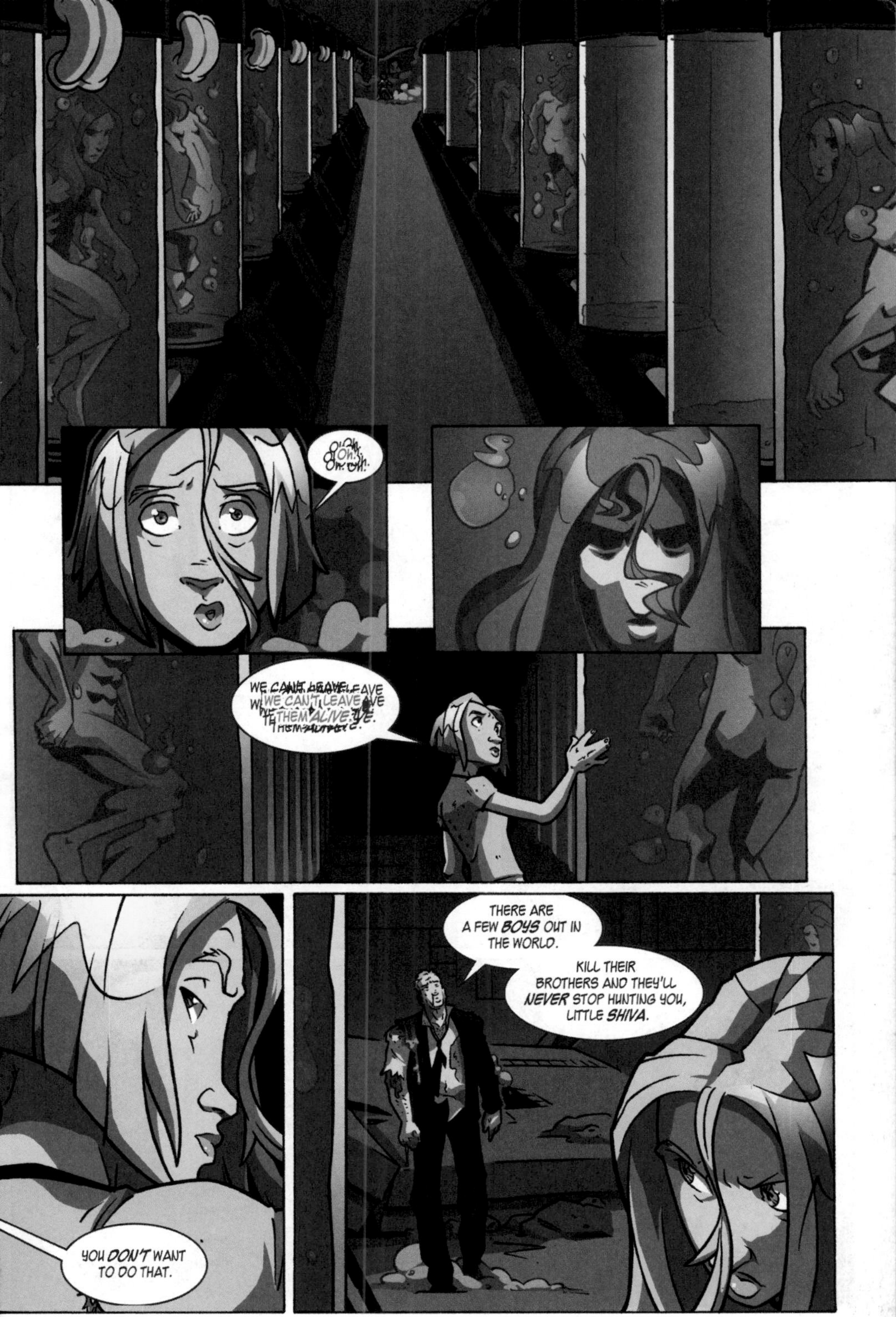
Oh.
WE CAN'T LEAVE THEM ALIVE.
THERE ARE A FEW BOYS OUT IN THE WORLD.
KILL THEIR BROTHERS AND THEY'LL NEVER STOP HUNTING YOU, LITTLE SHIVA.
YOU DON'T WANT TO DO THAT.

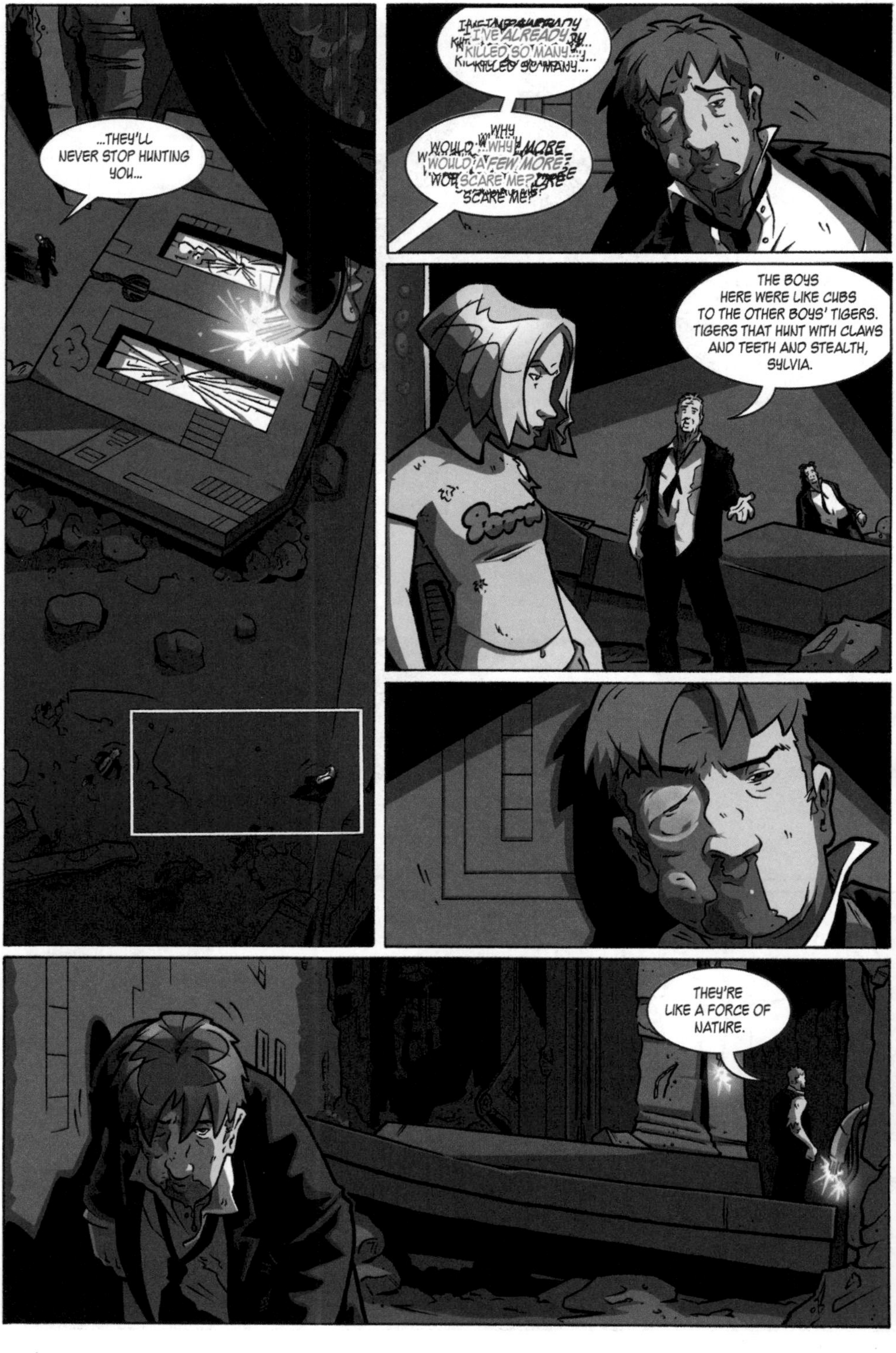
...THEY'LL NEVER STOP HUNTING YOU...
I'VE ALREADY KILLED SO MANY...
WHY WOULD A FEW MORE SCARE ME?
THE BOYS HERE WERE LIKE CUBS TO THE OTHER BOYS' TIGERS. TIGERS THAT HUNT WITH CLAWS AND TEETH AND STEALTH, SYLVIA.
THEY'RE LIKE A FORCE OF NATURE.

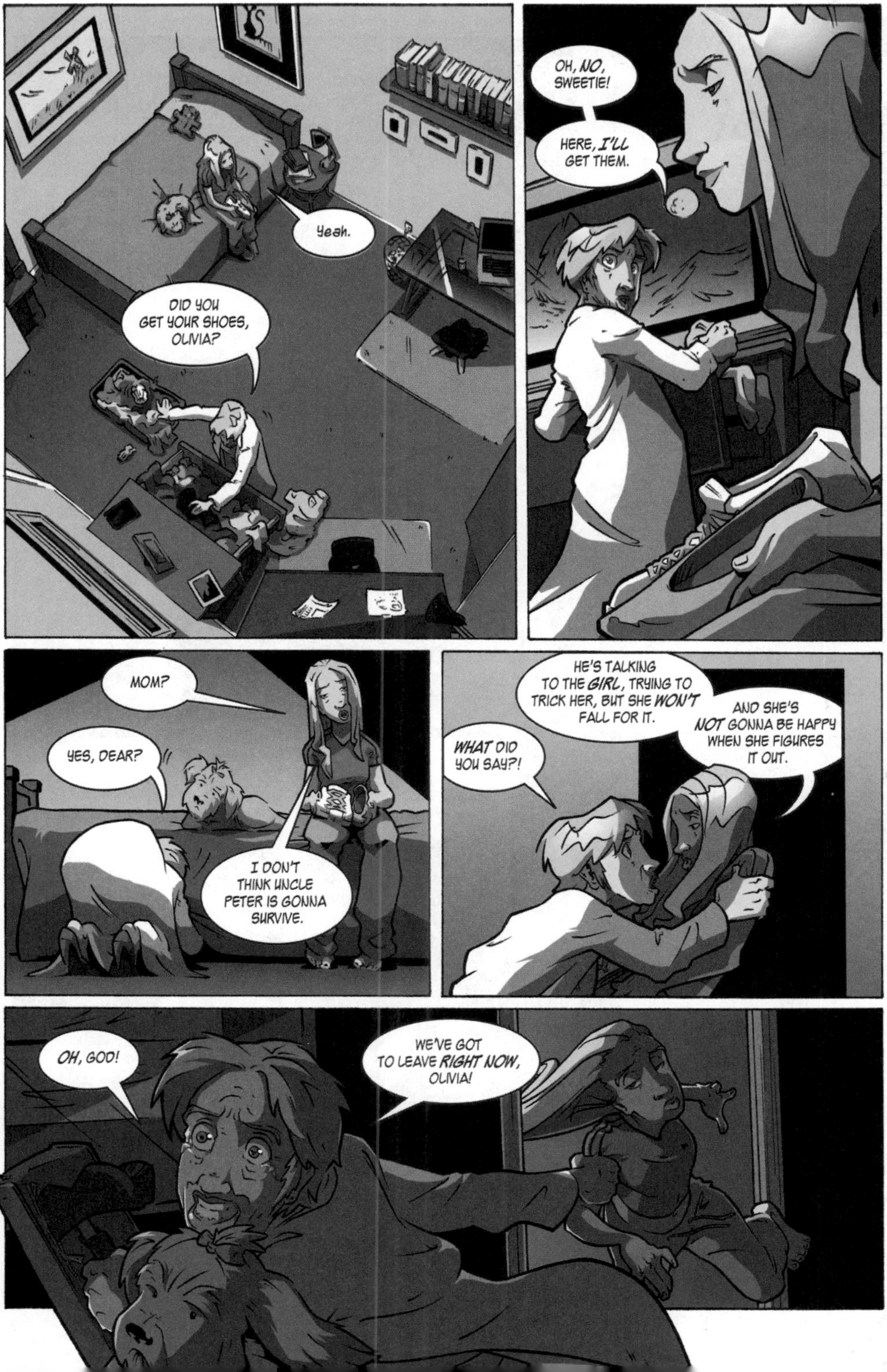
DID YOU GET YOUR SHOES, OLIVIA?
Yeah.
OH, NO, SWEETIE!
HERE, I'LL GET THEM.
MOM?
YES, DEAR?
I DON'T THINK UNCLE PETER IS GONNA SURVIVE.
WHAT DID YOU SAY?!
HE'S TALKING TO THE GIRL, TRYING TO TRICK HER, BUT SHE WON'T FALL FOR IT.
AND SHE'S NOT GONNA BE HAPPY WHEN SHE FIGURES IT OUT.
OH, GOD!
WE'VE GOT TO LEAVE RIGHT NOW, OLIVIA!

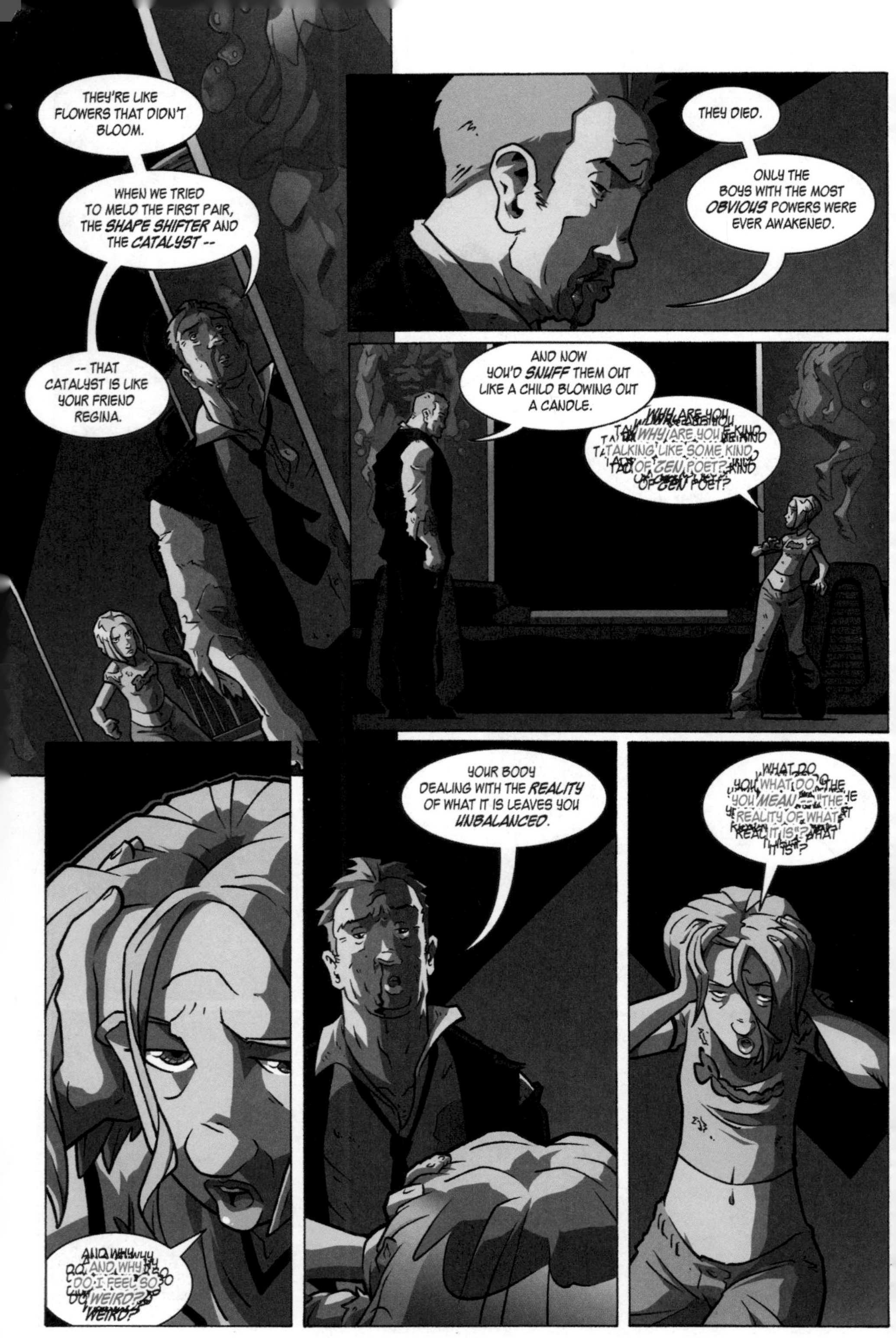
THEY'RE LIKE FLOWERS THAT DIDN'T BLOOM.
WHEN WE TRIED TO MELD THE FIRST PAIR, THE SHAPE SHIFTER AND THE CATALYST --
-- THAT CATALYST IS LIKE YOUR FRIEND REGINA.
THEY DIED.
ONLY THE BOYS WITH THE MOST OBVIOUS POWERS WERE EVER AWAKENED.
AND NOW YOU'D SNUFF THEM OUT LIKE A CHILD BLOWING OUT A CANDLE.
WHY ARE YOU TALKING LIKE SOME KIND OF ZEN POET?
AND WHY DO I FEEL SO WEIRD?
YOUR BODY DEALING WITH THE REALITY OF WHAT IT IS LEAVES YOU UNBALANCED.
WHAT DO YOU MEAN -- "THE REALITY OF WHAT IT IS"?

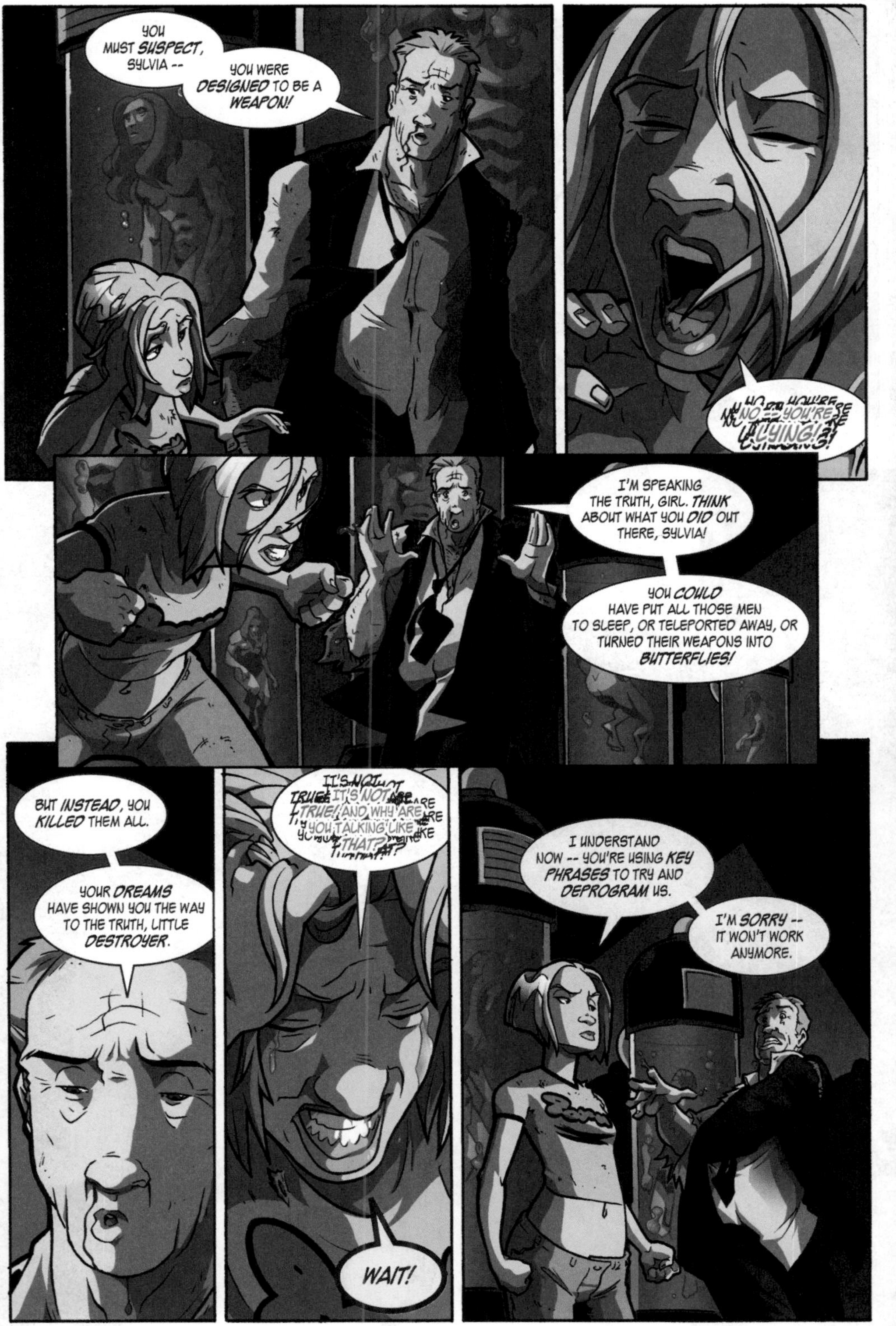

YOU MUST SUSPECT, SYLVIA --
YOU WERE DESIGNED TO BE A WEAPON!
NO -- YOU'RE LYING!
I'M SPEAKING THE TRUTH, GIRL. THINK ABOUT WHAT YOU DID OUT THERE, SYLVIA!
YOU COULD HAVE PUT ALL THOSE MEN TO SLEEP, OR TELEPORTED AWAY, OR TURNED THEIR WEAPONS INTO BUTTERFLIES!
BUT INSTEAD, YOU KILLED THEM ALL.
YOUR DREAMS HAVE SHOWN YOU THE WAY TO THE TRUTH, LITTLE DESTROYER.
IT'S NOT TRUE! AND WHY ARE YOU TALKING LIKE THAT?
WAIT!
I UNDERSTAND NOW -- YOU'RE USING KEY PHRASES TO TRY AND DEPROGRAM US.
I'M SORRY -- IT WON'T WORK ANYMORE.

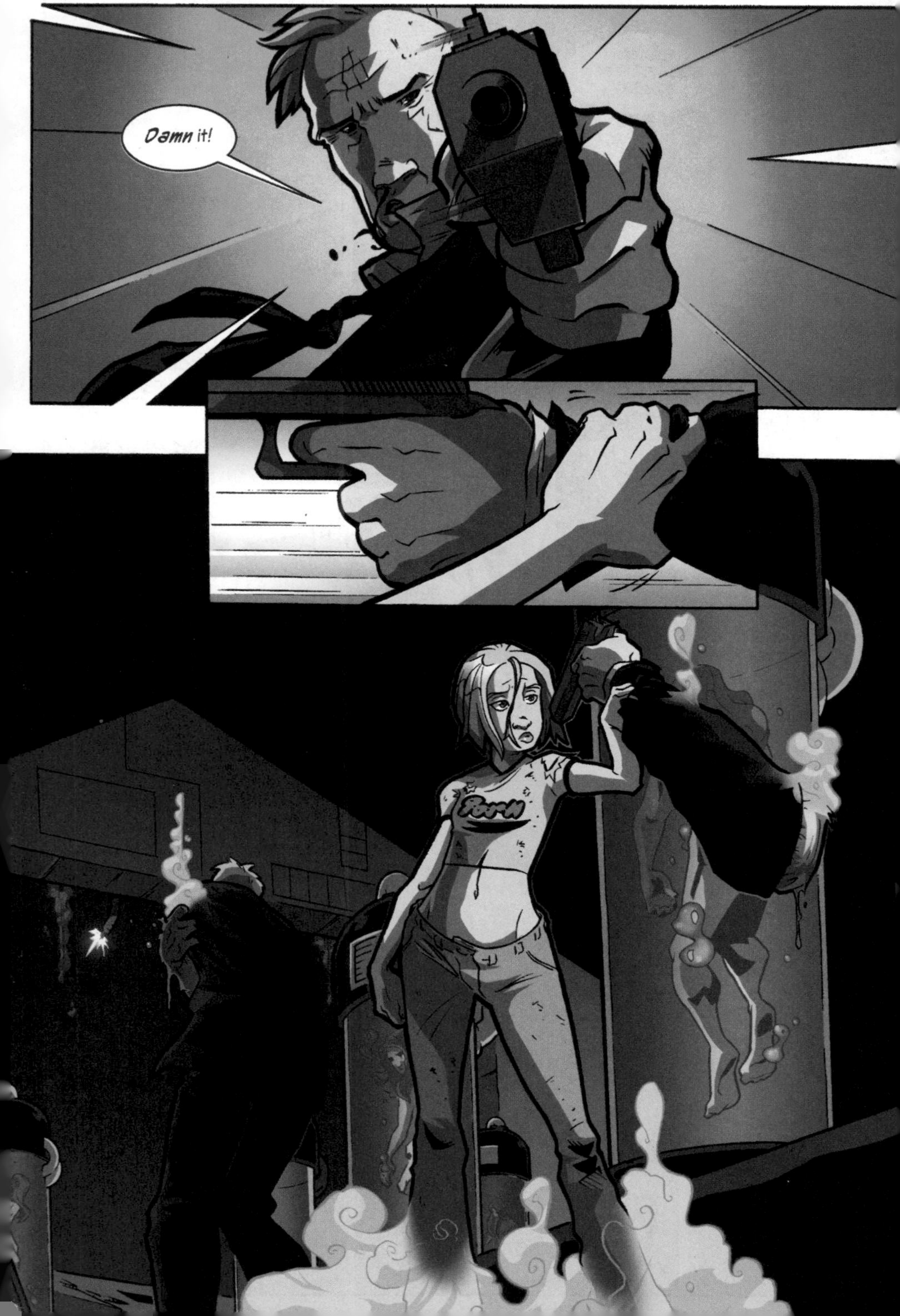
Damn it!

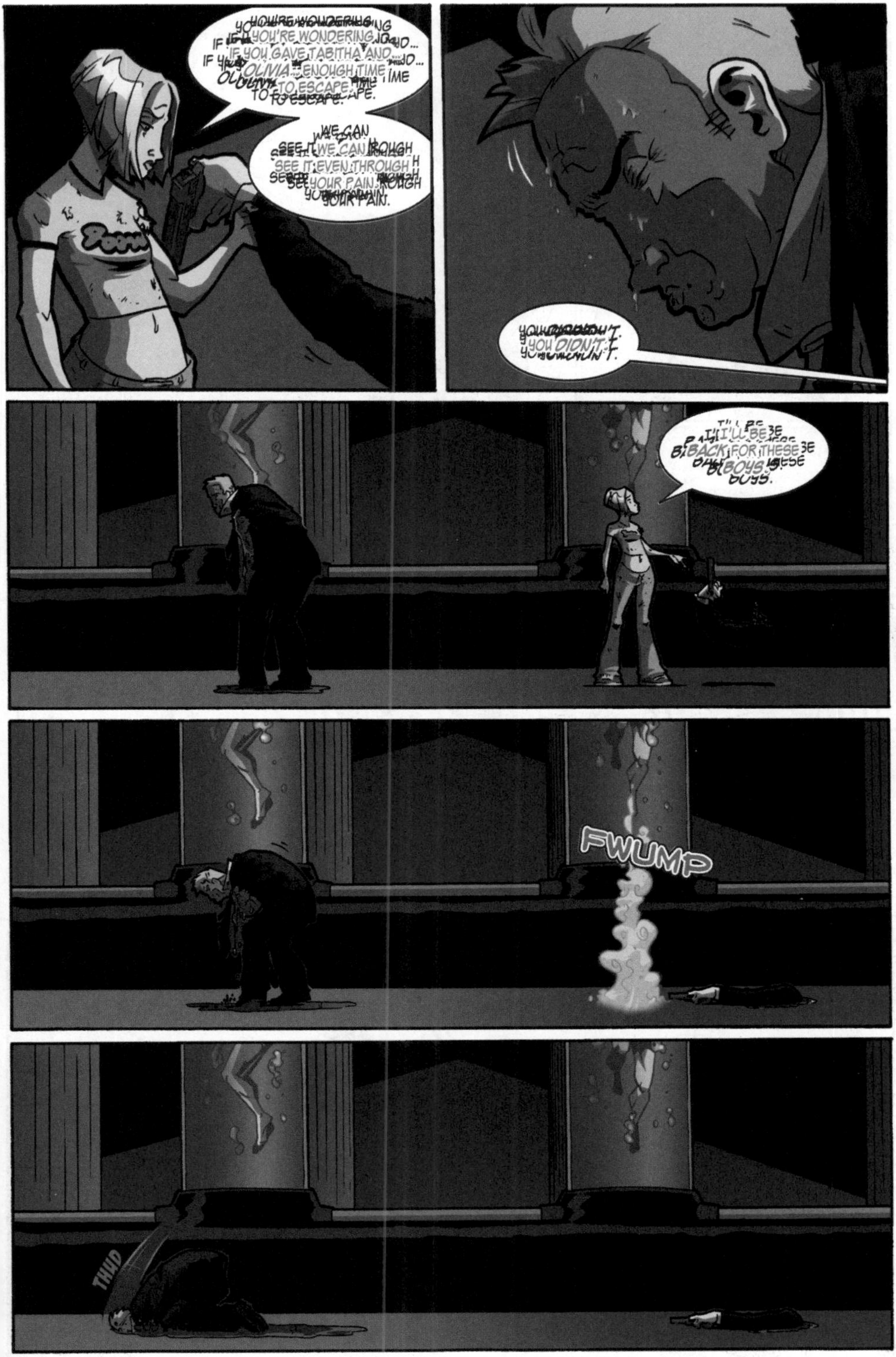
YOU'RE WONDERING IF YOU GAVE TABITHA AND... OLIVIA... ENOUGH TIME TO ESCAPE.
WE CAN SEE IT EVEN THROUGH YOUR PAIN.
YOU DIDN'T.
I'LL BE BACK FOR THESE BOYS.
FWUMP
THUD

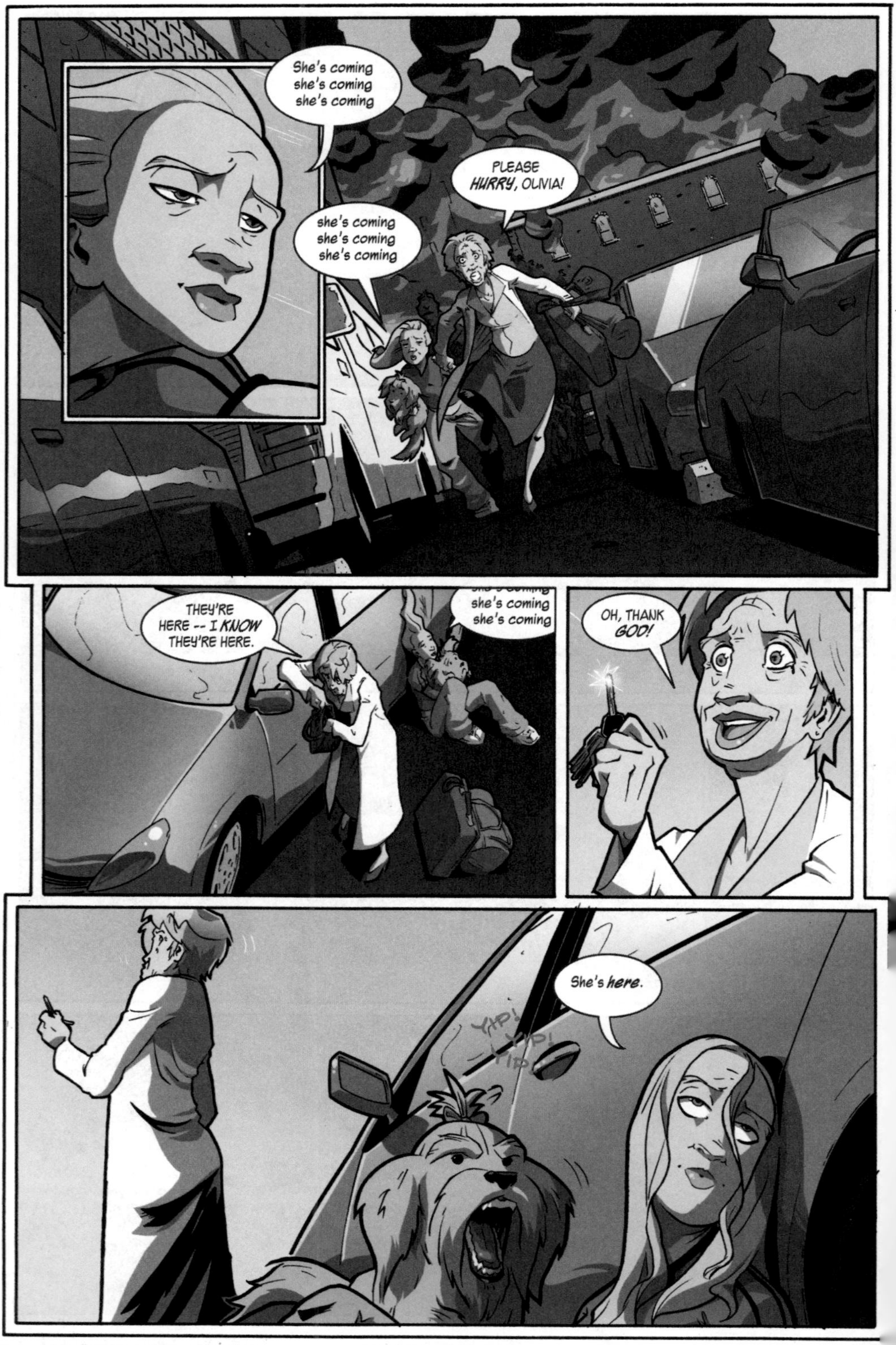
She's coming she's coming she's coming
PLEASE HURRY, OLIVIA!
she's coming she's coming she's coming
THEY'RE HERE -- I KNOW THEY'RE HERE.
she's coming she's coming
OH, THANK GOD!
She's here.
YIP! YIP! YIP!

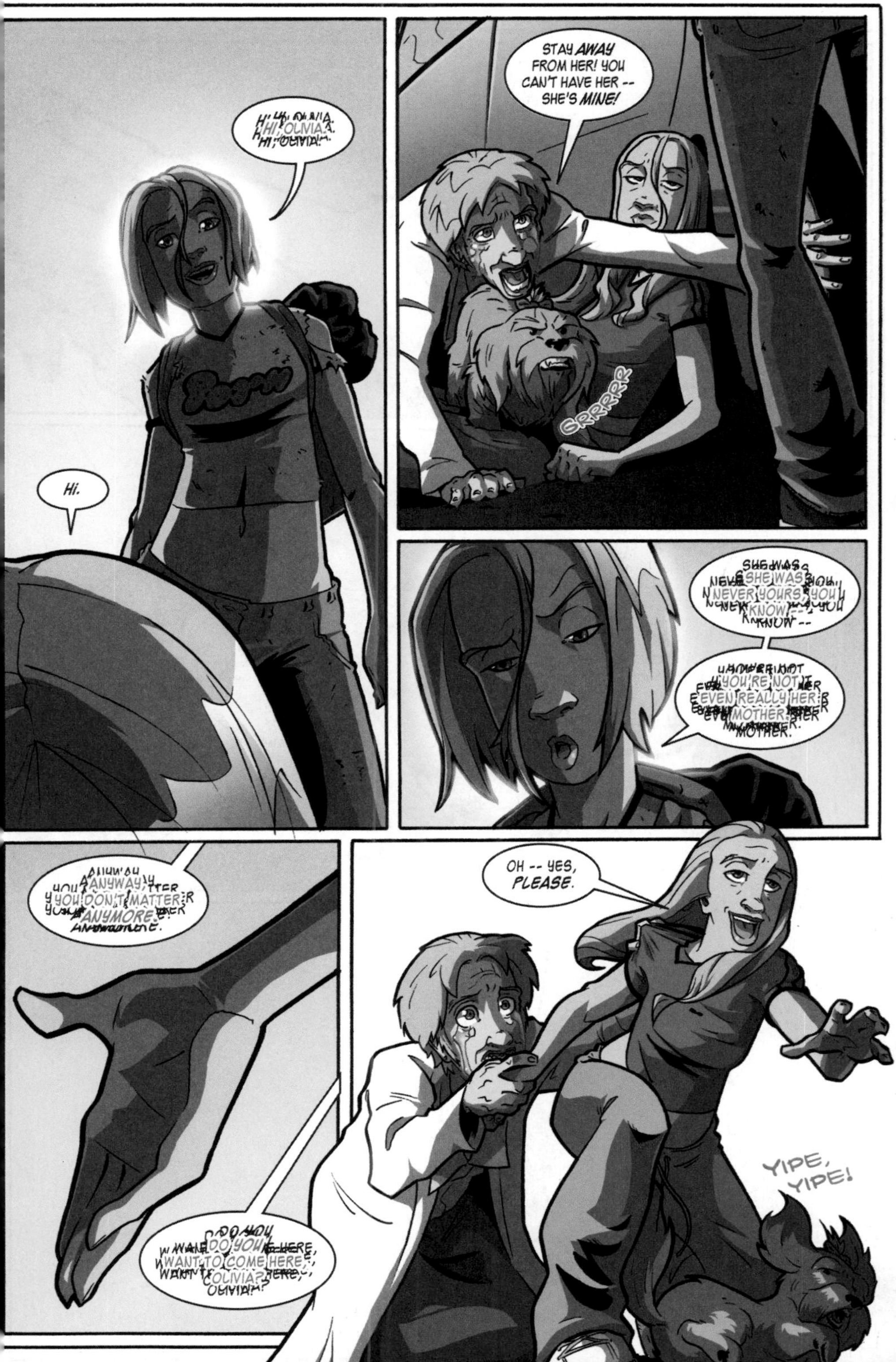
HI, OLIVIA.
Hi.
STAY AWAY FROM HER! YOU CAN'T HAVE HER -- SHE'S MINE!
GRRRRR
SHE WAS NEVER YOURS, YOU KNOW --
YOU'RE NOT EVEN REALLY HER MOTHER.
ANYWAY, YOU DON'T MATTER ANYMORE.
DO YOU WANT TO COME HERE, OLIVIA?
OH -- YES, PLEASE.
YIPE, YIPE!

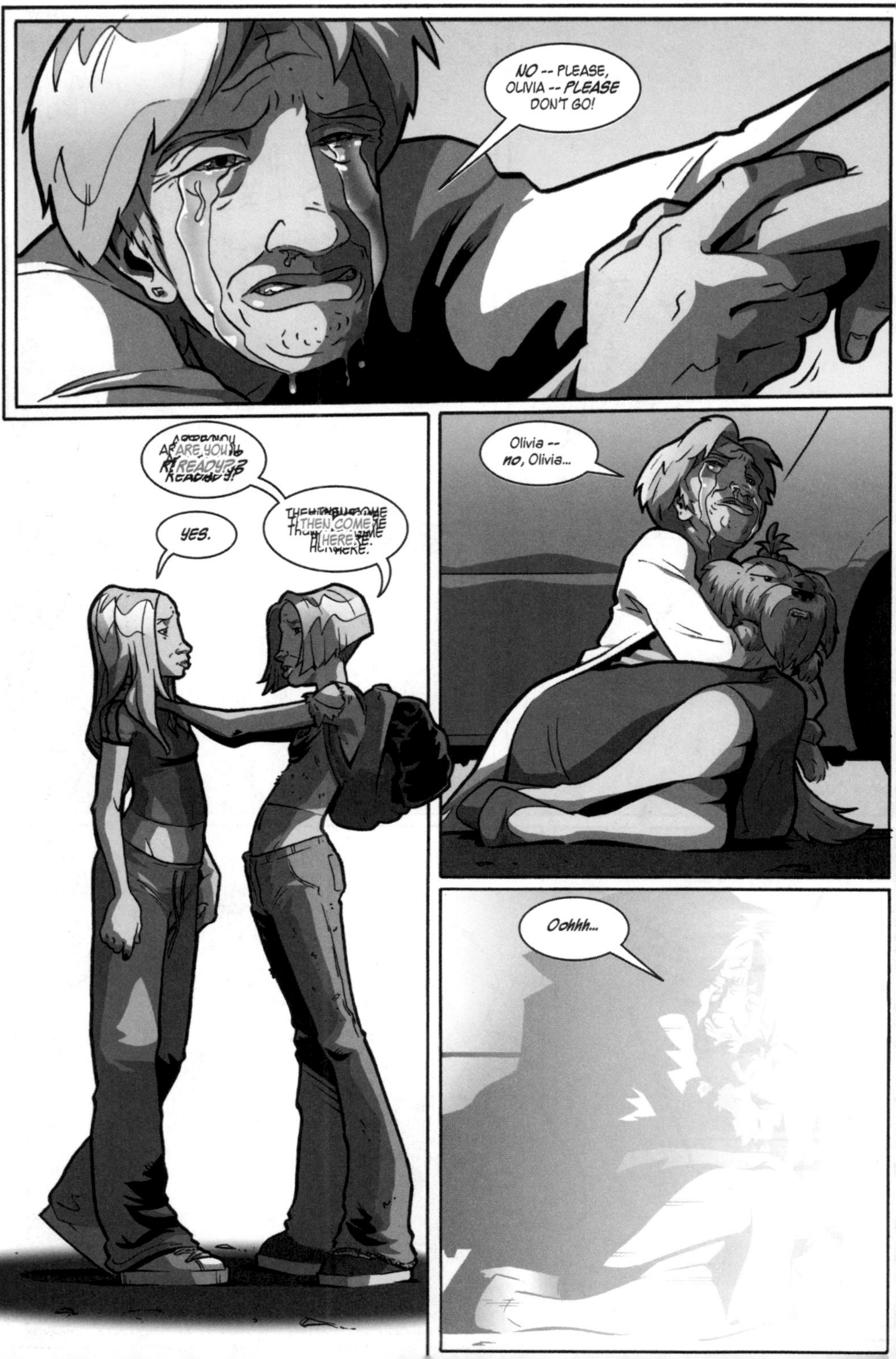
NO -- PLEASE, OLIVIA -- PLEASE DON'T GO!
ARE YOU READY?
YES.
THEN COME HERE.
Olivia -- no, Olivia...
Oohhh...

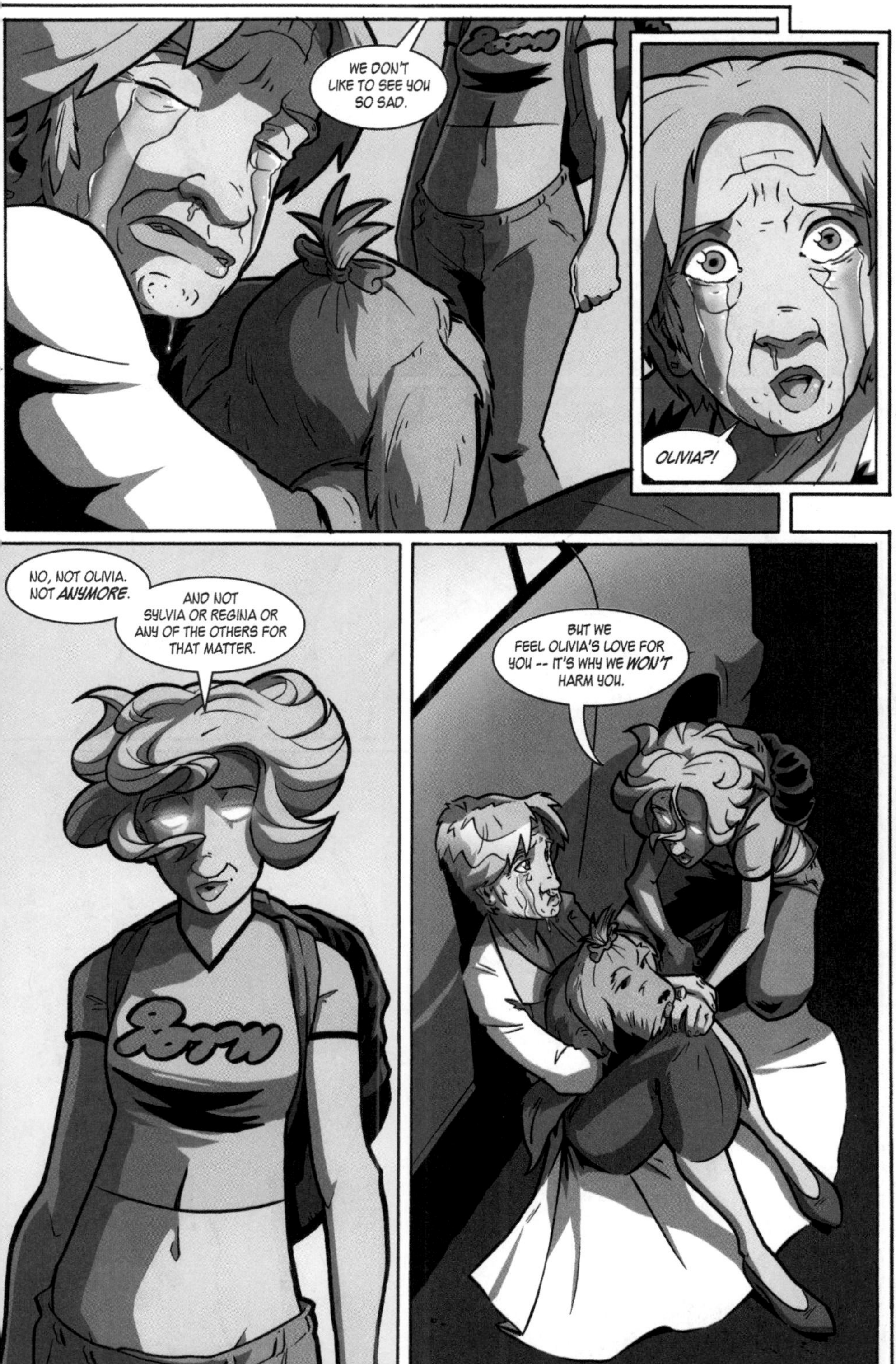
WE DON'T LIKE TO SEE YOU SO SAD.
OLIVIA?!
NO, NOT OLIVIA. NOT ANYMORE.
AND NOT SYLVIA OR REGINA OR ANY OF THE OTHERS FOR THAT MATTER.
BUT WE FEEL OLIVIA'S LOVE FOR YOU -- IT'S WHY WE WON'T HARM YOU.

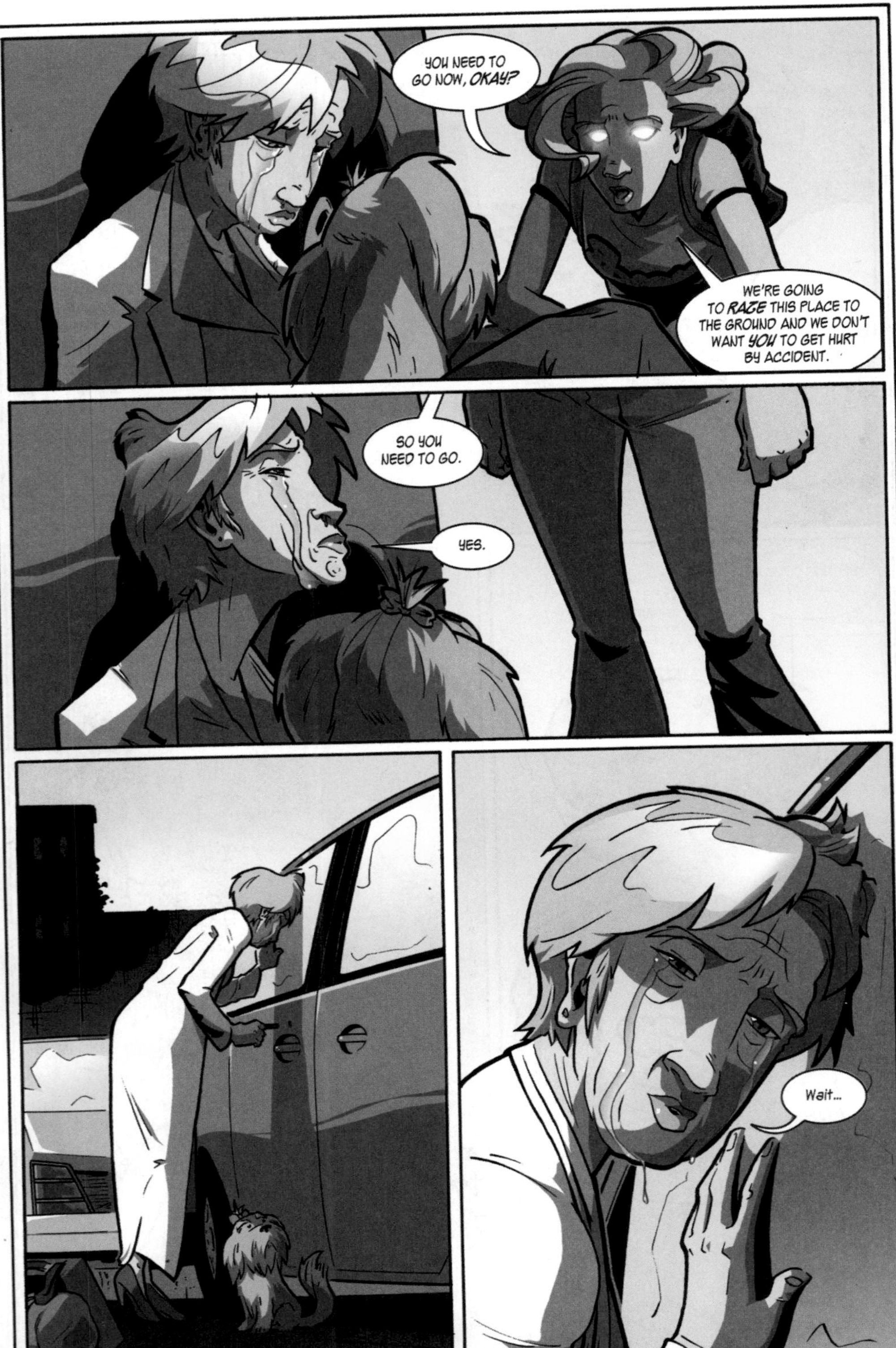
YOU NEED TO GO NOW, OKAY?
WE'RE GOING TO RAZE THIS PLACE TO THE GROUND AND WE DON'T WANT YOU TO GET HURT BY ACCIDENT.
SO YOU NEED TO GO.
YES.
Wait...

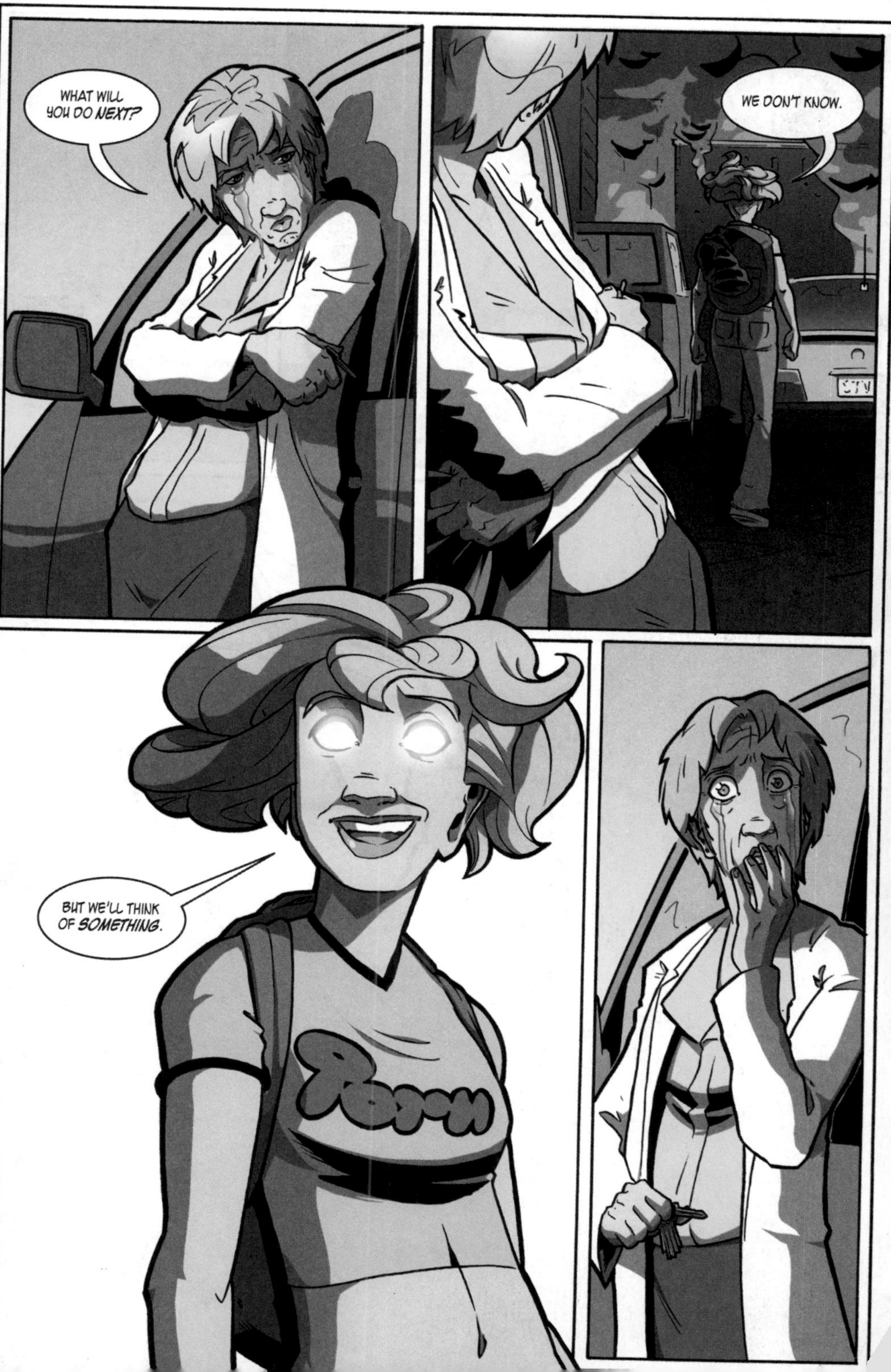
WHAT WILL YOU DO *NEXT?*
WE DON'T KNOW.
BUT WE'LL THINK OF *SOMETHING*.

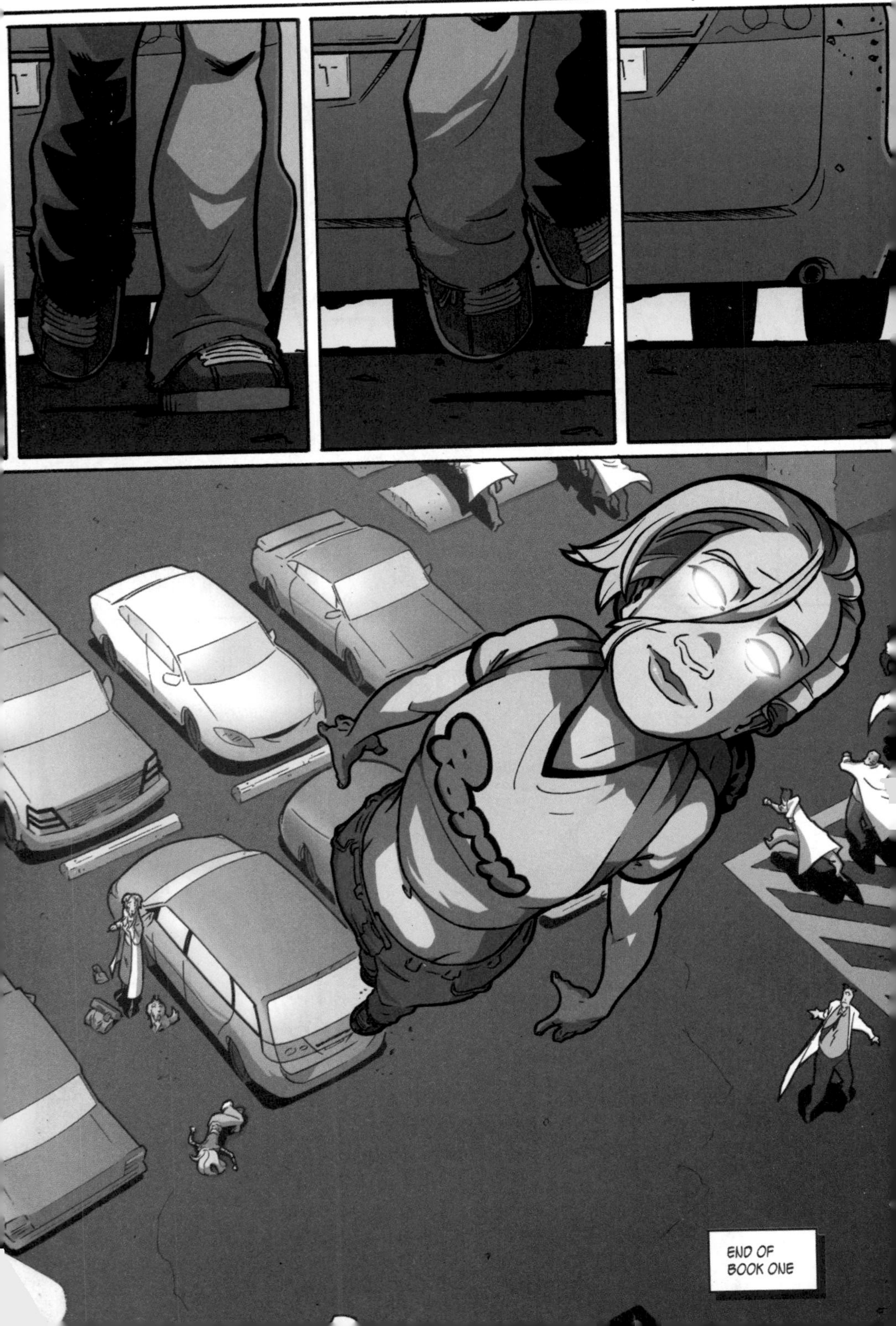
END OF
BOOK ONE